======

*It's a whole lot of Hudsons around,
you just haven't never met them.*

Hosea Hudson, 1978

The Narrative of
HOSEA HUDSON
·
His Life as a Negro Communist in the South

Nell Irvin Painter

HARVARD UNIVERSITY PRESS
Cambridge, Massachusetts
London, England
1979

Library of Congress Cataloging in Publication Data

Painter, Nell Irvin.
    The narrative of Hosea Hudson, his life as a Negro
Communist in the South.

    Bibliography: p.
    Includes index.
    1. Hudson, Hosea. 2. Afro-American communists—
Southern States—Biography. 3. Afro-Americans—Southern
States—Biography. 4. Trade-unions—Officials and em-
ployees—Southern States—Biography. 5. Iron and steel
workers—Southern States—Biography. I. Title.
HX84.H8P34   335.43′092′4 [B]   79-4589
ISBN 0-674-60110-6

I dedicate this to my late mother, Laura Camella Hudson Blakley, who died in 1965. When the FBI was running me around in the McCarthy period, she'd always want to know how was I coming along, was we making any progress. She had to slip and whisper to me.

Hosea Hudson

To Connie and Preston Williams and Jean and David Layzer for their friendship through the Cambridge and Philadelphia years.

Nell Irvin Painter

Preface

I FIRST saw Hosea Hudson in June 1976 in Atlantic City, where he lives in a small apartment behind a barber shop. I knew that Hudson was nearly eighty years old, a retired ironworker from Birmingham, Alabama, a longtime radical, but his youthful appearance impressed me and my friend Nellie McKay before he said much more than "Hello, ladies." After we exchanged introductory formalities, he recited without pause incidents from his life underground, until my recording tape ran out. Then he invited us to have dinner with him. He brought out a delicious chicken he had cooked, with vegetables from his own garden. At the table he talked for three more hours, and I cursed myself for not bringing more tape.

Driving back to my house in Philadelphia, Nellie and I spoke little, awed and exhausted by Hudson's energy of recall. It was clear then that I would have to go back to Atlantic City. But when I had first learned about Hosea Hudson from Nellie's colleague, Mark Solomon, I had no idea that we would meet more than once. Even Hudson's writing gave me no clue to the charm and humor of his life as he tells it. Obviously he had a great deal more to say, and I wanted to hear it. Hudson readily agreed to my returning, and we taped several more sessions before he started to pose some serious questions.

When he asked about my politics I feared that would mean the end of our work together, for although I admired his long years of dedication to radical change in the face of opposition, I had to admit that I was only a Democrat. To my surprise, Hudson was greatly relieved. His worry was not that I might be a liberal, but that I might belong to one of the groups he calls "left-splinter," such as the Socialist Workers Party. They are anathema to the Communist Party of the United States, infinitely worse than Democrats. So we continued talking and taping.

A few meetings later, Hudson had another question: What were my intentions for this rapidly lengthening interview? Until then, I had thought no further than recording Hudson's life for what I vaguely called history. As interesting as Hudson's story was, I did not plan to transcribe or edit it. I had asked few questions, satisfied to let him speak as he would about his childhood, the part of his life I then found most useful. After all, few informants can lucidly describe growing up in the rural South at the turn of the century. I am working on the South in that period, and he was contributing to my knowledge greatly.

Hudson suggested our making a book of his experiences in the Communist Party in the South, and I agreed. I was to be on leave from the University of Pennsylvania during the 1976–77 year to work on a book on American views of the South. Hudson accepted the limitations on my time and understood that I could only work part time on his life story. With that, I typed our first agreement on his typewriter, and we took it to an Atlantic City funeral director to be notarized.

During the remainder of the summer of 1976, I commuted to Atlantic City from Philadelphia almost every other day. In between visits, I transcribed and edited our interviews. As the material grew more familiar and I came to know Hudson better, I asked him hard questions. He answered nearly all of them candidly and completely. His first desire is to secure a place in the historical record for himself and the Alabama Communist Party, and so there are only a few areas in his life that he refuses to talk about for the record. It also helped a great deal that he has a fine sense of history, distinguishing firsthand knowledge from hearsay. And when he can't remember something or someone, he says so.

We've had two quarrels, both settled by mutually agreeable compromises. The first concerned the title and author of the book. Hudson wanted to be both. I wanted to be the author. We settled by making him the title and me the author.

The second difference concerned my introduction. We had decided that the narrative had to be acceptable to both of us, because I present it as Hudson's words. To make sure that he is in agreement with all I have him saying, I read every word back to him. The introduction was another matter, however, and so we have two of them. He wrote what he wanted and signed it; I wrote what I wanted and signed it. But later Hudson objected to my mentioning ex-communists in my introduction and bibliographical essay, particularly Harry Haywood, who had moved over to what Hudson calls the "ultra-left." I insisted that, as a scholar, I needed to review important works in the field, that my mentioning Haywood didn't necessarily indicate approbation. We both gave a little, and our solution is in note 21 to my introduction: Hudson's statement of his opposition to Haywood. Hudson recognizes my right to mention whom I please in my introduction, but he still doesn't like those people in his book. Otherwise our work has been harmonious and friendly.

THIS narrative is a collaborative oral autobiography, produced by a young historian and an old radical with an excellent memory and the ability to answer questions openly and honestly. The words are nearly all Hudson's, but the pruning and arranging that eased his spoken language into readable form are mine. I explain my preparation of the narrative at length in my introduction.

If this experiment works out, readers will come away with a sense of Hudson's life as a black workingman in a southern city in mid-century. I don't think that Hudson's view of his times is characteristic of southern Negroes of his generation in all aspects, but I'm convinced that it is valuable and worth recording in his own voice. At first non-southern readers may find the language cumbersome and strange. But it's easily mastered, and Hudson's story compels attention.

N.I.P.
Chapel Hill, 1979

Contents

Illustrations

Chronology

1898	Hosea Hudson's birth in rural Wilkes County, Georgia.
1900	Sophie Scroggs's birth in Wilkes County. (Sophie Scroggs is a pseudonym.)
1917	Marriage of Hudson and Sophie Scroggs.
1918	Hosea and Sophie Hudson begin sharecropping on their own.
1920	Birth of their only child, Hosea, Jr.
1923	Hudson moves from Wilkes County to Atlanta, works as a common laborer in a railroad roundhouse.
1924	Hudson moves to Birmingham and begins career as an iron molder. Family joins him a few months later. Between 1927 and 1937 he uses the name Will Holton.
1931	Hudson joins the Communist Party in the wake of the Scottsboro and Camp Hill cases.
1932	Hudson fired from the Stockham foundry, suspected of being a communist.
1933	Hudson attends national Party meeting in New York, his first trip outside the deep South.
1934	Hudson spends first ten weeks of the year at Party National Training School in New York under the name Henry Thornton.
1934–1936	Family moves to Atlanta, where Hudson does organizational work for the CP under the name Larry Brown.
1937	Family returns to Birmingham.
1938–1940	Hudson works on WPA, serves as vice-president of the Birmingham and Jefferson County locals of the Workers Alliance. Leads the Right To Vote Club and fills the office of recording secretary in Steel Local 1489.

1942–1947	Hudson is president of Steel Local 2815, chairman of the grievance committee, delegate to the Birmingham Industrial Union Council.
1944–1945	Hudson is vice-president of the Alabama People's Educational Association while the CP is reorganized nationally as the Communist Political Association.
1944	Hosea Hudson, Jr., marries.
1946–1947	Hosea and Sophie Hudson separate, then divorce.
1947	Hudson is expelled from the Birmingham Industrial Union Council, fired from his job, stripped of his offices in the local, and blacklisted for being a communist.
1950	Hudson organizes a United Political Action Committee in Bessemer, a suburb of Birmingham. A few weeks later goes underground, until 1956.
1951–1953	Based in Atlanta, Hudson works for the CP as liaison among scattered communists in the South.
1954	Hudson moves to New York City. In 1956 begins working again, as a janitor in a restaurant.
1962	Hudson and Virginia Larue Marson marry.
1965	Hudson retires from New York restaurant job. He and his wife move to Atlantic City.
1971	Hudson visits the Soviet Union for the first time. Virginia Hudson dies.
1972	Publication of *Black Worker in the Deep South*.
1979–	Hudson is still a member of the Party and still active politically.

The Narrative of
HOSEA HUDSON

Nell Irvin Painter's
Introduction

MY favorite photos of Hosea Hudson are the ones I took in Atlantic City in August 1978, just after we ate lunch on the boardwalk and shared a second bottle of champagne. We were celebrating the completion of our taped interviews, or so we thought—the taping continued on into the fall. After lunch Hudson stood before the chain-link fence that protects his neighbor's vegetable garden from dogs and children. I snapped several photos of him as he told me what a fine book this would be if they printed it like we wrote it. He was in good spirits, and it showed. When the photos were developed, I saw they were better than any I had seen of Hudson before.

The series of pictures I had taken earlier in 1976 resembles the portrait on the cover of his first autobiography, where, smiling under a collage saying "Free Angela and All Political Prisoners!" he looks too young, too ingenuous, and too open for a man who has lived his life. Another photo I don't like was taken in 1973. There he looks too old, sick, and angry. But in the 1978 photos, Hudson looks like the crusty and knowing man who speaks in this narrative.

Partly it's that I know Hudson well enough now to capture him on film. He talks to me instead of posing. But it's also that he's changed. The last two years of severe weather and his brother's death have taken their toll on him physically. When he was seventy-eight years old, he looked sixty-five. Now that he's eighty, he looks about seventy. The idea of death has made him seem older than before, but it has also encouraged him to drop his guard.

During much of our long conversation Hudson spoke as if his life were divided into forty-six years in the Communist Party and

I

thirty-three years of groping toward it. Recently, however, he has begun speaking of his youth as a time that is interesting because it was *his* youth. He put on record events that in the past he refused to let me tape, much less print. His youth is no longer simply an object lesson in the persecution of Negroes under capitalism; it is also the time when he learned to gamble.

HUDSON was born on 12 April 1898 in Wilkes County, Georgia, a cotton county near the South Carolina border. His mother, Laura Camella Smith Hudson, was eighteen when he was born; his father, Thomas Hudson, twenty-seven. Two years later, his brother Eddie was born. The parents were quarrelsome, and they chopped up their marriage with many short separations. After three years, Mrs. Hudson left her husband for good, taking her two babies to her parents in Oglethorpe County, four or five miles to the west. With these three new members, the family consisted of Hosea's grandfather George Smith, his grandmother Julia Smith, his uncle Ned, and his aunt Georgia Mae.* George Smith was born a slave and had failed to improve his fortunes very much over the years. In 1901 the family owned one mule named Bailey and sharecropped on Tom Glen's plantation. Like other poor sharecropping families, the Smith family moved often and owned very little.

Among Hudson's earliest memories is his grandfather's preaching to the trees behind the cow barn. An illiterate who never was pastor of a church, George Smith was only a jackleg preacher, but he solemnly considered himself a Methodist minister. Behind his back, the older members of the family laughed at his preaching to the pines but, for five-year-old Hosie, Smith's sermonizing was no laughing matter. At noontime, Hosie would have to go call his grandfather to dinner, terrified always that he would see a snake in the woods. That fear ended only when George Smith left home after Ned's difficulties with the law supplied a pretext for a quarrel.

Hosea's uncle Ned attended church regularly with the rest of the family, but somehow that young man always attracted trouble. One Sunday in 1903 when he was seventeen, several white men, includ-

---

* Hosea Hudson's family in Wilkes and Oglethorpe counties

Mother: Laura Camella Smith Hudson   *Father:* Thomas Hudson
Brother: Eddie Hudson   *Grandmother:* Julia Smith
Grandfather: George Smith   *Mother's brother:* Ned Smith
Mother's sister: Georgia Mae Smith

ing his grandmother's half-brother, waylaid him, stripped him, and beat him badly, forcing him to flee Oglethorpe County without going home. That night the whole family worried. Julia Smith stayed up, peering down the dirt road and calling her son's name. As soon as it got light

She went down that farm road through the forest and cow pastures until she got to the gate at the other side of the pasture near the church and near the pasture gate. She found his top dress coat, his vest, and his white shirt with blood stains on all of the clothing, and she cried out that Ned had been murdered . . .

It was a bright and sunny day about September. I can remember how I heard the old people there talking and planning to search the forest and drag Long Creek for my uncle's body.[1]

A few weeks later, Ned turned up thirty miles away. He was sent back to Oglethorpe County and charged with jumping the bond his landlord had posted to get him out of difficulties earlier in the summer.

As Ned awaited trial, George Smith grew testy and refused to take clothes to the boy in jail, as his wife asked. George and Julia Smith were "already at the breaking point" because of Laura's return and the strain she and her two sons imposed on the family. Swearing he would not support them all, Smith left home for good. Hudson remembers his departure as a minor loss. Even before then, Julia Smith had headed the household in all but name. Smith had begun "running around in his late years," Hudson says. "I don't know whether to say he wont no man or what."[2]

Ned spent twelve months in 1903 and 1904 on the county prison farm. The rest of the family moved to Dave Arm's place to sharecrop without him. After his release, Ned farmed near them and sometimes helped them out with the work. In 1906 the family moved to the Jones place, then to Burl Sill's place in Wilkes County. The main plowhand in these years was Georgia Mae, Hudson's hardworking aunt, ten years older than he. When she ran away and got married in the fall of 1908, ten-year-old Hosea inherited her job and plowed full-time.

What remained of the family—Hosea, his grandmother, his mother, and his brother—moved to Dr. Rail's place in Oglethorpe County in 1909. Crops were so bad that year that Ned left farming entirely to work as a porter on the railroad, depriving the family of women and boys of valuable assistance. They moved to Jim Allgood's place in 1910 and suffered a loss Hudson regretted keenly. Laura Hudson had mortgaged two cows to buy a sewing machine for $40 but was never able to pay off the debt. Allgood foreclosed, appropriating "two *fine* jersey cows." In 1911 the family lost even occasional assistance from Ned when he moved to New Jersey.

Hudson's mother married again in 1911. Her new husband, Bill Blackburn, added to the family's working hands and moved them to a promising situation, farming with a well-to-do friend of his, a Negro named Willie Pollion. Soon Blackburn's friendship with Pollion soured for the rest of the family, although Hudson never understood exactly what took place. Bill left Laura, moved in with Willie Pollion's brothers, then lived with one of Pollion's female relatives. After Blackburn left them to farm alone, the family rarely got enough to eat:

We was trying to pick out some cotton where we'd be able to sell some seed and get some food, cause we practically working without food. Eating roast ear, what you find from late corn planting in the corn fields, roast ear and apples, late apples, peanuts out of the peanut patch. Nothing to eat.

My grandmother got some roasting ears was too hard to make roasting ear corn out of. She took a piece of wire, a piece of tin, and put holes in it with a nail and bent it around, put it on a piece of plank and grated that corn and made something like grits and we had that for bread.

Before they were able to pick a single bale of cotton, Willie Pollion seized their crops, garden, and livestock. In court Laura Hudson lost the crops and garden but won the right to keep the cow and pig and to leave Pollion free of any further debt to him.

A black neighbor, Man Wallace, invited the family to live with him and pick his cotton in exchange for shelter and food. The food was still scanty. When Wallace's cotton was all in, they picked cotton for a white man named Bell, making 50¢ per hundred pounds.

One day as they were picking in Bell's field, "Willie Pollion came down there on his horse Sally," Hudson recalls. Pollion claimed that Laura still owed him money. Demanding payment roughly, he threatened to hit her:

My mother told him she wont paying no debt. He looked like a white man. You couldn't tell him from a white man. And when he started talking big talk at my mother, I told him—I wont but fourteen years old—I got mad, I told him, "God damn your white soul! You done took all we made up yonder on your place, now you come down here trying take what little we got down here!" I said, "I'll kill you with a rock." I said, "You hit her, I'll . . . I'll kill you with a rock!"

I was crying, I was so mad. He done took all we had made, we's hungry, and I just got mad.

Hudson had raised his voice to speak sharply to an adult for the first time. Willie Pollion left the family alone, but the hard times continued.

In January 1913 Hudson's family moved to Dave Arm's, where Laura cooked for the hands at the sawmill and Hosie carried water and chopped firewood. They earned no wages for their work, only room and board—"fried meat and clear grease and biscuit. I think we had white meat [fatback] sometimes and some peas. My mother cooked peas sometime. No money. Didn't know nothing about money."

Hudson's first accident at work occurred one cold morning. "All they's firing the engine with was green slab, pine slabs," and Dave Arm sent Hudson into the woods to cut some "fat pine" to kindle the fire. Splitting a piece of wood, Hudson struck his foot with the ax and cut three toes badly. "The toe next to my big toe, it like to unjointed it." He drove back to the sawmill, "Oh, it was long, about two miles, I guess, down in the woods, cold in the morning, frosty." From the sawmill he limped home with his shoe full of blood.

His grandmother bathed the foot and applied soot and turpentine. Dave Arm allowed the boy a few days convalescence, then ordered him back to hard work. Hudson's grandmother refused to let the injured boy work before his foot healed, and she sent him to stay with his aunt Georgia Mae. Then the family moved to Bob Johnson's.

Back on his feet, Hudson worked at Johnson's sawmill six days a week. They agreed on 50¢ a day in wages, but the wages turned out to be only food for the family. "The most stuff they fed my grandmother and them with was from the table and from his garden. He had a large turnip patch, and he just give her a bunch of those turnips ever so often, give her a piece of hog jowls or something, or some cornmeal. That's the way we made it, until we got able to start the crop, where she could open a account where we could buy some food on the crop to make the crop. Oh, it was rough."

Laura Hudson Blackburn made a lasting marriage to John Henry Blakely in 1913, leaving behind a family of Hosea, his grandmother, and his brother. At fifteen, Hosea headed the household and "traded" with landlord Jones Collins on the family's behalf:

I come in, say, "I hear them say you got a extra farm that you want to let out for sharecropping. I come to see could I get it."

Old man Collins say, "How old are you?" I was so young till he wanted to know "who did you have to work a farm with?" I told him me and my grandmother and brother. He want to know how old my brother. My brother then was about thirteen or something.

"Do you think you can work a farm?" I told him I *been* working.

"You reckon your grandmother mind you trading with me?"

"No, she don't mind me trading. I always do the trading anyhow for the farm." And that's the way I traded with them.

Hudson traded with Collins for three years, until the family moved to Taylor Hall's in 1917. That Spring Hudson courted Sophie Scroggs, and they decided to marry at the end of the year. After he sold the cotton early in December, his grandmother divided everything they owned into three equal parts. Hudson took his third and married Sophie on 31 December 1917. They remained with Hall, sharecropping until the end of 1922. Hosea and Sophie made good crops until 1921, paid their debts, cleared a little money, "nothing much."[3]

Boll weevils appeared in Wilkes County in 1921 and ruined Hudson's 1922 crop. He made less than two bales of cotton and very little corn—the bud worms got in the corn. Working on halves, he broke even. That was Hudson's last year of sharecropping. For the next seven months he hired out with Tom Jackson for $10 a month, intending to stay out of debt and save a little something to get started in the city. He planned to quit farming in the summer and leave Wilkes County.

But by May Hudson still had saved nothing and owed Jackson 50¢. Then he got an idea:

I began to go and find out who was it among the farmers that had peanuts left over after planting their peanut crop. I bought them at $2 a bushel* . . . I took the peanuts home and removed the rack from my little four-eyed wood cooking stove and made a hot wood fire in my cooking stove. I would put a peck of the peanuts in the stove at a time until I parch a bushel of peanuts . . .

I took a salmon can and shined it up very nice. I had a strap that I put on each end of the bag of peanuts. I would go out to Mr. Jackson's

_____
* Hudson bought the peanuts on consignment.

grocery store on Saturdays . . . where the Negroes would hang out . . . and sell a salmon can of parch peanuts, 5 cents a can.

I went to the church on Sunday and took a stand down to the spring where the people would come to get a fresh drink of spring water. There I would sell my peanuts.[4]

But at 5¢ a can, roasted peanuts netted little profit. Hudson had another idea: "I got me a pipe and a barrel and went out there in the fields and got some of that old syrup, what you mix with arsenic to kill boll weevils, and I buy me some meal and made me a barrel of mash, made me some whisky." Peanuts and whisky brought him $40. "That's the way I left the country," he says. "I come out of there and I didn't go back for nineteen years."

When Hudson speaks of leaving Wilkes County, he lists his gambling, bad company, difficulties with his relatives, run-ins at Jackson's store on Saturdays. The city offered both an escape from personal tensions and well-paid work. He focuses on the personal side where his own actions counted for something. Unmentioned are the evils he could not affect, the boll weevil or the iniquitous system of sharecropping.

Little wonder that Hudson did not return to Wilkes County for so many years. He had grown up materially and emotionally impoverished and spent his youth in unending hard work. School had been no fun either, but a place of high anxiety. Before he was old enough to be a regular pupil, he went along to Professor Hardiman's school at Rocky Branch Church with Georgia Mae. His grandmother had sent the five-year-old "just to learn the rules and regulations of the school." He remembers only that his grandmother had made him a little calico shirt, a "waist," with buttons around the bottom to fasten to his pants. "I used to go, set up in school, and I'd eat the sleeves of that calico, of that waist. I'd just bite it and nibble on it, just bit it. When I go home, I done had bit holes all in my waist sleeve." Julia Smith sent word to Professor Hardiman to whip him when he chewed his sleeves, and that broke the habit.

Even after Hudson began school in earnest in 1904, the whole experience remained disagreeable. Of these years he says that "it was just really a horrible frightening life for me." Rocky Branch Church was two or three miles from home, and he had to cross woods and pastures to get there. "I was always scared to death of seeing a snake or a mad dog. People always talking about mad dogs." He remembers vividly his return home from school one afternoon:

I was going home in the spring of the year, and a dark cloud was back in the East. The sun was shining here, and it was thunder back over here. You could just stand and look at the drops of water through the sky, and they was shining. And I just stood there, afraid to move. I just looked at it. I could see them drops ashining, falling against that black cloud here. I was just scared to death.

As he got bigger, plowing took Hosie out of school by late February or early March. He attended school in spells until 1912, but for all his years in the classroom, he only learned to read haltingly, spelling out each word before he could pronounce it. To explain his lack of facility, he usually says even now that he only had a few months of schooling as a child. His brother Eddie was a very different case.

Hosea's brother became a preacher and was obviously a better-educated man. Eddie was the favorite child of their grandmother and mother. Hosie was the hard-working older son, the "thick head," while Eddie was the baby, the pet. All the family and friends predicted that Eddie would become a preacher. He was the good boy who could "talk like a mockingbird," but he also tattled on Hosie whenever Hosie did something wrong. Hosie prepared the fields, mended fences, and cleared ditches while Eddie attended school every year from beginning to end—Christmas to Easter. "It was always something between me and him," Hudson says, and even as adults the brothers often verged on trading blows. Yet they never lost sight of one another. Hosea went to Atlanta to nurse Eddie during his terminal illness in 1977.

Of his mother and grandmother, Hudson remembers their "contempt" for him, which still puzzles him. They would hit him on the head with a piece of stove wood "when they got mad around the house." He says that his mother gave him away to his grandmother when she left his father, because Julia Smith often told him he "belonged" to her. When Laura married for the third time in 1913, she moved away with her husband and left the boys with her mother. When Hosea married, his grandmother and brother went to live with Laura and John Henry Blakley.

Despite his parents' early separation, Hudson recalls his father Thomas Hudson "ever since I can remember anybody." His father was a handsome man, outgoing, and a bit of a show-off. He sang and spoke in a fine bass voice and was a favorite for singing during collection or selling dinners at church. Hudson can still recapture his father's scent: "He always carried that good perfume on his shave and on his clothes, like men used to carry, 'Heart's Home.' I can smell it now."

The day Hosie and Eddie learned that their father was working on the Elberton Seaboard Railroad, they searched the line for him. To their pleasure, they found he was the boss of a gang laying pipe. He stood in the ditch with his overalls rolled up, ordering the other Negro men about in his rich deep voice, making a fine show of directing them. On the job and at church, Tom Hudson stood out.

He was kind of showish, all right. He'd have all the women, especially, at the church. He'd set his hat to one side, and he'd always have something to say.

People always admired Tom Hudson. "Tom Hudson! Tom Hudson!" He was known everywhere.

Church service at Winn's Chapel on the first Sunday of June 1907 gave Hudson special delight. His father was there in the choir, and he sang with him. "I was so small that he would stand up in front of the bench, and I was standing on the bench, standing beside him," Hudson recalls. The boy glowed with pride when the other men kidded Tom Hudson. "What you doing with that boy?! You know that boy can't sing!" Tom Hudson laughed back at them, "Yes, he can sing!"

His father's visits always pleased young Hosea, and he especially remembers one of them in 1906:

Poor man, I bet you he walked fifteen miles, walking, and these was swamps then, woods, forest. But he came over there one night to see us, and he brought a can, a baking powder can full of sugar for us, and he brought some canned goods.

He had me sitting on his knee, and he was letting me eat all the candy I want. And my grandmother said, "Thomas, don't be giving that boy all that candy. You make him sick."

"Oh, let him eat it," he said, "I brought it for him to eat." And he stayed there that night and he left, I don't know what time, going back, walking those fifteen miles back through the swamps and woods.

And the next morning I got up looking for some of that candy and them canned goods, and I haven't seen them yet. My grandmother took them and wouldn't let us have them. I asked about the candy.

"Shut up your mouth! Your daddy will spoil your guts out! You go around here and just eat everything he bring here!" She never did give me any more of that candy.

Hudson thinks that his grandmother's meddling caused his parents' divorce. Julia Smith didn't like Tom Hudson and never spoke kindly of him. Often she told Hosie, "Your daddy no good. He don't give you nothing." Eddie shared his grandmother's views and felt little affection for his father. Eddie "didn't care anything about him," Hudson says, but "I didn't feel that way against him. I always had a feeling I always wanted for a daddy." He feels that warmth in spite of ambiguous memories of his father.

One Sunday in the summer of 1913 Hilly Mount Zion Church held a fair where barbeque dinners were on sale. Tom Hudson smiled and winked and called to all the people to come buy barbeque. His oldest son stood off to one side, certain his father could see him:

I wanted some, but I didn't have no money to buy it. And my daddy didn't give me none, didn't offer me none. I don't remember how I felt, I didn't get mad, but I remember it very well how bad I wanted some of that fresh meat. I was *so* hungry. I wanted some of that food *so* bad.

Hudson says he was "kind of shy in them days" and probably did not ask his father for food. But he cannot remember his feelings that day and offers no good explanation for the incident. In the end, however, he sums up his father as "a great man. He was a good man."

UNTIL 1932, Hudson attended church regularly. His family were all believers, and none ever missed a Sunday at church. Meeting Sundays came only once a month, but there were several churches in the vicinity with different meeting days: first Sundays were meeting Sundays at Winn's Chapel, second Sundays at Rocky Branch, third Sundays at Jordan Chapel, fourth Sundays at Lionsville. Some of the churches were Missionary Baptist, like Hudson's family, others were Methodist, but many of the same people attended them all.

For several of his churchgoing years, Hudson wanted to be a preacher, but something was missing. "I tried to get the feeling like other people, but I never could get that feeling. I went to church regular. In them years there was nowhere else to go." What he enjoyed most about church was singing. On meeting Sundays a minister would conduct services and preach, leaving little time for singing. But on other Sundays when there was only Sunday school, the program would include five or six songs.

Hudson's family all sang: his mother soprano, his father bass, Ned tenor, and Georgia Mae alto. "My mother and them used to sing when I was a kid, way back there in 19 aught 1 and 2 . . . They was singing shape-notes then, and they had a song I never will forget. I know that song yet. I learnt to sing notes off of it." I asked Hudson to sing the song, and he sang it twice for me, first: "Sa do mi, mi re do, do ce la, do la sa, mi, mi da mi, mi re do." Then in words:

> There the sun never sets
> And the leaves never fade
> In the beau-ti-ful city of gold.

That's the way it went. I used to listen at them sing, and I was a small kid, and I learnt how to sing notes on that old songbook.

When Hudson says "sing notes," he means shape-notes, a method of singing that takes its name from the variously shaped notes used in a score. Each shape has a name and corresponds to a relative pitch. Singers can read a melody by the shaped notes, without contending with absolute pitch or different keys.

Shape-note singing (stemming from the British fasola system) originated in New England, where William Little and William Smith published the first shape-note songbook, *The Easy Instructor,* in 1802. This simple system of notation did not last in musically sophisticated New England. But it flourished in the frontier regions of the South and West. In the early nineteenth century, several types of shape-notation existed. Seven-shape notation, which Hudson uses, appeared in 1832. Jesse B. Aiken introduced the system of seven-shape notation that is standard today in the South in *The Christian Minstrel,* published in Philadelphia in 1846. Here is the kind of seven-shape notation used in Hudson's own *Golden Hours* songbook.[5]

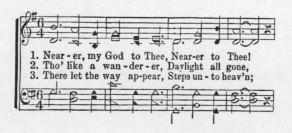

1. Near - er, my God to Thee, Near-er to Thee!
2. Tho' like a wan-der-er, Daylight all gone,
3. There let the way ap-pear, Steps un-to heav'n;

Shape-note singing did not become popular in southern black churches until the late nineteenth century. Spirituals and lined-out hymns had dominated black religious singing until then. According to Hudson, John Tiller, a preacher from South Carolina, introduced shape-note singing to Wilkes County before Hudson was born. It was popular in Wilkes County in 1902, when he heard his family sing. But in Oglethorpe, the next county to the west, there was no shape-note singing until after the First World War. A Wilkes County preacher named Tate, who lived in a place called Golden Star, introduced it.[6]

Georgia Mae preferred ballad singing to shape-note. Shape-note singing stressed the melody and printed score, but ballad sheets listed only the words:

It used to be ministers come out there—this was 19 aught 4 and 5 and 6 and 7. Preachers would come out, had what you call ballads. You have a song wrote out, verses and choruses, on a long sheet. They sell that to poor folks out in the country, 5 and 10¢ a sheet.

My aunt got very popular singing them songs. Taking up a collection, sing a song, everybody called on Sister Georgia Mae. She was about sixteen to seventeen years old then.

Didn't have no piano then. Nothing like that in the church then. And one of the songs she used to sing—I just about forgot it now—but

> My name is written, oh my Lord,
> My name is written, oh my Lord,
> My name is written, oh my Lord,
> My name is written on the cornerstone.
> If my mother asks for me, tell them I'm gone on to Galilee.
> My name is written on the cornerstone.

And the whole church would be singing

> My name is written, oh my Lord . . .

That was the kind of singing people had, see.

And in a community where gambling and drinking were sins, singing was the only kind of amusement good boys had.

Until his grandmother and brother moved out in 1917, Hudson was an obedient child. He attended church and sang and prayed and never stayed out after 9:30 at night. He had learned to keep out of trouble, partly through the negative example of his uncle Ned. He was "a good worker," with a powerful temper he seldom showed. "I didn't bother nobody," Hudson says. "I didn't want no-

body to bother me. I'd treat people nice. I'd be quiet and manner-
able, you know, tip my hat." But in the month of freedom before
his wedding, Hudson discovered drinking and gambling. He drank
"some" and "gambled a whole lot" until he went to Atlanta in 1923.

In Atlanta Hudson started a new life. "When I got in the city,"
he says, "I wouldn't associate with nobody, gamble, or drink. That's
why I stayed out of trouble." He didn't even sing. He wanted steady
work as a machinist's helper in the railroad roundhouse, since
helpers made nearly $5 a day. (He couldn't be a machinist, they
were all white.) Failing to get the job, he moved on to Birmingham, where friends swore a man could earn $5 a day regularly. In
Birmingham he became an iron molder at the Stockham foundry,
but he seldom earned $5 a day for a full week, even in the 1920s.
After the 1929 crash, weeks of one or two days' work were usual,
if there was work. Hudson was a good worker, proud of his skill.
He held his job until early 1932 when his life began to change.

He was disturbed to learn of nine young black men sentenced to
death in Scottsboro, Alabama, for raping two white women on a
train. It was to him a flagrant act of southern racial injustice. He
wanted to act, but there seemed little he could do or say about the
outrage—he was only one poorly educated, working-class Negro
with a talent for gospel singing. His minister was in a position to
protest the Scottsboro conviction, thought Hudson, but he would
not. Faced with pressure from his congregation, the minister recommended only that the law should take its course, that "God going
to take care of this thing." But one of Hudson's former co-workers,
a black man named Al Murphy, offered some compelling answers.
(Hudson explains Murphy's arguments and his own reaction in
Chapter 2 of the narrative.)

Al Murphy had been a communist since the summer of 1930,
when the Communist Party first became very active in Birmingham.
His background was not vastly different from Hudson's, although
Murphy was ten years younger. Born on a plantation in McRae,
Georgia (about seventy miles southeast of Macon), Murphy attended elementary school for four years. He moved to Birmingham
in search of work in the mid-1920s and lived with his aunt and
uncle. Before the Depression hit and things got worse, Murphy
attended night school.

One of Murphy's neighbors in Birmingham was Frank Williams.
Williams' wife was blind, and Murphy describes them as being very

poor. "I saw Frank walk along the street picking up cigarette butts. He would unwrap the tobacco and put it in an empty cigar box from which he took small amounts and gave it to his wife who smoked a pipe. He then would take some for himself and roll cigarettes." One Sunday in 1930 Murphy found a communist leaflet on his porch. He read it and liked it, but he mentioned it to no one. In the middle of the week, Williams asked him casually, "Say, Mr. Murphy, did you get one of them papers?" Williams said he himself couldn't read, but he wanted Murphy to see it. Murphy replied that he agreed with it. "A conversation began which was to seal our friendship and last as long as I stayed in Birmingham," Murphy said. He wrote to the New York address on the leaflet and received pamphlets and copies of the *Daily Worker* by return mail. Frank Williams took him to a meeting of the CP, "held in a standing room only smoke-filled room somewhere not far from the [Stockham] shop," where a white communist led a discussion about unemployment, political rights for Negroes, self-determination for the Black Belt, and the Depression. Murphy joined the Party that night. Later he joined the Young Communist League and attended Marxist-Leninist classes. Then he looked around the shop for other likely recruits.[7]

Hosea Hudson . . . had worked at Stockham for many years. He knew the workers and about their conditions. Hosea was a large hunk of somebody, about six feet tall or more, his complexion was medium brown. He was popular in the black community because he was well-known as a fine singer and music group leader.

I was cautiously optimistic about recruiting Hosea. He was too valuable to the Birmingham workingclass struggles to miss him. I was determined to reach him.[8]

Murphy led the discussion at the meeting Hudson joined. In turn, Hudson recruited people such as Henry O. Mayfield, a co-worker on the city relief-work project.

Frank Williams, Al Murphy, Hosea Hudson, Henry O. Mayfield, and all but four or five of the communists Hudson worked with in Birmingham in the 1930s were black, poor, and uneducated (in the formal sense, at least). They had been born on the plantations of Georgia and Alabama and grew up in the cotton fields. In search of work, they had migrated to the foundries, mills, and mines of Jefferson County. When there was work, they worked hard and made less than whites. Many of them resented their condition as blacks and as workmen.

Before the Communist Party came south in 1929, black steel-workers and miners lacked access to any protest organization, although members of what Hudson calls "the better class of Negroes" might join the National Association for the Advancement of Colored People or the Interracial Commission. The NAACP extended membership to all, but the organization's activities made it offensive to Alabama whites, and its membership made it uncomfortable for working-class blacks. Class lines in the black community were unwritten but clear, and men like Hudson did not associate with educated or well-off Negroes until the united-front period of the late-1930s.

"The better class of Negroes" numbered only a few among Birmingham's 100,000 blacks in the 1930s. (The total population was about 260,000.) Hudson says they were "teachers, preachers, little homeowners, big deacons of the churches," and they lived in a different world. The city's housing pattern drew the distinctions. Workers lived next to the mines and foundries—like Stockham Pipe and Fittings, which owned little neighborhoods—or near the whites they served. Blacks of the better class owned their own houses and lived where they pleased, within the acceptable areas in a racially segregated community. But Hudson has never owned his own home. In the Depression years, when he was out of work most of the time, his family moved every few months in the same poor neighborhoods.

In its appeal to radical black workers in the 1930s, the CP was occupying virgin territory. In Birmingham there were virtually no unions, no Socialist Party, no leftist parties other than the CPUSA, not even the Universal Negro Improvement Association. (Murphy said that he had read about the Garvey movement and heard that a chapter of the UNIA existed in Birmingham, but he was never able to find it.[9]) Between 1930, when the CP began to organize seriously in the South, and 1936, when the CIO entered the field, the CP had no competition on the left. Jim crow and hard times had created a radical black constituency in Alabama of men like Murphy and Hudson who did not find political sufficiency in church or lodge. They joined the CP gladly, at their very first meetings. "It look like the thing I had been looking for," says Hudson. When hundreds of Williamses, Murphys, Hudsons, and Mayfields became

communists, they also made the Party their own. In Alabama in the
1930s, the CP was a southern, working-class black organization, as
Hudson's narrative clearly shows.

The Scottsboro defense, jobs, relief, and civil rights were the
Party's short-term concerns. The long-range aim was self-determination for the Black Belt, a goal worked out in Moscow in 1928. The
theory held that the Negroes of the Black Belt counties of the Deep
South constituted an oppressed nation, according to Stalin's terse
and comprehensive definition.[10]

In books and pamphlets in the 1930s, the historian James Allen
explained that the Black Belt was the weakest link in the chain of
American capitalism. If the CP could educate and awaken the
peasant masses (black and white), a democratic revolution might
occur. Allen foresaw a revolutionary struggle that would create
"councils of Soviets of peasants and workers seizing power at first
on a local scale, extending their sphere, consolidating a number of
areas and establishing the hegemony of the new revolutionary gov-
ernmental power as the democratic revolution spreads." Only then
would blacks obtain their civil rights in the South. They would con-
fiscate the plantations and redistribute the land as collective farms.[11]
The policy of self-determination focused attention on racial oppression as part of a wider economic system that victimized both
black and white working classes in the South. It presented a "scientific" explanation for the pervasive racial discrimination that otherwise seemed to defy understanding. CP periodicals presented black
life as a whole national culture endowed with full dignity, not
merely a flawed and comic mimicking of whites. The CP's introduction of the self-determination slogan signaled a concentration on the
South and on Negroes that had not occurred in a national political
organization since the middle of the nineteenth century.

Translated into immediate goals like welfare and voting rights,
the self-determination theory was clear and attractive to Hudson.
However, the theory's tortured logic and the shadow world of revolution presented problems. It proved difficult for working-class communists to interpret the theory without reciting it like a catechism.
Making sense of self-determination became particularly awkward
in Birmingham, where the generalizations about the plantation
economy broke down.

One day Hudson tried to explain to me the substance of discussions he and his comrades had in the early 1930s on the application of the self-determination slogan to Birmingham:

We used to discuss quite at length about the places like Birmingham—was in the Black Belt—an industrial, a coal mine. What we going do about that? Well, we had a lot of discussion, and I can tell you the truth, I don't know how we come to, what conclusion we reached.

But we said, it meant putting it maybe in that particular area, like the industrials for the mines, the ownership of mines and mills, it might have to be after the workers take power before the Negro people would be able to enjoy they full rights in a place where these industrial is at.

These big industrials is owned by the North, northern capitalists, and they wasn't going give them up so easy without a real battle. And that's, that's what, we also discussed all that.

Out in the rural area, you know, the rural area of the Black Belt, where the Negro farmers was in the majority, we felt that there, many places that the Negro would be able to get, enjoy the land, the land would be, you know, the rights of the land, before socialism.

But then they, we know that they going have a big struggle in the big industrial towns like Bessemer Alabama, Birmingham, Gasden Alabama. All these places was in the Black Belt. It's a question of what was to do there. It just wasn't the farming area.

Really, what it meant, it meant the right of self-determination in the Black Belt, meant confiscating the land from the big landlords. It also meant confiscating the industrials from the big industrials, which was going to be a pulling of a eye tooth, but that was the correct slogan at that time, see?

It is not that Hudson is less articulate than other working-class communists in Birmingham—the theory was inappropriate. It depended on the Comintern's misapplication of Russian history to the American situation.

I doubt that anyone ever joined the Communist Party on the strength of the self-determination theory alone. It was the Party's more pragmatic activities that succeeded in attracting (if not holding) large numbers of southern blacks during the 1930s. Whereas fewer than 200 blacks belonged to the CP in 1929, over 20 percent of the new members in 1930 were Negroes—1300 of the 6000 recruits. In the Birmingham district, the CP enrolled significant, but not massive, numbers. In the late 1930s, between 1000 and 1500 people were "in contact with the Communist leadership" either in Party-related organizations (the ILD or the Young Communist League) or in the Party itself, which numbered some 250, nearly all blacks. In 1931, blacks accounted for a little over 7 percent of the national membership; in 1932, nearly 10 percent; and in 1935, 11 percent. In 1939 the number of Negro communists was 5005. The Party continued to attract Negroes in the 1940s, with membership hovering between 7000 and 8000—14 percent of the total—in the mid-1940s. The black membership has had a very high rate of turn-over, however, among the rank and file. Among the leaders, blacks were more likely than whites to stay in the Party.[12]

Hudson's experience both corroborates and disputes this attraction and loss of black recruits. Hudson's forty-seven years in the CP make perfect sense for him, in terms of both his ideals and his self-interest. He adds that his friends have been every bit as constant in their loyalty as he. Among his close friends, only two dropped out, Joe Howard, in an incident he recounts in Chapter 12, and John Beidel, who gave church activities first claim on his time after the Party sent him back to church in the late 1930s. The rest of Hudson's friends stayed in the Party until they died or left Alabama.

In a recent visit to Birmingham, Hudson rediscovered an octo-genarian comrade and his older sister who still think of themselves as communists. "Archie is just as strong—he ain't active—but he just as strong in his belief as he ever was, and also his sister. On the question of people leaving the Party . . . the Party people back yonder in them rough day that I talk about . . . practically all them people dead." The people from the early 1930s didn't leave the Party, Hudson says, the Party left the people. Well after the 1950s, when the CP went underground, Negroes in Tallapoosa County still considered themselves communists or members of the Sharecroppers Union. But the organizers, unable to "make contact" with large numbers of Party people, could not keep them together in groups.

Hudson surmises that difficult conditions in Alabama bred a tough kind of communist who did not appear in other places, or even in Birmingham in easier times. In "those rough days," as Hudson fondly terms the early 1930s, the Party in Birmingham was a tightly organized unit. Even on the national level, the workers were the center of the organization. For Hudson, the *Daily Worker* was at its best in those years, when it frequently printed workers' letters about conditions on the shop floors.

Hudson's own comrades in the South went to their graves as communists, but that was not the common thing. Only in the Deep South was the Party overwhelmingly black. In the North and West, whites have held the majority in Party units, and the CP has had difficulty in holding blacks. Hudson explains that Party people, black and white, tend to push Negro recruits into organizational activities before they are mature ideologically. This effort, he says, "has a tendency to swell that individual's head." Other Party members "pushing him and pushing him . . . but they don't take time to study that individual, to see what his level of understanding is. And by not taking that into account, they pushes these people too fast and too far. They push them clean up through the Party and out the Party." In his own case, Hudson says, he resisted the pushing. "If I had allowed the white comrades—and Negro comrades too—to push me like that, I would have been pushed the same way. But I always was like a mule going down a hill. I would always hold on brakes, proclaim I didn't know, act a little bashful. I took advantage of my not being able to read and write. And by that I learnt quite a bit."

Hudson's second explanation for high black attrition in the CP points to the "white chauvinism" (racial prejudice) of white communists:

that's another thing that cause a lot of Negroes, to my thinking, to leave the Party. Because when they come in the Party, they think they coming where everything hunky-dory, but you have to fight in there. You got the filth of capitalism, racism, and what-not, expressing itself one way or the other, in the Party, like it is out . . . just because people in the Party, don't you think that they been regenerated and born again. You got to battle them things and get that junk out of them, see. The only thing is, in the Party, you got a chance to fight.

Hudson finds fault with blacks who leave the Party over racist incidents without fighting back. The Party opposes racism, Hudson says, but individual comrades are not innocent of "white chauvinism."

Anti-communist writing on the CP stresses the Party's failure in regard to blacks and places great emphasis on high turnover as proof of that failure. The argument says that communists wanted to embarrass the United States by courting the most oppressed people in the country; but Negroes, downtrodden as they were, loved America too much to become communists; hence the CP failed in the United States. Now that the Cold War is thirty years in the past, it is possible to conclude that the Communist Party never attracted masses of Americans, even in the depths of the Depression, but also to see that among the small minority of the population that is radically inclined, blacks joined the CP in numbers proportionate to their share of the population.

The racial climate of the United States in the 1930s and 1940s, rather than a strategic failure on the part of the CP, provides much of the explanation for why blacks left the Party. American life was so thoroughly segregated that, until recently, few whites and blacks were likely to have personal contact with members of the other race, most certainly not as equals or co-workers. But in the CP, whites and blacks attempted to collaborate on a basis of equality. It should come as no surprise that they experienced difficulties working together comfortably or that black communists were annoyed by manifestations of insensitivity and "white chauvinism."

No matter how patient the Negroes or well-meaning the whites, cooperating interracially in a segregated world that assumed black inferiority imposed strain on both sides. For blacks, working with whites usually meant enduring slights or insults, something to be kept to a minimum in life, not to be sought out. In the CP, blacks voluntarily associated with whites who tried—not always with complete success—to improve on American race relations.[13] In attempting to organize interracially, the Party anticipated desegration by decades. Herbert Aptheker, Eugene Genovese, and Jessica Mitford have all observed that white communists were conspicuous in the 1940s and '50s because, unlike other whites, they associated with Negroes.[14]

Negroes felt out of place in the Party for other than racial reasons. During the '30s, '40s, and '50s, the CP was strongest in the big cities of the North and West. It drew few members from the South and many from New York and, as time went on, more from the middle class and more intellectuals. Working-class Party members included a large proportion of northerners in heavy industry who had foreign parents. During these years, blacks were almost entirely working-class, but comparatively few worked in industry. Blacks were native Americans of southern, rural background and upbringing. They shared an uneasiness with organized radicalism characteristic of most native Americans and southerners.

In Hudson's narrative, one of the most potent forces in keeping blacks away from the Communist Party was fear. They were usually poor and vulnerable to employers' reprisals against radicals. Time and again Hudson quotes his co-workers warning their peers, "Don't mess with that stuff, you lose you job."

The warnings were right, of course. Only visionaries were so foolish to take the risk, because communists did lose their jobs. Political and economic repression—usually expressed in racial terms—was so extensive and so severe in Alabama that most blacks and black institutions tended to guard their own survival. They carefully shunned even the appearance of militancy. Considering the formidable pressures against being both Negro and communist in the South, it's a wonder that any blacks at all joined the Communist Party in Alabama.

Hudson has has heard it said often that the CP only wanted to use Negroes to further Soviet ends, a charge he dismisses as class-biased fabrication:

I heard that, I heard it up all the way through from the early years, when I first got acquainted with the Party. That was in the papers, especially these better class of Negroes was using that slang.

Now you can see from what I say, from what kind of people *we* were, what kind of people was joining the Party and was active in these un-employed block committees and in the ILD. It wont none of these little people that got they hand in the pie, thinking they going get a dollar from their good white friends. It was the people out there who knowed they didn't have nothing but they chains of slavery to lose.

So any guy that say the Party was using Negro people is just lying, that's all. Because the Party is a working class, political party, and it takes in all workers, and the Negroes happen to be part of that working class. How they going use them? I mean, when these people raise the question about they "using" us, how they going use us when we're part of this working class? We play our part as the workers.

Despite Hudson's interpretation, the CP unquestionably used Negroes, as have the Democrats and Republicans over the years. What is important here is that blacks like Hudson were able to use the Communist Party in their turn. The Party supplied Hudson with a satisfying explanation for the oppression of blacks in America. It broadened his perspective by putting him in touch with communists across the nation and the world, people who often had far more formal education and social standing than Hudson and his friends. It is clear that his membership in the Party gave him educational advantages he would never have had in other circumstances.[15] Most important, the CP gave Hudson self-confidence:

What the Party was doing was taking this lower class like myself and making people out of them, took the time and they didn't laugh at you if you made a mistake. In other words, it made this lower class feel at home when they sit down in a meeting. If he got up and tried to talk and he couldn't express hisself, nobody liable to laugh at him. They tried to help them and tell them, "you'll learn." There was always something to bring you forward, to give you courage.

Every time Reverend [Jesse] Jackson comes on television, say "I am somebody," I thinks about it. The Party made me know that I was somebody.

Hudson was a leader in the Birmingham CP from the beginning. The eight others who joined with him elected him unit organizer, the equivalent of chairman of the group. When District 17 was reorganized and a political bureau set up in the spring of 1932, Hudson was appointed to the "pol buro" as one of twelve policymakers for Alabama. In the early 1930s, Hudson was responsible for the unemployed councils among all the Negroes in Birmingham, with several subordinates reporting to him. The Party practice of rehearsing procedures beforehand made Hudson more confident in public—for instance, in meetings of the Workers Alliance. The Party even helped him conquer his feelings of inferiority among the educated.

When the CP sent its people into liberal organizations in the United-front period, Hudson could not speak comfortably before middle-class blacks. He recalls his fear and the impact his presence made:

You know how you feel—shame I reckon. That's the way I felt, but I just fought againt it, went on in there. I just break myself in there. I just would go. Other Negroes scared to go there, go there and pull off they hat there, act like they lost.

And you know one thing, tell you the truth, me and Mayfield, just to be working type of people, me and Mayfield was the ones that woked them so-called better class of Negroes up that the lower-class Negroes had some sense.

They was shocked, they was surprised to hear what we had to say. They wonder, "where did that fellow Hudson come from? I didn't know we had people like that!"

That was the kind of miration they made. We'd get up and talk, and they'd just sit there with they mouth open. They didn't know what to say, cause they hadn't been used to something like that.

Hudson is right in his conviction that given the time, place, and his class and race, only the Communist Party would have provided him the patient encouragement he needed to master public speaking. In addition, painstaking tutoring from Jim Gray, an Appalachian white minister who is still his friend, led Hudson to read and write with ease when he was thirty-six years old. During the 1940s Hudson stood out in the Alabama CIO, thanks to more than a decade of coaching and inspiriting from black and white communists.

A retired official of the United Steelworkers of America in Birmingham insisted to me in 1978 that, if Hudson had not been irrevocably attached to the CP, he could have made a career in the union. I asked Hudson about that, and he thought back to the black union officials he knew in Birmingham, then contrasted his own life. Although he is poor, Hudson has published a book and met people from all over the world. His name and his life are known in countries he has never seen. He says it could not have happened outside the Communist Party:

Would the steel union white officials taken such pains to show me that I still could be somebody, at the age of thirty-six years old [and] could not read and write [?] I say they would not. I could have become their servant or yes-man. I would have been a great union Negro leader in their eyesight in and around Birmingham Alabama, just like Eb Cox who had a leaning, and many other Negro leaders in the unions.

Most of them has gone and the only record that is left of them is their names and a hump in the ground.[16]

The union men may have it good for a while, "the big time, nice home, nice car, and every woman I see I want, be out with her—that's the way they carry on, I know the life of them"—but Hudson is satisfied that he worked for a greater good, "to see things better for everybody," and has some permanence in the printed record.

HUDSON's joining the Communist Party in the early 1930s makes perfect sense in terms of the CPUSA's chronology, and it also fits into Hudson's own personal and cultural history. Although he had attended church since childhood and joined a Missionary Baptist church at eleven, he never underwent the religious experience and conversion that should precede baptism. He simply followed a girlfriend to the mourners' bench, to baptism, and to church membership. He watched people getting happy in church but never felt like shouting. He says, "I wondered how did people get that feeling, what did it feel like. I never did discover it." Nor did he understand

God and preachers: "I'd wonder why did God always talk with the preachers, didn't talk to other people."

Impervious to any religious calling, Hudson nevertheless for several years wanted to be a preacher. He went to church and prayed. Better yet, he says, "I had a voice. Still got a preacher's voice. A lot of people still think I'm a minister if I don't tell them different." But Hudson's interpretation of the Bible placed another obstacle in his way to the ministry:

I had a discussion [with] old man Spellman, a old man, every day he used to come down the house—that was when I had my leg broke. That was way back there in 1930. We discussing the Bible, and I was discussing about James. It look like it was First James or Second James. (I'm going get the Bible and read that chapter.) It says something about "servants obey your masters." And that, just reading that, I disagreed with that, cause I seed that, even up to that day, I seed that as the people have to serve the masters (was the rich), and the people was serving and wont getting nowhere.[17]

When Hudson joined the Communist Party, he says, "I began to drift off, and I lost sight of that preaching, I lost sight of the Bible."

Hudson says that the Party seemed to be a sort of alternate church at first, with restraints on worldly activity as strict as the Baptists':

We all thought, "Well, now, this is the real religion," cause they said that Party members shouldn't mess around with another Party member's wife or his daughter, and all like that, and live a clean life, get out and meet the public, people look upon you as a leader. So that was what we came up in the Party in, and not drinking no whiskey, not being half-drunk. (And tell you the truth, I didn't know that Party members drink until 1950, the month of December 1950, when I first come to understand that top Party people drink whiskey . . . My first time seeing Party people drink was at a Christmas Party.)

The parallel between the Party and the Baptist church runs even deeper than Hudson admits. He grew up in the Southern Baptist tradition that allows young men a period of wild youth between churchgoing childhood and churchgoing maturity. It is not unusual for adults to get baptized and join a church after having married and passed through a crisis. Hudson remembers that an adult named Merton Huff joined church at the time of his own youthful and insincere conversion. Joining the church as an adult is the public profession of one's settling down and pledging one's life to God and to a congregation. It marks a willingness to make a commitment to a community of believers.

Even though Hudson was never able to flesh out his religious commitment or experience conversion, his life divided into periods that were recognized by southern Baptists. He had his wild period, drinking and gambling in the years between 1918 and 1923—and committed occasional transgressions until September 1931. When he joined the Communist Party, he pledged himself to what was the equivalent of a congregation (his comrades in Birmingham) and a religion (communism). This conversion bound him through faith to the Party in the early years, before he began to realize fully the advantages to be gained from membership. Now when he explains his commitment to the CP, he draws a baptismal analogy:

When I started in, it's like you got water a foot deep here, and you don't know way out yonder the water's deep. The further you go in the water, the deeper in the water you get, the more you get out there, the more you learn out there.

So finally you get out in the real deep water. So then, it's best while you out there to stay out there.

A docile Party member who never raised questions prematurely, Hudson survived all the crises of the CPUSA. Like other black members, he has not been enough distressed by events in Europe to leave the Party.[18] Hudson easily explains away the Hitler-Stalin pact and argues the need to open a second front after Germany attacked the USSR. In 1944 he voted with everyone else in the CP to transform the Communist Party into the Communist Political Association. In 1945 he turned around and repudiated Earl Browder along with all the rest. He did not have to weather the white-chauvinism campaign that battered the Party in the North in 1949–50 because there were not enough white communists in Alabama, and because by mid-1950 the CP in Birmingham was underground. Hudson was on the Soviet side of the Hungarian uprising of 1956. But he did have some difficult moments after Nikita Khrushchev disclosed Stalin's mass butchery. Those revelations in 1956 divided the American CP on the related issues of subservience to Moscow and denunciation of Stalin. A faction led by *Daily Worker* editor John Gates repudiated Stalin and questioned the Soviet Party's hegemony in the international communist community.

Hudson held back his criticism, remembering that the Negro Commission that had mandated the Party's move into the South in

1930 had met under Stalin's chairmanship. Without the Negro Commission, Hudson would never even had heard of the CP. In the way most Americans attribute whatever happens during a President's term in office to the President, Hudson gave Stalin credit for the Comintern position on the Negro question:

Stalin had done more than anybody else for the rights of the Negro in the South, cause Stalin, way back there at the early stages of the Party, along about in the late '20s, first of the '30s, he called a conference of some of the Negro American comrades, and out from that, they discussed the Negro question in America. You know, how can we approach it. And they came out with the slogan of the right of self-determination . . . Stalin did something that nobody else hadn't done, to make it possible for us to be able to struggle.

On his death bed Edward Strong, a long-time friend of Hudson's agreed with him about the anti-Stalin resolution:

"Hosie," [Strong] said, "I'm not going against Stalin." Some of them [in the Party] wanted to come out, make a big public statement condemning Stalin. He said he wasn't going to do it. He took the same position that I took, that regardless of what they have to say about Stalin, Stalin had made it possible for the Negro in America to liberate himself, where none of the rest of them hadn't done . . . He wanted to be no part of going against Stalin.[19]

The resolution did not pass, but Stalin remains an awkward subject for Hudson. He disassociates himself from Stalin's activities in the Soviet Union and thinks of him solely in terms of the initiatives of the CPUSA in Alabama.

Hudson also considers the infamous "third period" of CP history its best. According to the Comintern theory devised in 1928 at the sixth conference, the third period followed a first period of revolutionary upsurge in the late 1910s and very early 1920s and a second period of capitalism's temporary stabilization in the 1920s. The Comintern had designated the third period as the crisis of capitalism before the Great Depression came, and it thereby earned a brief reputation for good economic forecasting.

The third period was also said to be marked by a danger of "imperialist war," in which troubled capitalist states would gang up against their socialist enemy, the USSR. The third period was to have been followed by socialist revolution, but the Third Reich came instead. The united front of the late '30s (the popular front in Europe) was a reaction to nazism, and because events in Germany broke the sequence, the united front was not called the fourth period.

Hudson does not use the phrase "united front," however. When he speaks of the 1935–1946 decade, he calls it the "New Deal period." The first two years of Roosevelt's presidency, what some historians call the first New Deal, were a "reactionary period," says Hudson. Only what is sometimes called the second New Deal merits Hudson's use of the name. He extends that period through the war, to include the whole time that communists were active in liberal organizations and when he worked in the union. Similarly, he does not mention the third period by name. He calls the early '30s "those rough days."

The third period appears in modern writing as a belligerent phase of ultra-left sectarianism, when communists labeled all noncommunist liberals "social fascists" and refused to cooperate with them.[20] The Party's southern salient is generally overlooked in such analyses. In Alabama, exclusiveness was not explicit Party policy, but the tone of the CP in the early 1930s militated against a dedicated communist's belonging to nonrevolutionary organizations. During this time, Hudson dropped out of his gospel quartet and left his church.

In Birmingham, where a city ordinance outlawed the CP, Party meetings were likely to be raided by the police in the early '30s, so communists went to great lengths to protect themselves. The Party, ILD, and unemployed councils were organized into carefully meshed committees and subcommittees. All prospective members were scrutinized before they attended their first unit meetings. Hudson boasts that, in perfect secrecy, he could cover the whole city of Birmingham with leaflets in one evening—the organization was just that tight.

For Hudson, the Party's preoccupations with the Negro question and self-determination were appropriate for the 1930s. During the 1940s, when he was absorbed in the union, he lost sight of the self-determination slogan. Although it was not formally rescinded, the Negro nationality question slipped away from the forefront of the Party's concerns. Self-determination came up again in 1956, when Hudson's friend James Jackson presented a thesis on the right of self-determination for the Black Belt. (Jackson is now the National Educational Director of the CPUSA.)

"Jackson's position," says Hudson, "was that you had to fight for

the rights of Negroes, jobs for Negroes, and fight for the unions to
bring the Negroes into jobs on equal basis. That was a economic
fight, along with the question of rights to vote, of political rights for
the Negro people, which they had never got." Hudson agreed with
Jackson that the old slogan for self-determination no longer applied.
"Them houses is growed up, them plantations is briar patches, you
know, and the Negroes is all in the towns." When Jackson's resolution passed, several black communists who opposed the change left
the Party, including the well-known leader, Harry Haywood. That
was the first instance Hudson knows of when many blacks quit the
Party on theoretical grounds.[21]

The next great Party crisis occurred in 1968–69, but for Hudson
the issue was not the Soviet Union's intervention in Czechoslovakia.
It was black power and, in particular, a resolution before the 1969
Party convention supporting Negroes' right to armed self-defense.
In the bitter and confusing debate, many older communists foun-
dered as black comrades argued opposite sides of the question. Hudson and Jackson together opposed the resolution on the grounds
that putting the Party on record for armed self-defense would play
into the hands of enemies who accused communists of advocating
violence. "You ain't have to worry about the Negroes down South
defending theyself, they going defend theyself," said Hudson of the
Louisiana Deacons of Defense who were already armed to protect
civil rights activists. For Hudson, the Party's duty was to reassume
its role of the early 1930s, when the CP and ILD championed the
Scottsboro boys and Angelo Herndon. "What you do," said Hudson
to the convention, "let's organize to defend them when they do
get in prison . . . That's the self-defense." Hudson's position prevailed, but several blacks he knew placed racial allegiance before
their commitment to the CP and left the Party.

At the same time, Hudson was fiercely opposed to the whole con-
cept of black power and nationalist separatism of any kind. He saw
black power as the evil corresponding to white chauvinism. Without
citing the slogan, "black and white, unite and fight," he insisted that
the working classes must unite to combat their mutual enemy, capitalism. Black separatism could only lead up a blind alley, he said,
and he had no time for African names and clothing. In the last year
or so, however, his position has softened in practice, if not in rhet-
oric. He is collaborating with a minister of the Nation of Islam in

Atlantic City to combat the resurgence of the Ku Klux Klan in southern New Jersey.

White communists left the Party at various times, often because of issues of policy that turned on foreign events. Hudson says that blacks felt more strongly about what happened in this country. Like blacks outside the CP, black communists cared most about domestic questions that related directly to black interests. They were not likely to become deeply involved with European issues.

HUDSON takes his longevity as a vindication of the course his life has taken. He looks back at what happened to those who let him down, crossed him up, or betrayed him and says, "All them dead now, and I'm still here to tell it." He says that often. Only two aspects of his life visibly disturb him still, the breakup of his marriage in 1946 and the loss of his union local and his job in 1947–48.

Hudson's first marriage lasted nearly thirty years. But in retrospect, Hudson remembers aggravations in the 1920s. Even before he joined the Party, he says now, his marriage had tensions. Sophie complained that he spent too much time away from home singing with his quartet. "She was just as bad about the singing as she was about the Party," he says. Hudson's nightly Party meetings were not the actual reason for her making trouble, he is convinced. "That might of been her excuse. It was just a part of her."

When we first began taping our interviews, Hudson spoke even more harshly of his former wife than he does in the narrative now. He blamed her entirely for the breakdown of the marriage, finding nothing in his own conduct that might have weakened the bond. During our conversations, however, I have come to sympathize with Sophie Hudson. But as she did not wish to speak about the past or give her side of a painful story, we have here only Hudson's half. Under my questioning, at least, he admits that his absorption in the CP and his spending night after night in Party activities strained his marriage. Although he says he suspects now that his wife was seeing another man in 1936, he also says that he continued to give his attention to the Party.

But all his and my reasoning about the issue thirty years later cannot blunt the surprise he felt when his marriage collapsed in 1946. He was enraged, and the rage lasted for two years. Hudson was beside himself with hurt and threatened at crosswalks and bus stops to kill his wife and the man she later married. He felt then and still feels the shame and anger of a betrayed husband.

The broken marriage was a casualty of ambitions that were Hudson's well before the CP supplied the broader ideals and the means to realize his aims. He had hoped in the days of enthusiastic quartet singing to make records and become famous. Later on he succeeded, making his mark in the Party and the union. His wife, however, did not share his aspirations. She saw only the daily hardships and his absences from home.

I spoke to Hudson's former wife and only son in Birmingham in 1976. The son is almost sixty, tall, slender, attractive but worn-looking. He has no strong political convictions, and yet he holds no brief against the Communist Party. He criticizes his father for caring more for the movement—which merely happened to be communism—than for his family. He was more communicative and less bitter than Hudson's former wife. Sophie Lester spoke with me only briefly, insisting—understandably—that she didn't want to review "all that mess." She blamed Hudson for willful neglect, but she was not particularly angry with the CP. In her eyes, the Party had only furnished Hudson with a pretext for leaving his family to shift for themselves in especially hard times. It is clear that all three of them, Hudson, Sophie, and their son, still feel keenly anguish they inflicted on one another in the 1930s and 1940s.

Hudson's other painful memory dates from the Cold War era, when the career he had gradually built as a labor leader in Birmingham collapsed, crushing aspirations he had nurtured for decades. Even before he joined the CP, the welfare of blacks had concerned him. In the 1920s and '30s he heard frequently that Negroes lacked leaders of courage who would not sell out. By the 1940s Hudson had the self-confidence to try for prominence:

I'd study. I'd maneuver and train myself to be the spokesman. And I got to be the spokesman at practically all the meetings. I see what need to be said—they all wallowing around—I get up and speak. After I found out I could be somebody around there in Birmingham, I set out to be a leader among the Negro people.

He succeeded by monopolizing the leadership of his local. He was the president and the chairman of the grievance committee and a delegate to the Birmingham Industrial Union Council and delegate to the state CIO and national Steel conventions. Judging from his power and determination today, I would guess that he did not absorb differing opinions very well. Even now he doesn't admit that his domination of the local might have cost him some support.

In late 1947 he was expelled from the Birmingham Industrial Union Council for being a communist. In the council meeting that voted to oust him, Hudson had the support of most of the black delegates, but all the whites and a handful of the blacks voted against him. Hudson lost, and he remembers those few Negroes very well.

Following his expulsion from the council, Jackson Industries fired him from his molding job. His local then called a special meeting to decide whether or not to appeal his dismissal through the grievance procedure, a meeting that more white members attended than had ever before turned out. They came with the express purpose of voting against Hudson, whose leadership they had long resented. As in the council, the great majority of the blacks voted for Hudson. The vote was very close in the local, but Hudson won.

When his support from blacks in the council and the local proved to be less than unanimous, Hudson was shocked and disappointed. He considered retiring from political life entirely:

I liked to throwed up hands. I went to some of the comrades, I told Lou Burnham, "Lou," I said, "I think I'll just give up this fight, won't try to push it through."

He said, "Hosie, you can't do that. You'd be letting too many people down. People is looking to you and depending on you. You'd let the people down."

He fought the appeal for his job but lost it as well as membership in the union. The Negroes, he says, let him down by "voting along with the white delegates, even when it came to voting me out the union itself." The whites, whom Hudson's leadership had offended for so long and who had taken advantage of the Cold War climate to ground him, he barely mentions. He never expected anything from them.

Summing up his experiences in the late 1940s and early '50s, Hudson speaks evenly and thoughtfully of FBI harassment, Bull Connor and the Birmingham police, and the myriad dangers of living underground. These were the risks a communist ran in those years, and he takes a certain satisfaction from having outsmarted the authorities. The historic Cold War, he knows, was a national thing, engineered by powerful whites outside the South. As an indi-

vidual, Hudson could not affect it. But in 1978 he still rails against
the Negroes in the Birmingham Industrial Union Council and in his
local who caused him to loss his seat and his job. Unlike the Cold
War, a handful of Negroes presents a problem of human propor-
tions. Their treachery, as Hudson sees it, very nearly destroyed his
life.

Recounting his disappointment, Hudson wonders why he still
fights for the rights of black people at all. "I said many times, I
shouldn't do *nothing*. Sometime I look back, I gets very bitter. I
shouldn't do *nothing*." For Hudson, the heartfelt meaning of the
Cold War is his betrayal by Negroes.

Thanks to the encouragement of his comrades, Hudson did not
give up organizing in the late 1940s. He worked in the Progressive
Party campaign in 1948 and formed a United Political Action Committee in 1950.[22] In mid-1950 he had suddenly to go underground
in Birmingham and then move to Atlanta. There he served as a liai-
son among scattered communists in the South until the Party brought
him to New York early in 1954. By that time he imagined every
white man in a suit, white shirt, and two-toned shoes to be an
FBI agent. He had trouble sleeping and was unfit to work for two
years. In 1956 he took a job as a janitor in a New York resturant.
Working at night, he attended Party meetings by day when he
could. But the combination of long, abstruse discussions and fa-
tigue proved deadening. He retains little of the substance of those
important debates, beyond the questions of censuring Stalin and
rephrasing the position on self-determination for the Black Belt.

Hudson married the widow of a New Jersey timber merchant in
1962. Virginia Larue Marson was a small, dark-skinned woman,
spunky and devoted to Hudson, as he was to her. To fulfill her life-
long wish to live near the boardwalk, they moved to Atlantic City,
where she died before *Black Worker in the Deep South* was published, dedicated to her memory.

Hudson began writing his autobiography in the early 1950s, when
he was underground. Sitting well back on the porch of friends in
New Orleans, he first put pencil to paper. But the manuscript that
formed the basis of the book dates mostly from the 1960s. The publishing process began when Hudson attended Ben Davis' funeral in
New York in 1964 and ran into a black Party member he had not
seen since Birmingham days. Eugene Gordon was a writer, and he
told Hudson he wanted to do a book on the South and needed his

help. Hudson replied, "I already wrote the book. I need somebody to edit it for me." They agreed that Gordon would edit Hudson's handwritten manuscript.

Hudson gave the manuscript to him, but Gordon did nothing. Hudson's friends would ask about the book's progress; Hudson would see Gordon and ask him; Gordon would stall. There was a falling out and Hudson took his manuscript back. Two high-ranking black communists, Henry Winston and William L. Patterson, stepped in and encouraged the project by sending Gordon $100 a month to edit Hudson's book. In fifteen months, Gordon finished his work. By then, says Hudson, it was 1968 and the book still was not ready to go to press.

[Gordon] turned it over to a Jewish woman writer, and she got it. You couldn't make out all the words, the way he had left it. It wasn't typed, it was handwritten. He done changed it, and I had to change some of it back. So this Jewish woman, the Party had her on it for about three months. She was an elderly woman and she could understand my writing better than Gordon could.

After this writer revised Gordon's version of Hudson's manuscript, she turned it over to James Allen, editor of International Publishers, the CP-related press. International held the manuscript for several months and then rejected it. Finally Henry Winston pressured the house to publish the book. A young black teacher from St. Louis made the last revisions in February 1972 while Hudson nodded beside him. In July 1972, *Black Worker in the Deep South* appeared.

The book reads like nothing Hudson said or wrote. Here is a section of the book as Hudson wrote it in 1965 and then as it appears in print. Hudson's manuscript goes like this:

the land lords Would furnish My Mother and grandMother pore land Which Was Meny times pore soild. Rockey. Washes across the fields of little ditches that had to be filled with green pine Bush to catch some of the soil and stop some of the flore of Warter from Heavy Rain falls. the land lord Would take What cotton and cotton seeds that We did make that year for depts.

these Depts Would be for the futlizes that we use in tryin to Make that crop.

In *Black Worker in the Deep South:*

The way it was with sharecropping was this: First the landlord would furnish us families with the most run-down, poorest land with

rocky soil and ditches cut crisscross every which way by rain water rushing from the high ground. Before we could begin to work the land, we
had to lay branches of pine sapplings in the ditches. In time, this acted
like a brake on the flooding waters, and the heavy rainfalls would then
partly fill the ditches with soil. But though all this work helped to keep
the soil from being washed away, it didn't make it any richer. It still
needed fertilizer, and that cost money. (page 9)

The paperback version of *Black Worker in the Deep South* appeared in 1972. Since then, Hudson always carries copies of it with
him to sell. When he addressed my University of Pennsylvania students, they remarked on the irony of a communist's selling books.
But they also understood that, for Hudson, selling his book is not
only a way to make a little money and an act of modest self-promo-
tion, but it is also a vehicle for spreading his truth. "I done made my
day, you know," he said in 1977.

When you get up to seventy-nine, you near about done made your time.
Why I want this thing to be told, because I know how hard that the
other people, my co-workers and members in the Party with me strug-
gled to try to live to see this day. Most of them has been long gone, and
I'm still here. So you know I have a right to talk.

Without the communists in the 1930s and '40s, he is convinced, the
civil rights movement of the 1950s and '60s couldn't have succeeded. He overlooks the important achievements of liberal groups
like the Southern Conference for Human Welfare, the Interracial
Commission, the Southern Regional Council, and the NAACP,
which also helped to change the South in his time. For Hudson, it
was CP and only the CP that took tough positions in the bad old
days.

The publication of his book marked a step in his personal growth,
although he was seventy-four years old when it came out. In the
past, he "wasn't exactly independent on my thinking and speaking."
But now, "I'm a little bit more independent than I used to be. If
I'm wrong, I'm wrong. I say it now." During our two years of taping
interviews, Hudson has also revised his estimate of the role the CP
played in his development.

Earlier in our work, Hudson gave the Communist Party credit
for changing an ordinary, illiterate industrial worker into a national,
even international, figure. He wrote me a letter saying that "The
Party Made Me To Be Come To Be What I Am What Eaver It
Is."[23] He spoke of his need to tell the story of communists in Bir-

mingham. If he was exceptional because he happened to be a survivor, he was no more than what the Party could make of any man.

At the end of one of our last interviews, I asked him if there was something special in him as a person that made his life turn out as it has—or was he Everyman whom the Communist Party had fashioned into a leader? He said that the Party certainly helped him become who he is now, but he feels he has always been a strong individual. "I don't know, but I always had people to respect me. It look like they just single me out." Then he told two anecdotes that displayed his natural leadership ability, long before he became a communist. In 1917 he led a gang of Negroes older than he away from a job cutting lumber when the quitting bell did not ring. In the second, which he recounts in Chapter 3, he led molders from the Stockham foundry to the Alabama Stove Foundry where they hoped to find better-paying work.

Hudson read his horoscope recently and it confirmed his estimation of himself. "According to my horoscope, I have a very strong mind and whenever I set myself to do something, it's hard to turn me around." Hudson does not believe in horoscopes, but he thinks it described him perfectly. The lesson was not that horoscopes are right, but that here the greatness was in the individual man, not in the organization. The organization only provided the necessary tools.

Hudson is still organizing people. In Atlantic City, he works with low-income people—of whom he is one—to protect their housing in the era of casino gambling and soaring property values. Since 1973 he has attended the conventions of the Coalition of Black Trades Unionists. But his consuming interest now is building a nonpartisan voters' movement that will make government more responsive to ordinary citizens, especially in the area of jobs. He speaks of this movement in his own introduction.

Hudson says that he does not expect to live much longer, but while he is able, he will work in the public arena to improve conditions for all the people, "Negro and poor white, regardless to whoever, but particular for the Negro." He is not optimistic about Negroes, however. While everybody else can stick together, he says, "our people's all wandering." He wonders "why is our people so far behind *everybody?*" and fears blacks may not be ready for progress. They're always "digging at each other" instead of concentrating on what needs to be done.

Maoists are Hudson's *bête noire*. Instead of organizing the working class, they pass the time "tearing apart" and criticizing the CPUSA and the Soviet Union.

They ought to try and be uniting people and work together. Now they may not agree with Gus Hall and them, but everybody is facing this high cost of living. Don't everybody benefit if they get together, fight against the high cost of living?
Everybody benefit.
But still they out here fighting . . . and they ain't doing nothing for people. That's why I call them counter-revolutionists. What they're doing, actually, they giving the enemy of the working class a greater chance to take a greater hold.

Agents of division on the left or squabbling and divided blacks, the foes are at least familiar: the forces of disunity. Luckily, for every one of them there exist ten good people who need only to be educated. Hudson preaches to anyone who will listen to him (Maoists don't listen), confident that if he talks to enough people, he will organize his movement. His model is the broad-based Scottsboro defense coalition of the Depression years. He can organize this movement among the people, he says, because "I know they respects what I have to say."

How the Manuscript Was Prepared. If I succeed in this narrative, my hand will be invisible. Hosea Hudson will seem to have sat down to tell readers everything they want to know of his life. It should not be apparent that in the interviews that formed the narrative's foundation, Hudson had little intention of telling me everything I wanted to know.

He wanted to tell the story of the Communist Party in Alabama. Only as the work proceeded did he come to see—or to admit—that his experiences beyond the Party held an interest for readers that equaled his importance as a symbol of the CP. Still, Hudson was recording a political autobiography. I wanted to write southern social history using Hudson's life as an illustration.

He is a unique informant, an expressive representative of the unlettered workforce that built the new urban South and peopled its cities. He draws a peerless picture of working-class black life in Birmingham, describing the workplaces, the neighborhood, the amusements, the police, the jim crow, the better classes. As a former member of the inarticulate, Hudson speaks for them with the nuances that only narrative possesses, and he gives humanity to lives that historians usually meet in the census tracts. The narrative is longer than planned, because to cut it I would have had to sacrifice either political autobiography or social history. I have tried to preserve the integrity of both our concerns.

I put the narrative together mainly with historians in mind. But I hope students of linguistics, folklore, and perhaps even psychology will find it valuable. My aim in making this an autobiography instead of a biography was to preserve as much of Hudson's speech as possible. It is specific to his time and place, and, like his generation, it is passing away.

Although I am not trained in linguistics, I realized that I must preserve Hudson's words and basic phrases as he uttered them. As much as I possibly could, I left the rhythm of his speech intact. Also I tried to frame questions that would reveal something of Hudson's psyche. But he was reluctant to cooperate here, refusing steadfastly to interpret his actions or those of others. Although he does not guess the meaning of actions voluntarily, he does relate his dreams and the voices that speak in his head. He is open enough about the supernatural to show something of his psychology, as well as that of the folk culture of Wilkes County and Birmingham. Very obviously, migrating to Birmingham did not strip him or his neighbors of the culture they grew up in. Alongside the steelworkers and miners of Birmingham lived the card readers and fortunetellers like Miss Lena and Pop.

The evolution of the opening pages of the book shows the tension between the book Hudson wanted to write and my conception of an autobiography. When we decided to do a book, Hudson gave me a manuscript about thirty pages long. His typescript began where he felt his story began, joining the Communist Party. This is as he typed it, as he types all his correspondence and public statements, with an initial capital on each word:

On Some Of The Early Party Orgnization in The South Potickly [particularly] In Birmingham And AlA. I Wont To Say A Few Words A Bout The Communist Party Orgazation, As I Knew It From Sept 8th. In 1931 Untell The Year Of Joe McCarthy, In The Early 1950S. Whin I Join The Party On The 8th, Of Sept 1931 With 8 Other Workers In Birmingham, 6 Of Thim Was From The Stockhom Foundary Where I Was Working At That Time, I Was Eleacted Unit Orgnizar Of Our Unit. All Of That Group Were Negroes . . .

Much of his typescript concerned the years from 1931 to 1933, touching on the unemployed councils and foraging coal along the railroad in the depths of the Depression. But Hudson's writing style lacks the richness of his speech. This is the basic weakness of *Black Worker in the Deep South,* which was a heavily edited version of what he had written. In this narrative we overcame that problem by having Hudson retell on tape the whole of the material covered in his typescript. That is now Chapters 5, 7, and 8, "First Demonstrations," "The Depression," and "Reverend Sears and the Reds."

I felt the need for introductory material to explain how Hudson left Wilkes County and what organizations he had participated in before he joined the CP. The new material my questions produced is now Chapter 1. The first versions of the beginning of the book were brief in comparison to its present opening. I asked Hudson, "When you left the country, how did you get from the country to Atlanta? Why did you leave? What time of year was it?" He answered:

I left, in order to be able to leave the country, I worked for Tom Jackson for seven months, for wages, $10 a month. I hired that way because I wanted to leave the country in the summer, while it was warm. I didn't want to leave in the winter. After my seven months was up at Tom Jackson's, it was a friend of mine in the country, we was buddies in the country, we sung together, and he had a brother working at the railroad, N. C. and St. L in Atlanta [Nashville, Chattanooga, and St. Louis]. And he left the country, my friend did, along about the first of year, just after Christmas, he went to Atlanta, and went to work at the railroad with his brother. And he knowing that I was planning to leave the country, he came back home somewhere along after it got warm in the spring or the summer, earliest part of the summer, say like June, and he told me his brother was going to leave, give up his job in August, and was going to Chicago, and if I could make arrangements to leave, to be able to get in Atlanta by the time his brother give the job up, [he] would try to see could he help me get the job.

So I . . . his brother was going leave around the 16th of August, and I got my business arranged, got my wife moved and everything, back over to her mother's, give my father my cow, give my mother and stepfather some of my things.

NIP: Excuse me, you left your wife with her mother?

HH: I left her with her mother and father, I had to go up there to work. I couldn't carry them [wife and son] with me, didn't have enough money. So she had to stay over there till I worked, went up there and got it arranged.

So I left home on Thursday morning, and I went to Atlanta on the train. I left from Tignall, Georgia . . .

In a later discussion about the agricultural depression in the 1920s, Hudson added material on marketing conditions when he left Wilkes County. I added that material to the quotation above, to make the first expanded introduction, which read like this:

I left the country in 1923, the second week in July, because the boll weevils had got to where you couldn't raise any cotton. That was the main source of livelihood in that area. The landlords wouldn't advance you for buying fertilize for cotton and natural soda for the corn. There was no market for corn, wheat, peas, and potatoes. You could sell a few bushels in trade at the store—you wouldn't get no money. You couldn't sell anything like you could sell cotton on the market. I was working on halves, and I went from good farming to hardly two bales of cotton at the last of 1922. So I quit farming.

This was also when the young Negroes were coming back from the war and the white hoodlums was whipping them up. And they wanted to get on to me, but they didn't know how to start. I was pretty firey back in those days. I didn't take nothing. One of them told my friends they wanted to get on to me bad, but they didn't want to get in trouble. I quit going down to the crossroads where we hung out on Saturday afternoon and commenced laying plans to leave.

In order to be able to leave the country, I worked for Tom Jackson for seven months for wages, $10 a month. I hired that way because I wanted to leave the country in the summer, while it was warm. It was a friend of mine in the country, we was buddies in the country, we sung together, and he had a brother working at the railroad, N. C. and St. L.

I asked Hudson to tell me more about the circumstances surrounding his departure. He had said he was "pretty firey," but up to this point I had no sense of that in his story. Then one day in the middle of summer 1976, he started to tell me more. Hudson was in the kitchen cooking dinner for us as we chatted about our work. The tape recorder was turned off in the living room. He told me he had shot a fellow, his brother-in-law, in fact. The white hoodlums who were after him were on the side of his brother-in-law. The agricultural situation—the boll weevil, the collapse of the cotton market—provided a distant background for his leaving for the city. The personal complications dictated an early departure. Despite my requests, Hudson refused to commit this personal story to my tape recorder during 1976. It was not part of the story of the Communist Party in the South or the struggles that prepared the way for black civil rights.

By January 1977, however, Hudson had agreed to repeat in detail the personal story of his leaving the country. Even then, he was reluctant to commit it to tape:

NIP: Now I want to ask you one other thing before we get to this [correcting the manuscript that was already written], about shooting the fellow in Wilkes County.

HH: Well, I tell you . . .

NIP: Do you want to put it on tape?

HH: I don't know whether I should or not put it in the book . . .

NIP: I think it makes a very dramatic contrast.

HH: Well, I know it, but you see, it's my wife's brother I shot. And some of them kinfolks get hold to the book, you know . . .

NIP: But we have to change some names anyhow.

HH: But even at that . . . It's so devilish much I went through till some things you just forget and they come to you. Now I'll tell you about that. I don't know whether you're going to put it on that [tape].

[Seeing that Hudson is not strongly opposed, I turn on the tape recorder.]

HH: There you go, doggone it. All right. Now see this guy, I think I told you one day.

NIP: No, it's not on the tape. You told me one day in the kitchen.

HH: Well, let me tell it on the tape, then. I'll tell it on the tape. What happened, my wife's brother—he wont but about nineteen years old, and he couldn't get along with his father. So he came over and asked me to let him live with me and Sophie, and work with me.

NIP: When was this?

HH: Oh, this was about along in 1919, somewhere in there, and I told him, I said, "Lump," I said—his name, called him "Lump" but his name was Charlie—but they called him Lump. I said, "Lump," I said, "Uncle Zack," that was Sophie's father, I said, "he needs you to work with him. I ain't going bother with this."

"I ain't going stay with him."

So I asked Uncle Zack, I told him, I said, "He came over there and want to live with me, Uncle Zack."

He say, "Hosie," said, "that boy, I don't want him at my house," he said, "you can't do nothing with him," said. "My advice is don't you let him come there."

So he talked to me and he sugar-coated and he talked, and I told him, I said, "Lump, me and you can't get along." And he, "Yeah, we can get along, we can get along."

It was in the wintertime, it was along about this time of year. It was along in January, before everybody started to working. So he talked with me and he kept on till . . . I talked to Sophie about it, that was his sister. She said, "Poppa say he don't want him there, him and his poppa, he just challenge his daddy, you know, want to fight, and all like that. Poppa say he can't stay there." So I took it.

NIP: You were about the same age?

HH: No, no, I was much older than he was.

NIP: You were only about a couple of years older.

HH: No, several years older, cause I was along in my twenties, he was about nineteen.

NIP: If it was 1919, you were only twenty-one.

HH: Well, it might have been, somewhere, I don't know, twenty-one or twenty-two I was. I can't get the year exactly, but what I'm trying to say is, I know what happened. I don't know, let me see, 19 and 18, that was the year me and Sophie worked on halves, that was the year I married, 19 and 17, December the 31st, so I worked on halves.

The next year, 1919, I bought a mule, and I went out to rent. I bought $50 worth of corn, fodder, bought a mule for $316, bought all my plow. My account was $716, mule and all.

NIP: How do you remember that!

HH: Wait a minute, don't you cut me off here. I ain't got nothing to do with what you all can't remember. I'm telling you the story.

My account was $716 with my fertilizer, my mule and the corn I bought. I paid for my mule and everything and cleared $700, me and Sophic. That was in 19 and 19.

So in 19 and 20—trying to get up in these years—my grandmother left me when I married. She wouldn't stay with me cause I married, so she came back to me, and she stayed there with me one year. That was along about 1920. So she stayed one year, and she left again. She worked thirds with me. She went off then, and everybody, and she told me, "I worked here . . . you ain't, you ain't give me nothing, you take all I got."

We made three bales of cotton. And when she paid for her fertilize— had one of my poor little cousins, eleven years old, Jesse—she paid for her fertilize and everything in thirds, and I took her bale of cotton and a bale of cotton I had and carried it to town and sold it, and I got the money. I sold it for 37¢ pound. And we didn't call a bale of cotton a bale of cotton until it weighed 500 pounds. The bagging and the ties weighed 25 pounds, so you had to have over 500 pounds to have a bale of cotton. So a bale of cotton was weighing 550, 575, 595, all bales like that, those was a bale of cotton, that was what a bale of cotton weighed.

Howbeitsoever, her third that she cleared out of that cotton was around $100. And I carried the money back home. I put mine in the bank and bought me a pistol for $30 and the balls, all, six-inch barrel.

And I went home, and I give her all her money. And I give her a a little part of the corn she had. She had a little corn there, and I give her all she had, hers, I give it all to her. Then she couldn't say nothing. "I'm going tell you about Son, he didn't take nothing, nothing from me." That's what she went around and told them, "Son didn't take nothing from me." She left me after that.

NIP: She was young, wasn't she?

HH: Who?

NIP: Your grandmother.

HH: She was around fifty. She wont no old woman. And so she left. That was along in around 1920. So when she left, Lump come in there and wanted to stay with me, along about '21. He didn't have no clothes. I went and took him to the stores and I bought him a couple of suits of overalls, shirts, underwear, shoes and everything.

All of the above is now encompassed in pages 56 and 57 of the book and was, until recently, the beginning. The present opening pages were only added in the summer of 1978. Of course the early pages were not the only ones where I had to sacrifice the full measure of Hudson's storytelling to advance the narrative. As we first planned it, the story was to have covered the years 1923 to 1954, Hudson's Atlanta and Birmingham years. But the detail I found attractive in Hudson's talking took up so much space that the narrative stops in 1948.

Obviously the richness of Hudson's narrative has suffered at my hands. I altered his story in this episode, for instance, by leaving out the grandmother, the little cousin Jesse, and the weight of the cotton. I also straightened out the bends and turn in the flow of his talk. Some of my readers have argued with me about deleting details and repetitions, but I decided that by cutting out small bits of information and squeezing in more historical development, I would better serve the reader interested in Hudson as a worker, communist, and unionist, and yet preserve his style of storytelling and a sense of his dialect. As a result, this narrative cannot be taken as a perfectly faithful rendering of Hudson's style—only the tapes and raw transcripts can be considered primary sources. Students of linguistics may consult them directly. But this is a faithfully crafted autobiography. Every page of the narrative was checked with Hudson, revised and corrected, checked with Hudson again, revised and corrected again, and read aloud to him again.

Adapting Hudson's spoken language to the printed page meant abandoning its sound, for Hudson does not speak as I have rendered his words. I use standard English spellings, with a few exceptions, in order to produce an easily read discourse. An attempt to reproduce his speech phonetically would have resulted in a version something like this:

In o'da to be able to leave th' country, ah werked fuh Tome Jackson seben months fuh wages, ten dollah a mont. Ah hi'ied that way be-cause ah wonted t' leave th' country, y'know, in th' summah, whale it wuz wahm. Ah didn't wanna leave in th' winner. Aftah mah seben months wuz up, at Tome Jackson's, uh friend of mine, in th' country, we wuz buddies in th' country, we sung together, and he hadda bruther werking at th' rav-road, N. C. 'n' St. L., in Atlanna . . .

This sort of rendition was unthinkable, not only because its fidelity depends on the reader's understanding of its system of phonetics. More important, it's condescending and difficult to read, and I wanted to respect Hudson's speech and make it accessible. To this end I have generally avoided apostrophes in words that would have them to show variations from standard usage. Thus words that would have been spelled 'cause, 'twas, and so forth, have no apostrophes in the narrative. Instead of writing "I'd 'ave been in jail," I wrote what Hudson said, "I'd *of* been in jail." I have made these choices because apostrophes and dialect in literature have long singled out characters that readers need not take seriously, ignorant folk who cannot speak correctly. With black people, the usage is centuries old. For all these reasons, I have not rendered Hudson's speech phonetically or stressed its deviance from standard English.

Nonetheless, I have used some unfamiliar verbs and phrases that are integral parts of Hudson's speech. The first is "wont," which Hudson often uses as a contraction of "was not," "were not," or occasionally "would not." It is usually a past imperfect contraction of the verb "to be," in the negative. I have deleted the apostrophe to avoid confusion with "won't," which Hudson uses as the usual contraction of "will not." Hudson says "wont" as I have spelled it, for instance, in speaking of his grandmother: "She was around fifty. She wont no old woman."

Hudson also uses unusual past tenses:

> Ben *driv* every step of the way.
> They *helt* about two bushels.
> We hadn't *et* no breakfast.
> The police *wrang* the stick out of his hand.
> That's the last time I *seed* him.

Hudson also uses the gerund "going" in two constructions. Sometimes he says "going to do something"; other times, he says "going do something." In the first construction, he would say "goin' to do something," in the second, "gwine do something," and "gwine" is markedly nasalized.

As I edited, I preserved Hudson's syntax and vocabulary, so that the narrative contains many usuages that are distinctly southern and sometimes oldfashioned. Often Hudson calls dates with a word in the middle, such as "19 aught 4" and "19 and 34." He uses the reflexive verb "to call" to indicate skepticism: "they called theyself had it sealed," meaning that they said they had sealed it but hadn't done a very good job of it. Hudson also uses an "it is" construction where "there is" might be expected: "it came a rain," and "it wasn't no Republicans." In this latter, as in other places, the double negative is probably familiar. But other southernisms may confuse. Often Hudson leaves words out where they are expected, as "say" and "of" in this quotation: "and he'd [say] 'you have to stay out [of] the cemetery.' " I hope that words like "onliest" (only), "nary" (none), and "carry" (take someone somewhere), and verbs used in more than once tense in a single paragraph are clear in their contexts. My favorite Hudsonism is "howbeitsoever," which I had never heard before.

Keeping Hudson's own phrases, I edited out much repetition but left some in to show how, with small variations, he uses it for emphasis and color. I also arranged his stories to progress chronologically with relative directness. For some, this pruning is objectionable tampering with the spontaneity of the unretouched transcript. For others, however, even the edited narrative is dense and strange. I have tried to remain as close to Hudson's language as possible without sacrificing readability.

Hudson's unedited speech is not lush, exotic, rural talk. Years of speaking in public, living in Birmingham, New York, and Atlantic City, and associating with communists outside the South have affected his way of talking. He uses several styles of speech in this narrative, corresponding to different settings. I have not tried to bring consistency into his styles or use of words, or to make his voice conform to what I might imagine as authentic southern speech. When he uses "they" and "their" and "fertilize" and "fertilizer" in the same paragraph to mean the same thing, I have left in both usages. I also resisted occasional pressure from Hudson to replace his "ain'ts" with phrases that sound more polished to him.

Hosea Hudson, Atlantic City, 1978

Hosea Hudson's
Introduction

I am writing this book today telling about some of the struggles and suffering that we old pioneers had to endure, in the South in the cotton fields of Georgia and steel mills and coal mines of Alabama in and around Birmingham, that made it possible for the black and white workers to be earning the present wages that is being earned today there on these jobs by the workers who are able to get a job, where many of us, particularly the black workers, was only making 29–30 and 40 cents an hour, with no overtime for overtime work, with the white workers working on all of the skilled and semi-skilled jobs where the Negroes who were working on semi-skilled jobs would not be classed as semi-skilled, some of them were classed as grease-wipers who were working on a machine, as it was reported in some of the T.C.I. [Tennessee Coal and Iron] steel mills as late as the middle-1940s. And many of the white workers were not earning top union wages on these skilled and semiskilled jobs.

This was the results of the long-time practices of racism that the white workers and white masses had allowed themselves to nourish among themselves, that had been put out by the big ruling powers of cotton fields, the mines, and steel mills in the South, in order to keep the black and white workers and masses divided, by teaching the whites that they were better than the Negroes, and at the same time teaching the Negroes not to trust the poor whites, because the poor whites were not to be trusted by the Negroes.

And these rulers was able to keep the white workers and masses blindfolded with this myth of racism, up until the 1929 Depression. It was only then in that Depression, when these white workers found themselves walking the streets with no jobs, nothing to buy food to feed their hungry children, nothing to buy fuel to keep their children

47

warm from the bitter cold weather, and pay their rents, it was only in these rough days of experiences that these white workers and masses began to wonder and to try to examine just what was wrong, because they had always been taught that they was a white man or a white woman, and that they were better than the Negroes, through their teachings. And now they were finding themselves treated by their rulers in the streets and in the courts when they were evicted out of a house when they could not pay their rent, just like the Negroes was being evicted out of landlord's house when they could not pay their rents. Because up until that Depression, in the early 1930s, there were no communication between the Negro and white workers. We work in the same shop or plant. Many times Negroes would be helpers of the white workers and hardly ever talk any important business together. When a white would tell a Negro something, that white would, in most cases, tell the Negro to keep this or that under your hat. That meant for that Negro not to tell anybody what he had been told. And in most cases if that Negro helper did tell anybody, it in most cases be someone that he was able to trust to keep what he or she had been told.

It was only the Communist Party that was the first to begin to raise the slogan in all of its leaflets and newspapers, that was put out by night in the working-class neighborhoods, white and Negroes, calling on the Negro and whites to organize unemployed committees in their blocks and communities, for unemployed cash relief for the unemployed workers and union wages on all jobs in the coal mines and steel mills, and for the right to the workers to organize a union in their mines and mills Negro and white together, without the raiding and arrest of the meetings by the police, and for full economic, political, and social equality to the Negro people, for the freedom of the nine Scottsboro boys. It was these basic demands, along with others, that began to open the eyes and minds of many of the white workers, as well as many of the Negroes who had been made to believe that it was the poor whites that they, the Negroes, had to watch. When we began to make a break-through in that mass of racism that the white workers had been nursing in their hearts and minds for the hundreds of years in the South, we was able to build the unions in the coal mines and steel mills and small iron foundries around Birmingham and through Alabama, and that unity of black and white organized together to build the CIO union forty-odd years ago, to bring about higher wages and better working conditions in these plants in the South, are still bearing fruit today in Alabama and the South.

But today we are living in a higher state of racism, a new stage. We are living in the stage where schools are being closed and children are being denied the chance to get a decent education. The young people coming out of school cannot find jobs, in particular the Negro youth, whose unemployed percentage is double.* Hospitals are being closed down, and the hospital expenses are climbing higher and higher. And the working poor are finding it harder to get medical care for their children. All of these sufferings which cannot be denied that is placed upon the people today because racism are still playing that role today, on a national level, that it was playing among the white workers in the South and Birmingham forty-odd years ago. That is the workers and people are failing to understand the burning need for a united people's movement around a people's program that addresses itself to the needs of all the people, regardless to their color, sex, or political beliefs, so long as such people and members are working to carry out such a people's program. Therefore the task before us all today to fight against the effects of racism is the building [of] a united people's movement around a people's program of all people.

Atlantic City, 1977

* Hudson wanted to add emphasis on jobs in 1978, so this sentence does not appear in the original statement.—N.I.P.

I Am Wrightin This Book To Day,Tellin A Bout Some Of The Struggles And Suffrin That

We Old Pinears Had To Endure,In The South In The Cotton Fields Of Ga,And Steeal Mills

And Cole Mines Of Ala,And In And A Round Birmingham,That Made It Posable For The Black

And White Workers To Be Earnin The Preasant Weages,That Is Beaing Earn To Day There On

These Jorbs,By The Workers Who Are Able To Get A Job,Where Meny Of Us Potickly The Black

Workers,Was Only Making 29-30 And 40 Cents An Hour,With No Over Time For Ever Time Work.

With The White Workers,Working On All Of The Skill And Sema Skill Jobs Where The Negroes

Who Were Working On Sema Skill Jobs,Would Not Be Class As Sema Skill,Some Of Thim Were

Class Os Greas Wipers Who Were Working On A Macheain,As It Was Reportead In Some Of The

T.C.I.Steeal Mills As Late As The Middle 1940S.And Many Of The White Workers Were Not

Earnin Top Union Weages On These Skile And Semi Skill Jobs.

(1) This Was The ~~The Long Time Standin~~

(Results Of The Long Time Practeses Of Racism)What The White Workers

And White Masses,Had Aloud Thim Selves To Nurach,A Moung Them Selves,That Had Bin But

Out By The Big Rulin Powears,Of Cotton Fields The Mines And Steeail Miles,In The South

In Ordear To Keap The Black And White Workers And Masses Devitead,By Teaching The Whites

That They Were Bettar Than The Negroes,And At The Same Time Teaching The Negroes Not To

Trust The Pore Whites,Be Cause The Pore Whites Were Not To Be Trustead By The Negroes.

And These Rulears Was Able To Keap The White Workers And Masses Blind

Foldead With This Mith Of Racism,Up Untell The 1929 Depreashan,It Was Only Thin In That

Depreashion,Whin These White Workers Found Thim Selves Walking The Streats With No Jobs

Nothing To Buy Food To Fead Their Hungary Children,Nothing To Byy Fueail To Keap Their

Children Warn From The Bittar Cold Weather,And Par Their Rints,It Was Only In These Ruff

Dayes Of Exprinces,That These White Workers And Masses,Be Gain To Wondar Be Gain To Try

To Examin Just What Was Rong,Be Cause Thay Had All Wayes Bin Tought,That They Was A White

Man Or A White Womman,And That They Were Bettar Than The Negroes,Through There Racist

Teachings,And Now They Were Findin Thim Selves Treated By Their Ruliars In The Streats

And In The Courts Whin They Were Eaoictead Out Of A House Whin They Could Not Pay Their

Rint Just Like The Negroes Was Beain Evictead Out Of A Land Lords House Whin They Could

Not Pay Their Rents,Be Cause Up Untell That Depreashear,In The Early 1930S,There Were No
Comunication Be Tweain The Negro And White Workers,We Work In The Same Shop Or Plant
meny Times Negroes Would Be Healpers Of The White Workers,And Hardly Eaver Talk Any

Emporton Bismueas To Geathar,Whin A White Would Tell A Negro Somthing That White Would

In Most Cases Tell The Negro To Keap This Or That Undear Your Hat,That Ment For That

Negro Not To Tell Any Body What He Had Bin Told,And In Most Cases If That Negro Heapar

Did Tell Any Body,It In Most Cases Be Some One That He Was Able To Trust,In Keap What

He Or She Had Bin Told.

It Was Only The Communist Party,That Was The First To Be Gain To Rase The Slogin In All

Of Its Leafets And News Papers,That Was Put Out By Night In The Working Class Nabor Hoods

White And Negroes,Callin On The Negro And Whites To Orgnize Unemployead Commijjes In

Their Blocks And Comunitys,For Unemployead Cash Releaif,For The Unemployead Workers And

Union Weages On All Jobs In The Cole Mines And Steeail Miles,And For The Wright To The

Workers To Orgnize A Union In Their Mines And Mills Negro And White To Geathar,With Out

The Radin And Arest Of The Meatins By The Police,And For Full Ecnomict,Political And

Socially Equality To The Negro People,For The Freadon Of The Nine Scotsbore Boyes It Was

These Basic Demands A Long With Others,That Be Gain To Opin The Eyes And Mines Of Meny

Of The White Workers,As Well As Meny Of The Negroes Who Had Bih Made To Beleave That Itt

Was The Pore Whites That They,The Negroes Had To Watch,Whin We Begain To Make A Brake

Through,In That Mass Of Racism,That The White Workers Had Bin Nursing In Their

Harts And Mines,For The Hundrads Of Years In The South,We Was Able To Build The Unions

In The Cole Mines And Steeail Miles And Small Iron Foundarys Ill A Round Birmingham And

Through ALA,And That Unity Of Black And White Orgnize To Geathar To Build The C.I.O.

UNION 40 Ard Years A Go,To Bring A Bout Highear Weages And Beattar Working Condishions
In These Plants In The South,Are Still Barin Frout To Day In ALA,And The South
But
But To Day We Are Livin In A Higheair Stage Of Racism,A New Stage,We Are Livin In The
Stage,Where Scools Are Beain Close And Childrin Are Beain Denide The Chance To Get A

Deasin Eaducation,Hospittles Are Beain Close Down,And The Hospittle Expinces Are Climan

Higheair,And Higheairy And The Workin Pore Are Findin It Hartar To Geat Meadar Ceair

For Their Wives Children,All Of These Suffrins Which Canot Be Denide That Is Plast Up

On The People To Day,Be Cause Racism,Are Still Playing That Role To Day,On A National

Leavle,That It Was Playing A Moung The White Workers In The South,And Birmingham 40Ard
Years,That Is The Workers And People,Are Falin To Undear Stand,The Burnin Knead For A
Unitead Peoples Move Ment,A Round A Peoples Program,That A Dreses It Self To The Neads

Of All The People,Regardlys To Their Collar-Sects Or Politeal Belaafs So Long As Such
People And Membars Are Working To Carrie Out Such A Peoples Program.

Hudson's family, Birmingham, Easter Sunday, 1941.
Hudson's wife, Hosea Hudson, Hudson's son.
Seated: Hudson's father

1

From the Country to the City

ME and Sophie messed around courting about four years. We wont going regular all the time. We'd fall out about other boys. Everytime she make me mad, I'd go off, stay off three-four weeks to a month, go back again.

One Sunday morning, it was in the spring of 1917, I went to her house, was going to church with her and her sister, and she told me she had something to tell me. She told me that the spirit spoke to her and told her, asked her why did she treat me like that, said, "Don't you know Hosie going be your husband some day?" She say the spirit spoke to her, it was a voice. (I've heard voices speak to me like that.) Sophie told me, "I wants us to quit falling out and go to live like we ought to live and be loving to each other." She also told me if we didn't marry Christmas, she was going to Atlanta to live. It was either be married or if I didn't, I might lose her.

So we made up that Sunday. I was the only boyfriend then. I got so I had it so good with her, it was like we'd be out—her and me and some more boys and girls—be walking. And a boy be with her. I'd be behind her, and I'd go to catch up with them. The guy look, see me coming, and he'd leave before I get there, say, "Yonder come Hosie. I might as well to go." I didn't have no more trouble then.

Me and my grandmother and my brother, we worked that year and we got through clearing the crop. We cleared about $300. My grandmother, she took a hundred for herself, a hundred for my brother, gave me a hundred. She give me a cow and a calf, and I had some chickens, give me a bank of sweet potatoes* and some

* [A bank of sweet potatoes was built like a tee-pee to keep 400–500 pounds of sweet potatoes dry in storage during the winter. About five feet in diameter at

53

corn, and I think a shoulder of meat and a ham of meat and a middling of meat* and quite a bit of home-made sausage. That's what she gave me. That's what I married on, married on that. My grandmother and my brother moved back down with my mother. She was living not too far, three or four miles from us with John Henry Blakely on a plantation.

So I got set up all right, and had everything ready to marry Sophie the 31st of December, last day of December 1917. It was on a Sunday, fifth Sunday. I went to Washington Georgia, bought the license that Saturday. It was cold as the devil! The wind was blowing, it was kind of snowflakes. When I got back home it was after dark. It had done snowed lightly, and the moon was out from under the cloud. It was cold that night I mean! The calf was in the lot. I had to turn the calf out and go hunt for the cow and put her up. Oh I had a time.

That was Saturday night. Then Sunday I got my aunt's husband's horse and buggy. I got the buggy and went and got Sophie and went up to old man Tom Jackson. He was Justice of the Peace. I already had done been up to Mr. Jackson that morning where he was coming to church. I already told him I'd be up there to marry, I had give him my license. He told me where he going be at his brother's house. I got up there in the buggy, went up to his brother's house. I got up there in the buggy, went up to this brother's and everybody, all the Negroes, seen me and Sophie in the buggy, knowed we getting married. They was kids and some women was running behind the buggy.

When I got up there to Mr. Ed Jackson's, old man Jackson came out. By the time the Negroes got to the buggy, he'd got through marrying us. That was some marrying. I turn right on around, left them all standing there.

Sophie's father wanted to have a wedding, but I didn't want no wedding. I didn't want to be bothered. I didn't want a whole lot of people be around talking. I just didn't like that kind of thing. I just didn't like it. I ain't never liked weddings.

---

the base, it had bark on the outside and corn stalks at the opening at the top. Inside, layers of sweet potatoes alternated with layers of pine straw.]

[The footnotes are Hudson's, except for the bracketed ones. Those and the endnotes are mine. N.I.P.]

* [From the middle part of the hog.]

I was at home by myself two or three weeks before I married, after my grandmother and my brother moved out. I lived in the house by myself. I was kind of got to be a man then, nobody to tell me to come home early. But I didn't stay out late at night. I still went home early. I never did stay out over 9:30–10 o'clock. I didn't hang out all night. About a Sunday or two before me and Sophie got married, me and Charley* and about two or three more boys, we went up and we went down to the spring, down in the woods, and they all got to playing cards.

They had a deck of cards, and they went to trying to gamble for a nickel. I had never played a card in my life, and I was nineteen years old. I stood there and look at them a while. I had some change in my pocket, and I took a nickel and went and bet. I took a nickel and won a dollar, and that started me to gambling. We were playing Georgia Skin. So from then on, I kept on. I'd go out to the game and I'd bet a little. I'd always win.

It ain't no bad game, Georgia Skin was a good game. I mean to say it make you feel good, picking up money and betting. Around home there you had all kinfolks, first cousins, brothers, sons, all like that. It was a large community. You knowed a lot of people, and the men would get together and they'd gamble on Friday night, especially Saturday, Saturday night, and some Sundays. Maybe if it was a meeting Sunday, you'd quit and go to church Sunday morning. I never did quit going to church.

I always kept my songbook, and I always was singing. I went to church every Sunday. I'd get all dressed up, go to church and Sunday school, and sing in the choir. At the same time, I was gambling. I'd slip around and go to church too. I wont public gambling, wont doing it publicly, but the old folks begin to find out. Some of them find out, say, "They tell me Hosie gambling!"

"You mean to say Hosie gambling?"

"Hosie gambling and he singing in the choir!" That was supposed to be a sin. It was a sin for you to go out and gamble and sing in the choir. I would go to church and when that was over, I'd go down in the woods and gamble. And I'd take a drink, but I never did get drunk.

* Charley Williams had just married Sophie's sister. He married about a month or two before me and Sophie did.

So that was 1917, 1918—all of '18—1919, 1920 . . . hmmmmm, I gambled a long time. I didn't quit. I gambled so much till I gambled with all kind of people. Some bad, some guys didn't do nothing but gamble for a living, like a guy came in there, Harry Porter. I heard talk of him a long time when I was a kid. Harry Porter was his name, and his mother was black. He looked like a half white man, had good straight black hair. He didn't do nothing but travel and gamble.

Them kind of people, gambling, they carried cubs, they believe in switching, marking the cards, had stripped decks, all like that. A cub is putting two-three cards together. It's just like take a deck, put two jacks together. And stripping the deck, a fellow take a brand new deck, take out four cards, take some sandpaper, go down the edge and smooth it down so it was a bittle bit narrower than these four cards, and then you put them back in there. We call that stripping the deck. All you got to do is catch hold of them, and you know where them four cards are.

My wife's uncle, Al, he keep some bluing, kept it somewhere in the pocket, and have a fingernail trimmed, stick it in there, and he mark his cards. He see that card down there, and next time he know that's a jack. That's called catch you on the turn. A lot of people got killed all about that stuff, and that's why I wanted to quit.

Two or three times I liked to kill somebody. Sometime you get a rowdy crowd, people who don't want you to win your money and you win, then they want to start a fight. A guy cut me on the arm, I broke his arm. He went and tried to clip on his shotgun. I seen him before he was able to do what he's trying to do, and I got my shotgun and dared him to raise his shotgun up. He wont no more than six feet from me. I told him, "If you raise it, I'll cut you half in two." I was just going do it. That was one of the run-ins I had. I had several run-ins. I didn't keep up no racket, I was quiet, but if you ruffle my feathers I was ready to fight with you. Take for an instance, I had some trouble with my brother-in-law and I shot him.

My wife's brother, he wasn't but about nineteen years old. He couldn't get along with his father. He came over and asked me to let him live with me and Sophie and work with me. I told him, I said, "Lump," called him Lump, but his name was Charlie. I said, "Lump, your father needs you to work with him."

I was much older than he was, several years older, cause I was along in my twenties and he was about nineteen. I can't get the year exactly, let me see. Nineteen and eighteen, that was the year me and Sophie worked on halves, that was the year I married, 19 and 17, December the 31st. That next year, 1919, I bought a mule for $316 and I went out to rent.[1] I bought $50 worth of corn, fodder, plow, fertilize. My account was $716 and I paid for my mule and everything and cleared $700, me and Sophie. That was in 19 and 19.

So in 19 and 20—trying to get up in these years—my grandmother came back to me, and she stayed there with me one year. She had left me when I married, and along about 1920 she came back, she stayed one year, worked thirds with be, and she went off again. I sold her bale of cotton for 37¢ a pound, and her third that she cleared out of that cotton was around $100. When she left, Lump come in there and wanted to stay with me, along about '21. He left his father, Uncle Zack, said, "I ain't going stay with him."

I asked Uncle Zack, I said, "Lump come over there and want to live with me, Uncle Zack. What's the matter?"

He said, "Hosie," said, "that boy, I don't want him at my house." Said, "You can't do nothing with him. My advice is don't you let him come there."

Lump, he talked and he talked to me and he sugar-coated and he talked. I told him, I said, "Lump, I ain't going to bother with this. Me and you can't get along."

And he, "Yeah, we can get along. We can get along."

It was in the wintertime, along in January, before everybody started to working. So he kept on till I talked to Sophie about it. Sophie was his sister and she was on Lump's side. She said, "Poppa say he don't want him there. He just challenge his daddy, want to fight. Poppa say he can't stay there." So I let him come and live in the house with me and Sophie and work with me. He didn't have no clothes. I went and took him to the stores and I bought him a couple of suits of overalls, shirts, underwear, shoes, and everything.

So here's the first thing he did. My mother give me a '38 Smith-Wesson pistol, and I had the pistol in a box. I just went on, had it laying up there, box was up there. I didn't never use it. It just laying up there. I didn't never tote a pistol. Finally one day I decided I'd look in the box, and the pistol was gone. Lump didn't know nothing about it. But somebody down there at the crossroads said that Lump had had the pistol and he sold it to somebody.

Then the next thing was over old man Hall's mule. Old man Hall was the white man I rented from, and he had a extra mule he didn't use, didn't need. So old man Hall, after Lump working with me, he let me have that mule for Lump to plow, to use him four-five days to plow his crop. Then I had to go back with my mule and myself and pay back old man Hall for the days Lump used that mule.

Lump went to whupping the mule. He would plow to the end of a row, and instead of turning around, go back, he go at it and beat the mule at the end, just beat him all over the head. I told him to stop beating the mule, cause I'm responsible for the mule, not him. So he turns and cuss me. That het it up a little bit more between us. He was staying in the house with me, he done took my pistol, now he done start to cussing me.

I told him, "Now you work your crop, but you ain't going stay in this house." He had to go back to his father. His father was right over across the branch* there about a quarter of a mile. I didn't allow him in the house.

Next thing was the wood. In January, when he first come to live with me, we went down and we cut down nine trees. Four trees over here, and five over yonder. They was long, good pine. We split them up, windrowed the wood. Over here where the four trees was, we burnt all through January and February, making fires in the house. But over here at the five trees, we didn't bother it. Then he goes over to the five trees and hauls nearabout all of it up there to Aunt Ethel's and throwed it off in her yard. Aunt Ethel was Uncle Zack's sister. He goes and sells Aunt Ethel a great big pile of the wood he and I cut down. Now she knows well that he shouldn't of done it, but she bought the wood from him. I don't know what she paid for it. I went and got the other, carried it on in to my wood yard.

That evening it came a rain, come a big thunderstorm along about 1 or 2 o'clock in the afternoon. When it quit raining, he come down to the house and asked me what did I go get the rest of *his* wood for? I said, "We split the four trees over there and you stayed here and helped to burn it, cooking wood and making fires. When you went and got all the five trees, I decided the rest of it was mine. I got it."

He was standing out in the yard there and I was setting in the door of the house in a chair with my songbook in my hand, looking over a song. My baby was about a year old, and he was just trying to stand up. The house was a old slavery-time house, two story,

* [Creek.]

with a chimney in the east and the west, and it had a hall coming through and two doors. I was setting this-a-way, and right here was a door going into my bedroom, and up over the door was my shotgun.

He was standing out there in the yard with two brickbats in his hand, and he draw back. I told him, I said, "You better not throw in this house." I said, "If you throw in this house, I'm going to kill you."

I was setting in a chair, and the baby was standing on the side, holding to me. And Lump out here. He draw back. I said, "I ain't going dodge you," said, "you throw in here, I'm going kill you."

He throwed it in there, sure enough. And when he throwed, I jumped up. When I jumped up, the brick hit the chair and knocked the baby over on the floor. I went right in the door and got my shotgun. He went off a little piece and stopped. He had him two more bricks.

My cotton was a little bit above knee-high, and he was standing straddle of a cotton row. He said, "You got your God damn gun. Shoot!"

I had a brand-new choke-bore shotgun.* You could lay a dime on the barrel, it was that steady. And it was a good, new gun. That's why I know the Lord or somebody been with me. Lump was standing about as far as from here across the street, it wont a whole lot. I throwed that gun up and I meant to kill him, I'm telling you, I did. I meant to kill him. I aimed at his body, but the shots hit him all in the feet and legs, none him him in the body. When that gun fired, it didn't sound like a gun. It rung like a bell. Everybody say that gun, they never hear a gun sound like that gun that day. It rung. It rung so much like a bell, till it took my attention.

Lump took out and run up the road. I went back in the house and got another shell. I runned at him a good while, and finally, as I runned, my nerve changed, and I quit running at him. He went on up to old man Jackson's, about three quarters of a mile. That was the justice of the peace. He went up there and told him I had shot him. I went on across the hill over to old man Hall's. Old man Jackson was up here, old man Hall over yonder. I went on over yonder.

They done heard the gun now, they done heard the racket. You could hear in the country a long ways off. Old man Hall said,

* When you shoot that barrel, all the shots go in a lump, just like a ball, for a certain distance, just all lumped together.

"Hosie, I heard that gun shoot. What you do down there? Did you shoot that boy?"

I said, "Yes sir, I did shoot him. He throwed a brick in my house at me and knocked my chair over and knocked the baby over," and I said, "I shot him."

Old man Hall said, "I told you not to fool with that boy. He's just like his daddy." He said, "I had his daddy here working with me a year before he ever married that boy's mother." And said, "He just stand up in the fields and cuss me all day, stop and fuss and cuss." He said, "I told you you couldn't get along with him." He went up to old man Jackson, told him not to get a warrant out for me. Old man Hall told him not to give Lump no warrant. So he didn't get no warrant.

Now mind you, when Lump done went to Jackson and I went up to old man Hall, when I come back, my wife had done locked the house up on the outside and was in the inside. I couldn't get in the house. She was on Lump's side. She was on Lump's side and knowed how he had been doing me, and he hadn't just started. He'd been doing it a long time.

Now the big thing's on. And this cotton is growing. It was rich land, land hadn't been cultivated in about thirty years, old man Hall told me. He had owned it thirty years and it had never been nothing on it but a cow pasture. That cotton got so high I could get on my mule and ride along and pick at the top of it without reaching down. The cotton was six feet tall, and I had the rows five feet wide.[2] When I got ready to lay by, I couldn't even put a furrow in the middle. The limbs done lapped over the middle. That cotton was right up to my house, so it was easy for Lump to come up there in that cotton, right up to that door, and I come out, and he kill me. All the balance of that year and part of the next year, I walked around that house and looked to be shot down.

Lump would go around and make threats, tell people, "I'm going kill that son of a bitch, I'm going kill him."

People come tell me, said, "You'd better keep your eye on Lump. Lump say he going kill you."

I'd say, "All I ask him, all I say to him, whatever he do, he better do it well," said, "cause if he don't, I'm going do it to him."

One day I went down the crossroads down there, three-four miles away, where the store is. I got off my mule. I went into Theo Brooks's store after some sugar. There was a young white man named Haney was there, looked to be about twenty-five or thirty. He wasn't married. He didn't have a thing to do with it, but he says to me, says, "What the God damn hell is that going on up there with you all shooting up each other up there, you and Lump?"

I says, "Nothing," I says. "Lump throwed a brick in my house at me and knocked my chair over and knocked my baby on the floor, and I told him not to do it," I said. "I had my gun and I shot him." I said, "What would you do if somebody come up there in your yard and you setting down, ain't bothering them, and your baby standing up side of your leg, and he throw a brick in there and knock your baby over. What would you do?"

"I don't know what I'd do, but I know one thing. You all better cut out that God damn mess up there."

That showed me that they was cooking up something for me. They had been talking. Old man Hall and them was on my side, but they wanted to move against me. They wanted to whip me. One of the young whites told one of the Negro men that they wanted to get on to me bad, but they didn't know how to do it without causing trouble, afraid I'd kill some of them—which I would if I had a chance. I commenced laying plans to leave.

Then the depression in the farm came on. That fall we couldn't sell no cotton at all. The landlords wouldn't advance you for buying fertilize for cotton and natural soda for the corn. There wasn't no market for corn, wheat, peas, and potatoes. You could sell a few bushels in trade at the store—you wouldn't get no money—but you couldn't sell anything like you used to could sell cotton on the market. I was working on halves, and I went from good farming to hardly two bales of cotton at the last of 1922. I decided to quit farming.

In order to be able to leave the country, I worked for old man Tom Jackson for seven months for wages, $10 a month. I hired that way because I wanted to leave the country in the summer, while it was warm. It was a friend of mine in the country—we was buddies in the country, we sung together—and he had a brother working at the railroad, the N. C. and St. L. He left the country, my friend did, along about the first of the year, just after Christmas. He went to Atlanta and went to work at the railroad with his brother. He knowed that I was planning to leave the country, and he came back home somewhere along after it got warm in the spring or the summer, say like June. He told me his brother was going to give up his job in August and was going to Chicago. If I could be able to make arrangements to get in Atlanta by the time his brother give the job up, he would try to see if he could get me the job.

His brother was going to leave around the 16th of August, and I got my business arranged. I give my father one of my cows, give my mother and stepfather some of my things and the other cow. I got my wife moved back over to her mother's. I left my wife and son with her mother and father. I was going to Atlanta to work, wouldn't be able to carry them with me, didn't have enough money. So she was going to stay over there a month until I drawed my first pay.

I gambled the Sunday before I left home that next Tuesday. The guy I was gambling with, he claimed he was only playing, but he wasn't playing. He told me, "Don't pick up my last bet." I picked it up. He snatched out a pistol. He was sitting up a hill, and I'm right here. He snatched out a pistol, and when he snatched out a pistol, I seen it and I grabbed it, and I happened to grab the pistol behind the hammer and was man enough to take it away from him. He couldn't pull the trigger.

That was the last Sunday I gambled in the country. That's when I quit gambling. I wanted to quit long before that. I didn't like it. But it's something you get accustomed to, it gets a part of you. It's just a habit, like a person that drink. Many of them would like to quit drinking, but it's a habit, he can't quit. Just like I'm chewing tobacco. I get where I just got to have me a chew. And the same way with playing cards. I wont afraid of nobody and didn't believe in nobody running over me. That ain't the half of it. I was getting badder and badder. I seen I was getting too deep in trouble, so when I got in the city, I wouldn't associate with nobody, gamble or drink.

I left home on Tuesday morning, and I went to Atlanta on the train. I caught the train from Tignall, a little branch line, over to Elberton. I got the train out of Elberton, the Seaboard. I got in Atlanta at about 6 o'clock that afternoon, and my friend and his brother, they met me at the railroad. I spent the night, and the next morning, when his brother was going out to tell the man he was giving the job up, I went out with them. They hired me in the place that his brother had.

The job they were doing was cleaning out the pits where the big engines run in the roundhouse. You see, these engines, they'd have to be gutted. At that time the engines—the firebox and the boiler—was lined with arch brick inside. Ain't just ordinary brick, special brick. After these trains would make these runs, a lot of these bricks would be done burnt. And thy'd have to knock all that lining of these bricks out, and they'd fall in this pit. And this pit is deep enough for a man to get in and stand up and work under the engine. They knock all these arch brick out and wash the boiler out. After they move the engine off the pit, all of that rubble has to be cleaned out. Me and this fellow, we had wheelbarrows, and we'd load our wheelbarrow and have to wheel it out on a dump. The dump was a high fill outside the shop, and we'd dump it on that fill. That was my job from August to along about the middle of September 1923.

Twas a fellow left the coal chute, I think he killed a woman or something, but anyway, he left the job. They came down and take me off this job in the roundhouse and put me on the coal chute, where you unload the cars' coal. You have an elevator bucket that carries it up over a big pit—you knock the bottom of the cars so the coal fall down in that pit, and you got an automatic bucket that dips that coal and carries it up and drops it in that chute. That chute hold about seven cars of coal. One side hold about four cars, and the other side hold about three cars. And we three men had to fill that coal chute everyday because these trains were regular running, night and day. You had a 7 o'clock shift in the morning, a 3 o'clock shift, and an 11 o'clock shift at night. So you had to keep enough coal in there to coal the trains. And also you had another space in there for sand.

Every so often we had to unload a carload of sand. This sand would be up in this hopper. You had some steam pipes and the sand would be up against these steam pipes. And these steam pipes would dry that sand. When your engine run on there, you put that sand on that train. You see these steam engines, they've got two big booms, two big knots, sitting up there. Well, that's where they put the sand in there. They had little pipes go down right under the wheel on the track, a little pipe. That sand would be dry, just like sugar. It would run freely, it wouldn't get clogged up, and anytime the man pull a lever, that would put that sand there, and the engine could pull.

So that was my job from along about September in '23 until November in '24, and I wasn't making but 30¢ an hour, no overtime, just made straight 30¢ an hour. In the wintertime, it was very hard to fill these chutes up. We'd have to work from 7 o'clock in the morning to 11 o'clock at night—cooooold days. Only thing was, it was under a shed, and the cold wind would be blowing in there.

We'd be working in that cold trying to get that coal in those chutes.

Under that pit where you run those cars, you'd have railroad ties about four inches apart all the way across that pit. We had hammers weighed about seven pounds, and we had to hit that coal, beat that coal, till that lump get small enough to go through that four inch space. Had to be like that because those engines had automatic stokers. Many times it would be raining and the coal would be frozen just like a rock. We'd have picks to pick that coal loose in the car to get it to fall down in that pit.

There was myself, Chan Henson, and a young man, he was married, named Hubert. Three of us worked the chute. The foremen was a white guy by the name of Bill Lavers, a real rebel, but he liked me, because I was a good worker. I always mastered my job. Whenever he wanted anything done, he would tell me, and I'd have to tell the other two guys. He'd always call me "Country." Said, "Country, take the boys and do so-and-so."

Now, if we fill that chute up, got our work done, by say 10 o'clock in the morning, we'd go in a little shack we had with a heater. We'd go in that shack and sit down all day. We didn't have anything to do till 2:30. When the switch engine come out of there at 2:30, we'd have to get up on that tender and smooth off that coal level all over with our shovels. Twas very hard work. Wont no play work. We had a long rod had numbers on it—that rod was about eight foot long, crooked at one end and sharp at the other, about half inch square. We had to run that rod down through that coal until it hit the bottom in that tender, and whatever the number was on the rod, we'd tell that old guy on the ground had a book and pencil, to know how much coal was on that engine.

I kept on there about a year. I left there for two-three reasons. One reason I left was because the relationship between me and Hubert had got just about to the breaking point. Hubert, the young guy, looked white. He had very good hair.* Lavers didn't like him because he was too much like a white man. He never spoke a decent word to Hubert. When Bill Lavers tell me, "Take the boys and do thus-and-so," I tell them, "the foreman say we're going to do so-and-so."

Hubert say, "Let him tell me. I ain't going nowhere until he tell me." He didn't want to take any orders from me. But Chan—I call

_____

* [Straight hair.]

him "Uncle Chan" because he was older than I was and because he was my wife's aunt's husband—Chan would get up and we'd work together. But Hubert always had to have a word to say. It near about got to where it was going to be blows between him and me. So that was one reason I left.

The next reason I left, that chute was 90 feet high, and the steps you go up were on the outside. You could get on the bucket of coal and ride up to the top, but when that bucket heist up, it would open up that bottom, so all the coal would fall out. You'd be standing on the coal. If you didn't get off of that when it open up, you'd fall down with the coal. Or else when the bucket bottom close up, you'd get cut half in two. One fellow they put on there, he fell down near about 15 feet into the coal and it broke him up bad. He had to go in the hospital.

I had to chain the bucket. It was my job to ride that bucket, but I wouldn't ride the bucket. I was scared of it. I'd walk up these steps. The steps were about 3 by 10 feet, great big piece of timber. Well, at the top up here, where it was nailed, it had been there so long to where them great spikes was driven here it had cracked open. The spike just sitting there and it just wiggle, wiggle, wiggle. I kept telling old man Kennedy, the roundhouse foreman (he was a devil), about fixing it. Two or three flights of stairs done got dry rot and them spikes done cracked open and it was just sitting there, nothing to hold on, just there. I was looking for that thing to fall any time. Now either I walk up the steps or ride the bucket. That's another reason I left the railroad.

At the same time, I was always over after old man Kennedy about promoting me to a helper. He would come up there whenever a machinist's helper lay off, and he'd put me to work with the mechanic. If I work all day, he'd pay me a helper's price. But if he work me three or four hours, he'd just pay me that regular 30¢ an hour. The helper's pay for eight hours was $4.68 a day. But they wouldn't give me a helper's job.

I had heard about in Birmingham you could make good money, you could make $5 a day.[3] 'Twas a fellow went over there and came back, and he telling me how much work was over there, plenty work, and you could get all the work you wanted, it was easy to make money. So I just give this job up at the railroad. First of November I told the man I wanted all my time. My wife and everybody, all my friends, was begging me, "don't go to Birmingham, don't go to Birmingham." People in Birmingham was bad. People in Birmingham would kill people. They take your wife or your husband away from you. Take each others' wives and husbands. "So-and-so, they went over there and some man took his wife away from him, some woman took her husband away from her." That was the way they'd talk, the people in Atlanta. My wife didn't want me to go either, but I went. Just like I left the country, I couldn't take my wife and son wih me.

I got to Birmingham that Monday evening. I went over to the house where the guy told me I could get a room—the guy in Atlanta what told me about Birmingham, his name was Willie. I went over to the house and seen the people. They taken me in. They had two or three sons working in that shop. As soon as they got off work that evening, they wanted to go downtown. I went downtown with them, and on our way back, up there at the railroad station there in Birmingham, the Ku Klux was in they hoods and everything, marching, about 25 or 30 of them, just marching around. That was the first time I'd seen them. I'd heard talk of them, but I had never seen them before.

The next morning they taken me up to the shop, the Stockham foundry.[4] Told them that I was a friend, that I wanted a job, so they hired me over everybody else. A whole lot of people was at the window. They told me to go around to the doctor's office, the doctor examined me, okayed me. Then I went down to the boss man, and he sent me to go to work down in the malleable department in the foundry. I had never seen no metal, no molding, in my life. Come out the cotton patch and the railroad shop and I went from there to the foundry.

The first day they put me to just piddling around there, moving boards, moving sand, moving this—common labor work, paying $2.90 a day. The next day they put me on the floor, molding. Every man had his own floor. At that time a floor was around about 12 feet wide and they run about 20 feet or maybe more long. You could line up about ten molds, something like about 18 inches long across here. And you'd set your molds in rows, row after row of molds. You have your walkway between your molds, your lines going across. You start at a point at the far end, and everytime you pour off, you turn over, and that leaves a space there. At that time it was one man on one floor. That was called ground floor molding, because you putting your molds on the ground.

They showed me everything: how to do it, how to make the sand, how to line my mold. The foreman made two or three. They really learned you. It's a real first-class skilled job, molding is. The foreman and the assistant foreman was white. All the rest, the molders, was black. The foreman name was Walden. I don't know if he was Italian or Polish or something. I couldn't understand what he said.

I was making a 4 inch tee and a 4 inch ell,* a malleable ell. I worked there for about a month or two. That was in '24. First of all, I left my wife and kid in Atlanta, and they wasn't paying me but $2.90 a day. I wasn't making enough to send back to my wife and son in Atlanta. I'd work all the week, and by the time I pay my rent and board, I wouldn't have enough to send after them. I was young then, and I was very crazy about my wife. Good God, I couldn't sleep at night and grieving through the day.

They was training me how to mold, and they told me they was paying me by the day. That's what I say about Negroes agitating. The Negroes were telling me "that job ought to be paying 50¢ a piece." But everyday the sheet would come out, and it'd have $2.90, $2.90. I go to the foreman, said, "I thought you paying me by the piece." I got mad and quit and went up to Virginia Bridge & Foundry and went to work. They're paying 32¢ an hour. I could make three dollars and something a day, because they'd work till about 7 or 8 o'clock at night, from 7 o'clock in the morning, straight time, 32¢ an hour.

When the end of the week come, I'd have a little more money than I had there at Stockham. I spent some time in December, and I worked about three, four days. I was working on a crane with a guy. I was standing up there, and then they took the chain off. I moved the chain with the left hand, and I had my hand on the angle, a long piece of steel. When I loosen up that chain, the angle slipped and caught them fingers. I snatched my hand, and since I had on gloves, it just stripped my fingernails off. If I hadn't had on gloves, it would have stripped all the flesh. So I went to the doctor. I wasn't able to work, and I forget just how many days I lost. Howbeitsoever, the days I lost coming up to Christmas, they paid me somewhere around $40 for the time I lost. So I went back to work there after Christmas.

Another guy from Atlanta, he came and he went to work at

* [The ell (short for elbow) and the tee, named for their shapes, are the short lengths of pipe used in plumbing fixtures; pictured in *Webster's Dictionary*.]

Stockham. Everyday he kept agitating me, "Man, I made $5 yesterday. You ought to come on back there!" He was working in the gray iron department, and I was working in the malleable department. So I changed my name to Will Holton and went back to Stockham. If I went back and used the same name, Hosie Hudson, they'd put me back in the malleable. I picked up Will Holton in 1925, and I used that name until I left Birmingham in 1934.

I was a good worker, that was what they wanted, but I was always kind of militant. I always had a feeling that I wasn't getting what I should have been getting. I felt that I wanted to make some money like everybody else was making. The other guys, some of them who had been there a long time, they was making $5 and $6 a day. The guy who had a job paid $7 a hundred for the mold, he put up a hundred and make the $7. But that was bogish work,* and I felt that the job wont paying what it ought to pay. These guys would go in there and they'd work fast. They gets money like a bunch of muddy hogs.

We called them "road men," that means a guy can put up more molds than the average man. We had a guy in there at Stockham named Charlie Cunningham, and he was making a 4 by 3½ inch tee wire. That job was paying 11½¢, that's $11½ a hundred. But he had to make all them pieces and put them together before he got his mold made. He would make his $12 or $13 a day, but look what he done. You couldn't pour but one of them things a dip. Every dip would be a ladle of molten iron, and that ladle would hold about 60 pounds of metal. Every time he carried a ladleful, he was carrying 60 pounds. Now the iron pourers, the men who were pouring the metal, they would give Charlie Cunningham breaks. The foreman would see to him getting aplenty metal. Every time they come around with the bull ladle, they give everybody one dip, they'd give Charlie Cunningham two or three dips. That helped him pour off, but at the same time, look at the metal he carried. Look at that 60 pounds 110, 115 times. See what I'm talking about?

Charlie Cunningham drinked hisself to death. All them guys like that. Time they leave work in the evening, they went to these blind pigs, places where they bought this bootleg whiskey. They has whiskey bills like grocery bills. They drink a lot and that's why so many of them die from pneumonia. They kill themselves.

* [Hard, rough work.]

That work was hot! They wouldn't have on nothing but a pair of trousers and a pair of shoes. Maybe have on a pair of overalls, wouldn't have on a shirt. But I wouldn't work that way. Get all hot, I just wasn't going to work that hard. I thought I shouldn't have to work that hard to make a little money. They was ripping and running. I didn't never rip and run on a job. I felt this as an individual —didn't know nothing about no union, nothing about no organization. But I tell you what I did do. I had a big scrap.

What happen was they had a three inch graded ell, two castings in a mold. And they got a rush order. So they wanted 50 good molds on that job a day. The job paid 11¢ a mold. Well, 50 good molds, you see, you be done made $5½. But they wont that easy, cause it was heavy work, and it took a lot of metal. Two big casts in there, and it would take a ladle of iron to pour it. And it's hot, liquid like water, but it's like a blaze of fire.

In this particular job, they had 2000 casts in a rush they wanted. They had a fellow by the name of Long Boy,* he was well over 7 feet tall. They put him on, and the first day, he put up 50 molds. The next day he put up about 35 or 40. That was Friday afternoon and Saturday morning. Joe Mays was the assistant super. He was Italian, and boy, he was the devil! So he came up to my floor, and he ask me would I help Long Boy to run that job. I told him yes.

After Long Boy made 35 molds, Joe Mays gave him the devil about it. I'm standing on my floor looking over at them. Long Boy was tall and Joe Mays was low, and he's shaking his finger at him. After he left, I went down and I ask Long Boy, I said, "Long Boy, what was that Joe Mays saying to you?"

"He tell me to wrap my cast and cut my sand, fix my sand and get out. Say he had another man to take my place, say if he was as sorry as I was, he'd go off and hang hisself."

"Yeah?" I said, "he asked me to help you run the job."

"He told me to get out of the shop after I pour off."

I said, "If you're not going to work, I'm not going to work." So when Joe Mays came back, I said, "Mr. Mays," I said, "I thought you told me you wanted me to help Long Boy run the job," I said, "but I understand you done told Long Boy to get out of the shop."

"Oh, he ain't no good. A man can't put up but 35 molds don't need to be in the shop."

* He been dead fifteen years. He died in Ohio.

I said, "If he ain't going to work, I ain't going to work."

"What you say?"

"I said if he can't work, I ain't going to work."

"By God, boy, if you don't work, you ain't going to have no job here."

"I came here looking for a job," I said, "and I'm going to go away looking for one."

"You get out of the shop too."

I said, "Give me my money." I was supposed to have went over to Long Boy's floor and got the pattern, brought it up and put it on my machine, but I didn't put up no molds that Saturday afternoon. I poured my floor off. I just got me a nail keg and sit down beside that post by the gangway. All the Negroes there said, "Hey! Big Red, I hear you, Big Red!" They called me Big Red.[5] I was sitting there, and finally Joe Mays come back. He said, "You ain't going to run the job?"

I said, "I ain't going to run it. I told you I ain't going to run it unlessen you let Long Boy work."

"If you can't do as I say, get out the shop."

"Give me my money."

"You won't get your money until Monday."

"If I don't get my money today," I said, "then I'll just stay around this shop till Monday." Joe Mays told this little Harold Darby, the foreman under him, to go get the watchman to throw me out. I said, "Get two, cause I ain't going nowhere." I just sat there.

Mays and Darby would come by, walk by, wouldn't say anything, just walk by and look at me. All the Negroes were working and looking up there at me. They seen it was getting serious between me and the foremen, so they quit hollering, went to mumbling among themselves. Some of them were right there around me. I just sit there. I told Long Boy, "Don't you go nowhere, you stay on your floor."

After a while, Len Argyle came by. He was the big super. Joe Mays said to him, "Mr. Argyle, don't give Will Holton his check today. He just raising hell here in this shop."

"What's the matter with you, boy?" So I told him the story. "You get on out the shop like Mr. Mays said."

"I will, when you give me my money."

So he walks away. I went around and took Long Boy. I said,

"Let's go get in his office." Len Argyle's office was right across the gangway, a little place there, and we just went in his office, stood around in it. After a while he come in and Joe Mays come in, wouldn't say nothing to either one of us. We just stood there. I said, "Long Boy, now you stick to me," I said, "I'm losing my job on account of you."

"I'm going to stick with you," he said. Then Len Argyle got Long Boy and carried him on the outside, away from me. When he got through, Long Boy left. He didn't come back and tell me what had happened.

Here I am by myself. I done give my job up and the future of my making a living for my wife and kid. After a while, Len Argyle came back in. I'd still standing there. He went out again. I'm still standing there. After a while he came back. He reach over there in his desk and got my statement. He said, "Come on here." I walked out with him, and we walked down to the floor where we was going to work, and he had Joe Mays. He said to me, "Is you going to work this job?"

I said, "Are you going to let Long Boy work?"

"Yes, he going to work."

I said, "If he going to work, I'll work."

"What time you come in here Monday morning?"

I said, "I generally get in here every morning about 6:30," I said, "I'll be here about 6:30."

Joe Mays said, "If he don't be here Monday morning on this job to work like he promise, don't ever allow him back here in this shop no more."

I got my sand all together, fix my floor up, got everything ready for Monday morning. Monday morning I was in there on time, singing. I'd sing and hoot and holler. The Negroes would say, "Why don't you go on back down there and plow that mule! You up here hollering like you in the country!" So I went in there, went down, and went to work, just molding, doing my job. I put up the 50 molds. The next day I poured them off, cut my sand, everything, put some more up this evening, where I wouldn't have to work so hard tomorrow. The next day I put up some extra again.

Now I was working over on my floor, over yonder, one half a day, and Long Boy was over on his. We'd be carrying that pattern up and down the gangway, over on my floor, back over on his. That thing was heavy. Long Boy had a big floor, it would hold 100 molds. Mine wouldn't hold 100 molds. So I said to Joe Mays, "Mr. Mays . . .

"What is it, what is it, Big Red?"

I said, "Long Boy got a bigger floor than my floor is over yonder. Why not let me and Long Boy just make all these 100 molds here on his floor? Then we wouldn't have to be carrying this pattern back and forth on the gangway."

"That's a good idea, Big Red. Wait and let me see Mr. Argyle." Finally old Len come on walking by. He had old gray eyes, and he wouldn't never smile. He come by. Joe Mays says, "Mr. Argyle, Big Red raise a question, a good question here. What about letting them pour all the molds on this floor and . . ."

"Any damn way they make that job, let them make it. I wants the job made."

So Long Boy make the mold, bottom and top, then I was making the core. I make the core and sit it over here. Long Boy set the drag, the bottom—we call it the drag. I take it and turn it over, turn it around, take my core box off and blow it out, and go back to making another core. All Long Boy had to do was make his top and blow it off, and put it on the drag, and close it up.

So we went to work. We put up around 105 molds, where even if we lose any as scrap, we'd have 100 good molds. But that job was very hard to make if you didn't know how to make it. But if you know how to make it, it was easy to make. I always was able to catch the slack of how to make a job. I showed Long Boy how to ram his mold. There was a certain way you had to ram it. If you didn't ram it hard enough, it would what we call "swell"—when you pour your metal, it would be thicker on the bottom than it was on the top. The mold would give away on the bottom.

Now you had to have your sand strong. If you didn't, your sand would give away, it would wash. You'd have to have it open, or your mold would blow—the gas wouldn't be able to come out. And you'd have to have your mold around solid, to make a perfect casting. You'd have to have your core made solid, but not hard. Then you'd have to have your metal hot. You couldn't pour chilly metal in that mold.

When you pour that iron in that sand you already got, it just about burn all the temper, all the saving power, out of the sand cause it was hot. When it burn all that temper out of it, when you put your mold up, when you pour that metal in there, by it not being stout, that metal would just wash that sand on into your mold, and you'd have a whole lot of scrap. You have to renew your sand. Then it's got to be wet a certain amount to be tempered. You've got to have it on the little too heavy side. If you have it on the too light side, it's like a dust, and metal, again, will wash your sand.

We had some sand we call "red sand." It wasn't red mud, it was red sand, and you could take that sand and put it together and it would stick like red clay. But at the same time, it would be open. You'd take so much red sand with your regular old sand, what you're already working with. And you get sea coal. Sea coal was like gunpowder, but it was like a dust. It was made out of charcoal, real black. First you wets down the sand you done worked in, it's hot, called them hot casts, it was steaming, it was like hot embers. So you take it and wet it all over with a water hose, take your shovel and hit the sand and twist it, twist holes in it and wet it some more. Then you put your sea coal all over. Then you take about half a wheelbarrow-load of that red sand and scatter it all over. Then you just come up here to the end and you start to throw your sand in a heap, make a heap of it.

But that red sand was precious. They wouldn't allow everybody to use that red sand. You had to see your foreman. If he said no, you couldn't get any. He had to give you a little slip to go get your red sand. All your sand was down in a bin, but they wouldn't allow you to use that red sand unlessen they tell you. But I'd get me a wheelbarrow, go down to that red sand bin, and load it up. Here I come up the gangway, ain't asked nobody. That's the kind of Negro I was. Come up to my floor, and the old foreman would say, "Hey there, boy! Hey there, Will! You can't . . . who told you to get that red sand?" But I'm just throwing my sand on my floor, and by the time he get there, I near about got it all scattered over here. "Who told you to get that sand?"

"Nobody told me to get that sand," I says, "didn't you tell me you wanted to get this job made?" I says, "If you want the job made, I'm going to make the job, but if I make the job, I'm going to fix my sand like I want it to be." Long Boy wouldn't say nothing.

Then it come down to the metal. Me and Long Boy catch a ladle of metal each. It would be hot, red hot. Well, this bull ladle runs on a trolley with a man handling it. He come in, and pour, pour, go on up the gangway, pour, and by the time he pull back down to us, this iron done got kind of dull. It would chill up before you finish pouring your mold. It would be kind of like buttermilk, you could see little white waves waving across the top of it. And if it did run, it would make your mold nappy, have a hole in it or something. I'd say, "Don't get that iron, Long Boy, leave it off."

The foreman would say, "Get your ladle out there, Long Boy, come on and get that iron!"

I'd say, "Don't put that metal in them molds!" And Long Boy would listen to me. If you want me to make that job, I'm going to make it like *I* want to make it. And when we'd pour off at the scrap pile, sometimes we'd have one piece, two pieces, out of that 110 casts. Come out just as perfect and pretty. That would kill them. They'd come and look. Now I learnt right out of the cotton patch, I just went in there and went to making jobs them other guys been in there for years couldn't make. I was a molder, sure enough.

"This here's the steel plant out there in Ensley. That's it. I know it when I see it. I got a eye like a eagle, I tell you."

"This here is that Ensley steel plant again. That's just the way them pipes was. And the cow, they'd have a cow grazing. A Negro would have a cow, to milk. Some of them have a hog haltered out there, so he could just eat around."

Outhouses near a foundry

"It look like the houses around Slosses ore mine, in Bessemer, on the red mine. That's the way them houses was built."

Double-tenant houses

"This plant look just like the plant I was working in, Jackson foundry [see Chapter 20]. They had double-tenant houses, and the houses come across the street just like that. Jackson foundry had little pipes standing up, and the foundry was sitting out just like that. Jackson foundry and the Alabama foundry. All them was right there connected."

"That would be a mining camp, that's right around these coal mines. This here is completely isolated from the city itself. See, the mines is out here, and they build these here houses. He must be a guard, must be a deputy sheriff. They carried guns or pistols all the time."

"These here is miners. I don't know whether they ore miners or coal miners. Them poor Negroes is sitting up on that timber. If they dig here, and they timber here, and they dig over here too far, and don't timber up, this here's liable to fall in on them. That's what they timber the mine with."

2
Joining the
Communist Party

BALL games and singing, that was the social life there at that time. All the major industrials had ball clubs, and they had a city league among the companies. The Acipco Pipe Shop, they had a club. Stockham had a club. McElwain had a club. Jules Goslin had a club. Edgewater Mine had a club. And Dofina had a ball club. Sayreton Mine had a ball club, the L & N railroad had a ball club, and the Tan City Pipe Shop had a ball club. I didn't play, I just was around there, around the diamond there at Stockham, but I didn't play ball. My ball playing was way before that time.

Now several of these clubs, like the L & N ball club, they didn't play in the city league. These clubs would play each other through the week. In the afternoon, after work hours, after 3 o'clock, they'd play. They always had a big crowd of people. Regular work hours was to 3 o'clock, and the ball players would be on a job where they quit work at 3.

The molders, sometime, we wouldn't get out the shop till dark. Ball game was over when I get out the shop. It was a real mess, I tell you, cause I love ball games. And the balls would go right out there next to the fence. I was working close to the edge of the foundry, and every once in a while I could peep over the paling fence. But I couldn't see much of anything because the ball diamond was a good ways out there across the field, and the grandstand was kind of on the side. You could see a little of the ball diamond, but you couldn't see the game because the people had you cut off, the view cut off. I'd hear them hollering and hooting, but I couldn't tell what's going on.

Sometime I could see a game on a weekday, but very seldom. I remember one weekday, I laid off all day. I lost a whole day's work

75

to go out to Ensley. Stockham's team was very good, and they were playing the Ensley steel plant. Ensley had a number-one ball club, but they didn't play in the city league. They played through the week. I lost a whole day's work to lay off and go out there and see Stockham play Ensley, to see that ball game. Everybody was talking about Stockham and Ensley going to play ball, Stockham and Ensley. Stockham had a guy pitching named Jesse Jeeters. He was the ace pitcher for Stockham, out of say three pitchers. They'd have a few pitchers, maybe one catcher, and a guy who's considered a good hitter. Jesse Jeeters was pitching for Stockham. He was among the best in Birmingham. The guy at Ensley also was a big ace pitcher. I didn't go to work that whole day.

That was the first time I see a white umpire in a game. The umpire at Ensley was a white guy. And Jesse was very hot-tempered. Very hot-tempered. That day, he throwed the ball, he thought it was a strike, and this little white umpire called it a ball, and Jesse mumbled back at him. The white umpire told Jesse, "By God, you better not dispute my word." Everybody around the diamond, just crowds of people. He walked out to the mound and told Jesse, said, "You better not dispute my word!" Quite naturally, Jesse had to shut his mouth. Quite naturally, he was sullen. But he knows he better take it, better kind of stay cool.

On Saturday, the main clubs what was in the city league, they played each other. One Saturday, Edgewater would be playing Acipco—next Saturday, Jules Goslin would be playing Dofina. They played every Saturday. Then at least two or three times during the week, that was part of the practice. It was open field game. It wont nothing you pay to see. The city league didn't play each other through the week, they played these clubs that wasn't in the league. And on Saturday, I think it was about six clubs was in the city league, they'd play round each other. They had some very good ball players too, but none of them boys reached the top. They did get far as the Negro clubs. There was one boy, James West, first baseman at Stockham in 1925. He went to Cleveland in '26 or '27 —it was a black club, it wont a white club—and that's the last time I seed him. That's as far as they got then. Willie Mays, to my knowing, was the first Negro that was able to make the major leagues from Birmingham out of all them good ball players. All the rest of them fell on the wayside.

I met John Beidel in about 1926. Beidel was just above a midget.

He was a very low fellow. I don't guess he was five feet tall. I reckon about four and a half feet, if he was that tall. Cause he just come up to about half along about my shoulder. He was stout. He wasn't bulky, but he was stout-built like a man. He was very strong. He was very strong. He was a grinder when he was at Stockham. He ground the fittings in the grinding department. And he was very lisp-tongued. He couldn't talk plain. He'd talk, "Blah, blah, blah." He'd make his words, but he couldn't get all his words out very plainly. I don't think he was quite as old as I was. He was in his thirties. He was very funny, very fun at a ball game. He knew every player. He was always a ball game fiend, all the way up. He had a little softball club there he played in. I played a little in that, but not no major baseball. But he followed all the ball games.

I really got to know Beidel around the ball diamond, in the afternoon, when we get out the foundry. He was working in the Stockham foundry there and we lived in the same community together. We'd meet around the ball club and talk with the other guys. Beidel used to be a great ball fan, and he loved singing quartets too. I had built up quite a reputation in the foundry because of my singing, and he was one who used to follow the quartet around about the singing every Sunday.

All these guys in the foundry from all parts of Birmingham, they knew me. They knew me by my singing. We had a very good quartet, the L & N quartet. It was named after the L & N railroad, because the leader, Sid Hudson—he wont no relation—Sid worked at the L & N railroad. All the rest of us worked at Stockham, but we named it after him. Everybody knew that I was the L & N bass and I was among some of the best bassists was there. I wouldn't say I was the best, but all the others had to recognize me. Those guys would come through my floor all through the week, asking, "Where you going to sing Sunday, Big Red?"

"I'll be going such-and-such-a-here."

"I'll be there." Just like that. Sometimes it would be in Bessemer. Some fellows would follow me everywhere we went.

I sung in Georgia until I left the country in 1923. In Atlanta I didn't find nobody that was singing much. But in Birmingham I became acquainted with a lot of people out of south Alabama, down below Montgomery, people who was all out of the country. So I went back to that singing again. I went to singing quartets—singing quartets were very popular in Birmingham. We would sing for some of the big white politicians who'd have banquets, and they'd invite us down, pay us. We had good business in 1927 and 1928.

When I was singing, I wasn't a bad-looking person. (I was a little rowdy in them days, you know, before I got in the Party. The Party learnt me a whole lot.) I was looking pretty good, I reckon, because all kinds of ladies was always making marks or shaking hands and scratching me in the hand and making eyes or something. So I would try to find how to chance to make contact, in a quiet way. I didn't have no close friends. I didn't do much talking. What I do, I went on and done it, keep going. (After I joined the Party in '31, I quit. I quit. I understood that I was supposed to live a respectable life in order to lead people. So I laid all my lady friends aside.)

I always had a mind to try to venture, and I wanted to make a career of singing. I kept hearing a lot of programs on the radio, on the WAPI, Columbia Broadcasting, so I kept on till I found out where the station was at. And one day I just stayed off the job and went down and went up into the office.

The man who was there asked me what did I want. I told him I came down to see if it was possible to get on the radio. (I don't know, but I always believed that was Bull Connor, the same Bull Connor what put the dogs on Reverend King, because at that time he was broadcasting ball games.[1] He became famous as a great umpire on the radio for baseball.) So when I went there and told him what I wanted, this guy told me, whoever he was, he said they didn't fool with colored talents because they wasn't dependable. He said, "You know our time is organized on the radio, and if we give you fifteen minutes and you all come up five minutes late, that's five minutes that's destroyed. And therefore, that's why we don't fool with colored talents."

Well, I talked there with that racist—that's what he was—until I convinced him to give me a chance. When I got through, I said, "We can be on time."

He said, "When can you get your group down here?" He said, "Can you get your group down here by 6:30 this evening?"

I told him yes. Now I didn't have no guarantee I could get them down there, because, see, Sid Hudson was working at the railroad as a switchman, and the tenor and the baritone was in the shop. I hadn't seen them, hadn't told them I was coming down. So I told him if I didn't be able to get them I'd call him ahead of time. That's the way I nailed that down.

I went back down to the shop, I got out there about noon. I chanced to see the tenor and the baritone singers. Willie Bogans was the tenor and John Mitch was the baritone. I got them and told them what I had done, so it was all right. Sid got off that evening at 3 o'clock, and he had to come from the L & N railroad shop on the number 22 trolley and transfer onto the Eastlake car, number 21. Well, I got up there and stayed up to the station until he stepped off the car, and I got him. So at 6:30 we were down there.

They put us in a glass room to try out our voices. We started one song, and he stopped us, said, "You don't have to sing no more, it's okay." He put us on and give us fifteen minutes then, and after that he give us a regular time, every Sunday afternoon at six o'clock. That was in 1927, because we sang there at the New Year's '28. We went down in a big snow, and we just could get there, the snow was all around, just about half knee-deep. We got there at 11 o'clock at night, and we had to stay there until 2 o'clock in the morning before we chanced to sing. They was having a New Year's program. At 2 o'clock it turned on in London England, and they wanted us to come on the program to be heard in England as well. So we sang three numbers.

We went back there Sunday afternoon, and they had another young fellow there, and he said, "Boys, you all sure made a hit there the other night. We got checks here from everywhere for you boys." He said, "When you all get through with your program, I'll get them for you." When we got through singing, walking out, feeling good to know we had some money, he came round looking so dry. He look like a different person. He said, "You know, I can't find those checks of you all's." We were going to be back on Tuesday night. We came back, and we sang, and we got through singing. We asked him about the checks. It was another guy, and he said, "We got them signed already." That's what he said, "We got them signed."

You see, what they were doing, they wont paying us to sing, not anything, but that's why we got chance to sing at these big banquets for white folks. They pay us at the banquets. They contact us at the station, and the station would contact our leader, and that's the way we'd set up our program. At the station they had never offered us anything for transportation, but at that time they give us $5 between us for our transportation. We went back on two or three programs after that, and they give us $5 again. Now I was bullheaded and always had people following me, so I said to the other boys, I said, "Let's us don't go down no more. They done taken our money and they ain't never offered us $5 and now they going to give us $5. They done taken all our money. Let's just mess them up." We didn't go back to the program no more.

We were the first Negro quartet got on the radio in Birmingham. I was the man that made the breakthrough for Negro talents to be on the air. After we went on and quit, then every little quartet got on the radio.

In the late 20's I didn't have any mind about racial issues, but I always did resent injustice and the way they used to treat Negroes, whip them and mob them up and run them with hounds. I came up to that from a kid. I always did feel that if the older people got together, we could stop that kind of stuff. My grandmother used to talk about these things. She was very militant herself, you know. I didn't have no understanding on the race question, but I did wonder why the Negroes were doing the same work as the whites and yet the whites getting more pay than the Negroes. I couldn't understand that. I used to talk with John Beidel about that.

Before I knowed anything about the Party, I took an interest once in the presidential election. I think it was Harding, the one who died. The first time I began to try to pay attention to anything about what was going on, politically speaking, was about the tariff bill.[2] That tariff bill, I think it was about foreign trade. I think it was the time of Coolidge, when the great majority of Negroes was working one and two days a week, and that big discussion was about that tariff bill. I heard them talking, so I was like they was, I was waiting to see what was going to happen to the bill. The Negroes thought that if the tariff bill got passed, the jobs would just open up. I don't know why, but that was what everybody was saying.

You see, all of '25, '26, '27, in that gray iron department at Stockham, we was working what you call the "stagger system." You work two days this week, three days next week, maybe one day the next week, and maybe the next week, not nary a day at all, year in and year out. The malleable department was running six days a week, but the gray iron department was working that two days, three days a week. I don't know myself how I lived. We done just that work, nothing else. When we was off, we'd walk around the street, talking to each other. We wont doing anything. Maybe the other guys was working, but I didn't try to find anything. It wont much there to be found.

You see, the Depression—people talk about the '29 Depression —but that Depression was all the way up through the years after World War I. And I didn't go into the shop, really, until 1925. And that gray iron department was working the stagger system until along about when they put that conveyer in. They took most of these jobs off the ground and put them on the conveyer. And they put in the Bedeaux system.[3] In other words, they time you—how many molds you make an hour, how long it took you to go to the toilet, and everything. When they got through toting the watch on you for a day or two, they'd average how many molds you'd make an hour, say about 25 an hour, that would be about 200 molds, that mean 200 *good* molds, a day. Say for an instance that job I tell you about 11¢, the ell. They took that job and put it on the conveyer. They put two men on the job and cut that job from 11¢ down to 4¢ a mold. Then they come around again, they taken it off the 4¢ and put it on what you call "the Bs," and you got to average so many good molds an hour for the eight hours, and if you have them good molds go over, say, 8 or 10 over, you making 18¢ Bs, call that premium, as your percentage. But you wasn't making but 32¢ an hour. That was the base rate. Now wasn't that going some? You was really taken. You wasn't making nothing. Just rob you, work you to death.

The first thing I tried to set up, twas somewhere along in 1930, somewhere along in there. There was an old building in Birmingham, called the Penny Savings Bank. This was a bank for Negroes, they claimed, way there before I went to Birmingham, and the bank busted, but they still had the office building. There was a Negro there, call hisself from Washington. I don't remember if he contacted me or somebody told me that he told them that he wanted to see somebody from Stockham. I got three, four guys I thought was dependable and went and seen him one night. We went down to his office.

We went down there, and he talked to us and talked to us. He explained to us and told us to go back to the shop, "just get you together a little social club, where you have some representation." He told us don't tell it was a union, don't say nothing about no union. Just say it's a social club. And he was going to take it up in Washington about what they's paying us on the job.

And I went back out there, took them three, four guys back out there in the shop and went and built a club, a social club in the shop, about thirty-some members. We was meeting on Saturday. Now all of this was under my influence, and they was doing just what I said. But after we got organized, some of them wanted to turn it into a business club, wanted to go into business. The guys wanted to build a store. I never was much interested in Negro business, somehow or another. I'm talking about Negroes going into business, cause you know, they always go to fighting.

I wasn't interested in no store, and I quit meeting. I seen where it wont getting nowhere. It was a waste of time. So I quit. I went back to my singing for several years. Then that dissolved, the whole thing just fell apart. They had about $30 or more in the treasury. I don't know what become of the treasury.

At the same time, the Communist Party was putting out leaflets, but I didn't know nothing about the Party. I'd pick up the leaflets, but I didn't pay them much attention, because I was only interested in singing. Several leaflets came by. The people were always putting them around the community, but I didn't know who they was. They'd drop by at night and you'd pick them up in the morning— there'd be a leaflet on your porch. Sometimes I'd get my wife to read it, because at that time I couldn't read. But she never was too interested in politics, even when I got real all out into it.

The Party people, they first came into Birmingham I think it was along about in 1930 when they had the first meeting.[4] They went to the officials of the city for a permit to hold a meeting in the park, and told them what they planned, what everything was, and they give them a permit to hold the meeting. The whites was ignorant about it too. So when these Party guys got out, right in the Depression, and started speaking about the unemployed conditions, talking about the bosses and the capitalist system, and Negro-white unity and the rights of the Negro people, the officials told them, "Now you all leave these niggers off," they said. "You all get the white folks together, we'll take care of the niggers."

So the Party people said, "No, we have to organize the Negroes too."

The city officials wouldn't give in on that question. They said, "well, now if you won't leave the niggers off, we going to fight you."

"You'll just have to fight, cause that's our Party policy. We can't go back on the policy." Then the police broke up the meeting, run them out the park. They went to hounding them and trying to arrest them. Then the Party went to going underground, to stay in Birmingham.[5] All that was before my time.

I didn't pay no attention to any leaflets till the Scottsboro case, when they took the boys off the train, and then the sharecroppers' struggle in Camp Hill.[6] Those two was about the first thing that claimed my interest. I don't remember which one of these cases broke first, but I know well how I felt.*

The first break I know about the Scottsboro boys was in the Birmingham *News* on Sunday morning—had big, black headlines, saying nine nigger hoboes had raped two white women on the freight train, and Attorney General Knight† said he was going to ask for the death penalty for eight of them. The boy, twelve years old, he was going to turn him over to the juveniles, and when he come of age, eighteen, then he'd try him for his life. That was the first of my knowing about it. I began to buy the papers then, so my wife could read the paper and see what was going on—the Birmingham *News,* I hadn't seen any other newspapers.

Whenever Negroes was frame-up, I always would look for somebody else to say something about it. I wouldn't say nothing because I didn't think there was nothing I could say. I'd look to some of the better-class white folks. Dr. Edmunds,[7] he was the leading white minister in Birmingham, he'd always come out with some nice statement about race relations, so I didn't figure the better class of whites as being the enemies of Negroes. I thought it was the poor whites, and that was the regular stand. "It ain't these better class of people," you hear it even now every once in awhile, "it's this here poor class of whites doing things." I didn't see the hidden hand was doing the devilment. So I was looking to the whites. Sometimes it was some white woman would come out and make a statement. But it wouldn't amount to nothing, because they would continue to do the same things they was doing, until the Scottsboro case, when these people from all over the world began to talk. Then I could see some hope.

And then more and more I was trying to keep up the best I could. There was a fellow there by the name of Tommy Clark, he run a little grocery store that sell sandwiches right down outside the shop down there. (Clark had been selling his sandwiches in the

* [The Scottsboro case began in March 1931; the Camp Hill shootout occurred in July of the same year.]

† [Attorney General Edmund Knight, Jr.]

shop, but a fellow bought a sandwich for a dime and wouldn't pay him. Clark shot the fellow about the dime. And that's what broke him about selling inside the shop.[8]) The boys would come out and go down there and buy a sandwich. When the telegrams was really pouring in, that place was where we'd go down and congregate and talk about the Scottsboro case and the telegrams, down there in that little shop. We wanted to see what the outcome was going to be.

Then they had this gun battle, these Negroes down there had that shoot-out at Camp Hill. The papers came out about it, and about fifteen of the leading Negroes, preachers and some businessmen, issued a statement in the paper condemning the action of the sharecroppers' union down there in Camp Hill. They put up a $1500 cash award for the capture and conviction of the guilty party who was down there "agitating and misleading our poor, ignorant niggers." (Later I learnt that Mack Coad was the man who was down there, that they put up the $1500 reward for, and he was a steelworker, Negro, from the country just like me, couldn't read and write.*) I thought the better class ought to been putting up the money trying to help the Negroes who's trying to help themselves. I had some wonder about it. I couldn't understand it.

They had filled the jails at Camp Hill full of these Negroes, and telegrams began to come in from all over, demanding they not be hung. I wanted to know what's happening to them, what's going to happen to them, what's going to be done? It was the first time I ever known where Negroes had tried to stand up together in the South. I tried to keep up with it, asking people about it, and "what you think about it?"—getting other people's opinions among my friends and people of my stature, all working people. I didn't have no contact with no better class of Negroes. A whole lot of them was sympathetic to the sharecroppers. They wanted to see something done, too, to break up the persecution against the Negro people.

Everybody in the community had seen the Party leaflets, but nobody was much involved. The general word was it was "these

---

* Mack Coad fought in the Spanish Civil War. In 1936, it was three of them left Birmingham and fought on the side of the Abraham Lincoln Brigade, helping the people's army. One of these white boys was named Red, but I forgot the other one. Mack Coad came back about the first of '39, and he was telling me about a lot of people crossing this border over this valley. He came back to Birmingham, lived in Birmingham from then until 1967. He dropped dead of a heart attack on May 9th, 1967. He was going out to feed his dogs when he died, fell in the yard.

Mack Coad in the 1930s—union organizer,
wounded in the Spanish Civil War

Al Murphy in 1977, the year before he died—
recruited Hudson into the Communist Party in 1931

Reds." It was the Reds' leaflets. We'd pick them up and try to read them. They'd sound good, but so far as I was concerned, it didn't never jell in my mind. I was sympathetic to the Scottsboro boys, but I still didn't grapple with it to try to find out, cause, as I say, I'm concerned about singing. "Where we going to sing at tonight?" or "Where we going to sing at tomorrow?" We had went on the radio in 1927, and this here was in '31. And I was very popular and having fun with the girls. I had to push them off.

At first I just look at the leaflets and keep going. I wasn't scared of the Reds, never was scared of the Reds, but I just wasn't interested. Other people were scared, said, "better not fool with that mess, you'll lose your job." But I never was scared of losing a job. I lost five jobs.

Somebody approached me, that's how I became interested. I met a guy who had been working in the shop, Al Murphy. I think he was about twenty-six years old. He was slender, not skinny, but slender, and about 5½ feet tall. Somewhere along the line before I met him, he had got a pretty good education. I don't know whether he got his like I got mine, in the Party, but I think he had more schooling than me. Murphy was with Herndon[9] and them one time in Birmingham. They got arrested once in a meeting. Now that was along there in 1930, but I didn't know nothing about the Party then.

The first time I met him to come to know him was somewhere along about 1930 or '31, there in the shop. He wasn't a molder. He worked in the coal room. You know if you be around a long time, you see a guy, you say "hello, hello." You don't know his name, but you know his face. So I had done knowing him long enough to recognize him when I met him in the street. Whether I knowed his name then or not, I don't remember. I hadn't seen him in a good while and I ran into him, asked him, "You ain't working in the shop now?"

"No, they fired me."

"Fired you, what they fire you for?"

He said, "They fired me because I was participating in that organization for the defense of the Scottsboro boys." He said, "I just came from New York."

I said, "Yeah? What is they saying?" Now I'm looking for somebody to say something. I'm looking to see what is going to be said out of all these telegrams. "What is they saying about us?"

Murphy said, "They asking why the Negroes won't organize. I

told them they wasn't organized because they don't have nothing to fight with. So they asked me which is it easier to do, organize or fight, and I told them it was easier to organize. They said, 'Well, you go back down there and organize, and then if you get when you need guns, we'll see what we can do about helping you to get some guns.' "

When he said that, I said, "You all got an organization here?" Up until then, so far as organization, I never heard anything about no organization. No NAACP, no nothing, no union. I only know I had heard them talk about the railroad union in Atlanta when the railroad workers went on strike, and I heard them talk about the coal miners' union when the coal miners went on strike along about '22 in Birmingham. I said, "You all got something here?"

He said, "Yeah, we have meetings here in Birmingham."

"Is that what you a member of?"

He said yeah.

I said, "When you going to have another meeting?"

He said, "I'll let you know." Then he became suspicious of me. Everytime I'd see him, I'd say, "When you going to have the meeting?"

"I'll let you know." He became suspicious, and he shunned me a good while. He told me years after that he thought I was one of the company stoolpigeons.[10]

Finally he came by and left word, came by my house. He done got fired, now, and I'm living in the company house. That shows you how much damage people who's inexperienced in the Party can do to a person who has a job. Now here I'm living in Stockham row, and all the company stoolpigeons on here too.

Here's Tom Truss, the guy in the dispenser's office, call hisself "Dr. Truss." On the same row is George Smiley, the custodian around the office. And here is John Mitchell, he's on the head of the ball club and the YMCA at the shop. All these are stoolpigeons. This here is just one block. It wasn't no long neighborhood, just one block, and all these houses on one side the street. Out here is the ball diamond, over here the houses. And here come this guy Murphy they done fired out the shop. He know he been spotted, they know who he is. And he come busting up to my house and yard with an armful of papers in broad daylight. He brought me papers, come strutting up the street, everybody know him, ain't nowhere to hide, and he come there, leave me a paper. So I take the paper, try to read it. It was called the *Liberator,* on the right of self-determination for the Negro people in the Black Belt of the South.

Then he told me there was a meeting that night and I went on to the meeting. It was just over there across the shop. I'm living on this side the shop, and you go around one block, turn over there, come right down over on that side. That's where we had our meeting. We went to a small house of the man who had the meeting, and he was working at the shop. When I got there, it was two guys I didn't know, and the rest of them, like Beidel and Anderson Harris, all the others I knowed. They was working there in the shop with me. I didn't say anything, but I'm a little let down, cause I'm looking for a big something, important people. And here's the guys working in the shop with me, regular guys. Those other two were working in the U.S. Pipe Shop, up there in the same community.

We was sitting there, and Murphy got to outlining about the role of the Party and the program of the Party—the Scottsboro case and the unemployed and the Depression and the imperialist war. You had all that he was talking about that night. In the biggest part, I didn't know what he was saying. All I know is about the Scottsboro case. He was explaining about how the Scottsboro case is a part of the whole frame-up of the Negro people in the South—jim crow, frame-up, lynching, all that was part of the system. So I could understand that all right, and how speed-up, the unemployment, and how the unemployed people wouldn't be able to buy back what they make, that they was consumers and that it would put more people in the street. He went through all that kind of stuff, and I understood it. I understood that part. He took the conveyer, up there where we mold, took that and made a pattern, said, "How many men been kicked out in the street after they put that conveyer machine in there?" I could see that.

That was the beginning. I didn't do much thinking about it. When it come ready to join, I join, that night. Everybody there that night signed up, right there that night, the 8th of September, 1931. I don't know how it came to be, but I didn't never kick against nothing. They elected me as organizer—they didn't call it chairman—they elected me as organizer of the unit. They elected a guy named Will Cal as literature agent. His job was to get the literature, and see do everybody have his own literature to put out among their friends. That was the two main jobs. We didn't have a treasurer or nothing. If I had of kicked, I wouldn't have gotten so deep into it.

But I didn't kick, I accepted, and they told me I'd have to go to the unit organizers' meeting on Friday night. I was told by Al Murphy that it would be my task to meet with all of the unit organizers of the city of Birmingham each Friday night, to make reports on our unit and its work in the shop. My job was to see Murphy. He'd tell me where the meeting's going to be at, and Friday night I'd go there.

At that unit organizers' meeting it was myself, from Stockham, a fellow by the name of Knox, out of North Birmingham, worked among the coal miners, and a fellow named Bradley—I never did know anything about Bradley—and an old man from down the southside named Mr. Harris, and they had another guy, I think his name was Phillips, and they had another guy from out there from what you call East Thomas (I forgot what his name was), and a fellow named Fred Walker, and a Negro woman by the name of Addie Adkins. Her house was nearabouts the headquarters for all the meetings, Addie Adkins and Fred Walker. We did all the meeting at her house and at Fred Walker's house.[11]

The first unit organizers' meeting that I attended, where I was looking to meet with a large group of people on the south side of Birmingham, I met with seven other people, all Negroes. I did not know of any white members of the Party then. (The first one that I met was Harry Simms, the young white comrade that was murdered up in Kentucky early in 1932, in the coal miners' strike.[12]) I was somewhat surprised, to see such a small group of people. I was looking for a large group of people.

At these unit organizers' meetings we all would make reports on our unit activities as to what been achieved by our unit members' work among the workers and community people since our last meeting, such as passing out our pamphlets, *The Daily Worker,* putting out leaflets on the success of the Scottsboro boys' case, and recruiting new members, or making new contacts for the ILD branch or to become a member of the Party, and checking up on things that we had reported on in previous meetings.

Then we would have a discussion on some issue, or some new developments that had arisen since our last meeting, and the new tasks that we had to tackle in the coming period, such as leaflets, sending in post cards to the judge or governor on the Scottsboro case, or some case of police arrests or brutality against some Negro or raiding of an ILD branch. This was how we was able to get all of our members to become active one way or the other in Party assignments, by a strict check-up and also collective criticism, where everybody had to take a part. Everybody had to say something on the subject.

At that first unit organizers' meeting, I wondered why they made such a miration over me that night. I'm an industrial worker, from Stockham. Well, they was concentrating on industrial workers, and they didn't have any. Of all these people, wont none of them industrial workers. All of them was people from community units. Wasn't none of them from a shop. They's all from little units out from different spots in Birmingham, but I'm from strictly an industrial unit, out of the shop. They thought that had a gold mine on their hands. And I'm wondering why they making such a miration at me. So it would come time to report what we all doing in the shop since our last meeting, but none of them would never report nothing about no shop. I began to wonder, "How come they don't make no report about somebody from a steel mill or something?" It was all from the community but I didn't understand it. But I would be on time to my meetings, I wouldn't give up. I'd go every Friday night, rain or shine. I'd come back and tell the unit guys, "We done pretty good."

We done all right. We decided we wasn't going to have over five or six in one unit, and we had got to where we had about six units in the Stockham foundry. I was only responsible for one. Murphy was getting the others together.

There was also a young Negro fellow, we called him Ted Horton. He was a YCL* guy. Horton and Murphy was the onliest two guys I knew and looked upon as kind of special. People like Bradley and Knox and them never talked about nothing but just something around they area in Birmingham. That made me look upon Horton and Murphy as knowing a little more than Bradley and them cause they met different people. They could always talk about a certain meeting over yonder. "We went to a certain meeting in Chattanooga," like that. Murphy always left you with the impression that he was meeting with somebody from New York, somebody coming through. At that time we didn't have no district leadership in Birmingham. We only had a guy, Harry Jackson, from New York was assigned to work in the South. The headquarters, as I understood it, was in Chattanooga Tennessee. And this guy went from Chat-

* [Young Communist League.]

tanooga Tennessee, through Georgia, Atlanta, down to Florida, Tampa, and Miami Florida. And he took in Mobile and New Orleans and Birmingham. He just took his rounds. He didn't have no organization, just had little contacts. And Murphy and Horton was meeting with him when he came to Birmingham. Eventually this New York guy began to visit our unit organizers meeting, but he was still just running through there like that.

Before we was able to get the representatives from the different units in the Stockham foundry together to set up the leading committee, we all commenced to getting fired. We put out a leaflet there in Stockham what stirred up the whole thing. We give Murphy a whole lot of information about what happening in the shop: the foreman's cussing men, make one man do two or three men's work in the heat, didn't have no relief to cool off, all the grievances. The leaflet said, "Herb,"—didn't call him Herbert (Herbert Stockham was the big chief of the plant)—"we going to hit the first lick, you can hit the second." We went on down, talking about these conditions. We put the leaflets in the shop, put them all around, put them in the toilets. And I talked a lot, I done a lot of talking. I guess it was easy for them to know who I was. I'd go around to the toilet and have a leaflet in my pocket. I'd drop a leaflet between the toilets.

The toilet had about eight or nine stools, right down the side of the wall, cause you had a lot of men there. It was the kind of toilet, you sit on the stool and the tank fill up. You get up, they flush theyselves. And I'd go in and drop one there, you know, between the toilets. I'd go back later and say, "You all seen that leaflet them folks putting out here?"

"Yeah, I seen it. Somebody going to get fired about that mess."

Everybody who changed the pattern on the machine, they go out to the assistant superintendent's desk, and they had a wrench. You go out there and get the wrench, change the pattern, and put it back. I went to that desk and got a wrench, and to show you how big a fool I was, I puts a leaflet in the desk, in the assistant superintendent's desk. Went on, got my wrench, put it back there. So I goes down, and then I make like my pattern had got loose, I goes back to the desk to see had anybody got the leaflet, like I'm looking for a wrench. When I pulled the drawer open, this foreman walked up and asked me, "What you looking for?"

I said, "I'm looking for a wrench to fix my pattern, my pattern done got loose."

He said, "So-and-so has done got the wrench." But now I figure maybe he might have seen me put that leaflet in there and might have knowed I'd go back there and see had it been got. The leaflet was gone. That was the kind of chances I took.

I'd say, "I wonder who putting them papers around here? I seen papers around here this morning." I just want to see what they going to say, get a conversation about it. That was the way we'd do it. If the guy said, "Yeah, I seen it. That leaflet was talking all right." Well, then I know I can give the guy my opinion. That's what we were told to do and that's what I did. But I overdone the thing.

One day we was all sitting down talking on a little platform in the shop, eating dinner. One of these same guys was in the unit with me the night they made me chairman. I don't remember what I was saying, but he said, "You going to run your mouth round here till you get everybody fired out this shop yet." That's the way I was, I was overambitious. When I did get into it, I went on into it.

One night, me and Beidel went to a unit meeting. On our way back home, in the community where we was way over behind Stockham, we met this Negro, Tom Truss, there in the dark in the street. I don't know whether he had business over there. He was working in the doctor's office, he was supposed to been the helper in the dispensary. We met him, and we knew him in the dark, we recognized him. We didn't speak to him and he didn't speak to us, he just stopped. As we passed by him he just stopped and looked at us in the dark. Me and Beidel kept walking. I asked Beidel, said, "Beidel, you see, you know who that is?"

He said, "Yeah, that's Tom Truss."

I said, "What he doing way back over here?" over in that community where we was at. Now whether he's walking around looking for us or had seen us going on over that way or what, we didn't never know. Just before Christmas 1931, Beidel was fired out of the shop. I kept associating with him.

Then one night I was laying down sleep and didn't go to bed with nothing like that on my mind. That was in January '32. I don't argue about dreams because I don't understand them. But in my sleep I seen a big, black shiny snake come out of the top of the ceiling, and he was about the size of a saucer, a large saucer, and his head had done got down, come all the way from up in the top of the ceiling, come down side the wall, and his head had all went under the bed and his tail hadn't got out from up yonder. He was shiny, like a brand-new patent-leather shoe, real black. So I jumped out. I was on the side there next to my wife, beside the wall—I was sleeping on the right side of the bed—in my sleep I jumped out the bed over her. She woke up and asked me what was the matter, what was the matter. I told her, "Don't you see that snake come out from there? He's under this bed!"

She said, "Ain't no snake there. You just dreaming."

So when she did get me to my senses, I said, "That ain't nobody but Tom Truss." That Negro, he was shiny black.

Along in January of '32, on a Tuesday, I was told by the personnel officer, his name was Nibbley, to give up my company house. He said he wanted somebody in the house he knew, he didn't know me. He told me, "I don't know who you are."

I told him, I said, "I been here seven years. You ought to know me."

He said, "I know you, but I don't know of you." That was Tuesday.

That Friday I came and I went back to Nibbley and told him I didn't have the money to move. I had a house, but not the money. He loaned me $10 that Friday to move. I moved that Saturday, and Anderson Harris helped me to move. That Monday when I came back to the shop, that's when Harold Darby left word for me to stay in the shop, he wanted to see me. It was very cold that day.

Everybody was gone, and I waited there in the shop. Shop began to get cold. Finally he took me on the outside, where nobody couldn't hear, and he wanted to know what was I in.

I named bits of names, different church groups, and my Sunday school.

He said, "Ain't you in some mess?"

I told him no.

He said, "They fired you up at the office."

I said, "Somebody had to went up there and told them something then. I don't know anything about what they say. I have no way of defending myself." I said, "They told me at the office they wanted the house. Now you say you done fired me out the shop." I said, "Do you have my time?"

He said yeah.

"You might as well give it to me," I said, "cause ain't nothing I can tell you. I come here looking for a job. I guess I'll leave looking for a job." And that was it. Monday afternoon, the 21st day of January. Anderson Harris was fired with me, and Smiley was fired the same day as me and Anderson. They accused him also, as I understood it, of being a member of the Party, but he wasn't.

The big top stoolpigeon, Mitchell, had another guy he wanted to get on the job, Willy Wilson. He was one of the ball players, and he was one that could be trusted as a good stoolpigeon. Mitchell took some of our Party leaflets—so I was told—and put them in amongst Smiley's tools where he worked in his place, and then he went and got Nibbley and carried him there and showed him the leaflets. That's the way he got Smiley fired.

Then Tom Truss was running around. He come to my house, tell my wife to tell me he wanted to see me, he wanted to talk with me. I stayed out of his way. I never would let him get a chance to talk. He died later on that spring.

When Beidel and Anderson and I was read out of that foundry, all of the rest of these members became frightened and wouldn't come out to a meeting. They also wouldn't come around us. We didn't know just what to do. There we were, fired out the foundry. We couldn't see anybody to tell us what to do. It was cold in the heart of the winter, and everybody was unemployed.

3

Sticking to the Party

So I got fired the 21st of January 1932. I went home and I told my wife they had fired me. She said, "We'll be able to make it somehow." She was working for a woman, a white woman, at that time—not no rich woman—just doing day work. It wont paying but about 50¢ a day. This white woman claimed to be a great friend of my wife. But then one day Sophie came back home, told me that the woman asked her, "Didn't they fire your husband at the shop? Didn't they fire him about something?" The news had got out that Will Holton was fired at the shop. This white woman told Sophie that she was going to have to let her go. She'd try to do her work herself, said, "When you have people in your home, you don't know who you got in your home working." That's what Sophie told me she told her.

Sophie asked me to quit the Party several times. In '32 she asked me, "Why don't you get out of it? What you getting out of it?" and all like that. My brother came over to Birmingham, him and his wife, spent two-three days with me. My brother was from Atlanta, he was working for the railroad. (He's younger than I am. He's a minister.) Him and his wife and my wife, they talked to me about a couple of days there, "What you get out this thing? Done lost your job cause of this here mess, and you don't know nothing about it. Why don't you get out of it? You got a family to take care of."

Verdella, that was his wife, she said, "I wonder what is these folks giving you? How come you love them so well that you got to throw away your job and go hungry and suffer to stay in this thing? I don't see nothing in it for you."

So my wife, she talked. And my brother, he talked, and I stuck to my point. My position was it was freedom in it for me.

94

The last morning at the breakfast table, my brother finally said to me, said, "So you don't change your mind, eh?" He talked like a minister. "So you don't change your mind?"

I said, "No, I don't see anything to change my mind for."

So he said, "Verdella!"

"What is it Eddie?"

"Get up and let's pack our suitcases and let's go back to Atlanta." Then he said to me, "So far as I'm concerned, you and I is blood brothers, but our relationship is dissolved here and now."

"Suit yourself about it," that's what I told him. "Suit yourself about it. That's your business." He left and went back to Atlanta and I didn't hear from him. He didn't write me and I didn't write him, I guess a year or more.

I wasn't developed then like I am now, quite naturally, but I had learned enough in the Party to see it was something that the Negro people needed and would have to have if we got our freedom as all other people have.

My position was that in the Party I would be bettering my condition by helping to get conditions better for other people. And I wasn't the onliest one suffering. I was suffering along like all the rest. Everybody else was unemployed. I had learned enough to know that the working class have their own problems. But we all going to have to solve our problems together in the struggle. I stuck to that argument and I stuck to the Party.

I wasn't afraid about the white Party people coming in from New York. Many of the Negro leaders and the Negro newspapers talked about "the Red agitators all agitating the ignorant type of Negroes and misleading them." I didn't feel that way. I didn't wonder if they was getting anything out of it. I didn't have that kind of thought. Because way back there in the years when I was a small kid—that wasn't long after slavery, you know, the old slave people used to talk about the Yankees whupping the South. They used to sit around and talk about the Yankees. It used to be some Jewish peddlers to come through with bags of things to sell on their shoulders, and they would talk about the North. I heard that talk so much until I always looked for the Yankees to come back one day and finish the job of freeing the Negroes like how the old people talk about.

Before the Party, I hadn't had much relationship with people from the North. The onliest relationship I remember having with them was in 1927. I took them to be from the North because they spoke different from the whites in the South. Twas a company came down and opened up the Alabama Stove Foundry. I was working that stagger shift at Stockham, and I went over there before it was ever opened up. I got some idea about what day they would be putting men on. I went back to Stockham and I told several guys about this job over there—a fellow by the name of Quincy Elias, another fellow by the name of Johnson, and a fellow named Sooner. It was several of them I told about it, and they told they friends. I carried a great number of them Stockham molders over there to the Alabama Stove Foundry.

The day for them to open up, it was a host of Negroes over there. We all got hired and went to work there. The old man that was my foreman, he spoke kind of like a northerner, and I was interested to made conversation with him. I tried to talk with him about the conditions, about how the Negroes was treated in the South—we wont making no money, such like that. He would kind of casual say, "Well, it's bad . . ." But I noticed he wouldn't do much talking against it.

I'd say, "I'm glad you all down here," I said, "where we can be able to make some money. We ain't make no money." I thought I had met some friends from the North, these guys. All of them spoke this northern brogue, they didn't speak like southerners.

When they opened up, it was a whole lot of us. We's all lined up. Twas a big, large place. They put everybody on the floor, we got lined up on the floors. We got to working. Guys making good parts of stoves. We worked all day, put up the job today, poured off. I was making the flue door for the stove. After that day's work, we want to know how much the job going to pay. No price. Everybody grumbling.

So the next day, we went back to work. No price. They hadn't brought the price list out yet. We wouldn't put up too many, cause we didn't want them to know how many we could put up until we first found out the price, before we putting up a whole lot.

About the third day, we went in, went to work that morning, everybody lined up. So we raised the question again. They brought out the tally sheet with the price of the different jobs. One fellow next to me—he making a long stove leg. I guess it must have been for a range, just one leg in a mold. Three cents! Ha, ha! My job, 3½ ¢! Lo and behold, them northerners come down paying lower wages then we was making down there at Stockham.

Them Negroes—including myself—we cleaned that shop out that day. We had our own shovels and whatever our molding tools we had. Everybody got their shovels and their tools and just left and went away from there. More Negroes left that shop that day! The foreman stand looking—the guy's been a friend to me and here I'm walking off, leaving my good white friends from the North.

That give me to do a lot of wondering about this Yankee thing. You see, I didn't understand the class question. It's the class, you know. It was the North that owned the wealth in the South, these big steel plants. They was the ones making the profits, the northern industrialists. We went on back to Stockham.

WHEN they fired me in 1932 I didn't have but $8. I got on the city welfare. Had to set up there and wait and wait and wait, but I finally got a piece of white paper valued at $2. I took the paper, went to the market—wont no A & P down there—and I traded that piece of paper in groceries, which allowed me to get a 24-pound sack of flour for 45¢ and get a piece of streak-lean salt pork*—it was 6¢ a pound, and other things like that. Everything was cheap then.

Then they begin to mail me that white slip out to the house so I didn't have to go down there every week after it. They mailed me this white slip to my house for a while, then they sent me a note to come to the office. I went to the office. They gave me another white $2 slip, but they told me this would be the last one I'd get. They were going send me out a work order. When I go to work, I would get my groceries at the supply house. Then they sent me a blue card in the mail. I went to work at the Eastlake Park, there in Eastlake Birmingham. It was a very large park, way out near the outskirts of East Birmingham, back on the road to Tennessee. We was remodeling the park, white park, city park for whites. (The Negroes didn't have no park at all.)

A whole lot of them big shots, the better class of Negroes, they found theyself on the welfare, out there on the welfare, digging in a pit for a grocery order, to get that grocery they hand out. I'll never forget a man here, I call him Uncle Henry, great big brown-skinned man, had high cheekbones. He was a deacon, one of the big deacons of the 16th Street Church.† All before the Depression, he had his own home. But when the hard times hit the better class, they got

* [Salt pork with streaks of lean meat in it.]
† Where them kids got killed.[1]

on city welfare making gardens. They was out there digging up in the park.

They was out there digging up in the gardens, and old man Henry was out there, and these guys was working with him, these little Negroes what knowed him. They said, "Here you out here? A big shot! You know the time you wouldn't pay us no attention, and now you out here on the welfare like us is, digging up this here park. Big deacon of the 16th Street Church, and you out here, lost your home like us is."

He couldn't say nothing, he had to take it. He couldn't fight. He said, "Boys, I just have to agree with you. You all telling the truth."

I worked there about a year, the balance of '32 and until April in '33. You didn't work every day of the week. You work so many days in the week. Work say three days, from Wednesday till Friday, or from Monday till Wednesday. They paid us script for a while. I didn't have enough money to get around.

That Eastlake job is where I worked with Mayfield, and Beidel was out there for a while. Beidel was very conscientious. He was talking on about the Party all the time. I was always telling him I thought he was talking too open to the guys when he was in the shop. He was talking about the conditions and things so he was fired along about the first of December, before they fired me.

I remember just after I got put out the shop. It was very cold and frosty. Me and Beidel went to a unit meeting and didn't nobody show up. Beidel and I was standing on a little foot bridge over a ditch, and I said to him, "Beidel, I believe that I will go back to Georgia." He asked me not to go and leave him there alone. He was from Columbus Georgia, but he didn't have no people to go back to. His grandmother and grandfather had raised him. He would always talk about his grandmother. His mother died when he was quite young, and his father, he didn't know where his father was at. He remembered seeing him once or twice when he was a small little kid. He went off and Beidel never seed him no more.

Me and Beidel talk about it for a while, and I told him, "All right, since you and I can't get none of the rest of these guys to meet with us now, let's you and I see if we can get some more of the guys together out of that shop and set up another unit." Beidel agreed with me.

Still in the same winter months, coming up near spring—it was still cold (that was in '32)—Beidel and I began to build up our

Party units again. He said that he would work on Joe Howard and DeBardeleben, and I said that I would work on West Hibbard and Henry O. Mayfield. Joe Howard and DeBardeleben and Hibbard were still working in the shop. Joe Howard was in the galvanizing pit. Mayfield was out on the Eastlake job with me and Beidel.

Mayfield and me worked together on the welfare job, but we was already friends. We had both been in the shop, at Stockham, and also we knew each other singing. He was in the East Birmingham Stars. But we wont close personal friends. We got more personal on the job, to where we trust each other, talking to each other about things. I would talk about the Scottsboro case, talk about the leaflets to him. Ask him did he see what the paper said yesterday or what the leaflet say. That's the way we Party people would do it. We wouldn't go up and say we were a member of the Party. We'd just talk. So I was talking with Mayfield and feeling around trying to find a certain place to come in, to approach him about the Party.

Mayfield didn't read the Party paper, but he knew a lots going on. We gets to talking, and I continued to talk, until I said, "You know, I met a fellow that knows something more about the Scottsboro and the unemployed, that would like to talk to us about it."

When Mayfield said, "I'd be glad to meet him," well then we met with Murphy. Murphy was still there. And then Ted Horton. He was the YCL guy, he was also a Negro. So we got Mayfield. I think we got Joe Howard before we got Mayfield. And we contacted Hibbard. Hibbard, me and him was the same age. His name was West, and his wife was Cornella. We got him, got his wife. And then after they joined, Hibbard talked to Hunt, Hunt was Hibbard's landlord —he had a double-tenant house. Hibbard was renting from Hunt, so Hibbard talked to Hunt, and Hunt joined. So we just kept aspreading out. We had this unit with Hibbard and Howard and Beidel and myself and DeBardeleben and Mayfield. After a while, we had another unit, a neighborhood unit over around Hibbard in Greenwood. Then it was another unit in Greenwood. Joe Howard brought them in. He recruited a man named McGee, and then Mr. Dixon, and then Mr. Fowler, Ben Fowler. We was spreading out. This was the results of me and Beidel's talk on the bridge.

Unemployment kept getting worser, conditions worser. And these people, everyone I'd contact, he would contact somebody else, and this way among the Negroes. And this was just one area where we lived, ain't got nothing to do with the southside, where Walker was living, or where Bradley was living out in Woodlawn. This here was right around the Stockham shop, where we done lost all we had. Most of these people wasn't in the shop anymore now, people just unemployed.

The main thing that attracted people was unemployed relief. That was the main thing we talked about in the units. Unemployed relief didn't just mean food. It meant getting some coal, it meant also paying the rent, cause a lot of people couldn't pay the rent, and the landlords would be threatening to put them outdoors. We'd get us a postcard, get the landlord's name, go to writing down, demanding not to put the people out the room.

Now I never did burn any houses as lumber, but other people did. Most houses were wooden, and the people was tearing up houses so bad. When they'd put a family out, the people's like eating them up, just like a fire, eating them up. They tear them down so quick, so fast, to make firewood out of them that the landlords got scared to put people out. That's how I got a house over in Collegeville to stay in from April '33 to July of '34 for $2, just to keep the house from getting tore up.

We got started with the Party units the second time, we began to move out among other people, all Negroes again. We had several people around us, reading the *Sunday Worker* and the *Southern Worker* about what was happening around the Scottsboro boys' case, which was the hot issue at that time. This was our main activity, getting these papers and leaflets out among the people in our communities.[2] Some of the leaflets we would pass out of our hands, some of them we drop them on people's porches at night or stick them in their gates. Many times we would put them on the various church steps on Saturday nights before the Sunday service. We would go back in the communities and see what the people had to say about them. This was how we could know the people that we could make friends with, for new recruits. We would not try to recruit people right at one talk, because police pimps was also very active trying to find out just who was a member of the Party for the Birmingham police. So we had to know just who we was talking with. We didn't tell no one that we didn't know to be a Party member that we was members. We also didn't tell a member of another Party unit any other member's name.

Our struggle was around many outstanding issues in our Party program in the whole South: (1) full economic, political, and social equality to the Negro people and the right of self-determination to the Negro people in the Black Belt of the South, and the outlawing of the jim crow laws in the South that was on the statute books that prevent the Negro and whites from meeting together to discuss their daily problems together;[3] (2) was for the freedom of the nine Scottsboro boys; (3) the right for the Negro and white workers to organize and meet together without being arrested by the police (that was a big issue); (4) the right to vote for the Negro people and to hold elected public offices; (5) the right for the Negro people to serve on the jury roll; (6) no discrimination against the Negro people and women on all public jobs; (7) unemployed cash relief for all unemployed workers and part-time workers and separate demands for each dependent and whoever could not find suitable work; (8) direct cash relief with a certain amount to all youth who could not find suitable jobs; (9) free government housing; (10) unemployed and social insurance for the old people who were too old to work; (11) death to lynchers; (12) equalization of education for the Negro youth in the South; (13) against police brutality against the Negro people and the white workers who attempted to organize a union; (14) the right for the sharecroppers in the rural areas to sell their farm products after they had raised their crops; (15) union wages on all public jobs.

In every leaflet that was issued by our Party, these basic demands was raised. Among the "lower class of niggers," as we were called in those days—and many of the "better class" ones and some of the whites also would whisper to our people—they were saying, "we are with you all," or "I am in favor of what you all are working for, but you know I cannot stick my neck out, but I am with you. Here is my little donation, but just keep what I say and do to yourself, and don't ever call my name to anyone."

They had a old doctor over up in the Negro Masonic Temple, Negro doctor. Old Dr. Thompson. He was the head of the Young Democratic Club. He went for a dentist, but I don't know how he lived. He sit up there, but he never did have no customers. He'd say, "I'm with you. I'm with you all, boys, but you know these God damn white folks." He'd cuss a whole lots. "They ain't going to let you all do it. These northerners come down here and give their time and all that, but these God damn white folks here ain't going get with you all like these northerners do." That was his position. We had all kind of arguments. But he'd give little donations, give $5 or $2 on the side. (He's dead now.)

We was having classes in the units, with Mayfield, Beidel, Hibbard, Howard, and DeBardeleben. When we got together, we discussed and we read the *Liberator*. The Party put out this newspaper, the *Liberator*. It carried news items on the whole question of the oppressed people, like Africa—this George Padmore, that was where I learned of him, the first I hear about George Padmore was in this *Liberator*. Also William L. Patterson, who was the executive director of the International Labor Defense in the early period of the Scottsboro case. It always was carrying something about the liberation of the black people, something about Africa, something about the South, Scottsboro, etc., etc.[4]

We would read this paper and this would give us great courage. We had classes, reading these articles and the editorials in the *Liberator*. We'd compare, we'd talk about the right of self-determination. We discussed the question of if we established a government, what role we comrades would play, then about the relationship of the white, of the poor white, of the farmers, etc., in this area. If you had a government in the South—they'd give you the right of self-determination in the Black Belt—you got whites there. What would you do with the whites? We say the whites will be recognized on the basis of their percentage, represented on all bodies and all committees. But the Negroes at all times would be in the majority. All parties would be elected. We were talking about electing people to committees. Our position was that on committees, if you had a committee, the majority of that committee would be Negro. But you'd also have representatives in all committees by all factions, not exclusive Negro, see.

Back in those days, we felt and we discussed it from the point of view, and from our instructions, that setting up a Negro government, exclusive, there again we would establish Negro capitalists. And Negro capitalists, number one, would be exploiting the Negro masses just like the white under such a system. This was the basis that we discussed the question of integration instead of separation. We might not could be sure some white people would run for office, but at least we sure what we're fighting for, which way we going. It was the comrades' job to try to educate the people on the importance of this and not a complete separate government from the whites.

The role of the communists, Negro communists, was to try to educate the people against setting up another same old system that we had. The question of the people educated—education just don't come from books, it comes through struggle. While they're struggling to get the right of self-determination, they also learn through the struggle of the importance of not separating. We had no guarantee, but twas our job to try to convince them. We couldn't make people be communists, it wasn't a question of making people. It was a question of being able to educate them to the point where the people themselves would take the correct path. It wont a question of force. The question of the right of self-determination was the *final* goal. But all these economic questions we struggling for each day: the right to vote, against lynching, police brutality, the right for poor rural Negroes to sell they products, that was immediate.

I remember one time, eight or ten of us was meeting there along in July, and it was thunder and lightening. It was in a tight-room house.* We had to talk low, because them houses wasn't sealed but just outside weatherboarding with no sealing inside. Anybody pass along on the outside can hear you talking on the inside. That's why we had to talk low and get in the house in the summer and sweat. A white fellow from New York† was meeting with us in there, and someone asked him, "Do you think the Negro people will ever be able to enjoy democratic rights under this present set-up?"

He said, "I think it will all depend. It depend on how well we able to organize mass pressure. If we can organize sufficient mass pressure of Negro and white workers in the South, there will be many democratic rights that the Negroes will be able to enjoy under this present government, before socialism."

I stopped him and I said, "I don't know what you mean by 'democratic rights.' I hear you all talking about 'democratic,' what *is* 'democratic rights'?" I'd been listening at it, setting up in the meetings, and they talk about "democracy," and "democratic rights," and it was just like talking about China to me. That's how much I knew. But I set up there, I set till I got tired, then I came out and asked the question. He explained it to me, what it meant.

* A hot little house with no air conditioning.
† [Don Rose, later the CP district organizer in Alabama.]

He always took time to explain to people, see. Didn't get mad, say, "You ought to know," or stuff like that. He stopped and explained it in detail, said it means the right to vote, the right for Negroes to serve on a jury, to hold public office. That was democratic rights. In the present set-up, everybody supposed to have the same rights, but we didn't have no rights. It was a bourgeois democracy, not a working class democracy, like there was in the Soviet Union. That was the first time that I learned what democratic rights was.

In the spring of 1932, there in the community of Kingston, part of Woodlawn, out there where I lived, and also where Murphy lived (he was living with his uncle), a case come up. There was this white man. See, the white community and the Negro community kind of joined. The whites start here and go one way, and the Negroes start here and go back the other way. Maybe they have a alley to separate them. They didn't live on the same street, and the backs would be fenced in. This white man walks over here about a block or so, over in the Negro community. He went to a Negro woman's house. It was a rainy afternoon, it wasn't night. I don't know whether the woman had a husband or not, but she had a twelve-year-old girl. This white guy went up there and told that woman he wanted to get the girl to stay with his wife, his wife was sick. This Negro woman let the girl go with this strange man. (That's how big a fool she was.) He took her, and the woman let them go, going to his house to stay with his wife. The man led the girl on off to the outskirts of that community, to where the bushes starts, into the swamps.* He raped the girl. The girl came back home, all muddy and wet.

They called the police. The police came out and they made their investigation, and the police hadn't never made no report, hadn't never arrested nobody. Murphy came and went around to individual Party members, got about five or six of us together. We went down to Birmingham that next morning, which was Saturday morning, to see about the case. We didn't know that Murphy had done met with some ILD lawyers had come down from New York and told him and some of the rest of them, said, "You all get something started here. You all ain't doing nothing. We want to start something. If you get in jail, we'll come and get you out. Don't worry about getting in jail. Get something started." I didn't know about the meeting with the lawyers until later. I wasn't there.

* That's where part of the airport is now.

Now this case done been two-three weeks since the incident happened. We went to the chief of police, walked in, wanted to know what had they done about this case. Murphy was the spokesman, he and Horton, the young guy. These was the leaders of the group. I was just with the crowd. It was about six of us. We went into the police department and asked them questions. The police looking around, they thought something done happened last night. They got all excited. We said this had happened now three or four weeks ago out there and, we said, "We want to know and the neighbors wants to know, what's being done about it, about tracking down this man who raped this girl?"

So when they found out it was about three weeks ago, they said, "You have to give us time. We still investigating that." We didn't put up too much argument, but at least we went there. We left then, and we went down to a place down there they used to call the Little Masonic.

This Little Masonic was down on 7th Avenue, about 15th Street. It was a headquarters of the Negro World War vets and where the Negro preachers hung out at, to chew the rag, you know. Robert Durr had a paper called the *Weekly Review,* and that was where the preachers hung out at. (This here wasn't where the tip, big preachers was. It was kind of the next layer. You had two so-called ministers' organizations in Birmingham. You had one that met on Tuesday, at 16th Street Church. That was Reverend Fisher and them. Then you had the other group that met down in that church on 11th Street, St. James Church. That was the other group. All the preachers belongs to the "better class of niggers," but Reverend Fisher and them, they was the top—Goodgame,[5] Reddicks, all them was the big shots. They used to meet with Dr. Edmunds in what they called the Interracial Commission.[6] They might of done something, but we considered they was just doing what the white people tell them to tell us to do. It was said that they go there on Tuesday, and they would discuss the sermon they going preach the next Sunday. That's what was told to me. The white ministers would select out the sermons. They discuss the sermon the Negroes going preach in church. Then these top big Negro ministers come out and then this other second crowd had a layer with the big crowd. They would hand it on down. And when they get to the church, whatever they had to talk about, everybody talked about the same thing. If it was anything important, they'd bring it out in a certain way they had.

This was especially true around the Party and the Scottsboro case. There was always one of them big preachers, would get up and say, "Them Reds send down a lot of agitators among our ignorant people to break up the peace and happiness of the South. They kicking up all this trouble, putting out all these papers.")

So we walked into the Little Masonic and Murphy said we were the Liberation Committee. We began to ask questions: "What about this colored girl's rape out there in Woodlawn?" They didn't know about that. Then we want to know what they was doing about the Scottsboro case. They know about that. It was things like that we asked them about. Murphy and Horton was the ones doing all the talking. I'm just with the crowd. Horton was very militant, and he began arguing with them about "you all call yourself leaders, and you ain't doing nothing." One of them says, "I'm still sticking with the 'old gold.' " "Old gold," that means the government. "I'm sticking with the 'old gold,' " he said. That means with the money.

That was all we did. I never did hear no more about that case, never did hear what happened, whether they caught the guy or whether they ever did try to catch him. But that was the first thing we did.

The next thing we did, we went to this mountain where the city welfare was opening up a highway. This was in the spring of '32. Three of us went down there on the mountain. We wasn't working there, we just decided to go over there and start something. We went on over there and walked all the way across that mountain, went way to the far end. Then we came back where the crews would be all worn out. One of us would say, "Man, you working here, digging these rocks, doing this work and ain't drawing no money." Then the second one would come along behind. He'd talk about what you've got to do, you've got to organize. And the other guy would say, "Tomorrow evening at 3:30 we're having a meeting at the Kingston school to discuss this question, how to get money for this work." We done that all the way up the line. It was myself, Andy Brown, and Joe Howard. Beidel wasn't in that.

The next evening there at the schoolhouse, we had about 250 people to show up out of the community. We had some women to show up. Al Murphy was the chairman of the meeting. He was the general spokesman, but he called on two or three of us to have some words to say. And in my way, the best I could—that was the first meeting I spoke at in my life out in public—I spoke. I don't remember what I said, not word for word, I might exaggerate. I know practically what I said. I talked about the importance of we organize, about the unemployed and the demands we was always talking about, more relief for the unemployed and this was the only way we was going to be able to get it. I think maybe Al Murphy might have talked about Scottsboro and Camp Hill, but I didn't talk about that. I was ascared then, cause in the crowd, standing there listening, was a guy, John Mitchell. He was one of the top stoolpigeons from the shop, and he was standing right where he could hear everything that was said that afternoon, him and some others from Stockham. It wasn't too far from the Stockham shop, it was in the community around there. I had done been fired then, but more and more then, they seeing just who I am. They wasn't sure before, but now they know for sure, they hear me.

The next morning we had about 150 show up to march to the city hall. We left there, headed down to Birmingham. At that time it was down on 19th Street and 4th Avenue. We had one white guy going with us, Turner. He was a local guy. We had three or four there at that evening meeting, but he's the only one came the next morning, and he was one of the Party members. When we got down to Birmingham, our crowd had done dwindled down. They friends was stopping them on the way, "Hey, where you going?" "You in that crowd?" "Man, you better come on out of there!" on like that. They kept on adropping out, adropping out. So we did have about 50 or 60 people when we got down there. This was from at least three miles from town. We was walking four deep, side to side.

We got down there, and city hall had a large front, a pavement. We told everybody to stand back next to the curb where we wouldn't block the people trying to pass. We already done chose about six people, and this white guy made seven, that were going up to see Jimmie Jones. He was the mayor. Our people all stood back, orderly, didn't bottle up no traffic, and we went in the city hall. We's going up the steps, we got up about the first flight of steps, and old detective Mosley run up in front of us—he was head of the Red Squad—he run and pull out his pistol, asked, "Where you niggers going?"

Horton said, "We going to see Mr. Jones."

Then he asked this white guy, "You with these niggers?"

And he said, "No, I'm going to the Health Department." He had a can of some kind of something, of beans or tomatoes or something. He wanted to ask some questions about the health department, and he had that can when he came that morning.* Detective Mosley told us, "Get back down them steps!" Right about this time Police Elliott came on around, pulled out his pistol and hollered, "Get out of here!" So they wouldn't let us go by, and we had to go back down the steps.

We walked back on outside, and we got back to where all our people standing, and Mosley and Elliott's walking behind us. Horton says, "Fellow workers, these white gentlemen won't let us go see Mr. Jones. We'll have to go back and reinforce our strength and come back. We are going to see Mr. Jones."

When he said that, Mosley run up and hit him side the jaw, said, "God damn you, I told you to get out of here," and he hit him right upside his jaw with his fist. He had on one of these hard straw hats, Horton did, and when Mosley hit him, his hat fell off on the ground. He walked up the sidewalk looking back, feeling the jaw and looking back at the hat. I picked up his hat, told the rest of them, "Come on you all, let's go."[7]

So we went on up at the corner of 2nd Avenue, went on up 2nd Avenue and went on out where we came from, back to the community. We didn't have much to say. We's all pretty let down. We wont marching then, we's just walking. Everybody's talking about it one way or the other, said, "Well, what we got to do, we got to organize more strongly." Some people wont members or nothing, they was just with us. But they all had pretty good courage.

The police at city hall was looking for us to come back that evening, though, so we were told. They mounted police with sawed-off shotguns, machine guns all around, waiting for us to come back. That evening they took Mayor Jones, took him in an ambulance and

---

* We said among ourselves—well, I wasn't developed then—but I know Murphy and them said, "That damned Turner deserting us." Like that, going back. He wasn't expelled or nothing to my knowing, I saw him several times after that, but I never was able to see him any times involved in meetings. You see, at that time you had a lot of whites, they would join and maybe give a little money on the side. They take some literature, but the Party among the whites wasn't organized like among the Negroes. Because you have one white here and nobody but hisself. If he attend a meeting, he didn't have nobody else around him, and he would join hisself, but he's scared to open his mouth to other whites to try to get them to be members.

carried him home, with the motorcycle guys guarding him, protecting him from the Reds. The Reds would be back. The next time we went back was November the 7th, 1932, when Turner and Alice got arrested. But by then we got a stronger leadership, and a lot more people.

4

A Party Leader
in Birmingham

ALONG in the late spring of 1932, May or June, Harry Jackson brought in the first Party district organizer to Birmingham. His name was Don Rose. (He was a white guy from New York.) When Jackson first brought him in, we met out there in Woodlawn, in Nelson's house. Wont but three or four of us there that day. I don't think it was a unit organizers' meeting. It looked to me like I might of been told to come out there. Jackson had Don with him, and he introduced him to us, told all of us, the Negroes, said, "I won't be with you all no more, soon." Said, "He'll be working here with you all. I'll stay here awhile, I'll be around a while, I ain't going right now, till he get on to everything. Then I'll be going to the West Coast." So Jackson met with Don once or twice in the meeting, just with us.

Very shortly after our first meeting with Don, he organized a one-day conference on Sunday, and all of the unit organizers was asked to be there. That conference was attended by Otto Hall,[1] from Atlanta Georgia, and Angelo Herndon. Hall and Herndon had just led that unemployed march of Negroes and whites on the city hall, and they was all telling us what a great success that they had had. (We got the news that next week that Angelo Herndon had been arrested at his mailbox picking up his mail.)

We had maybe ten or fifteen people there at that conference that Sunday when we organized the Southern Section Committee. We had people from Oxford Mississippi, from Georgia, from Montgomery, from Reeltown, Camp Hill, and Walker County Alabama, and then people from around Birmingham. From Birmingham it was Bradley, Andy Brown, Knox, myself, Beidel, Mayfield, Joe Howard,

Parker, Murphy, and Horton. All of them's Negroes. Then there was maybe a couple of whites.

Out of that conference of the Southern Section Committee we organized District 17. District 17 was Alabama, headquarters in Birmingham. We had representatives from Birmingham, mostly, but we also had representatives from Montgomery, from Camp Hill and Reeltown and from Walker County. All that got to be one person from down there. And from Selma, we had a person from Selma Alabama. I don't know if Mobile was included in that. I don't remember we having nobody attending from Mobile—the D.O. would go down to Mobile. We also had people from Atlanta to come sometimes, or from Oxford Mississippi. Sometimes we invite a guy from Chattanooga Tennessee. We had a little organization in Memphis Tennessee, but it never did get to the point of having nobody from there to come in from Memphis. District 17 was the best organized in the southern section and Birmingham was the strongest place, so we just invited them in from outside sections when we met in District 17.

A little bit later on we elected a bureau for District 17. That bureau was seven members, along with two or three alternates. Elected on that Party bureau was Don, the D.O.; Knox, a coal miner, he represented coal; Henry O. Mayfield, and a white guy from New York named Sid, they represented the youth; Sol represented the ore miners, that was Mine Mill;[2] Joe Howard was the steelworkers; representing the unemployed was me; Cornella Hibbard represented the women; then there was a guy, Al, represented the ILD. He was a kind of alternate. Let me see now, the mine-mills person was a black person. Coal was a black person. Steel was a black person. Unemployed was a black person. The women was a black person. The youth was two people, black and white. And the ILD was a white person, southern white. That was the bureau that met with the D.O.

The bureau met every week, *every* week. I was a member of the district bureau until the Party dissolved itself, when Browder liquidated the Party in 19 and 44. In order for us to meet, white and Negro Party bureau members together, we would have to meet all day long, mostly on Sundays, in private homes of Negroes.* In most

---

* It was strictly forbidden by the jim crow laws in Birmingham, for Negroes and whites to meet together, except the better class of Negroes to meet with their good white friends, such as the leading Negro ministers meeting with a few of the leading white ministers.[3]

cases they were not members of the Party, just good wishers in what we were trying to work for.

We would not tell all of the bureau members where the meeting was to be held, just some of us would know and have the other one to meet one of us who was responsible, to get that person to the meeting. We'd meet on a certain corner of a street at a certain time, early in the morning in most cases, about 6:30, at a time we felt that the police were changing shifts. If the member was more than five minutes late, we would not wait, and that member did not get to the meeting that day. He or she would have to have a very good reason for not showing up on time as they was supposed to. If they didn't have a good reason, we all would give him hell, in a constructive discussion. That way we did not ever have too much trouble with members being late whenever they had to meet someone on an appointment.

We would go into a person's home early before their neighbors were getting up. We went in one by one, two by two, so no one could hardly tell that there was a meeting taking place there. We would stay in the house until dark where the neighbors could not see us leaving the house. We left there one by one, five or ten minutes apart, until we all finally gotten out.

We would have the Negroes all to leave the meeting first, because we thought that if the police happen to see the whites leaving out of a house in a Negro community they might become suspicious. If the whites had of left first and the police came in, they would pick up everybody left in there. The whites always left last, and we never hardly had any trouble with the police raiding our bureau meetings or our members getting arrested leaving meetings.

Because the bureau met only once a week you had to have somebody there would get with the D.O. between times, if you wanted to get out a leaflet or make a statement or something like that. You couldn't run around and get everybody on the bureau together just any time. So the bureau elected three people to be a political bureau, we call it the "pol buro." I wasn't on the pol buro. It was the D.O., Sid, a young white guy representing the young people, and then you had the guy from the ILD, Les.

They was all three white, cause these people, under the conditions, we had to practice segregation. We wasn't working under the best possible conditions. Sometimes it just meant the whites meeting. Sometimes it was impossible for them to meet with a Negro, cause the police was watching. If the police see a white in the Negro community, the first thing, he going to stop and want to know what your business out here. Cause he's looking for Reds, you understand. It was just difficult. It wasn't so easy to get by. It made it very difficult for whites and Negroes to meet together. It wont because we wont trying to do the best we could, but it was a question of saving hides. So the pol buro was three white guys. Sometimes they have a meeting, just the three together, and they come back and tell us what they took up and what they talked about. Nobody didn't kick about it, not in that period. It wont much to kick about. Maybe it ought to been kicked, but look at what the conditions was—that was 1932, '33, '34.

They couldn't afford to make the whole bureau all white. That was against Party policy. We had to have white and black on the bureau, regardless of what the cost had been. But we had quite a time having meetings together.

One evening in a meeting, something came up about working among the Negroes. The D.O. was there, Horton was there, Murphy was there, and myself, and I believe Joe Howard. Jackson was there, and we was discussing the question of different people giving a report. This was still while Don was sitting around along with us just catching on. And Horton, Ted Horton, this militant young black guy, he had promised to do something or he had pledged to do something, something he was going to do. That evening he was making a report.

Horton didn't have nothing. He hadn't did nothing on what he had promised to do. So Jackson, being the leader, he began to question Horton, and pinning him down on why he didn't do so and so: "You promised that in the report you made last week that you had these contacts, and what you were going to do. Now you giving us the same report this week! When are you going to bring in a real report when you done made some progress?" Jackson cornered him off about it. Said, "You always making long reports, but you show no results." Said, "What happened from last week? What did you do?"

I'm not exactly sure what they was arguing about because I wasn't all that much developed then, but I know Jackson was talking about how Horton was always making long reports, political reports, but he never show no results. Horton could talk, he could talk a half hour. Many the time we'd get tired of him talking. He'd start off, and he'd make long reports. But when he get through, he ain't done anything—still the same thing it were last week. He ain't got nothing to show what he's doing.

Instead of Horton answering the question what he going try to do, he turns around and begins to get mad, and commenced to hollering, whooping and hollering, Horton did. He starts to cussing at Jackson, "What the damned hell is you doing to bring some white folks in? You always telling us to get Negroes, but you don't get no damned whites!"

We said, "Hey, hey, hey, cut out all the whooping and hollering in here, cause somebody hearing will have the police in on everybody."

Now it certainly was three or four times easier to make contacts with Negroes than it was with whites. A white really had to be sticking his neck out to contact whites, and yet we didn't negate the importance of contacting whites, of the role the white had to play among the white. That was on our agenda all the time, the question of concentrating among the white workers. We raised the question many times that the Party and the ILD too, was too far balanced, too far onesided, all black and no white. But actually, the Negroes was easier to recruit. They was ready to come. The whites had a whole lot of hang-ups. The ordinary whites in Birmingham, they was sympathetic, but they could not turn that racist sugar-tit aloose. They just couldn't see themselves coming all out and joining up with the Negroes. You just had a few of them to participate. Most of the white leadership in the Party there was from the North.

Up in the top years, in '33, '34, '35, the Party in Birmingham and Alabama was dominated by Negroes. At one time we had estimated around Birmingham about six or seven hundred members. And in the whole state of Alabama it was considered about a thousand members. We only had a few white, and I mean *a few* whites.*

After that day, I never seed Horton at another meeting. He was just trying to get around the criticism. He became very subjected to criticism and he was fighting back. If he'd been real honest about it, he'd a come back, kept on. But he didn't. I met him once or twice and asked him why he didn't show up, I said, "I don't see you at the meetings, how come you don't come?"

* Out in Tarrant City they said they had a unit of whites. They never did bring one of them into the Party leadership meetings. They had a few scattered whites around there, in Fairfield, in Pratt City.

"I'll be there. I'll be there."

I haven't seen him at another meeting.* That day with him and Jackson was my first see a run-in with Negro and white in the Party.

By the last of 1932 I had to go to bureau meetings once a week, unit meetings once a week, and Collegeville section committee meetings once a week. (We organized the neighborhood sections down towards the end of the year.) Then I was also active in the unemployed block committees and we also had other meetings to go to. I didn't have nothing to do, wasn't working, just going to meetings.

Plenty times my wife begged me, cried, asked me to stay home, "Please, please stay home tonight."

I'd say, "I got to go out. I be right back. I ain't going to stay long." That's right. She was, I guess, feeling romantic. (We wasn't so old then.) But I couldn't see . . .

One night I was getting ready to go to a meeting with Mack Coad. This was after he was at Camp Hill in that big struggle down there in '31. The Party had sent him to the Soviet Union. He stayed there about three years. When he came from the Soviet Union in 1934 and came to Birmingham, he lived with me for a good long while, for three or four months or more. He wasn't married, and I was undeveloped—politically speaking—and my wife used to get at me. Me and him be going off to a meeting, and she'd say don't go. She'd say, "Hosie, don't you go tonight. Stay here with me, stay at home. I want you to stay at home with me tonight." Once she asked him, "What are you trying to do to me? Why don't you go alone, let Hosie stay here with me?"

Mack Coad said, "What do you want? Why you want him to stay with you?"

She said, "I'm in love!"

He said, "What is that? Ain't no such a thing as love." That's what he said. That's the kind of thing was going on. Well, I can see it now, but I couldn't see it then. I made my mistake. I was paying attention to what he was saying, and he didn't have no wife. And I had a wife.

I loved her. My love didn't change towards her. It's just a matter

* The last time I seen Horton to my knowing was the period of World War II. This was way out of the '30s now, way up there in the '40s, and he was in uniform, had on a soldier's uniform and cap. I saw him on the highway, on 1st Avenue.

that I believed that I had a responsibility to carry out, to be at my post on time. When I get through that, I'd be ready to go back home, but she didn't see it like that. When I got home, it'd be 10 o'clock, 11 o'clock. She tell me many times, said, "I wanted you here, but I'm sleepy now. I don't feel like it. I don't feel like I was feeling." I was being busy, the Party keeping my mind occupied, and she couldn't see and feel like I was. By she not being politically developed, not being developed along with me, it just pulled us apart.*

Many times I tried to carry her to meetings, and she, "No, no, I know what you all trying to do, and I understand. But I don't want to go." Some of these large meetings, when we got to having open meetings, I carried her. One time she cooked a cake, and everybody just went wild over that cake. She was a very good cook.

She'd sew sometimes, but mostly she didn't have nothing to do. That's one thing maybe I made a big mistake. I never did want her to do a lot of hard work for low wages like other women. I didn't let her work in the white people's house for nothing like the other Negro men was letting they wives do. They wont paying but 50¢ a day, working all day long. I'd tell Sophie, "I can make enough to feed you and this boy. No use you going out there working for white folks for nothing. Stay here at the house if you can't make no more money than that." She worked when she got ready. But if she had of been working, her mind would of been kept busy. Cause if you working, you come home, you feel like relaxing some time. But everyday, day in and day out, doing nothing but just in the house, relaxing, don't have to work, her mind wasn't occupied. She would work for a few days, come back and say, "Hosie, I was out there working hard. I don't like that old job."

"I didn't send you out there. You wanted to work."

So she come back home and she sit down. This was the way it was for years, not just one time, but years and years, till the Depression. (When the Depression came and I didn't have no job, no money, that's when she *had* to go out to make her some money. Her work never did help me in the house. She never said, "I'm going work and I'm going buy some groceries." She never did do that. She'd go work and hide her money.)

One thing I told her, I said, "Whatever you do," I said, "when I

* She sitting in Birmingham today by herself, and I'm sitting here today by myself.

come home, don't be sitting up around with a dirty dress on," I said. "I want you to be dressed up real nice when I get back from work." And that's what she did. I got home, she'd be at home. Maybe she went to town. She'd say, "I went to town today. I went down, looked around the streets." I didn't pay it no attention, and I don't know where she had been. I didn't watch to see where she's going, cause I thought I had a true-loving wife.

Once I was living in a double-tenant house next to this old man. His name was Saunders, Reverend Saunders. This was in 1927. Me and him worked in the shop together, and he'd come round the house. We'd sit and talk. He wanted me to show him how to sing, try to sing a song for him. One day he said, "Will, come here, I want to tell you something."

I said, "Yeah?"

He said, "That friend Lee Bowman of yours . . . you watch him, cause I don't like his booming around your house, with your wife, while you're away."

I didn't want to hear it. I didn't want him to tell me. I said, "Okay," but I didn't want to hear nobody tell me nothing. My position was if I didn't see nothing, nobody tell me nothing.

Now to show you what I'm talking about, the year that I was living in this house where Mack Coad came from the Soviet Union and stayed with me, it was a old man, old man Whistnam, lived close by me. My house was facing the avenue here, and his house was facing the street here. His back was to the side of my house. He was a old man, worked at the railroad, and this man Goodwin, he was a old man. All them old friends. This man Goodwin was buying his house, and he had done got unemployed, and he lost out on his mortgage, and the mortgage had evicted him and taken over the house. After they take him out, they want someone to live in the house, keep people from burning up the house—people was burning up houses for firewood. Twas a five-room bungalow. I went and lived in that house from April in '33 until July in '34, and paid only $2. I paid $1 down when I went in. The man for the house said, "Give me a dollar to show that you rented the house, I give you a receipt," he said, "now you stay there and don't let them tear up that house, until you get a job to make some money where you can pay rent." I went back down there—it was a long time and nobody didn't come out there from town to see, so I went down there. He asked me did I have any money. I said, "I still ain't got no money,"

I said, "I ain't got but $1 yet." He said, "Give me that." I give him one dollar. I went back out there, stayed on there in that house.

Now Whistnam done broke up this old man, old man Goodwin and his wife. Whistnam was his friend, next-door neighbor. He had broke them up. I noticed Whistnam, he had a son, and his son's wife used to come over to my house, come around and come in there, talk to my wife, on a secret, secret, "Ahchachacha," whispering and going on. I wasn't paying no attention. She'd never come to visit—that was some people was not of my associatings. They was a little better class, cause the railroad guys was looked upon as better class.*

I didn't pay Whistnam no attention, and this was in the time Sophie was begging me to stay at home too. Now this was in 1934, and I went back in that community in 19 and 74. It was a woman in that community, Mrs. Washington, her and her husband. Her husband was a member of the Party, she wasn't, and they had about five or six sets of twins; that's right, she had about sixteen in all. She had some individual, but these here was sets, and they all lived together in one house. (I used to devil her about it, and she, "Oh Will Holton! You shut your mouth!" and all like that. I used to tell her, say, "You trying to raise you a little army all at once, all your own, ain't you!" She'd just laugh it off, cause I was joreeing.†)

So I went back there in '74, and I walked back down there to her house, me and a old Party member, friend of mine, Homer Martin. I went down there and Mrs. Washington, she said, "Will Holton, I want to ask you something. Did you and your wife ever go back together?"

I said, "Nooooooo. We ain't never . . . I don't guess we'll ever go back together."

"Well, I want to ask you something."

I said, "What?"

"Did you know when you living out there, in there where Goodwin's house, old man Whistnam would go at your wife?"

I said, "No, I didn't."

"One day," she said, "one day you come home." Now she back

---

* Women used to look upon the railroad men as being the money men—any railroad men, like my job in Atlanta. The railroad jobs was superior, it was a better job than ordinary other men working. So it was said around, as I know about it.

† [Joking, making fun.]

up there on this street and I'm down on the street over yonder, and the people over here could see below. It's all open. (It ain't closed up like New York.) She said, "We was watching. Old man Whistnam was in your house and we seen you come in at the front. We was just hoping that you'd catch him in there," she said. "You come in the front and old man Whistnam come out the back and run up that alley. All us was just hollering and laughing about it. And you didn't never know it?"

I said, "No, I never did know it."

My friend was with me, Homer Martin, he said, "We all know that old man Whistnam was going after Hosie's wife, but Hosie always said he didn't want nobody to tell him nothing if he didn't see hisself," he said. "We didn't tell." And this was in '74, and this was back there in '34. Forty years! And that's when it was brought back to me. When they told me, I thought about this son's wife of his used to come over, never sit down, but come in in a rush, like she come to tell her something, and they be whispering.

That's some of the results of the things I had to pay for and sacrifice for, trying to carry out this one thing, that was my duty as a Party person. The Party was a political party, and only the most developed, the most developed and class-conscious, the people who's willing to sacrifice, to take the sacrifice, to make the sacrifice and would be willing to accept the discipline of the Party could be members of the Party. Take that first Stockham unit I joined. Murphy had done picked us.

He talked with us and he picked us. He didn't just invite everybody in the shop. He started with me maybe in July, and it September before he brought me around. He avoided me because he thought I was a stoolpigeon for a long time.* It was always dangerous, cause if you got arrested, they liable to not take you to jail. They carry you out to the fields and whip you up and leave you for dead. That's the dangers we's faced, and yet we felt that the job could be did if we organized and planned our work right. And that's what we did, the best we could.

The ILD was a little different. The International Labor Defense was looked upon as the legal organization. So it worked out in the open, they had their office, a public office, and they had their peo-

---

* See the Party ain't that strict now as it was back in those days, as we was back in Birmingham. It never was that strict in other sections of the country as we was in the South, cause we never was a legal party in the South.

ple up there in the office. Now the leaders of the ILD, more or less, was members of the Party. But everybody members of the ILD wasn't members of the Party. They was just members of the ILD. It was easy to become a member of the ILD. You join, you pay your joining fee. They had branches in different communities. If you out here where they had a branch and you had leaders there, you meet in private houses. They wont meeting in the office. They had to slip in to meet, because the ILD, in the eyes of the police, was considered to be Reds. If we met in a house here, say, everybody didn't just come in here. You'd come in one by one and two by two till everybody got in here. We'd have our meeting and when we got ready to leave, everybody didn't just bulldoze out here. This was the ILD too, in many places like Birmingham and like Bessemer, because, as I say, the ILD, the police would raid them, would raid the ILD meetings and break them up. They didn't want you to meet, period!

But the ILD was legal. You'd have pamphlets and leaflets and material like that we'd pass out. People'd take that, pass it out to they friends. Some of the pamphlets we sold, 5¢, 2¢, 3¢. Through that we making new contacts. And the Party would do the same with the Party materials, but we didn't just jump on anybody.

We'd see how you talk first, how you talk about the leaflets, how you talk about the Scottsboro case. We come to be chummy, come back again and talk. And along that line we judge there whether you good for the Party or not by your reactions. We would ask you, "What do you think about these communists?" You don't know what I'm up to, you maybe speak out for or against, and along that line I'd be able to judge.

I never was scared to ask people to join, but many times they wouldn't join. It wont all our fault. But we still said if we don't convince, if I don't convince you, it ain't your fault. It's my fault for not being able to convince you why you should be a member. That was our position in them days. It was taking on a heavy responsibility, but we took on that. And I guess it had to be, we had to take on that because we was up against some pretty rough terror. Those days was rough. You couldn't pitty-pat with people. We had that that we'd tell people—when you join, it's just like the army, but it's not the army of the bosses, it's the army of the working class, organizing to make things get better. That was at the heart of the

Depression. People couldn't pay rent, people couldn't get coal, people couldn't get food, so we was in a battle. We was the onliest ones to tell the people, trying to fight through it to get better conditions for the people.

If you want to join the Party there with us, you didn't just join and come in. I would take your application and maybe it's somebody else would know you, and two of us would sign that application and carry it in. And if it's voted that we accept you as a member of the unit, then the next meeting, we bring you to the unit meeting. Now your outcome, your conduct, whether you going to prove good or bad, it's me and my friend's responsibility. If you go bad, we the ones got to tote the load.

To be a member of the Party, a person would have to meet the approval of certain standards that was laid down in the constitution of the Communist Party: (1) to attend their unit meetings regular, (2) to pay their membership dues, (3) their willingness to be active in carrying out their assignments, (4) accept discipline and collective criticism, (5) living a high standard of life in their moral conduct among the people, (6) honest in their handling of all finance, (7) their guarding against excess drinking, (8) fighting against all forms of discrimination and white chauvinism. These was some of the basic principles that a person had to live up to to be a member of the Communist Party. And we live up to these basic principles. That is why everybody were not eligible to be a member of the Party, because the Party was a political party and not a mass organization where everybody could become a member.

If you come to join, you part of a unit, maybe five, six people. At unit meetings you'd have to report on plans to recruit members, and maybe nobody hadn't did anything. Well, we was honest about it. We'd say we hadn't done anything. We wanted to know why is we ain't done no recruiting. Not individually, but we discuss on the grounds of political approach, why we ain't doing it. We came to the conclusion it's Red fear we's all suffering from, afraid we'd be called a Red, afraid for anybody to know that we're a Red. It was among all of us, Negroes and whites. I suffered from it too, all of us suffered from it.

The officers we elect in each unit would be a unit organizer, a literature agent, and a membership director—we didn't call them secretaries. They would keep the records of everybody who paid dues. The dues at one time was 2¢ per month. The joining fee always was 50¢ to join.* Your dues is based on your income, and everybody was unemployed, so this 2¢ was unemployed dues. People who was employed, was 10¢. They had little stamps called 2¢, and you had a book, and you pay your dues. You put that stamp in your book every month.

The unit organizer and the unit literature agent from each unit would be subject to meet in a neighborhood section committee. Say for an instance, out there in Collegeville you had North Birmingham, you had Vulcan City, and you had Poole's Quarter. That was down there next to the Price's Stove Foundry. We had a unit in Vulcan City. Vulcan City is just part of Collegeville on the lower side. Then we had another Party unit there in Poole's Quarter—same Collegeville. Then we had another unit over in the place there around what they call Beyer's Hill. The unit organizers from these three or four units would meet together, separate from the unit meetings, and this would be known as the section committee. A member from the bureau would be assigned to that section. You had to be a member of one of the units in that section. Also the same from the other sections: the southside, the Woodlawn section, Greenwood, Avondale, Ensley, Fairfield, Renona, Bessemer, Irondale.

This is how we organized it. We could pull a string and put leaflets all over the city. When leaflets went out, they went out from the bureau through the section committees. The section committee representative didn't have to carry the leaflets, but it was his taks to get arranged and make plans for a certain place for the leaflets to be delivered and see to everybody getting these leaflets to the different units. It went on down, on down, out to the streets.

Sometimes in the unit meetings we had to straighten out some kind of personal situation. Some of the Party members would have domestic arguments and fights. They didn't come in there perfect. They brought all the bourgeois filth with them. I've been in many a discussion with man and wife about they just about to crack up. We'd try to save them, keep them together. One or two times I had to help straighten Mayfield and his wife out, cause she wasn't developed like Mayfield and she couldn't understand Mayfield didn't

* And it's still 50¢ to join today. Don't care how much money you have, far as I know, you pays 50¢ to join the Communist Party.

have no time to be with her at home. That was the kind of stuff people carrying on.

Then Hibbard and Cornella was another one. We had to go in there and have a big discussion on that cause. Cornella went over to the Soviet Union, in the winter of '32, stayed eighteen months.

The D.O. came to me and wanted me to go, and I didn't want to go away. Beidel was the first one who pledged to go. But when he got ready to go, he backed up. His wife didn't want him to leave home that long, he couldn't leave her that long, he was sorry but he had to resign from the trip. So when Don came to me and asked who I would suggest, I said I didn't know, "I don't know who I could recommend."

"I suggest you," just like that.

I said, "I don't see myself leaving my wife and family that long."

He said, "You know, you join the Party, you was told you'd have to make a sacrifice. We'll see to her having food and everything from the welfare until you get back." I had to be gone eighteen months to go to school. So he said, he put it up to me, said, "If you can't go, you get somebody. If you can't get somebody, we going have to send you, cause we done promised to send three Negroes from Alabama."

I went over to Greenwood one night to see Mayfield. He hadn't been long in the Party. He had two kids, but him and his wife had separated. He told me years after that that her family got after him with knives and cut him up the time they separated. He had to run for his life. Anyhow, him and her had separated, and he went back home to Greenwood to his mother.

I says to him, "Mayfield," I says, "I got a trip for you, man."

He says, "Where, where to?"

I says, "To the Soviet Union, to Russia."

He says, "Man, to Russia?"

"Will you go?"

"Yeah, I'll be glad to go!"

I said, "You have to be gone eighteen months."

"That's all right. That's right down my alley."

So the night when we got ready to have the discussion about who we going send, I carried him to the special meeting with me. But the white guy who worked with me on the unemployed, his name was Mac Kurth. He was a Birmingham guy, and he was working among the white unemployed and I was working among the Negroes. Me and him was joint leaders. So that night, when the question came up, Mac Kurth wanted to go.

Don asked me what was my position about Mac going. I told him I didn't think we had got sufficiently organized enough among the unemployed white workers for him to go off. I thought it was much better for him to stay here now and we build the unemployed movement. He was the onliest contact I had to work among the white. I thought he should go at a later date. All of them agreed but Fred. He got mad. He got bursting mad, Mac Kurth did.

He thought he ought to go, said, "I think it would help me a whole lot to go," and so Don was very sharp with him. (He could be very sharp when he got sharp.)

Don said, "Hosie has spoke, and I think we should respect what Hosie has to say, cause he's working on the unemployed, and he knows how well he's able to do without you here now, working on the unemployed."

It was my position that Mayfield go, and they all agreed that Mayfield go. And Mac Kurth, I ain't seed Mac Kurth at another meeting since.*

So Cornella, Mayfield, and Archie Mosley went to the Soviet Union. Archie Mosley was there in Greenwood. He became active among the unemployed, the ILD, him and his sister. He looked like a pretty forward-looking guy to develop. We picked him on that grounds. We didn't put him through no 33rd degree. We'd look at a guy and more or less tell what kind of material he was. He was a ex-railroad worker, had been working, but was unemployed. So we sent him.

When all of them got back, Mayfield went back on the district bureau and Mosley was added on the bureau. The people down in Bessemer signed Mosley to work in Bessemer from the bureau among the ore miners on Red Mountain.

Cornella came back with a lot of crazy ideas about West, that was her husband, about accusing him of going with women and all like that. She was the one that stayed away from him for eighteen months, and he done take care of the house and stayed here. But she come home raising all this sand.

---

* I understand out there he turned stoolpigeon. Somebody had a whole lot of leaflets come in and he turned information in to the police. Police got all the leaflets. That's what these elements will do, you know.

Now they say, I don't know, but while she was gone, the landlord's wife was next door, Hunt's wife. I never did see nothing to know, but Cornella told me that she's suspicious. Here's three Party people. Hunt was a Party member, and Hibbard a Party member. Mrs. Hunt wasn't a Party member, but Cornella was a Party member.

Mrs. Hunt caught the trolley and she went to town and Hibbard, he left and went to town. So Cornella followed them to town. Downtown, she found Mrs. Hunt and Hibbard. It was near one of these rooming houses, the trolley didn't go too far by it, about a block by it.* Cornella found Mrs. Hunt standing on one corner, she caught the trolley on this corner here, going home. The trolley goes up here about the next block, and here Hibbard stands, where he catch the car. Cornella was on the car. So she got very suspicious.

We tried to keep it from getting so bad. We said, "What did you do while you gone eighteen months?" We were afraid that she would start something—she was pitching a fog—and we would have two comrades to want to kill each other, Hunt to kill Hibbard about his wife. We had to go over there and help to settle that thing, get this worked out, not to justify what Hibbard was doing and the wife, but to keep down maybe murder right there among them, which would have been a bad smell on the Party itself.

I was involved in a lot of things like that. There in North Birmingham they had a guy come in and claimed he was from New York. They called him Fess. He was a little old brown-skinned Negro man. He wont no young man, he's about a middle-aged man. This was along about the last of '32, first of '33. He was in this ILD branch telling about God had sent him down, he was coming down on the assignment of God. He wont afraid of fire, and he wont afraid of this, he wont afraid of that. He got over there to one of our old comrades had been one of the early members of the Party when the Party first got started, Mr. and Mrs. Thomas. That's where he got in there, got in and made a home with them. Mrs. Thomas and them lived down kind of out in the edge of North Birmingham, down at the lower edge of Eanon Ridge, back in there. It's very difficult down them hills where people lived. That was on a big gully. You just go over a little rise here and you all the

* They didn't have no hotels there, wont no hotels for people to go to in Birmingham where people could rent rooms. They had to go to a rooming house.

way at the foot of Eanon Ridge. He was staying with them, and he'd do all that talk all the time.

One night me and Beidel went up to the ILD branch where he was carrying on all this stuff. You had a lot of different people in the ILD branch that don't be in the Party. He started the same junk again. "I eat fire. I ain't afraid of death. God has done this and God done that." He wouldn't be talking about nothing, but everybody sit there and listening because he saying "God." They just go head over heels because they believe in God so much.

We wanted to talk about the Scottsboro case, what they ought to take up, and he talking all this stuff. So I challenged him, trying to get them straight. I begin to ask him questions: "Where did you come from? Why you come way down here? How come, you got the same people unemployed up in New York, same people being beat up by the police, why you come way down here for?" He always had to try to have his answer, so we tried to do it in a way to expose him, show the people this guy's a fake.

What showed him up was this unemployed meeting we had on May Day 1933. We had done told everybody how to come to the meeting, don't bring no sticks and no knives and what. And he telling all the people now, about he could eat fire, he wont afraid of the police, they could put him in jail, God would get him out. That day when the Negroes and the police really was fighting up there in the corner, and I mean fist fighting, they found that Negro way down over at that church down there about 7th Avenue, 8th Avenue, somewhere down there.* And the meeting was about 6th Avenue.

The people seen him, and they wanted to know if he's so bad and he got so much nerve, "How come you way off down here?" Some of them come up asking questions: "Thought you said you wont afraid of the police? What you doing way over there?" He tried to find some kind of answer, so I was told. But I never did see him no more. After they exposed him so bad, he left there, left out of that area over there.

* This was down there in the same park where Bull Connor put the hosepipe on Reverend King and the Negroes in '63 in May (and this was the first day of May in 1933, which was thirty years). The church was over at where the kids got bombed in '63.

5

First Demonstrations, 1932-33

THE first meeting we had was November the 7th, a unemployed meeting. We attempted to have it on the courthouse lawn. My part was just to put out the leaflets and be in the crowd. You just had certain people to play a certain part. Everybody didn't get exposed. The first speaker attempted to speak, his name was Turner.* He was a young white fellow, a Birmingham-raised boy. They arrested him. Then a young white woman went up to speak after they drug him off the lawn, was named Alice, they drug her down. That meeting wasn't a success. They was able to break that down.

We didn't put no Negro up to speak, because it was felt that a Negro, right at that time, it was too dangerous for a Negro to speak. They whup him. If he get in the jail, they might beat him to death. The speakers take a chance of getting arrested, so put the whites up there. They's the ones got arrested.

We always had some whites, but they was just in a small minority. The D.O. was white, but he didn't speak. You don't get your leader in jail. The leader don't jump up in the front. You have other people to take the positions, because if the leader in, you got nobody to see about getting the others out. That's the way we were operating then, cause we knowed somebody would get arrested.

That same year, in '32, the ILD had a open meeting in the Negro Masonic Temple, auditorium department. We got a contract from the Masonic Temple people, paid them for their auditorium. Then after we paid them for the auditorium we put out the leaflets announcing the meeting. The city officials went there and tried to

* [Ward Turner was the son of the man who had gone to the city hall with a can of vegetables in his hand.]

make the masonics cancel tne meeting, but they couldn't cancel because we had a contract.

After they couldn't stop the meeting from being there, the city officials then put out word that the Ku Klux was going to shoot up the meeting. The auditorium part of the Negro Masonic Temple, it was on 17th Street and 4th Avenue. It's on the second floor. When they got ready to have the meeting, they had police lying on the building across the street—the buildings wont but two or three stories high—and they's up on top of the buildings, had sawed-off shotguns and rifles, going to "protect" the meeting from the Ku Klux. All that was to try to intimidate, to try to keep the people from going to that meeting. The people went to that meeting all was in overalls and half-raggedy. You couldn't get none of the big shots. Big shot Negroes didn't go to that meeting.

The police, then, couldn't intimidate—Negroes just walked all under them rifles, just went on in the door and on to the meeting—had them standing on the corner too. People just walked on by. We had done instructed everybody in the units how to conduct themselves. We said, "If the police there, don't pay them no mind, just go on about your business, go on in the meeting." We packed that auditorium out. I'm sure we had three or four hundred people.

Alice spoke, this white girl spoke in the meeting. And Burt, he spoke also, as a leader. And they had Uncle Ben Fowler, he was a jackleg preacher,* wont no pastor, just a preacher. He was a member of the ILD branch over there in Greenwood. So they had Uncle Ben Fowler, he was the onliest one who would take the platform with these two whites and speak. The meeting wont all blacks. There were some whites, like Mary Stevens and one or two others like that, five or six. They was working-class whites, Mary Stevens and them. (She was from Birmingham.) They wont no big class. We had her and one or two others. Don's wife was there. At least it wont a solid black meeting.

The police came in and stood around the walls inside the building, "guarding." We just went on. They had to set there and take what the speakers had to say like everybody else. That was the first meeting, first successful Scottsboro defense meeting, was held in Birmingham. After that you had several meetings and some in the churches. Some of the churches would open their doors and min-

---

* [Jackleg preachers are called to preach by God. They have no formal training, are not ordained, and do not lead congregations of their own.]

isters would allow speakers, like the Negro Congregational Church and the church down in what they called Greymount, on 8th Avenue. We had a meeting down there once. Three or four places had mass meetings. That was just about what went on that was public in '32, excluding regular putting out leaflets and attending unit meetings.

In our unit organizers' meeting we'd discuss what we could do. We'd say, "Let's work in the church," and "let's get speakers in the church." I was a member of New Bethel Baptist Church in East Birmingham, and Reverend Patterson, he was the pastor.[1] So I went to Reverend Patterson and asked him about a speaker coming into the church to speak on Scottsboro.

"Oh, no, no, Bro' Holton, we can't have that. White folks'd break up this church." So I went on and didn't say no more. It was like throwing cold water on it. Then I figured out a way I could get a speaker in there.

I was singing in the quartet, and I give a quartet program one night after he had said no. This was the first of the fall in '32. It wont deep in the wintertime. I give a quartet program, invited five or six quartets. It was a big house full of people. Cornella Hibbard, she's mistress of ceremonies. (We were all members of the church there.) I told her to let everybody sing around, and then when all the quartets sing, stop, and take up a collection. Then right after the collection, make an announcement: "We have a visitor with us who would like to have a few words to say right here. We'll call on Mr. James." That was his name, David James. Nobody didn't know him.

So David James, he got up there, and he got to talking about "the communist party, the communist party . . ." to tell you the truth, I didn't know what he was saying. "The International Labor Defense and the Scottsboro case and what they mean to the Negro people . . ."

When he got through, a guy in my quartet, Moore, he ask a question: "I want to know, if we join your organization and we get fired, can your organization give us a job?"*

David James said, "No, we can't give you a job," he said. "We can't guarantee that the workers won't lose their jobs, because they fighting the bosses. But at the same time, if you have the workers organized, and the workers educated to develop an understanding

---

* That was a regular saying, a regular question.

of how to stick together, you might lose your job," he said, "but you ain't just one individual. You got the other people will support you, will back you." He tried to put it on that level.

But it was a little guy, his name was Reuben Patterson, was about nineteen years old, was a high school graduate, he gets up and he says, "I'm going to tell you all people, the day you all turn your back on these good white friends, that's going to be the darkest day for you all in America."

I couldn't get into what's in his mind, what he meant, cause I wasn't in his mind. But what his words was meant to do was to mislead the people against what James had said about the Scottsboro. That's frightening the people, cause nothing was clear and people was undeveloped politically speaking, and they was further in the dark than they was before. It was confusing the people. I would say that that's worse than lying. Because first of all, it wont a question of turning backs, it was a question of trying to wake up and get some of the things belongs to you. I don't think that was going be a dark day.

So David James said, "What you mean by dark days? Tell the people exactly what you talking about."

The Deacons all jump up, "Shhhh! shhhh! We ain't going have that here! We ain't going have all that now! Let's have quiet! Let's have order!" So everything cool off after that. That was on a Friday night.

The next day, the pastor put out word that he knowed that nobody had that fellow there but Brother Holton, cause he had asked him about having one of them speakers there, and about the Reds and about the Scottsboro, and he told him he couldn't have it. He said he knowed it wasn't nothing but about Brother Holton. "What he going to do, he going to fool around here and get everybody in jail. I'm going downtown and I'm going tell the white folks who it is responsible. It isn't me in there. I ain't going to have this church ruint on account of one person."

Some of the members run over, told me, said, "Bro' Holton," they said, "they say Reverend Patterson say he going downtown, going tell the white folks you's the cause of having that fellow at the church last night."

So I went out to Woodlawn. I went out to Nelson's place to see Bradley, Brown, and them, and I told them what I had heard that

Reverend Patterson said, that I was the cause of the man being at the church. I done got in trouble now. I need some help. These was my Party people, and I went and told them.

What they told me was, "You go on in the morning and you get ready to go on to church like you been going." I went back on home. Sunday morning bright and early, before 9 o'clock, about three or four of them got together—I don't know whether they were in a car or not, they might have been in a car—but they went to Reverend Patterson's house.

Everybody in the church was in the "lower class of niggers." We was in our overalls and we figured we didn't have nothing to lose. This was in the heart of the Depression. You up against the wall and no way you can go but come out forwards. You had to come out in the struggle. But was a whole lot of people was afraid. Don't think everybody was with us, cause it was a lot of them among our own ranks, right in that lower class, was against us, just as much as them in the other class was. We had to do a lot of straightening up. We had to have a committee[2] to go from this community over in another community, unknown, to talk to stoolpigeons, to tell them to keep quiet. Sometimes they'd go late in the afternoon. They didn't threaten to kill them or nothing, but they'd say, "If you ain't going to be with what's going on, keep your mouth shut." Our main man to do that was a fellow by the name of J. T. Watson. He was on the southside. They say he was one of these South American guys. He was real tall, *black,* slender, had long arms, a nice mustache, and black hair. He was real black, a beautiful dark color, slick black. Now he was a fearless man.

J. T. Watson was a very militant guy, he was one of these leftists, what we might call a extreme left guy. He believed in fighting, he wanted to fight. He believed in shooting it out. We had to always keep him down. We had to talk him down when we talk about taking drastic action against people. He was ready to shoot up people. He believed that stoolpigeons ought to been killed, put out the way.

They say he was in some part of Texas the time they had that race riot there in World War I, and he used to talk about how they had this shoot-out.* He was upstairs, he said, in the window, and one

* [The riot occurred in September 1917 in Houston, after police had harassed Negro soldiers at Camp Logan. Seventeen whites were killed, 13 Negro soldiers hanged, and 41 Negro soldiers given life sentences.]

of the bullets hit him right in the head, right at the edge of his hair, and it went under the skin, between the skin and the skull. And that bullet was still in there, it was a little knot. He kept it, never did have it removed, kind of a souvenir of that race riot.

He had him a committee of four or five, and that was his job. If we heard something going around, people saying, "I heard so-and-so was talking against the Party and he said such and such and such," over in Collegeville, over in Woodlawn. If we thought it would be worthwhile, we'd give J. T. the word, him and his committe, and give them the address. Now nobody in the community don't know it, just two-three leaders here know J. T. coming. He'd go over to the guy's house, knock, ask "Is this Mr. So-and-So?" He wouldn't threaten, just talk to him nice. We shut up a lot of mouths.

This time was just after breakfast, and the committee went, said they wanted to talk with Reverend Patterson. He invited them in and wondered what their names was, and they said, "Our names are not important. We came out because we want to talk with you. What we came for out here is to tell you we heard that there was a speaker in your church Friday night, representing the Scottsboro case. And because he was there, you had made the remarks that you's going downtown to tell the white folks it was Brother Holton had caused the man to be there, that you had been trying to prevent it from happening. Now we came to tell you, if you can't do us no good, don't do us no harm if you don't know what it's all about. We fighting in your interest like we is in ours. And if you don't understand it, don't know what it's all about, just keep your mouth shut. If you can't do anything else, just keep your mouth shut. Cause we going to keep on doing what we doing."

So I went on to church. When Reverend Patterson got up to preach, he said, first thing, he wanted to make an announcement. He said, "This morning I had three men, four men come to my house. I was sitting there reading the scripture lesson when they come in." And he said, "They come in very nice, they didn't threaten me, talked to me very nice. I asked them what was their name, and they wouldn't tell me what they name, said the name wasn't important. They came out to tell me that they had heard that I had threatened to have one of the members of this church put in jail on account of that man up here Friday night speaking about Scottsboro." He said, "But I didn't say it like that. I didn't say it like they said it. And let me tell you all something. If you going to tell a thing, tell it like you hear it, don't go back and put nothing to it."*

I don't know if he's talking to me or what. I'm sitting right there in the church. He say, "And I want to tell you all something else. You all leave this thing off. Quit talking about it. If you don't know what you talking about, just keep you mouth shut. Don't say nothing about it, cause you don't know what this thing's all about. You don't know who you talking to." That's what he told the whole audience. Everybody said, "That's right! That's right!" they said.

He said, "Don't go around talking about it," he said, "if you don't know what you're talking, you don't know who these folks is you're talking about. You just don't know what it's all about. So don't say nothing. Just keep your mouth shut." That's what the pastor told all the people.

I was just as quiet, but everybody knowed who was Party members. They know there were three or four around me. I was there. Hibbard was there. Cornella was there. And another guy named Will Cal, he was a member of the church, and Anderson Harris was a member. That was about the four or five most outstanding. So they couldn't say who done the talking, but they knowed all us.

I went there again a few months after that, in the spring of '33, the Sunday of the meeting at Sears's church. It wasn't too far, and I went over there and I had some of the leaflets. I carried some over there to the church and hand them out to people, and I went in the church. Reverend Patterson got up there: "You know, we got some members of this church, they don't never come here, but every time they come to this church, they politicking, politicking. I wish they'd keep that devilment out the church. You don't have to come to church to politick. If you ain't going to do nothing but come here and politick, I'd rather you to stay away from this church."

And all the people said, "Amen! Amen!" It looked like everybody might have been looking straight at me by now. So I said to myself, well, I wouldn't go no more. And I don't remember going no more until along about '37–'38. I went to going back out there again, but I had several years when they called me a infidel.

I challenged one or two deacons one Sunday afternoon. We all sitting around talking. I told them, I said, "It ain't no such thing as no God. You all go around here singing and praying," I said, "and

* He never did tell what he had said.

they regular lynching Negroes, and you ain't doing nothing about it."

They all jumped up: "I don't want to talk to you." "You saying that kind of stuff." "I'm scared of you." I don't want to talk with you." They all got up and walked away from me. I didn't know how to conduct myself. I had heard other Party people talking. Some of them had never been members of no church, talking about there wont no such thing as God: "Where is he at? You say it's a God, where is he at? You can't prove where he's at." Negro Party people said that to me, Murphy and Horton and Raymond Knox. We'd have big discussions. One Sunday I said I was going to church.

"What you going for? What you going for?"

I said, "I'm going to serve God."

They said, "Where is God at? You can't prove it's no God nowhere." They said, "Where is God?"

I said, "In heaven."

"Well, where is heaven?"

Everytime I try to answer the question, it carry me further and further, and when I got through, I didn't have no answer. It's true. But now these people, like Murphy, had never been members of church, had never been active in no church.[3] Had a fellow by the name of Raymond Knox—he's one that give me such argument. We were walking along, going to a meeting one day, and I said, "I'm going to go to church Sunday."

He said, "Oh, Hosie, what you going to church for?"

I said, "I'm going there to serve the Lord, to sing and pray." I went on to church, but it weaken my beliefs, they throwing rocks at me about "here they lynching Negroes— if God's all that good, how come he don't stop the police from killing Negroes, lynching Negroes, if God is all that just?"

I just didn't have a answer. And them was the kind of questions they put. "If God is such a just God, and here you walking around here, ain't got no food. The only way you can get food is you have to organize. So if you have to organize to demand food, why you going to pray to God about it? Why don't you go on and put your time in organizing and talk to people?" Them was the kind of arguments we carried on.

I never did finally stop believing in God. I haven't stopped believing yet today. I don't argue about it. I don't discuss it, because it's something I can't explain. I don't know whether it's a God, I don't know whether it's not a God. But I know science, if you take science for it, and all these developments, I can't see what God had much to do with it. Take the scientific approach to the Biblicals; from a Marxist point of view, all this religious stuff is utopianism, it ain't got no foundation. It's just like you say Santy Claus. Ain't no Santy Claus. You say it's a heaven, but where is it? Here the guys been millions and millions of miles to the moon, and they ain't come across heaven up there. So it's something beyond my knowledge to deal with. And I don't deal with it. I don't try to deal with it.

But back there, though, we was always in a fight in them days. We just speak it out, and we made enemies. We turned a whole lot of people away. I tell you about people what followed me singing. Them same people, when I come round saying there ain't no such a thing as God, I left them just standing, looking. They didn't know which way to go. "What kind of guy is that?" They said, "He done turned into a infidel." That word, "infidel," it means you was out, you was a terrible something, a infidel. That's somebody don't believe in God. He's dangerous. And that's the way they looked upon the Reds, Reds didn't believe in no God. They's dangerous. That was all whipped up in the minds of the people, just like the ruling powers whipping up in the minds of the people today.

I was singing when I met the Party in '31, I sung all down through '31, into '32, and going to church. But more and more I was involved in going to meetings. And it got to the point of whether I'm going to meeting or whether I'm going to singing. In the quartet, Hudson and Mitch didn't like my politics whatever. They talking about "that mess you messing around with. You better get out of that mess. It ain't going do nothing but get you in trouble."

My brother organized a singing program for us in Atlanta. We went to Atlanta, and that Sunday night we sung. We got the train out of Atlanta at 11 o'clock at night, on our way back to Birmingham.

We was all sitting on our way back to Birmingham, hadn't had no words, no nothing, everybody's talking, on the train back home. Then I don't know, it was kind of like a bolt out of the clear blue sky, I said, "Well, boys . . ." and all of them stop talking.

"What is that, Will?"

"You all get you all a basson* now."

* [A man who sings bass in a quartet.]

"What you mean?"

I said, "I ain't basson no more."

"What's wrong, what happen?"

"I decided I ain't singing no more now."

"Man, don't you know we can't do without you! You just talking crazy."

"I said, "You better get you a basson." I didn't say no more.

Got off the train, went home, and when they come out there for me having to practice singing, I said, "I told you all I ain't singing no more." I quit, just like that. I seed I wont getting no where, and I decided ain't no use me keeping on fooling around there, losing my time. I'm going over here and come more active in the Party and try to carry out my assignments, see what's going be in that.

DEEP in the winter of 1932 we Party members organized a unemployed mass meeting to be held on the old courthouse steps, on 3rd Avenue, North Birmingham. It was for the purpose of raising to a high the demands for more relief for unemployed people around Birmingham. It was about 7000 or more people turned out to the courthouse steps and on the sidewalk in front of the courthouse that afternoon, Negroes and whites.

We had a committee of nine to go up to talk to Jimmie Jones, the mayor of Birmingham. Mary Stevens was the spokesman for that committee. She was the onliest woman, and Jimmie Hooper Sr. was the onliest Negro on that committee of nine. The rest of them was white, because we didn't expose too many Negroes.

It was reported at our bureau meeting afterwards that Jimmie Jones asked Mary in the course of his remarks to her after she had opened up their case to him, he asked her, "Do you believe in social equality for niggers?"

She told Jimmie Jones, "Yes, why not? They are just as good as you and I are. Why not?"

Jimmie Jones stopped her and told Mary Stevens that he didn't want to hear any more from her. "That's enough from you," and he told his police and plain-clothesmen to go up there and get all of these people from the courthouse steps.

These big strong-arm men rushed up there ahead of Mary and the committee and made the announcement to the crowd that there would not be any meeting here this afternoon. When they said that, the police who was standing among the people in the crowd began to shove and push the whites who was a little stubborn about moving, because this was the first time that many of them had ever been pushed around like that by the police. They had always been made to believe that they were better than the niggers was, because they were white people. That was a great eye-opening for a many of them that afternoon.

When the police went in and commenced trying to drive the whites, they had some pretty good scuffles between the whites standing there and the police. They were just ordinary white people, didn't know what was going on, they wont involved, they just there, standing, they just onlookers. The police pushing them too, so you had quite a little hassle there. That's where they learnt their lesson. They learning, many of them that day, that they were no more than the Negroes in the eyes of the ruling class of Birmingham and their police.

After that meeting, we called a Party bureau meeting, led by Don, the D.O., to make an assessment of that meeting and to lay plans to keep the spirit high among our Party units and members of the unemployed block committees and the ILD branches. At that meeting, it was a great discussion about the success of that meeting that afternoon after the people was pushed and shoved by the police. We took the position that these whites being pushed around in the streets and having no employment and no food, when the Party was coming out demanding these things for them and they was being pushed away from the meeting of good and peaceful speaking, we thought that wouldn't drive the people farther back. It would build up more fighting spirit in these people. They want to seek out in order to find out more about the Party, more about the ILD, more about the unemployed block committees, ask, "What do they stand for? What is this thing for?" That was how we came out about that big meeting on the courthouse steps.

In 1932 and '33 we began to organize these unemployed block committees in the various communities of Birmingham in a big way. We set up section committees, and from these various section committees, we set up a city committee. That city committee came to be known as the unemployed council of Birmingham. We had a network of organized leadership among the unemployed people. All unemployed Party members who was not members of a shop or mine unit was eager to belong to a unemployed block committee, but everybody who was a member of a unemployed block committee was not automatically a member of a Party unit.

We Negroes who was members of the Party was fair in advance in an understanding of how to organize the people more than the rest of the Negroes or whites. We was able to meet among ourselves in the Party and discuss the problems and plan out our tactical approach, utilizing our Marxist and Leninist understanding on how to go about trying to bring the people together. We was always busybodies. We didn't wait for people to come to get us when they didn't get they grocery order or they coal order from the welfare. We would go around to see what the conditions was.

If someone get out of food and been down to the welfare two or three times and still ain't got no grocery order, quite naturally the people talk about it. We wouldn't go around and just say, "That's too bad." We make it our business to go see this person, find out what the conditions was. And if the person was willing for the unemployed block committee person or the Party person to work with them and help them get something, we'd work with them.

Some people wouldn't want us to do nothing. "No, I'd rather handle it myself." We had a lot of people didn't want us to help them, think they could get by better by theyself. They figure we's the Reds and don't want nothing to do with us, afraid we might hurt they chances. If they want to go by theyself, we'd hands off. We wouldn't bother them. But people who were cooperating with us, we'd help them. We get the neighbors rounded up and try to have a little meeting on this, not no whole big lot of people. Sometime it would only be one or two of us Party members would get together four or five or seven or eight people, enough for a committee. It would be some of the neighbors, maybe the people next door, the people right around the person can't get no food delivered.

We'd go to the house of the person that's involved, the victim, let her tell her story. Then we'd ask all the people, "What do you all think could be done about it?" We wouldn't just jump up and say what to do. We let the neighbors talk about it for a while, and then it would be some of us in the crowd, we going say, "If the lady wants to go back down to the welfare, if she wants, I suggest we have a little committee to go with her and find out what the conditions is."

If she say, "I would appreciate it," then we ask who would volunteer. We don't just up and say we'll go, we ask, first for volunteers. We'd try to get some non-Party members, then we try to have a Party person to go too. It would be say three, four people. We ain't going out with a great big crowd.

Now when we get this committee set up, maybe one or two persons there we think we can depend on that we take aside, because you can't just walk out and go down there. You got to know what you want to do when you get down there. You have a discussion, not everybody, it's a discussion with just the best people on the committee. We always taught our Party members and people who went on these committees to keep a calm head when they talk to these welfare officials, but at the same time let the welfare officials know that the neighbors in the community was waiting back there to see what the results that the committee would have in getting the person some food or coal. In the private discussion, we tell the best people, "When you get down there, you all try to find out if the welfare agent say she can't get a grocery order, find out why she can't get it. Don't just take that and come back. Find out, ask questions, and then let them know that the people in the community, the neighbors, elected you to come down and find out why Miss Jane—don't say 'Miss,'—why Jane can't get no food."

When the committee get down there, the welfare official might say, "But I done sent her grocery order out." Sometimes they tell them that.

So the committee say, "She said she was told last week the food order was in the mail, but she hasn't got it. We been trying to help her along, we can't continue to feed her. We want to find out why can't she get it now." All such discussions in there. We didn't go out there, "We *demand* this! We *demand* that!" We talk with them like people, and in most cases we'd be able to get results. We seen the welfare agents as tools of the bosses because they doing the bosses' work, doing what the officials want them to do, but they wouldn't tell the people "I can't" or "The white officials is trying to give you all the run-around." Usually we was able to get results, because the welfare agent, Negro or white, he know he still got to come back in that community out there. He wouldn't want too bad a black eye out there among the other people. So that was the results of mass pressure.

After the committee go down to the welfare office, we come back to the neighborhood, pass the word around that this committee done gone downtown. Everybody wants to know what happen. But we wont going walk around tell everybody what's happened. We call a meeting. Sometimes we'd have 25–30 people in a room—wont no hall, we didn't have meetings in a hall, we had meetings in a room. We'd sort of have to raise the meeting kind of careful, because we didn't want the police to run in and break it up. Irregardless of what you was, they'd call you Red. But people's condition would force them to want to come in to get the report about the results. They'd take a chance of getting arrested cause they know that they time may be next.

We would conduct the meetings in a businesslike way. We would have one in the committee to make a report on what happened at the welfare office. The person who'd been the victim would explain the best they could. People was very bashful in talking back in those days. Then after that, the floor be open for the people to ask questions or anything they wanted to ask, the people that didn't go down there. Then we'd throw the meeting open for discussion, let them say what they think. The purpose of it was to let them say they thought it was a good thing, that we ought to keep this up, all of us come together to be a regular organization. If there wasn't already a neighborhood unemployed committee on that block, the floor would be open for membership. All they had to do was sign up, sign a card, and didn't pay no dues.

Block committees would meet every week, had a regular meeting. We talked about the welfare question, what was happening, we read the *Daily Worker* and the *Southern Worker* to see what was going on about unemployed relief, what people doing in Cleveland—you had regular struggles in Cleveland, struggles in Chicago. And we'd talk about what the workers up there was doing or we talk about the latest developments in the Scottsboro case. We kept up, we was on top, so people always wanted to come, cause we had something different to tell them every time.

I was a chairman of the unemployed council for all of Birmingham. It was two of us was responsible for working among the unemployed. I was responsible for the Negroes, and they had a white guy named Mac Kurth was responsible for working among the whites. We had one or two block committees among the whites, but we had the majority, overwhelming number of them was among Negroes in the Negro communities. It was organized in section committees like the Party was organized, so I wasn't doing it all myself. I had a committee.

I was also a member of a local block committee, a member like anybody else. I went down to the welfare office. One time I went down there when we had a white family out there on 29th Avenue, down where people got the coal. There was a white school that divided the Negro community and the white community right down the railroad. Twenty-ninth Avenue come down and cross the railroad, there at that Grayson Lumber Company, and the whites up here and the Negroes down here. This guy was just above the avenue there facing the railroad.

We had been talking with him, he hadn't actually joined us, but he was kind of friendly. (Whites was afraid. They agree with what we were doing, but they's afraid to stick they neck out, to "join up with them niggers," because that automatically would make them a Red. When the white and Negro got to cooperating together, that was "them Reds." That was the regular saying.) We didn't just go there, that wasn't the first time. He was for what we were doing. He was talking up.

He got evicted out of his house for house rent. I couldn't get over to Mac Kurth, the white guy, so I got two or three of we Negroes and went there, put his furniture back in the house after they done evict him. Then we got him to go with us down to the welfare, talk to the welfare officials about his rent.

I was the spokesman for that committee, it was between me and Joe Howard. Joe Howard was a pretty good speaker too. It wont but about three of us went with him. We didn't say we put his family back after they had put him out in the street, we said the neighbors went and put them back in.*

We talked from the neighbors in the community point of view, but the welfare officials didn't want to be outdid. They wouldn't give him money to pay his rent for him to stay in that house. But they did make arrangements for him to go get another house, cause the real estate company had sent out the bailiff. They had a special little deputy sheriff, that's his job to evict people out they house. He'd have two-three Negroes with him, and they'd go around and put your things outdoors. The welfare put him in another house, so he moved out of that vicinity, four or five blocks further over, and I lost contact with him.

Then I went down where it was a railroad man they was about to

* The white neighbors seen us, but we didn't have no white neighbors involved. They figured "there's them Reds." Their position was "I'd rather not get involved."

foreclose. He was buying his house and he had been unemployed a long time. This was a Negro man. (I forgot his name. He lived down there below Stockham.) He was working at the L & N and he got unemployed and quite naturally, he couldn't keep up his notes. So after so long a time, they was going to evict him out of his house and give him a certain time to move. So Joe Howard and myself and two or three more others, we got him and we went down to that real estate company where he bought the house from, and we told them that we was sent down by the people from the community, come down with him, cause he's one of our neighbors. He's been living there and he spent his money and now he's unemployed, threatened to be evicted, foreclosed and evicted out of his house. We came to see if there was some arrangements could be made about it. We always said the neighbors is anxious to know.

We talked around there and said, "We know he pays his notes when he's working, but everybody's unemployed now." We talked there to that real estate agent, and I says, "The question of it is, if you foreclose him out, you know what's going happen. The house going be burnt up. We have no guarantee of stopping it. You just only will have the land. The house going be burnt up for wood." He had a nice house.

That real estate agent said, "I tell you what we do," said, "his notes are due on the first," he said. "If he come down here every first of the month, just to report, and let me know if he still unemployed," said, "I'll let him stay there till this thing open up to see whether he be able to be back to work." So that was the agreement they had. And this old man went down there and reported. It was two or three years he went down there every first of the month to report. Finally the L & N commenced to putting people back to work and he went back to work. He stayed in that house until he died.*

THE unemployed committee of Birmingham went and received a permit from the city to hold another mass meeting on May 1st 1933 in that park between 5th and 6th Avenues, 16th and 17th Streets.† When the leaflets was put out announcing the time of the meeting—

---

* That come to be one of my headquarters for meeting. It was out by itself, it wont no more houses built around there.

† In front of that church where those four little girls was bombed there in 1963.

3:30 p.m., carrying the demands for the complete freedom for the nine Scottsboro boys and all the other demands, the city officials revoked the permit and issued a statement in the Birmingham daily press that the meeting would not be held. But our block committees was organized pretty well, with captains and sub-captains, with the members of each block committee instructed to listen only to their captains and no one else. So we all went to that park for the meeting. The police and plainclothesmen was standing all around in little groups of four and five in the park. People could walk through the park, but no one was allowed to stop and talk.

As the hour grew near for the meeting, some of the leading block captains began to talk among themselves. What was the next best step to take? We all decided to move as many of the people as could be moved across 5th Avenue, corner of 16th Street, in front of some mail trucks against the curb. Our captains of the block committees had told everybody that if the police try to stop the person who attempt to speak, that they will yell "Let her speak, let her speak!" When Jane Spear* was put up on the bumper of one of the parked mail trucks, a motorcycle police walked over and told her to come down from there, said "Come down, little lady."

The unemployed people, mostly black women, began to cry out, "Let her speak! Let her speak!" Some of those women wanted to tear up the police. I wouldn't call them radical, I'd call them militant, cause they wanted to fight. They just wanted to fight.

I said, "Let that woman speak." I said, "We getting damn tired of you breaking up these meetings." And about fifteen little black women there was saying to let her speak. It was only me and two more men there.

By that time, when we said, "Let her speak," people was coming across the park. Uncle Ned Goodman he walked up with a stick.† He said, "Yeah, yeah, let her speak!" and he just hauled off and hit the police upside of the head with the stick. He wasn't really in the meeting at all. He wasn't right at the spot at first. The police had everybody stood off, but people was rushing over, and he happened to rush over.

When he slammed the police the side of the head with a stick, by that time two or three plainclothesmen, they run in. Everybody was

---

* A young white woman from Montgomery.

† Uncle Ned, I don't know what he was. He talked like a West Indian or something. He's the first I've seen talk like that. He whine when he talk.

running in. Then the plainclothesmen was dragging Uncle Ned
Goodman by the arm. When they got him by the arm, this police
wrang the stick out of his hand. They were pulling him away from
the police. That made him have his back to this police. And the
police had the stick down in my face, going hit Uncle Ned in the
back of the head. I reached up and snatched the stick, and went to
change hands. Another guy hit me with a blackjack (not one of
these little old sticks, but a blackjack) right in the bowl of my head,
right in the forehead. I buckled, but I didn't fall. Some of them little
Negro women went to wailing at him, "Turn him aloose, turn him
aloose," and come up here and there with their parasols. They broke
him aloose, when another plainclothesman had me by the collar.
He had his pistol, was fixing to hit me in the back of the head with
the butt of his pistol. (So they said. I didn't see it.)

When this police was coming up with his pistol to hit me on the
back of the head, Uncle John Beard (his hair was white as mine is
now or whiter), he didn't make no noise or fall. He just hauled off
with his fist and hit the police in his eye and knocked him down. His
pistol, what the police had, went up under the running board of a
automobile. He rolled up under the edge, side of the fender, with the
pistol out here. When the pistol had fell loose from him, Uncle Ned
and some other Negroes was trying to get the pistol, so they tell me.
I didn't see it cause I'm over in my wrangle. There's two or three
plainclothes trying to beat them to the pistols, just like kids scrapping over a dime on the ground. The police beat Uncle Ned and
them to the pistol.

One guy I throwed as far as that door had a nickel-plate automatic. He come up with his pistol like that, and the other one said,
"Shoot that son of a bitch."

I said, "Shoot and be damned." He aimed at me, and just as he
did that, the sergeant hollers, "Put them guns up, use them sticks!
Put them guns up and use them sticks!"

The police said, "We can't do nothing with these damn niggers
with these sticks!"

"Put them guns up and use them sticks!" That was all that saved
me, cause he had that pistol up and it looked like it was about that
long, shining like a silver dime.

I got loose and went down to the alley, went round to the back
to 17th Street, come out the front of the Masonic Temple. I figured

they got me singled out, so I got out. I wasn't running, but I walking fast, so the police couldn't see which way I went.

I didn't see Beidel and J. T. Watson cause I was up there in all the racket, but Beidel said he and J. T. was down on the corner of 4th Avenue and about 15th Street. (The battle was on 16th Street.) They was on the corner, and it was two white men in front of them was standing and waiting for the light, and they wont paying them no attention. They was looking up there and seen where the Negroes was scuffling with the police. One of these white guys—they looked like businessmen—said to the other, "Look at those niggers up yonder fighting them police. Let's go up there and help them." And J. T. was standing behind them.

When they said that, J. T. said "God damn your soul!" and hit one of them upside the jaw and knocked both of them down in the street. And J. T. was behind them, cussing and kicking at them. Beidel say he was so scared he didn't know what to do.

The outcome of that May Day battle was Jane Spear was arrested. A young Negro man was arrested with a switchblade knife. Uncle Ned Goodman was arrested for hitting that police upside of the head with a stick when he went up to arrest Jane Spear. Two police went to the hospital. One was hit in the eye by Uncle John Beard, when the police went to hit me in the back of the head. The other police went to the hospital with a switchblade knife wound in his hip.

We were told later that the police in a meeting at the city hall that night called to discuss what to do with the Reds in such a mass meeting, was told that they could not shoot these Reds, they could not use their guns on the Reds if the Reds did not use guns. When the police was told that, fifteen of them walked up and turned in their guns and badges, saying that they were not going up against those Negroes with their sticks. We forced the Birmingham police to change short stick billies into long sticks. They didn't have them before.

6

Reeltown

BEFORE the shoot-out, I knowed they had the sharecroppers union and they had the Party down there at Reeltown and Camp Hill too. Whenever we'd have enlarged bureau meetings, we'd have representatives from down there, and they'd make reports of these things. This man Clifford James, he was a member of the sharecroppers union and also a member of the Party. I don't know about Milo Bentley. He might have been a member of the Party too. But Clifford James was a member of the Party, cause I had seen him in a meeting there in Birmingham.[1]

Al Murphy was working down there. He was the regular Party leader down there in the rural, about three counties, at that time. It was a good long distance from Birmingham, and when you get down there you had a good distance to drive. You had a circle in a big area there. You had Reeltown. You had Camp Hill. And you had another place farther up called Sandtown. We had members in all these places in the countryside around Montgomery.

We had an enlarged bureau meeting one Saturday in Old Man Thomas' house—over there where the man who said he came down from New York was and claimed he could eat fire. Murphy was instructed by the D.O. to bring two or three members up to visit and attend the bureau meeting. So this fellow James and another man by the name of Gray, Ralph Gray's brother, they was at that meeting that Saturday.* That was before the shoot-out was in Reeltown, somewhere along in the fall of '32. It was kind of cloudy that Saturday. It wasn't a clear sunny Saturday.

When the shoot-out happened, we was expecting trouble because

* [Ralph Gray had been a member of the sharecroppers union in Camp Hill, Tallapoosa County, and had been killed in the attack on the SCU in 1931.]

we expect trouble all the time because we had some. We expected people to get arrested, because all these was secret meetings. The sharecroppers union wasn't no public open meeting. They had to slip to hold their meetings just like the Party. Everything was secret. All of them was Reds in the eyes of the big landlords and sheriff officials down there. But we wont expecting trouble like that.

It was told to me at the time that Clifford James, he had his own little land. In those days, Roosevelt and them was paying the farmers to plow under so much cotton. They received back what they called the parity check for the land they let lay out. I think it was every third row or something. So Clifford owed this little white grocer $6. He mortgaged a mule or a cow or something. He put up something to lien against, something of what he had, for the $6.

Cliff had got his parity check back there through the summer, through the spring, but he didn't pay then. When he cashed the check, he didn't go pay the $6. He put that money, I guess, in the bank or something, cause he already know the the mule or the cow stand good for this fall when supposed to pay it, so he didn't pay it. When the time came to pay, the price of cotton was very low. He had three bales of cotton laying on the yard. And he told this old white merchant that he'd pay the $6 soon as the cotton price went up where he could sell some cotton. I don't guess he agreed with him. So what happen was the grocer sent the deputy sheriff to level on his livestock. Got the deputy sheriff to go to take the livestock for the $6 debt.

Various members of the union sent the word out around about what's going on at Clifford James's. So Monday, all the neighbors and the members went up there that morning. The Party and the ILD would always instruct people, anybody, in case if you have a confrontation with the law or the police, a certain way to conduct yourself. Try to talk, try to reason, reason out the guy. So all of them was standing there, and when the deputy sheriff got there, they went to talking with him: "Don't take the livestock for $6. Give the man time to pay." The deputy sheriff wouldn't stand no reason. He just want to take the mule. He had a Negro with him, and the deputy sheriff and this Negro started up to get the mule and put the bridle on him, and Ned Cobb said, "Don't you go in there."

When they see he was going to resist, wouldn't allow them to take the mule, that's when the deputy sheriff cursed him, he said, "You dirty son of a bitch. By God, when I come back I *will* get it." Then this deputy sheriff and them went for reinforcements, for help to come back.

Everybody, all the neighbors, got in the house. In the house they formed a electoral committee of three men, including, of course, Clifford James, to go out and talk. This committee of three, Milo Bentley, Clifford James, and Jug Moss, they was elected by the people to talk to the deputy sheriff and them when they came back. The others stay in the house with the shotgun.

When the deputy sheriff and them came back, James was the first one out the house. He started out, and they commenced to yelling and hollering and cussing Clifford James, the deputy sheriff and them did. He was trying to talk with them, and they wouldn't stand no talk. Milo Bentley, he walked out in the yard behind Clifford, toward them, and they shot Milo, they shot him. And then Jug Moss, he got to the door. When he got in the door—he was the third man to go out, they shot him out the door. They killed him dead on the spot. Bentley was wounded, but they didn't take him in.

Then when that happened, these Negroes in the house opened fire and went to shooting. The sheriff and them run away from there all full of shot.

Bentley got away, and the way I heard it, they didn't shoot Clifford James right then. They shot Clifford James that late afternoon after everything was over. He went back there to see about his livestock, about night, and that's where they ambushed Clifford at, when he went back to try to see about his mules and cows.

Then Clifford and Milo Bentley went to Tuskegee, to the doctor there who they considered to be the family doctor. And the doctor, he tipped off the police that these two men was in his office.

I know that our Party claimed that the man who was president of Tuskegee Institute at that time, Professor Moton*—well, the Party strictly held him responsible, him and this doctor, for turning these Negroes over to the authorities. Moton and this doctor was held highly responsible, for the death of these two men.

The police picked them up there in Tuskegee and carried them to Montgomery, to Kilbrook prison, and that's where they claimed they died of pneumonia on the cold floor without beds. They just about beat them to death, that's what happened.

When that news reached us, then we had a meeting on it. I know

* [Robert Russa Moton, successor of Booker T. Washington.]

it was snowing and sleeting, but I don't remember who brought the message that they had that big shoot-out down there in Reeltown. It was decided in the Party bureau meeting that we get out this leaflet about the shoot-out, get out 20,000 leaflets. Don assigned me the task of seeing to the leaflets being run off.

That was the first time that I met this man, Mathis, who the leaflets was being made in his house. They had put the paper already there, and the machine was already there in his basement. All I had to do was to get these two girls, two young women, rather (I call them girls), to carry them there to make the leaflets. One of them was a Young Communist League member. I don't know if the other one was a YCL member or not. They was friends, and one of them was one of the Party members' wife. She was a young woman, and he was very militant, Mack Wade, a Negro steelworker. She had been to school. I don't know whether she'd been to college or not, but she could cut stencils. These was the onliest stencils I knew was cut by Negro girls. Usually some of the white comrades made the stencil at the begin with. So I got the girls, and we walked over there that night, first night, wont late, first of the night, to that man's house.

When we got there, Mathis told me, said, "You all can't make no leaflets here tonight." I asked him why.* He said, "It done sweated down my basement. It's just water everywhere."

I just didn't see how it was possible we couldn't make the leaflets, you know. I said, "Oh yeah, I think we can."

He said, "You come on, go down here and look down here and see, but I don't think you going to be able to make any leaflets down here. I covered the machine up, covered the paper, where it wouldn't get wet." Oh when I went down—all you had to do was walk down a little flight of steps, wont no way down in the ground—got down here, and them tits of water, just drips of water, hanging all over the ceiling. Twas concrete, and all the wall was wet. On the floor the water had done dripped there until the water was standing all in the floor. You'd have to stand on a board or something, not

* I didn't know why he said we couldn't make them there, but I knowed it wont the police, cause in those days you'd have someone to go to someone's house, they say, "You can't do so and so and so on." Maybe they tell you, "I heard someone said the police watching my house," or something like that, cause it's always a criss-cross, talkng, one way or the other. That's the way it's always be. When he said, "You all can't make any leaflets here tonight," why he come out and told us why.

to stand in the water. All where he had a canvas over the paper, and the other things he had covered down there, it was all wet. It was a mess. So now it's a big job, what can I do now? What is my next step? Supposed to make the leaflets tonight.

I went back upstairs and told the girls. This girl was married said, "You move the paper and machine to my house, we'll make it over to my house." Now we had to go from one community to another, from Kingston over to Greenwood. How we going get over there? I didn't know who to go to, so I went out in the weather, went down to a friend's house what used to work with me there at the shop when I was working at Stockham, Will Smith. He had a car. I went down and told him what I was up against, and I wanted to get the paper and the machine back over to Greenwood to one of these girls' homes.

Stockham workers, they didn't stay up long at night, because they just tired, had to go to bed. I told him, "If you want to go on to bed . . ." He was sitting there at the fire.

He said, "Will, I ain't a member of this organization, so I don't know what it's all about," he said. "But just to help you out, I'll take my car and go up there and get your paper and I'll carry it over there, get the girls."

I asked him, "How much you going to charge me?" I didn't have nothing to pay with, but I'd go back to somebody else and tell them I owe him so much and so much, pay for the car.

He said, "I ain't going to charge you nothing, just so long as you keep it to yourself. Don't tell nobody."

So he went up there and loaded up all that paper, stacks and stacks of paper. It was four reams or six reams. And he carried it and all us and the machine back to Greenwood. That ice was slush. It wont snowing, just slush, like sleet, rain, just slushy, just real slushy.

We made leaflets all that night. They had their stencils and everything all ready, stencils already cut. They cut 3–4 stencils, cause 20,000 leaflets, after you run so many, they would get worn. When one stencil get worn and tear up, we'd put on a new one. As they made the leaflets, I'd take them off, straighten them up, stack them together, pile them up and tie a cord around them. That was some night. The next day, about 9–10 o'clock, we got through.

When I made the leaflets, me and the girls, now we had done our job. We didn't have to carry them around, give them to nobody.

We made them, pack them, and somebody else going to be responsible come and get the leaflets and decide on what they do with them. That was somebody else's job. I ain't worrying about that.

I don't know where Murphy was located, whether he was in Camp Hill or whether he was in Sandtown. He was down in there somewhere. About that same time as the bureau meeting, he gathered up two or three fellows, all members of the union or the Party, and they going over to Reeltown as relatives of these people to see what happened.

When they got down there—it was in the day, it wont in the night, I don't know what time of day it was—these white people stopped the car and wanted to know where was they going. And they told them they heard about the shooting and trouble, they come down, was relatives, to see what happening and what they could do. Some of the whites wanted to lynch them. They made them get out of the car. After so long, Murphy was the spokesman and they all was calm, they talked and after they explained to them, some of the hotheads wanted to lynch them anyhow and the others told them no, don't lynch them, just make them leave here. They made them get in the car and turn around and get out of there and not look back.*

Andy Brown went down there into the Reeltown area to contact the wives and see, number one, could they bring the bodies to Birmingham, and number two, would the wives agree to let the ILD handle the funeralizing of the bodies, to have a mass funeral. So Andy did that first. He got the wives back to Birmingham, they's placed in Joe Howard's hands to take them around to different preachers and leaders and things to try to solicit support from the Negro leaders in Birmingham. They got a little bit, not much. Especially the big preachers, the pastors of the big churches, they wanted hands off. The wives stayed in Birmingham quite a while, it was more than a week or so, cause it was a question of their safety.

Andy went to the Welch brothers undertakers to get them to go get the bodies when they arrived in Birmingham. The bodies was coming up on the L & N railroad from Montgomery at 6 o'clock, arrive Birmingham at 6 o'clock. When the bodies came in that Sunday afternoon, they was unloaded off on the pushcart down in the shed. Didn't nobody show up to get them. The undertaker didn't

* Murphy told that in the meeting when he got to Birmingham. It was in my presence.

come. So some white ILD leaders went out, goes to Welch and them to find out what happen, why they didn't come get the bodies when they promised they'd come. Welch's answer was they had been visited by some of their good white friends and had been advised not to bother with them bodies. They's afraid to bother because it would hurt their business of burying people. (That was their business, to bury the dead, yet they afraid to bury them.) Some of the ILD leaders told them wasn't nothing could hurt their business no worser than the ILD and the Communist Party if they expose them for the action they taken. "But since you're Negroes," they said, "we won't bother you. We'll let you off." So they went to Hickman Jordan.

Jordan said he owned his place from hell to heaven, said, "You all take care of the living, I'll take care of the dead."

So they went and got the bodies, put the bodies there, and they told Jordan when they wanted to have the funeral.

Jordan's wasn't no fancy place. It was a wood-structured building, old and two stories. The front of it, you go in—the front faced the sidewalk—and the porch covered over the door as you going in the front. It had some posts sitting on out here next to the gutter on the sidewalk, and posts holding the porch part up. Around under there on the ground, it was benches on each side of the door where people sit on, but the benches was sitting on the ground, instead of sitting up on a wood porch. He didn't have a wood porch in front of the place.

Jordan wasn't so tall. He was kind of a chubby man, I guess about five feet, kind of stout, but not bulky, real black. He had a mole on one of his cheeks, a big black mole. And he was real black. Around fifty or sixty years old. When you'd go into his office to talk with him, he'd shut his eyes. You'd talk awhile: "Poppa, you sleep?"

"No, I ain't sleep." You'd talk and think he sleep. He'd have his eyes shut. "I understand every word you say." You have to talk with him with his eyes shut.

The officials of the city tried to make Jordan go take the bodies and bury them right away. They had two big red hammer and sickles made out of red ribbon. The ribbon about as wide as your hand, and twas pretty red, deep red. And that hammer and sickle was right across the bust of each one of these caskets. The caskets open up about half way, where you could look at them. Wasn't open the whole way. They left them open a long time where everybody could view them. They had a glass in the casket. You could look through the glass and look at them. They looked just like they was sleep. Now where they was bulleted up at, I guess that was the part they covered from the public. They looked just like they was sleep. It was two of them, Clifford James and Milo Bentley. I don't know what happened to Moss. I never did know the whole story down there. That was a rough time.*

The Friday they was to have the funeral in Birmingham there at Jordan's, twas two or three white women went up in the funeral parlor upstairs where the funeral was. Mary Stevens was in that crowd, and I think it might have been Jane Spear. But I know Mary Stevens and two or three more of them went in there. The police told Jordan to go up there and get them to bring them out, get them out from there. Jordan said, "Now if you all want them folks up there," he said, "you'll have to go up there and get them yourselves, cause I ain't going up there bothering poeple."

So the police went up—so I was told, I wasn't up the stairs, I was out there in the crowd—they went up and told Mary Stevens and them, "All right, come out from there, little ladies," said, "You all come out, you can't sit up there among them niggers." Mary Stevens and them looked at them and turned their nose up at them and didn't get up. Then a lot of the people commenced to screaming and going on over the dead, and the police got scared and come out, left out of there.

They couldn't get no preacher to preach. The onliest one who would say anything at the funeral was some of them's cousins from

---

* But now all this Nate Shaw business and all this other stuff they're talking about, Nate Shaw told them that he was down there, that he had left, went to his doctor, had got away, got way down to his cousin's somewhere, and they brought his boy down there, going to throw his boy in the well, so he tells it in his book. The boy brought them where his daddy was. At the same time, his brother-in-law had already gone down there, had his shotgun, and he asked him, "What you come up here with this gun for?" He said, "You don't need that gun." And when they seen them coming, he run out the back door, and that's where they shot him out there. I didn't understand whether Nate Shaw said whether Milo shot at them or shot him or what. But anyway that's where they shot him down. That had to be Milo Bentley from the way he told it. He said when he all shot up, they made him and his boy put his brother-in-law in the car. They carried them all back to jail, and when they got ready to take them he told them to turn his boy aloose. That morning they got ready to carry him from that place to another jail, his brother-in-law was begging, telling him "don't leave me, don't leave me." And he heard that they gave him a black burial, that had to be Milo Bentley, cause it wasn't but two they brought to Birmingham.

down Reeltown. He was a preacher, but not from Birmingham. Some of the Birmingham Negro preachers was standing around there in the crowd, but they wouldn't have nothing to do with any of it. A fellow by the name of Christian, he was a World War I vet, he was a local leader of the ILD at that time in Birmingham. He made a talk. Now I wasn't up there, so I couldn't know what they were saying, but I know what some of them said he said. Along with some of the things he said, he talked about how the Negroes had shed their blood in the world war to save this country, how they shed their blood and braved the battles to defend this country, and to come back and get all lynched and all.

After the funeral, they went to the cemetery. The people in wagons—you had a lot of wagons and buggies in them days, still didn't everybody have cars, and Jordan's hearse, was two horses pulling the hearse. Behind the hearse was people in trucks and buggies, and in the front was a whole lot of motorcycle scouts, police, escorting, cars and everything.

All the police in town was at the funeral. Everybody was saying anybody could of went on downtown, take everything they wanted, because seems like all the police in town was out there in North Birmingham. All the funeral procession was lined up, and the police with all their red cars was behind. It was quite a line-up. They bumped traffic, the police stop at the traffic lights and stopped the traffic. That was one time one Negro funeral was recognized in Birmingham. They carried the funeral through Birmingham to go to the cemetery over at Grace Hills, where they were burying them at that time. That's on the southside over beyond Titusville, three-four miles.

After Jordan buried those bodies, then the people all see. It allowed a lot of people to know that Welch and them backed off. A whole lot of their members quit their burial policies and joined Jordan's policies. Welch Brothers wanted to try to sue Jordan for taking their members away from them. We had burial societies there, burial insurance, and all the undertakers had a little burial society. When a member died, they go get that member and bury him. Jordan told me hisself, one day when I went back there. It was something we trying to collect money for, and I went down there, asked for a donation. He ran his hand in his pocket, give me three $1 bills, he said, "You all made me." He said, "You all made me what I am." He strictly said that. That's all he said, "You all made me." And I know one thing that they said, that he put on a lot of agents collecting, writing insurance after that. He hired several young people from my church as insurance writers.

Hickman Jordan, I think a person like Hickman Jordan pretty near know what it was we was after. He know what the score was. A lot of people understand, you know. A guy ain't going all out there, all out, unlessen he have a pretty good understanding, especially in a business. And to tell you the truth of something else, we found out, according to the records in Birmingham, all the Negro undertakers, practically, was supported or backed up or controlled by whites, white business, except Jordan. That's the reason Jordan was able to do what he did, cause these whites would come in and close the others up. One time it was strictly and generally said, among all the undertakers—you had many undertakers in Birmingham, that was the biggest business among Negroes was the undertaking business—all those was owned, practically owned, by whites, except Jordan. He'd scuffle along and hussle along. Had his horses—the others had done got them a automobile, a hearse.* But many of the undertakers had done had to borrow about $2000 from some white firm, some good white friends, to do business. They had to play it real safe.

I'll never forget when Reeltown happened because that day— nobody working hardly—it was a minister, a little jackleg preacher, old man, member of the church where I was a member, Reverend Love. He'd be at the church all the time. So they had opened up a cotton mill over there. That was in East Birmingham. And Reverend Love and his daughter was working over there at the cotton mill that day. That's the reason I know so well, how I can remember a whole lot of that pertaining to Reeltown.

Reverend Love and his daughter was walking down the railroad track, walking home that afternoon, about 4:30–5 o'clock, and all

---

* First they had these trucks, you seen these black, closed-in-trucks, metal closed-in trucks with a back door, well that's the way they first started off with. It wasn't no fancy fancy thing. They eventually worked up to hearses like they have at the present time. But it wont always like that. And practically every undertaker had a ambulance. The ambulances, the Negro ambulances, it was some made like a stationwagon. You hear the ambulance coming, you know, a stationwagon! Feature a stationwagon like that. Negroes got shot or killed; get shot, carry him to the hospital. Get killed, carry him to the undertaker. When the doctor say he dead, there he have a chance to make some money out of him. That was big business for them.

that ice and snow and sleet was on the track. They didn't know the switch engine had some cars behind it, was coming down. The girl, it hit her, and knocked her off the railroad, down the fill. The man claimed the switch engine didn't have a cow catcher. It had a board where the switchman stand on the front of the engine. They claim Reverend Love walking in the track, and they got on to try to hold him to keep from getting under the train, but he couldn't hold him. That's what the whites said. And he just got cut up. Didn't know what happened. It tore him all to pieces. The daughter, she always looked kind of queer after that. Her mind wasn't good after that. All that happened on that same day, Christmas Eve day, 1932.[2]

7
The Depression

IT was rough. You talking about a rough time, that was a rough time. Birmingham is a cold place when it does get real cold. It got cold in those days. It got to where you could not find a stick on the ground as large as a baby's wrist to make a fire out of in your house. The ground was clean of any kind of anything to make a fire. We used to get coal off of the trains. Sometimes the Negro firemen would throw coal off the trains coming through North Birmingham from Slosses By-Products back to Slosses furnace over on 1st Avenue.* When they'd be shoveling coal, they'd come along and they'd just take they shovel and throw they coal all over the ground, just like they was shoveling into the engine, for people to get coal.

You would hear men say, "I believe I'll go down and meet the train." It would be already dark, and the train come along a branch-line through East Birmingham. This branchline was going down through Avondale, on out from the DeBardeleben mine, over to the Slosses By-Products. That's where they make the coke at. When it get on that track, going down, it goes through East Birmingham, and then the people down there would be getting coal. Come along about 8 or 9 o'clock at night, the train cross 1st Avenue. It stop, the freight train would stop because it would cross the avenue. The switchman had to get out to flag down the traffic. When he flagged down the traffic, we'd go and get on the train on the cars. The train run slow, then run just normally along where we lived, about half a mile or more from 1st Avenue. But when it got down to the L & N crossing, it had to stop again. It was a long train, so that it wont too

* [The Sloss By-Products plant was in North Birmingham, the Sloss Furnace in Central Birmingham, and the DeBardeleben mine on Red Mountain, on the southeastern edge of the city.]

far from where we had to get off and walk back to the house. So we get up there at night and we just roll the lumps of coal off the train by where we live. It was white and Negro both. We just roll that coal off.

We couldn't see it at night after we roll it off, but soon in the morning, just as soon as we could see that coal, by light, we get out there with buckets and bags. When day begin to break where you could see the coal on the ground, we get out there, cause we didn't wait till sun-up. By then everybody be done cleared up the coal. Everybody knew somebody done throwed off, cause they'd look for people to throw off coal. And it was whosoever will, let him come. Nobody fighting over "this is my coal" or nothing, but everybody trying to get what they can get. It wasn't any jim crow line around that coal, and there wasn't any fights among the Negroes and whites.

Sometime the Birmingham police would ride by and cross the railroad there at the Grace Lumber Company in their blood-red cars just down below where we all would be gathering up that coal. They would just look up that way and keep driving. I never did know of them stopping to bother people about gathering that coal.

One morning I went out there. It was so dark it hadn't got light good. Twas a large, great huge lump of that coal, covered with frost. It was white, and I looked at it, and I didn't know what it was. I couldn't tell whether it was coal or not, it was so large. And that lump of coal, I couldn't hardly get it up to put on my shoulders to carry it to the house. I finally just banded it up and put it on my shoulders—by myself—I didn't have but about a short block to the railroad. Just walk to the railroad right across the avenue, that's where I lived. I got out early that morning, got me enough coal to last me a good while, cause I not only got that lump, I went back, and it was several lumps smaller than that.

A fellow there named Will Caldwell, I had to go right by his house, just walk by his garden, right beside his house. He had a boy, the boy about twelve or thirteen years old. He got to calling him, he's calling his boy, say, "Get up, get up there!" He heard me walking and he knowed it was somebody getting coal. "Get up there and get out there and get some coal! Git!" He was a man who had a bad heart, so he couldn't do it hisself. This boy come out there, putting on his clothes. He's cold, he's half sleepy, and just falling around, trying to get him a lump of coal. Just racing, and he was racing at it. That was the way we had to get it.

I got my piece of coal into the house. I reckon that piece of coal weighed about 175 pounds. I took my hammer and broke it up. It was easy to break up, cause that was red-ash jelly coal. It would open like a eggshell. But finally just before I moved away down to Collegeville, the railroad detectives began to arrest people there at night riding them trains. One Saturday night, two Negroes went out there and got on the train. They just got on there and throw some coal off. But this night the detectives caught them and carried them, put them in jail, but they turned them loose. Somebody done told the detectives about how we was throwing the coal off, cause we were taking coal.

Me and Anderson Harris also went down to where they used to dump all the ashes from the Slosses furnace. We'd start early in the morning, take shovels and a little pushcart Anderson had, and a sieve. People take this screen wire, the heavy screen wire like you put your finger through, and take them a piece of 2 by 4 and put two sticks like that with 8 inch wire on them. Make a cross and make a sieve out of it. We'd have a shovel, and we go over there and we dug holes out. We pile the dirt on it and sieve, sieve, sieve, get all of the dirt cleaned out, clean out the rocks, and get down to nothing but the real fine coal, fine coke. We pick out all the rock and sometimes we find pieces of coal big as a egg, find maybe a piece of coke that large. Then we put it in the sack, in the bag. They was a sack like corn sacks, larger than a bushel. I think they helt about two bushels. They wont oat sacks. Oat sack's a large sack, corn sacks were small. Back then you could buy oat sacks, sacks of corn, back in the country. So we'd get about four or five sacks, fill them up, we tied a mouth on them, and stack them up on that cart.

A whole lot of people had these carts. They take two little iron wheels that was off a wheelbarrow, and take a iron pin as large as would go through that wheel, like a axle. You get a wheel on this side and a wheel on this side, and you build you a little body on there with a tongue to it, where it would push. The body built out of wood. That would make these little pushcarts. That's the way the people made them, out of these wheels. I don't know where they got them, so many people got them it's a wonder they didn't run out of wheels. You have a little body made about four or five feet long on it, not a high body, just a little flat built on there and the siding on it.

It wasn't no two or three little people out there, it was several people out there. We'd work all day, and we wont the only ones. Them people were coming all the way across there from East Birmingham. It was about two and a half miles across. We used to go out there and stay. We didn't run out there and run right back. You go out there and spend three or four hours. When you come back, say you'd have several sacks. It would take two men to push it when you going home.

We push the cart home, and it'd be real heavy, cause it's coming out the earth. It wasn't dry, it was wet. But when you dry it out, it would last a good while. If you get two or three sacks of it, it would last about a week or more. I would even use some of it in the stove to cook. You'd have to get you some paper to start it. Where the wind blow tarpaper when tarpaper was old, a wind come, rip a piece off, it fall on the ground somewhere, you pick it up. You put that in your stove and it start the coal to burn, put that coke and coal in there together. It soon get hot.

Coke makes the best heat, coke will last longer. Coal will burn up quick, but that coke'll just sit there after you done burnt it. That coke sits there and gets a cherry red coal, sit there a long time. But it'll burn your grates up quick too, burn your heaters up. A grate will warp and buckle, and your stove will buckle with that coke. That's what we had to do for coal lots of time. It was a hard way, but that's the way we had to live.

Sometimes we get coal from the welfare, city welfare. In the first of '33 I was in there in the Woodlawn section of East Birmingham. I was living over there around Stockham foundry, in that area. I'd been to the welfare office in Woodlawn, but I couldn't get no coal. They had their headquarters in the city hall. It was about three or four miles from where I lived. I had to walk. So I'd been down there and asked for some coal, and the woman told me where they'd be coming out.

I go back home, pick up a good piece of tarpaper, pull it off a house, something like that to make a fire with. There wont nothing to find to burn. People done got it all. When I got home, no coal. So the next day, I went down, walked down again, see about the coal. That morning it look like it going snow—big pillars of cloud, and *cold!* Wind blowing.

They had the office in the lobby of the city hall. In the front was a big, open, great big open space, helt a whole lot of people. But the back end of it, they had done took cardboard or plywood or something and made a little office out of it. So this woman named Hallie Moses, she was a Negro woman, that was her office, and people just lined up in this line here, had to stand out till she called. They give them all numbers. She call the number, the next person's number, and you would go in. Everybody lined up against the wall.

She had a white guy. He was keeping everybody in line. So I walks in the door, and when I walk in the door—the line all this side of the wall—he meets me at the door and say, "All right, big boy, you you have to go upside the wall, get back over side the wall. I SAY GET BACK SIDE THE WALL! EVERYTIME YOU COME OUT HERE GET BACK SIDE THE WALL!" That's the way he told me before.

I said, "Everytime I come out here, 'Get back side the wall,' and when I get in the office, they tell me 'your coal's on the way.' When I get home, I ain't got no coal to make a fire." I said, "I'm getting tired of getting back side the wall!"

I was talking loud. That was just loud-mouthing. Let the people know somebody had some courage to speak. And several guys in the line there knew me, had worked in Stockham foundry with me, they said, "Tell them about it, Big Red!" "I hear you, Big Red!" cause I always raising the devil in the shop anyhow. There was about 75–100 people, it was a lot of people there.

Hallie Moses look out, said, "Who is that man out there?"

The white guy said, "It's somebody out here raising the devil. I don't know who . . ."

"Let that man come in here." That's what Hallie Moses said. I walked from here on in there. She got a client in there, but she stop waiting on him, said, "What is that you saying out there?" I told her the same thing. So she said, "Well, now listen, er . . ." then she said to me, "Ah, how many children you have?"

I said, "I have one boy."

"How old is he?"

"He is twelve years old."

"You are not entitled to any coal," she said. "You ain't supposed to have coal unless you have children under ten years old."

"Then why didn't you tell me before when I was here? I was out here before and you," I said, "you asked me the same question and you said coal was coming out to me. Now you tell me I ain't supposed to have any." I said, "If you can't let us have coal, why don't you tell us, 'you can't have it'?" I was just regular talking.

She said, "Now wait now, Mr. Holton, wait now, Mr. Will, wait Mr. Will, wait, now, wait. Now, Mr. Will, I'm going to tell you what I'm going to do for you."

"What is it?"

She said, "I'm going to send you out half a ton of coal, but don't come back no more, cause you not supposed to have coal, but I'm going to send you this coal this time, but you remember, you can't get no more after today."

"Well, send me that then." So we was about through with our argument then. I went on out. Guys all in the line kept ahollering about, "I hear you, Big Red, I hear you, Big Red!"

And when I got home—I walked back to my house—that coal truck had been there and my coal was on the back porch. I didn't go back no more, but I got that. I wouldn't get no more by being quiet, and I wouldn't a got it that fast.

So they sent me a half a ton of what we call "egg coal." Your egg coal something about, about not quite larger than the size of your fist. You had "nut coal," "egg coal," and "lump coal." In the yard where they sold coal at in that community, we'd have coal there, what you call "white-ash coal." Your ashes, when you burn it, it wouldn't be many ashes, it'd be real white. It'd burn right up like a piece of paper. It didn't have any jelly. This other coal, jelly coal, when you burn it, this wax would just tear, run down the lumps of coal. But this coal burn up to ashes, wouldn't have no wax in it. The red-ash jelly coal helt the longest heat, cause it didn't burn like paper like that, but they didn't sell that jelly coal in the yard in that community.

The welfare agents would come into the communities to see if the people was getting anything off the welfare they shouldn't of got. If the people was working they not supposed to get from the welfare. Many times when these welfare officials came into a community, first thing they do, was go to a individual person's home before they go round to see anybody else in this block. We considered that's a stoolpigeon if the welfare agent come here last week, come to his house, come in, stay and stay, come out, then begin to go from house to house. Come back next time, come back here again, and go down, from house to house, and could near about tell you if you had done anything to earn any money from last week until this time, because that's what these stooges in the community would do. Check up on people, find out what they doing, if they worked any, see if a person leave home soon, "He must be going to work."

Then the welfare official come to you, "Did you work any last week, did you work such-and-such a day?"

"No, I didn't work."

"Well, where you going when you left home so early Tuesday morning?" Stooges done know exactly your movement, see. That's the kind of stuff. So if that agent come in this block and go in that house too often, automatically, whether he's a stoolpigeon or not, he's a stoolpigeon in the eyes of the neighbors, you know. That's why when we had one we pretty near got him down pat to know he's a stoolpigeon, then we had this unknown committee to come over—J. T. Watson's. They'd come over just about evening, walk around, walk in, not walk in but come to the gate, come to the door, knock, wouldn't come at night, hardly, then talk with the people: "We understand that you's informing the welfare officials out here on the other neighbors."

"I don't know nothing about it."

"They say the welfare agents is always in your house, more so than they is in anybody else's. Now we advise you to stop that, because we as a people is got to stick together."

And if it continues, we start to bombard them with postcards. They don't know who send them, don't know where they come from, all they know they come to they house.

In the neighborhoods, the police had they pimps. Take for an instance Collegeville.* In Collegeville, we had out there a police called Police Dukes. I don't know whether he was Italian or Greek. He had real black hair. We called him Italian. And Police Dukes, he was just the king in Collegeville in North Birmingham. Dukes— they call him Dukes. Lot of time he arrest Negroes, and they had a ice house up there. He wouldn't carry them to jail. He arrest them, he carry them up there, give them a good whupping, turn them loose.

Say you selling whiskey. It wont no whiskey in Birmingham, nothing but homemade whiskey. And you'd sell your little wildcat whiskey to make a little money. Dukes, he had a lot of Negro pimps. I'll say several, not a lot, and some of the stoolpigeons get holt to you selling whiskey and they turn your name in to Dukes. Dukes

* [Hudson moved to Collegeville in April 1933.]

would come and raid your house or raid your place and maybe
he'd find two-three gallons. He'd take about a pint and carry it
down against you for evidence and carry the other to his Negro
pimps to sell.

We Party people in the community, we found out. (Sometimes
we had to pimp—we call it "pimping," to tell on somebody, we call
that "pimps," some say "informers" now—to break up the pimps,
we had to pimp. But that's the way we straighten up a lot of things.)
We got on to it, all the names and everything, and all the lowdown.
We got us some postcards. We sent these penny postcards in to the
high sheriff's office, and we named out the police pimps' address
who's selling the whiskey. We broke up a lot of police pimps like
that. And nobody didn't know who's doing it, nobody couldn't go
out and tell you, cause they couldn't tell who's doing it.

In the fall of 1933 before Christmas, in Collegeville, it was two-
three brothers. The mother and father had passed away when they
was quite young, I understood. The older brother was named Eddie,
Eddie Powell. He was a member of the ILD, wasn't a member of the
Party. This Police Dukes went to his house, search his house for
whiskey. He didn't find whiskey. But he found some ILD literature
he had, was reading, and a winchester. Now he didn't have no
search warrant to search for literature or take his winchester, but he
wanted to take the winchester.

Eddie told him, said, "You come here looking for whiskey," and
said, "you didn't find whiskey. You found my winchester, found my
material that I read." And said, "You ain't going take my winchester."

Dukes didn't have no right to take his literature and his gun, but
that was just the way how the police was about Negroes. They done
what they pleased. In most cases they would have tried to beat Eddie
up, but Eddie was a guy they was afraid of. He was not only strong,
but he was a man they know would fight. Anytime a Negro would
fight, why they'd respect him. They didn't try to get tangled up with
him if they could help it. So Eddie told him, "If you take that rifle
out of here, you'll take it over my dead body."

Dukes told Eddie, said, "You going die with your shoes on."
That's what Dukes told him, said, "You going die with your shoes
on your feet."

Eddie said, "By God, let me die with my shoes on my feet!" He
said, "You ain't going take my winchester." He said, "You come

here looking for whiskey. Now you find whiskey. All you find in here that ain't whiskey, you leave it here."

So Dukes left. He didn't take the gun, but he still had it in for Eddie, see.

Twas several of the Negroes out there in Collegeville had went to Nashville Tennessee and got jobs in stove foundries in Nashville, cause stove foundries was plenty plentiful in Nashville Tennessee. They found work up there, so they go up there and stay, work and come home every once or twice a month, ride down in cars. So one particular weekend, Eddie came home. The other two brothers, they's grown, both of them was grown and married. I don't know whether they had any children or not, but they was men. They wont boys. Eddie was forty-five years old. They looked upon Eddie kind of like they father, cause he'd raised them. They give a welcome-home party for him one Saturday night after he come home Friday. They going give a little party for him at the house, and he go back Sunday afternoon.

Out there in Collegeville, they didn't allow parties without they notify Dukes that they going to have it. Church clubs couldn't have little parties without they tell him that they going have a church club. If they didn't, he would come there and break up they little special party. I ain't never knowed, but I guess that was because the Reds was holding meetings, and he wouldn't know one from the other, so they'd have to tell him they holding a church club meeting, where he wouldn't break it up. That was the regular saying—"have to notify Dukes"—through a stoolpigeon, "We going hold a church club." (In the Party we didn't notify nobody. We's holding our meetings in secret. They couldn't catch us.) So when Eddie come home and the brothers pitched that party for him, they didn't ask Dukes and them for permission.

That Saturday evening I met Eddie about 4 or 4:30, walking on the railroad. I was going up North Birmingham, he'd been up North Birmingham, walking down. I met him and spoke to him and we got to talking. Just a week or two before that twas a carload of them came down from Nashville, and on the way back up there, the guy was sleep at the wheel and went over a fill there. Some of them got killed, and all of them got buggered up. All them what done got hurt lived right down in the community around us. I said, "You wont in that wreck going back up there?"

He said, "No, man." Said, "You know, I had give them my $3

and a half on that trip, but my mind didn't leave me." And said, "I took my $3 and a half, and I backed out. I'm glad I didn't come."

He told me about his brother and them was having a little party for him, for me to come over. I told him, I says, "If I be able to get off, I'll try to come." But I didn't go to parties in those days. I didn't go.

Somehow it got out they was having this party and Eddie was coming home, and Dukes had told his Negro stoolpigeon, this Fat Harsh. Twas another guy with him. I didn't never learn the other guy's name. Dukes told Fat Harsh to go there and kill Eddie that night when he come home.

They say everybody was there in the party in the house that night. It was maybe 9 o'clock, 10 o'clock, and Eddie was setting at the fire. Twas a bungalow house with a large fireplace. This Fat Harsh come on in the door. The door was open for everybody to come in, didn't anybody knock. So Fat Harsh walks in, his buddy walks in first. Fat Harsh walks in and push the door behind him, had the door like this, and says, "Hold down the house! Hold down the house!" That's what they said he said. And he shot up in the house, shot up through the ceiling. Eddie was setting at the fire over here.

When Fat Harsh shot up in the wall in the ceiling, they say Eddie got up and walked up to him, say, "Fat, now don't come here breaking up my brothers' party." Just like that. Fat cussed at Eddie. When he cussed at Eddie, they claim, they say Eddie had his knife, and he throwed his knife round Fat's neck.

Fat said to his buddy, "Buddy, you going let him kill me?" And this Negro shot Eddie in the heart, from the back. Eddie fell over in Fat Harsh's arms. When he fell over there, he shot him up off him, from the front, Fat Harsh did. They killed him dead.

Then another brother back here in the kitchen, he come in through the door, just like coming in. He just looked in through the door and looked around. They shot him in the eye and killed him. And the other brother back there, he heard what's going on. He's trying to get out the window. He's raised the window to get out the window in the back in there. They went on back there and found him trying to get out the window and killed him in the window. They killed all three of the brothers. I went and looked at all three caskets, them three brothers laying side to side.

We all knowed it was Dukes behind it. So the ILD branch then, we got our postal cards, and we sent them down to the high sheriff.

We then went to the city commissioners, just all over the city. We's flooding the city hall with postcards demanding that Dukes be discharged off the police force and be prosecuted for having Eddie Powell and these brothers killed. We also was demanding the death penalty for Fat Harsh and his buddy what done the shooting. We had these cards wrote and we put out leaflets also. We stirred such a stink that all the leading Negroes, the NAACP, they called a meeting at the church.

One night they had the preachers, all the doctors, at a meeting. Dr. Macklin was there, all the big shots. The house was full of Negroes. One of the doctors, he got up and he was talking up towards the front. He was talking up to the front, and he's saying, "I'm telling you, I don't care who hear what I say!" And he look back at the door. He standing up facing up there, but when he talk everytime he say something, big words, he look back, he look back. We was sitting there, about four or five of us Party people sitting there in the meeting, and we said to ourselves, "Look athere. He looking for the police to come in." Oh, they was just atalking. They said they was going do this, they was going do that.

Me and Mack Coad was right there together.* It was me and him and somebody else, was three of us. Mack Coad got up back there and told them we was from the International Labor Defense and we was concerned about this murder also, and we were demanding the death penalty for these guys done this murder. We said we were willing, anytime they want, "to cooperate with you all and unite in the struggle to see to these people being prosecuted."

The answer they give us, "Brother, we're glad, we appreciate your interest, but right now we'll just try to go on by ourselves. We appreciate your interest, but just let us do it by ourselves right now. We'll let you know." So we left, cause we know they weren't going do nothing anyway. But we put on a whole lot of pressure on the city about Dukes.

They had a woman named Miss Lena, she was a great, big, brown-skinned woman, wont so tall. She was a card reader. She was supposed to be one of these people that could do things, this what you call hoodoo work. I knew her personally. I got to know her by my wife. Sophie went to see her once cause Sophie had a condition she had been had for a long time, a pain in her side. She went

* He was living with me then.

to her once for that. I didn't never go to her, but she was good. She could read. She always tell you things, whether people believe in it or not. She always told me, said, "Ain't nobody never going bother you." She always told me, "You just keep your business to yourself," said, "won't nothing hardly ever come upon you."

One day I went by her house, in the time of all this. She called me in, said, "Come here, boy, come here." She called me "boy."

I went in and walked in the house. She knowed me, knowed some of us was members of the ILD, and she was wishing us well, but she wont no member. She says to me, "Boy, what is you all doing?"

I said, "What you mean?"

She said, "You know you done near about run Dukes crazy," said, "you all near about done run that man out of his mind."

I said, "Run him crazy how?"

She say, "He come here telling me, he come here crying, said he didn't tell Fat Harsh to go there and kill all the brothers. He told him to kill Eddie. And Fat went there and killed all of them."

Dukes come to her asking, "What can you do?" said, "please help me." He want her to do some whatever she could do in a underhand way, cause he didn't want Fat Harsh to be electrocuted. He was paying her *big* money to keep him from going to the electric chair. I don't know how much it was, but she said, "He paid me well."

She said, "I gots to do something, but I wants the Negro hung myself," said. "But since he's paying me, I got to try to keep him out of the electric chair. But I ain't going try to keep him out of prison."*

And Fat Harsh did get fifty years. Dukes got removed out of that area. We didn't get him off the force, but we did get him out of that area.

---

* Miss Lena died since I left Birmingham. She was on the way to a funeral in a car on a Sunday, going down out from Birmingham to Bessemer, coming down that highway, and they had a wreck. Miss Lena got tore all to pieces. That's the way she died. That's the way she left this world. But she could read.

8

Reverend Sears
and the Reds

MANY of the leading Negroes in Birmingham in the early '30s was speaking out on every turn that these northern Reds was coming down into the South, agitating among the lower class of ignorant niggers and stirring up the peace and happiness among the Negroes and their good white friends in the South who had always been feeding the Negroes, giving them bread and meat when they were hungry. "And now these crazy, ignorant niggers are turning their back on those who had been their friends all the time."

In Collegeville in 1933, the Reverend Sears, who was the pastor then at the Bethel Baptist Church out there, would warn his congregation. Reverend Sears was a middle-aged man, he was mangly grayish, not full gray, but half gray. I guess he was in his fifties. He was brown-skinned, had kind of a long face, didn't have a round face. He weighed about 150, I reckon; he was about five feet. Wasn't a large man, just a medium-sized man.

Every Sunday a.m. when the leaflets was put out around that church on Saturday night, telling something about the Scottsboro case and Sears would find the leaflets around his church, he get up in the pulpit in the morning and have something to say about them to his congregation. He would make an announcement about the leaflets. "If I find my members fooling with this mess, I'm going to turn you out the church." We had several members in his church were members of the Party or ILD. When Sears say that, some of the congregation would say "Amen." Some of the people sitting there, members of the Party, wouldn't say anything. When they get back to the unit or the ILD branch, they would tell what he said, they tell what the Reverend had to say that Sunday.

We let him talk his big talk all he wanted to. We didn't bother

169

him. I was the section organizer of the Party and the unemployed committees out there at that time, and the Party members of that church would make it their duty to be at the church every Sunday to see what the Reverend were going to say in his service about the Party or the ILD. Finally the Reverend fell in his own trap.

We had several Party members working out there in the neighborhood of Greenwood on a city welfare job in the spring of 1933. You had "Sandbelly" there, "Sandbelly" one of them, and old man Jimmie Hooper Sr. was on there. Beidel was working out there, and I don't know whether West Hibbard working on there or not. I was living over there in Collegeville, and right cross the L & N railroad was Greenwood, about half a mile maybe, quarter mile. I learned about this thing what happened from some of the Party people was working on the job. It happened on a Wednesday.

A Negro named Doc Carter was a few minutes late getting to the toolbox, where all of the workers had to be at 7 o'clock a.m. to get their tools to work with, such as picks and shovels. When Doc walk up after all of the rest of the men had left the tool box, a big old white straw boss (he was a big old devil) cussed at Doc, and Doc cussed back at this straw boss. This boss pull out a pistol and shot at Doc Carter—he didn't hit him—and ran to a corner grocery store there in the community of Negroes and call the Birmingham police. A flying squad of police, about fifteen or twenty, came out with their sawed-off shotguns and rifles, very calm in talking to the Negroes, tell them not to raise any disturbance: they was out there to keep the peace, they did not want any trouble to arise on the job.

After their soft talk, they all left, and this big old straw boss came back on the job with his big .38 pistol out where all of the Negroes could see it sitting up in his hip pocket. Before then, he had been keeping his pistol hid. They didn't know for sure, they thought he had a pistol before, but then he took his pistol, stuck it up where it could be seen.

They had a lot of young fellows working up there. They's crowded up working, digging up rocks and all. They call this straw boss over to where they was digging up a big rock, to have him to give them some ideas on how best to get that rock up out of a hole. He went over among that group of Negroes, with that .38 sticking up out of his hip pocket, and they grab him, throwed him down, took the pistol. That was the last time that he had a chance to feel the weight of that .38. The one took the pistol, he run. But the straw boss didn't know who grabbed him, now, was a whole lot of Negroes out there. So he run back to the store and call the police again.

Then the police come up again. There so much confusion now, till the welfare officials came out from the office and they just knocked everybody off for the day. This done ruint the day for work.

That night, several Negroes, including some of our Party people, went and sat up with Doc Carter. They lived in the community and some of them was involved with the block committee members. That is why they so close to it. They stayed with him that night in his home, thinking that maybe some white hoodlums might come to get Doc Carter out of his house, but nobody came. And the next afternoon, which was Thursday, Reverend Sears come over and told Doc's wife he wanted to see him. Now Sears wont living in Greenwood. This happened in Greenwood. Sears was living over in Collegeville.

Doc went over to see what did the Reverend want. The Reverend told Doc that he was a member of a committee to go out and try to settle the troubles on the welfare jobs, such as what had developed on his job. He wanted to know from Doc just how did the trouble start Wednesday morning, and Doc told him the full story. Reverend Sears ask Doc who had took the .38. Doc told him he did not know who had the .38, because he had left the job when that straw boss shot at him and that he did not go back to the job any more that day. The Reverend told Doc "If you don't know, then you cannot be held accountable for it. The law might come out and question you about that gun. They might carry you down and put you in jail, but it won't be nothing to it. But if you don't know who got it, no one can hold you accountable for the gun and it won't be anything to it."

So Doc talked with Reverend Sears and he came back home, he made hisself satisfied. That Thursday night, the fellows went there to set up with him again, and Doc told them, "It ain't going to be nothing to it. You all go on. You all don't have to set up with me again. They ain't going to do nothing," cause he done went over, talked with Reverend Sears. So everybody went on home.

That Friday, the next day, four big white men came out and arrested Doc, carried him to jail. And that night, he didn't come back from jail. So Saturday, Doc's wife went to the jail to see about

him, go down and check on him. They allowed her to see him—
he's in the southside jail—and he's all beat up. He told his wife to
go out and tell all them that wont members of them Reds, they
might as well to join them, "because they done near beat me to
death here, trying to make me say I'm a Red, and I ain't nary one.
If you ain't in it, you might as well get in it, cause they going to beat
you up anyhow if they get you." And he wasn't a Party member,
wont involved at all. He didn't believe in nothing. In other words,
he had talked against the Party. He changed his mind when they
put him in jail and they beat him up. Doc Carter didn't come clear.
He got six months in the city jail, that was on there about that pistol.

When his wife came back and put out the news that he was all
beat up and what he said, that's when these people in Greenwood
got in touch with me. They notified me cause I was the chairman of
the unemployed committee in that area. I got a fellow there by the
name of Harper, a young fellow. I didn't consult nobody else in the
city. What we had, we called them people together in Greenwood,
got them to organize a committee. We told them we going organize
a meeting and we wanted David James to speak over there in the
community, over there in Vulcan City, in Collegeville. David James,
the spokesman, he lived there in Greenwood. He was a Party person.* Me and Harper got the leaflets out ourselves, mimeographed
them off, distributed them all. Got some in Greenwood and some
there in Collegeville, right in Vulcan City, all round Sears's church
that Saturday night, inviting everybody that Sunday afternoon out
there in the ball diamond to a open-air meeting.

There was several of the ILD and Party members in the Greenwood community, where all of the trouble started from. We agree
among ourselves that although I was the local Party leader out
there, I should not speak in the meeting. If any arrest was made by
the police, I would be free to see to them getting out of jail. We
decided that David James in his talk would ask the question to the
people at the meeting, "What would you all want to do about this
Reverend getting Doc arrested?" Then someone would make a
motion that we elect a committee here at the meeting to go and call
on this Reverend and find out from him just what role did he play
in getting Doc Carter arrested.

At 3 o'clock on Sunday, it was hundreds of Negroes out in that

---

* David James was not so well known in Collegeville. That's partly why we
chose him to be the spokesman for the meeting.

ball park. Jerry Meriweather spoke, he was a Negro World War I veteran of the community. At the close of James's and Meriweather's remarks, the motion was made and seconded by the great majority of the people there, and the meeting was dismissed.

We had already picked out a committee of seven from the Greenwood community that we wanted to go to call on the Reverend, but they were not exposed to the crowd there in that meeting, for fear if they were known by everybody there, and should things not come out too well, they could be very easy spotted out by the police pimps that were bound to be there among the people. And the Reverend also had members of his church, and they would also carry him all of what was happening there.

Many people was asking who was the people that was to serve on the committee to see the Reverend, some ask me who was they. I told them that I didn't know. One of the Reverend's deacons ask me, "How come you are not on that committee? Ain't you one of the leaders?"

I put the question back to him. I said to him, "Why don't you go on it? You are one of the Reverend's deacons. He will listen to you," and left him with that. We had found out that that Negro was one of the Reverend's right-hand men, and he was a member of the ILD branch there in Collegeville community. We had to play it very careful with him. He was very nosy that afternoon at that meeting, but we worked things out just as we all planned it. On that committee was voted to go to see the Reverend, among others, was John Beidel, Jimmie Hooper, West Hibbard, "Sandbelly," David James.

Many people left that meeting and tear up to the church, where a BYPU program was in session.* It was held before the evening service, at about 5 o'clock, and some women always be at the head of it.

I was at the mass meeting in the ball diamond, but I didn't go to the church. I didn't tell nobody what I going to do. (We didn't tell anybody what we had to do.) I told them I had to go away, I had some business I had to go see after. So the rest of them went to the church and I went on to the southside to this meeting with this person from New York was in there. It was about three or four of us met with a fellow called hisself Jim Allen, we called him in those

---

* [Baptist Young People's Union program.]

days—I don't know whether he said he was the Jim Allen who wrote that little pamphlet called "The Black Belt." There was a little pamphlet put out, had the Black Belt map on it, it was red, and the man wrote it was Jim Allen. (I thought he was Jim Allen, but he wasn't Jim Allen. His name, I found out in later years, was Joe North.[1])

He was just coming through. We had people in them days, they just coming through. I don't know what they business was, where they been or where they going. When they hit in Birmingham, they contact a certain Party person and tell the person to get one or two people together, "I'd like to talk with them while I'm in town, before I leave."

So the first thing they do, they run me down, notify Hudson, maybe Joe Howard, and maybe one or two others, say, "Be at such and such a one's house," more than likely, be there at six o'clock. We know it's something going on. So that evening we had this meeting there at this fellow's house in Titusville called Thomas. We was discussing. We got together and we told him what's happening over in Collegeville, about Doc Carter's arrested. At that same time, he was discussing with us the questions of the ILD and what the lawyers doing with the Scottsboro case, all that. We stayed there to about 9:30 or 10 o'clock, talking with "Jim Allen."

Whether he left first or whether we left first, I don't remember. He had somebody with him, to go back with him to maybe stop at a hotel. We didn't know where he stopping. All we know, when he get through, he disappear. So I came back to Collegeville, and I got home about 11 or 11:30.

When I got home from my meeting on the southside, my wife told me what happened. She said, "Hosie," said, "you all have raised the devil out here this evening."

After the meeting in the ball diamond, lots of the people went to Reverend Sears's church. Some of the church members who was at that meeting rush ahead of the crowd of people and told the Reverend that a committee was coming to see him. The Reverend had someone to bring his double-barreled shotgun into the church, and had placed that shotgun behind the pulpit desk.

Many people who had left that meeting in that ball park and went to the church went just to see what were going to happen there. Them people were living in that community, but never visit that church, but they went out that afternoon. When they all crowded into that church—some with their overalls on just as they were going to work—when they all crowded into the church, the Reverend stood up in his rostrum and told the mistress of ceremonies to close out the BYPU, to close that program. And when he told everybody to stand for the dismissing, David James rose to his feet and told the Reverend, said, "Reverend Pastor, we's the committee elected by the people in the community to come over and find out what role did you play in having Doc Carter arrested?"

"What did you say?" the Reverend ask James. And James put the question to him again. And the Reverend said to James, "I will not hear you."

Beidel was over in another place. He gets up and he come walking down the aisle, "We demand a statement out of you!" Then the other members of that committee who was scattered in different places in the church rose to their feet and told the Reverend, "We demand a statement from you!" "We demand a statement from you to carry back to the people that elected us to come to talk to you!"

By that time the deacons come toward Beidel, and another committee member jumps up—it's about six of them, "We wants a statement!" Beidel walking down this aisle. Some of the women members began to scream, "Don't you all hurt our pastor!"

At that point the Reverend went down behind his pulpit and came up with his double-barreled shotgun, waving it from his pulpit, "Let them come on! Let them come on! I'll stop them!" So much turmoil, and the deacons trying to get between the Reverend and the committee, trying to grab Beidel and them. Reverend Sears said, "Don't you hold him, I'll hold him!"

Then all the people said "Aieeeeeeee!" and began to scramble for the church door. They tell me that when he raised that shotgun there everybody went to falling and running over each other, trying to get out of there. That church was way up, was big, high steps, and them people was falling down the steps. Some was jumping out the church windows, including Beidel, Hibbard, and "Sandbelly." It's a wonder they didn't have a real stampede and hurt somebody bad. The committee all left the church, and as soon as they hit the ground they headed back to Greenwood.

Reverend Sears and them called the police and they arrested twenty-nine people. We had two people arrested. It wont but two of our people was in that crowd. All the rest of them was spectators, gone to see what going happen. Our people was the man who spoke at the meeting, Meriweather, and old Mr. Waters. He was a old man that carried the *Daily Worker* every day. He delivered the paper, so they know he was one of the Reds, cause he carried the Reds' paper. He was there, so they got him.

My wife told me, said, "A lots of people has been arrested and are still in jail. People been regular coming here asking for you. They want to know where you is. They want you to see about going down and see about getting these people out of jail."

I said, "Late as it is now, I won't get up about it. I ain't going down there tonight," I said. "There's nothing I can do about it tonight. I wait till the morning. I'll go and see someone tomorrow morning down at the ILD office." I went to bed, but I couldn't sleep much that night for looking to hear the police knock on my door. I was looking for them because I was looking for someone to tell them that I was the local leader out there in the neighborhood. But none of them came to my house that night.

That next morning early, I was aroused by some of the neighborhood members to see what I was going to do about getting the people that had been arrested out of jail. I told them not to worry, I would go down to the ILD office and see someone as soon as the ILD office open at 9 o'clock. And also I told them to go to the post office and get some penny postcards.

I had to walk to downtown Birmingham to the office because I didn't have the carfare to ride the trolley car. I had to walk about three or four miles to get to the ILD office. I went down and told Bob Binkley and Attorney Schwab, a young attorney who had come into Birmingham from New York to work with the ILD there in defense of the members of the Party and the ILD when anyone get arrested.[2] I made my full report to them about what had happened out there that Sunday afternoon. They told me to go back and tell the people in the community not to worry, they would go down and see about getting all the people out of jail. I went back and delivered the message. Some of the people who were not our members had already got them a lawyer and was out of jail. Mr. Waters and Meriweather and one or two more stayed in jail until Binkley and Schwab went down and got them out that morning.

The lawyer that the other people employed was a white woman lawyer by the name of Mrs. Thompson. I had never heard of a woman lawyer before. That was something new to me. At all these people's trial—they was tried together, ILD members and nonmembers—lawyer Thompson and Schwab was on the cases together. In fact, Schwab did not have to say too much in the courtroom. This white woman lawyer did all of the arguing before the city judge. (Oh, she was a rabblerouser.)

She went for a hot mama there in the police courts. She curse like a man in the courtroom. That was why these nonmembers of the ILD all got her, because she was looked upon by many of the Negroes what knew her as being a great defender for them in the courts against the police, when the police had framed them in false arrests in the past times.

So when this Reverend Sears got on the witness stand and began his testimony against the Negroes who was at his church that Sunday afternoon when he wave his shotgun from his pulpit, she was rough with him while he was on the witness stand. He was fined $250 for drawing that shotgun in that church on these unarmed members of that committee. All of these people was set free.

We, the ILD and Party members all over Birmingham, began to mail postcards to Reverend Sears, telling him to stop working for the police of Birmingham against the Negro people and to leave Collegeville community.* It was said that when these penny postcards began to flood into him by mail, he would take them down to the city hall of Birmingham.

He carried so many of them down there, until finally some of the police told him, "Reverend, the Reds are not threatening your life, they are just telling you go move out of that community." The police had been guarding his person day and night, protecting him from the Reds, until that point of discussion. The Reverend told them that he had built his home there to live there until his death, and he were not going to leave his home. The police told him that they were not going to risk their lives fooling with him and stand chances of being killed from their wives and children by these damn Reds, and that they were not coming back out there, guarding him at night. They gave him permission to deputize some of the deacons of his church to guard him at his house with their guns against the Reds.

We had Reverend Sears to where he was afraid to put his lights

---

* We wrote postcards to the city officials all the time, whenever something develop against the Negro people. But at no time did we ever write any violence threats. That was one thing that we would always warn our members against, making threats of violence in writing these postcards.

out at night. He had drop cords with lights all around his house and in front. It was lit up like a little city. He had his deacons, armed, sitting up on the porch with winchesters sitting propped up side of the house on the porch by they side. They sitting up there, "waiting for the Reds." We would walk by there at first dark and look at them sitting there and have fun to ourselves, just looking and laughing and talking. And we were walking by there in front on the sidewalk about twelve foot from them, having our fun.

Now them was some fools, you know. All that big, bright light, guns sitting up side them, rared back against the house, and we walk on out there just like in the edge of the shade there, out of the light, and look at them. They call theyselves "guarding," and we laughing.

Some of his best church members was living all around us and we were getting all of the news about what they were saying and doing all the time, and they did not know who we was.

That thing tore that church up, though. All Reverend Sears's members got to fighting among theyselves, some says Sears was right, some say he's wrong. His membership, they said, was about 2000 members, dropped down to just 300 or 400 members. People went and left church, then joined other churches.

He did live there in that house and pastored that church until his death. That occurred around the early 1940s. But that scar of the role that he played in that Doc Carter struggle stayed with him until his death. He never did hold his heavy hand over his membership any more like he did before that struggle that took place at that church that Sunday. But the word went out after that struggle at that church that Sunday that the Reds was out to break up the church—they was the devil's imps—they did not believe in God.

I lived under terror in 1933 myself. Police would ride by. I'd come home this evening, and I'd look for the police to raid my house before day in the morning, just like going to bed. I was right there, and some of Reverend Sears's members, best members was living in rock distance of where I was living, right back here behind me. My house faced the avenue out here, and 34th Street come up here, and my house face here, and right back here's 33rd Street, and this here's a alley back here. You had space between the houses. Some of them was double-tenant houses, had one family on each corner, wont two-story houses. But we were so well trained, our Party people so well trained, they didn't tell nobody who I was. And I was the real leader. I'd come out and walk around in the daytime, walk about and speak to people, just natural. That was organized, wasn't it!

The police was riding around, just riding around, patrolling through the community. They was regular raiding different Party members' houses all over the city. I didn't know them to raid anybody's house in Collegeville over literature, and they never did raid, never did come to my house. They'd ride by, and I'd be setting on the porch. Sometimes they'd ride by, and I'm just looking for them to say "Stop!" They'd drive by in that blood-red car, and I'd set there. I wouldn't make it no regular thing, setting out there on the porch. I'd stay in the house, more or less, but sometimes it's so hot, I wanted to sit outside on the porch. I had a nice porch out there on that bungalow house.

They never did bother me. I was careful, but the question was not so much careful. It was a lot of people around, Party members, and they knew me. But nobody didn't tell the police who I was. They never did stop by my house. Never happen. My house has never been raided. I better knock on something, knock on wood. That's luck, though, ain't it?

9

To New York and the Birmingham Jail

I found this Party, a party of the working class, gave me rights equal with all others regardless of color, sex, or age or educational standards. I with my uneducation could express myself, without being made fun of by others who could read well and fast, using big words. I was treated with high respect. I had a right to help make the policy. At every convention, maybe some policy question would change at the convention and we have a discussion from the floor. After a thorough discussion, decisions are arrived at by majority vote. Then all members, including those who disagree, are duty bound to explain, fight for, and carry out such decisions. When that decision is made, everybody got to fall into line.

I've been to many Party conventions. The first one I went to was an extraordinary plenary session called in New York by Earl Browder. That was in 1933, the 4th of July. That was the first time I got out of the South.

We left at night on a Monday, left out of Birmingham in a old piece of car, went over to Atlanta, me and Don and the rest of them. They taken me in the car from Birmingham to Atlanta. When we all got to Atlanta, we put down their car and we all got in Ben Davis' car and pulled out for New York. We went up with Ben Davis.[1] That was the first time I met him. Ben Davis was in Atlanta, he was then involved in the Angelo Herndon case. We drove to New York from Atlanta. I don't know what model of Ford it was, but twas seven of us packed up in that Ford. All the way from Atlanta to New York City. It was *hot!* That was the worst trip I ever had in my life. Seven people, seven grown people—wont no children in the crowd—it was seven people. Twas three Negroes: me, Ben, and Al

Murphy. We went up in the front seat together. In the back seat was the D.O. of the time, Don, and his wife, and another guy from Texas name of Lee, and another guy name of Ted Mebber. All four of them was white. Now you know that was some ride.

I was just looking for us to get picked up any time for white and black riding together, that was number one. And number two, the car being packed up there was uncomfortable. And number three, what they were talking about, I had to keep my mouth shut because I didn't know how to express myself. I just ride along listening and looking at the country. Every once in a while they'd ask me, say, "Hosie, you sleep?"

"No, I ain't sleep," like that, night and day, night and day. We never stopped, running about 30 miles an hour, I reckon. We got to where we could see the Blue Ridge Mountains before night. A dark cloud, it look like, on the side. Every time I looked at it it looked like a dark cloud. That was the first time to see a mountain as I knew a mountain. (We had mountains as hills in Birmingham, but this was a mountain you could see for miles away. That was a mountain to me.) I then was thirty-five years old.

Then we begin to see these tobacco fields before night, before dark. We went all through Gastonia, after that big strike in North Carolina of the textile workers.[2] We went through Gastonia, I know, cause they was talking about that big strike that they done had there before we got there. I don't know whether it was dangerous or not. We took the chance, is all I know.

One place we stopped where they made apple cider. The whites went out and brought some and we stayed in the car. They had to bring it. We wont allowed to go in the place. They brought cups out to the car and we all had some refreshments, drinking. Got tired of riding.

We rid all night that night, rid all day that next day, got into Philadelphia along about that next night, it looked like it was about 7 or 8 o'clock. We got into New York sometime before day that morning, late Wednesday morning. Ben driv every step of the way, all the way up there and all the way back. He never took a wink, night and day.

I didn't get to know Ben Davis too much on the trip. We's going up, riding. I know he was a lawyer, and I felt at that time that he was superior. I wasn't used to being around that kind of people,

Negro lawyers. And everybody was talking. Him and Al Murphy, they done a lot of discussing about everything, the country and the conditions. Ben Davis was a friendly guy, he was friendly to me, but he was driving the car, and Murphy sitting between me and him. I'm over on the side and the whites back here talking. Everybody talking and riding, try to keep encouragement. I was just listening, because at that time my development was very low, practically zero. I wont doing no talking.

We went on, got to New York, and we all got off. Some went in different places. Ben didn't go to that extraordinary plenary session. He didn't attend Party conferences. I presume, I never did know, I never questioned, but I presume he was up there to discuss with Patterson and them something about the ILD and the Herndon case in Atlanta, and also the Scottsboro case, which he wasn't involved in, but he did play a part in the Scottsboro case in Alabama.

That was the first big conference, first big meeting of the Party I was in. They had fraternal delegates at that particular meeting. They were there from Chile, and they had fraternal delegates there from Germany. The guy that Hitler killed—I can't think of his name right now—but he was the leader of the Party and Hitler killed him.* His name was very familiar with me. He was at that meeting. He spoke. About four or five fraternal delegates was there. I didn't meet them personally, I just was there when they spoke. It was a lot being said I didn't understand. I was still in the learning stage. I was just sitting quiet, listening. Some I understood what they said, and some I didn't.

After the meeting was over, it was a Negro woman there at the convention from North Carolina, and she was living in a big housing project there in New York, call it the Coop. I forgotten her name. She taken me on the trolley down to the waterfront down on Broadway, we rid all the way down there. It was real cold.[3] It was on July 4th, and it was cold enough to have on a overcoat. It was real chilly like the fall of the year. I seen a big ship there with peep holes and they was playing the music and everybody around right there at the water. That was the first time I seen ships.

I didn't see Ben anymore until we got ready to come back to Atlanta, and we all came back in the car together. Murphy stayed in New York, but all the whites came back. Lee sat in the front with

* [Ernest Thaelmann.]

us coming back, so it was still a question of I was looking for some one to stop us. It wasn't worse, though, cause Lee was smaller than Murphy was and it wasn't quite as tight up.

That was a trip! When I got back home from riding that trip up and back, I had some knots to come on my hip, under the flesh, and it was like a itch. I don't know where I picked that thing up. They say it was a seven-year itch. It was something, I tell you. It got all on my arm, all on my hands, all around my neck. I was in bad shape. I don't know how I got rid of that stuff, but it was way in the winter before I got rid of it. It was somebody, I don't know who it was, some old person in Birmingham told me how to get rid of that seven-year itch. I got some pokeberry root and some mullen and put it on and boil it. Put that stuff in a big pot and boiled it, put it in the bathtub and I bathed in it, real warm. And it brought all that stuff out. While I was in the water, all my flesh, under my arms, them whelps just knotted up, great big whelps. I just got all knotty all over. I kept doing it, so finally it just dried up. That was the worst stuff I ever had in all my life.[4]

THE coal miners and the ore miners was the first ones begin to organize in the NRA days. I never did know the whole thing, but in that period, the NRA, it was something worked out between John L. Lewis and Roosevelt, I think. That's my thinking. And whatever the agreement was, when they come out with the NRA, John L. Lewis came out organizing the coal miners.

We began to build the Party among the coal miners and the ore miners when they began to reorganize their UMW locals. Many of the miners were living in Birmingham, particularly the Negroes. We had some big struggles.

The bosses had all the coal mine communities guarded. They had deputy sheriffs in the coal mine areas. We didn't call them deputy sheriffs, we called them company dicks. Now out there in that Sareyton mine, out in North Birmingham, the guy out there, his name was Self. If a guy would be sick and he wouldn't go in to work, Self would go around "shack rousting." He go around, knock on those doors, see who all at home, who all in, who all out. If someone didn't go to work, Self want to know what's wrong. He'd tell the Negroes, "By God, if you ain't sick, when I get through with you, you will be sick." He was the shack rouster hisself, called hisself deputy sheriff of the company. Any stranger going in the mine quarters, especially through the week days, would be questioned, stopped and questioned by the company dicks.

I went out to Sareyton many times, but I'd pick my time to go. I always was able to dodge them. I'd go out there on a Sunday afternoon, that's when they wasn't working. I didn't go out there hardly during the week. We had three-four Party people we recruited, and if I had to see any of them during the week, I'd go up there to Sareyton mine where they came out the bath-house in the afternoon, when they get off work. Everybody's out there then. I didn't go bumbling through the community there when the people supposed to be working. I'd move when the people move. That's always my way of moving. That's the way we discussed it, how we going to work in places. That was our way of moving.

In Birmingham in the month of November of '33, we Party members call a meeting of workers from some of the mines and steel plants and iron foundries one Sunday afternoon, to organize a committee to begin to build rank and file committees in some of the coal and ore mine union locals around Birmingham and Bessemer. What these committees was doing was bombarding some of the unions, the top leaders, calling for industrial unions, *industrial* unions.* Because our Party position was the onliest way you going to get out of this present oppression, you got to organize the industrial unions and organize the unorganized workers, organize the Negro. The Negro hadn't been organized in unions before. They was all lily white unions. They wouldn't take Negroes in. This meeting, we had planned to hold it in the old Negro Penny Saving Bank, down on 2nd Avenue and somewhere between 15th or 16th Street. (Since that time this bank been torn down.)

Some of us had just began to go into that hall and arrange the chairs, early waiting for the other workers to come. Only nine of us had got into that hall, four white and five Negroes. A young white worker, Ward Turner, was to chair that meeting. Ted Welbaum, a young white YCL member from New York, was there with us and two other white workers. (That was the whites.) Then Joe Howard, myself, Homer Martin, and Sol Norman, and another young Negro coal miner by the name of Mosley was there. Mosley and I went down on the next floor below our floor, the third floor, to the men's

---

* All the unions was craft unions.

room. When we got to the second floor, we found city detective Mosley, the head of the Red Squad, and three other police standing down there questioning the Negro who was in charge of that building. The young coal miner Mosley just kept walking on down to the ground floor, right past that group of officers, and I turn around and went back up to our hall and told the rest of the boys that was up there that the police was down on the floor below, asking that Negro a lots of rough questions.

Ward Turner told everybody to get them a seat and sit down, and we sat down in the different places in the hall. Turner took his seat at the table where the chairman was to sit at. After a while, all of that bunch of police began to rush up the stairway, headed for our hall. Detective Mosley walk over to Turner and asked him what kind of meeting is that. Turner told him that this is a Socialist Party meeting. Mosley pick up all of the notes of paper that Turner had on the table and told all of us to get out of this hall. We all headed down to the ground floor. When we got down to the door at the sidewalk, the police had backed a paddy wagon up to the curb and form themselves into a line from that door to that police wagon. And we all walk right straight into that police wagon from that building.

As we were hauled away from that hall we could see several of our people standing on the corner who was headed to the meeting. But by the police hurrying into that hall to break up that meeting as they did, they saved many of those workers their jobs.

The police took us eight to the southside jail and lodged us Negroes there in a cell with other Negroes that was in there for that Sunday night. We didn't know what was going to happen to us, cause it had been the custom when they arrest any of the members of the ILD or the Party to take them out after a certain time of night —so we were told—and whip them. We didn't know whether they was going to whip us or not. We were just there. So I didn't throw my clothes off all that night. I just laid on the bunk, on the old bunk they had there, in my clothes. That was Sunday night.

The next morning the four white workers who was placed in a different cell and all us Negroes was hauled down to the city hall separate and placed into a different room and mugged one by one. Our pictures was taken and we was fingerprinted. They kept all four there until late that afternoon. Then they put us in what they call the "bull pen" where all the misdemeanors was, like you arrested for drunk or something like that. Not no bad crime. Everybody put out here in one big old place together. You sit around, sit on bunks, anywhere you can find. Ain't none of them decent, but you ain't got no particular place to sleep, just bunk up and do the best you can on the cots. That was where I seed a crap game for the first time in my life. A old man there had some dice and playing craps for a penny. He'd take them dice and work his hand around and shake them and "crack, crack, crack!" and throw them dice. When he throw them and the dice turn up, every time they turn up, he'd hit. He was a real dice shooter. He was a old man. We just set there and looked at him.

Didn't nobody bother me, nobody asked anybody what they was there for. We four, me, Sol, Homer Martin, and Joe Howard, we four was together. And quite naturally we sit around together, but we didn't talk. We always was told not to do no talking in jail, cause you never know when the walls are bugged or not, so we didn't talk about none of our affairs. They kept us there till Tuesday.

Now Sol, they tried to hold Sol for a while, cause Sol when they first arrest him, they asked him what his name was, he wouldn't tell them what his name. Old Detective Mosley hit Sol in the face around his eye. He had a red, very bad bruised face. I didn't see him when he got hit. All I seen was afterwards, and he had a big bloody place on the side of his face and his eye was all bloodshot.

Tuesday they taken us back for trial, put us in separate cells, except me and Homer Martin in a cell to ourselves. I don't know what time they had Joe Howard or the white guys' trial.

I had heard that whenever we was arrested that we were not to ever plead guilty when we went before a judge. I had told Homer Martin that we were not to plead guilty when we were asked by the judge. We was all lined up in a long line of Negroes. Some of them had been picked up by the police for drunk that Saturday afternoon. As they march up, they were asked the question by the judge, "You are charge of being drunk, are you guilty or not guilty?"

In most cases these Negroes would say, "Guilty, Judge."

And the judge would say, "$13 or 13 days." Most of them would be led off by the police to jail to begin serve that 13 days.

When Homer Martin and I got up before him, I was in the front of Homer. We were told what our charges was—that was meeting to overthrow the government. "Are you guilty or not guilty?"

I said, "Not guilty, Judge."

He said to me, "Stand aside."

Homer Martin told him the same thing, and he was told to stand aside. We were finally taken back into a room and the door was locked. And we sat there all the rest of that afternoon until just about night, from early that morning without any water or food. Finally they call us out and took us back to the southside jail, and then we were given water and some of that lousy black-eyed peas and hard cornbread with all of the corn husks and other filth in it. But we had to eat it because that was all that we could get until the next morning.

About 1 o'clock Wednesday the key-boy come to the bull pen and call us and told us to get ready, we were wanted down at the warden's desk. We walked out and we all walk down to the desk sergeant. He had a great big double forehead, a great big wide double forehead and smoked a pipe. I guess he might of been a Irishman, he had big feet. (He was called to be the good police among the Negroes there in Birmingham after that time. They said, "He's a good man, that boy, he's a good man." The Negroes called him nice cause when he caught them in their misdemeanors, he'd give them a little break.) This sergeant told the key-boy to unlock the outside iron gate and he said to us four Negroes: "You God damn niggers get out of that gate and get out of town. You damn Reds better not be caught in Birmingham any more. If you do, it will not be good for you."* We all walked out and went to our various homes. (Joe Howard passed from this life in Birmingham some time in 1939. I stayed there and built steel local 2815. Homer Martin passed there in 1974.)

Sol Norman left Birmingham. I heard that he went back to Selma Alabama. That was his home, down Selma. He worked with the sharecroppers union, but something happen to him there in around '35. Down in 19 and 65 I was talking to some people and they was around the area of Selma the time of that terror in 1935. It was a husband and wife, and the husband said they had some rough times down there, "but down in our part, where we live, they didn't never come down there and bother us cause we was so well organized together till they was afraid to try and come in there to mess with us.

---

* That was what he had to say to us Negroes knowing that we was considered to be Reds. He showed his real colors with us.

We was just too hot for them down there." The deputy sheriffs and the Ku Klux and them didn't come in there, but it was up in some other place where they was terrorizing and beating and arresting Negroes. Negroes was coming up missing.

Then I was talking to a preacher in 1953, Reverend Rivers (he's dead now). This preacher was a pastor down there in Selma at that time, and twas a white man, a merchant, had a blacksmith shop. He took this preacher out in his yard and showed him eight or nine things that was made out of concrete that looked like bears standing up. They had a solid bottom, and the top was a lid, was a piece of sheet iron with a lock on it, to lock it. They was just the size enough to put a man in.

Reverend Rivers kept asking this white man, talking like a preacher, said, "Boss, what is this? I just like this thing. This is a pretty, pretty thing. I just like to have one of them."

The white man said, "No, Reverend, you don't want that. That's for these people that won't listen at you and won't listen at us. That's made for these kind of people."

Reverend Rivers, he said it made him so sick that he went home and went to bed, had to have a doctor. He could just see all these people he knowed done come up missing, and they done put them in them concrete things and dropped them in the Alabama River. And he couldn't tell nobody. So when he got able, when he got well enough to move out, he left there and come to Birmingham. His wife said, "I bet you that's what happened to Willie Foster." He was one of the local leaders of the ILD there in Birmingham, and they sent him down there to see about some arrests. He never did come back. "They about put him in them barrels and dropped him in the river, cause he turn up missing and we never did hear from him."

We didn't never know what happened to Sol Norman to know the truth about it. It was hard to say if he left out of there or not, because we none of us at that time used our regular names when we went to a new different place. He might of left and used a new name someplace else. Or they might of put him in one of them concrete barrels Reverend Rivers was looking at.

But didn't none of us leave Birmingham according to the instructions of that old desk sergeant in '33. I heard about what happen to him there in Birmingham. It happened in the late 1950s. It was told to me that a old Negro man played a number with a Negro woman and he hit the number. He hit for $20 and he went there to get his money, and she claimed he didn't hit the number. She wouldn't pay him his money. He got the bus and went back home and got his pistol and he came back there and he made her pay him his money. She give him the $20. When he got it, he took his $20 and walked out.

He walked up to the corner of 8th Avenue and waited for the bus to come. She called the police. When the police got there, she pointed him out. He was still standing out there at the bus stop waiting to get the city bus. This bad old police what cussed us back there in '33 stepped out the police car and told this old man, "Hands up!" This old man, when he come up, his hands up, he come up with his pistol, shot the police down, shot him dead. Soon as he shot him dead, his buddy jumped out the police car and shot the old man dead. So both of them died there on the street, the police and that old Negro man left this life together. And they say that the Negroes all night was saying, "Oh, they sure did kill a good police. I'm sorry they killed that guy."

In the early 1930s, it started in '33, we in the Party was concentrating among the miners and industrial workers, we call it "Party concentration, industrial concentration." By "concentration" I mean contacting individual people, making it a regular responsibility. If you see a person seems like he's interested, give him a leaflet to read, a *Daily Worker* to read, and if he talk interested, not to go off and stay two-three weeks before you go back. Go back while he's interested, before he lose interest, to keep cultivating, and you can tell by his talk whether he's making progress or whether he's standing still or whether he's not interested. And that's the way we would be able to choose who's best for a certain place, who's the best for the Party, who's the best for the ILD. Some of them didn't know the ILD wasn't the Party. But others knew the difference. They think, "The ILD a legal defense organization. I'll join that. I won't join no Party."

We had to use our judgment on each person. We didn't just grab anything and put him up here. If we find a person may be overanxious, we kind of let him rest a while, we didn't push him up here, cause he might be a stooge. We had to judge. We were teaching our comrades all the way down through the units, we'd teach how to approach people, how to recruit. We'd have recruiting meetings, classes on how you recruit. Because you just take a average, ordinary worker in those days, especially a steelworker, a coal miner, he wasn't like a worker in some kind of domestic job. A industrial worker, a domestic worker like that, they got two different outlooks. Maybe the worker in the mine is a guy who don't talk much. He know how to dig coal, he know how to do everything in that steel plant, but he come out here, he don't have nothing to say. He don't express hisself. So you got to take all that into account when you recruiting, when we talk about industrial concentration.

Now you take a guy working as a chauffeur, he see a lot, he got a lot to talk about, right, but his outlook is not like the guy working in the steel plant, because he ain't facing that hot steel or facing that coal everyday. He's doing light work, right? It's a question of how they work. The railroad guy, he don't have the outlook that the coal miner have. He have a different outlook. You take a guy redcapping at the railroad or a porter at the railroad, he don't feel like a steelworker. He's tipping his hat, you know, kind of flunky-like. So you got to take all that into account to deal with people. Yet it's a many of them good people. But I'm trying to show the different thinking.

A guy, down here, the railroad guy, here the insurance writer, here a schoolteacher, they're workers. But they got a party somewhere they going to tonight. Old coal miner, he going to bed at night, cause he ain't able to make it to the party. They workers, but they line all different altogether, big time, big parties, having big outings somewhere. They ain't got time to talk about working class oppression. But you talk to a steelworker, coal miner, he got time to talk about it, because he got to face it every morning, got to go back to the mine.

I'm showing you why it's important to work on the steelworkers, coal miners, the basic industrial workers, because they know how it feel, they all have the same feeling, see, they go in that mine, every one know that feeling in that mine. When they go in that steel plant, everyone know how it feel, facing that hot steel. Maybe he doing a different job. Some may be punching, some may be trimming steel, but they all know how it feels to be in hard work, dangerous work.

But now you take out here, the guy, bellhop, you know, schoolteacher, people like that, they don't know how that feel. But they workers. I ain't said they ain't workers. You ain't going to negate these people, because they schoolteachers. You work with them too. Interest them, them that you can. But this worker, if you don't get that basic worker, what can stop the wheels of production, you lacking, you still lacking.

Efforts on industrial workers, that's your main baby. You got to nurse that baby, but you ain't going to let the baby over here go hungry because you trying to nurse this one. You try to give him something too, but you got to be sure of this one. You find out what they problems are, find out what they mad about. The basic industrial workers always grumbling about something. And on the basis of they dissatisfaction, you pick out one or two of the issues, and you try to sample this one person, these two, few people, you draft a leaflet on just that one grievance.

The leaflet don't have to talk about everything, just talk about one thing. You tell what's going on, tell how it's happening, but let the workers help to write it. Don't you write it. Involve them all the way through. Make them believe that they somebody. In other words, make them feel that they doing it, and not you doing it for them.

Then you sit down and show them how to fold up eight or ten leaflets, fold them up with the headlines on the outside where they'll draw attention. Then show them how you put them separate in they ·pocket, then when they go in the shop they drop them so don't nobody see them drop them. Drop one here, drop one yonder. Maybe they don't get but two or three in the shop. But them two or three is valuable cause if enough workers get to reading it and looking around, you start something. You sow the seed. That's the way we were working with the ore miners and the coal miners.

We put out a paper, called it the *Hot Blast*. It was a coal and steel paper, two or three pages of it, like a bulletin. And in that it was written about certain grievances, or certain things that happen in a steel plant. And this group over here at the steel plant could write they story, and over at the coal mine, write they story, and it would appear in this *Hot Blast,* came out every month, once a month. Maybe William Mitch[5] had a general statement made coming out in the newspapers, and maybe what he's saying we considered was contrary to the interests of the rank and file members of the mine. The *Hot Blast* would criticize Mitch.

During that time in 1933, during the time of the NRA when we was organizing coal miners, I was active in Collegeville, I was living there. I was the bureau representative for that section. We had a section committee in there. I was foreman for the section, and the section got two or three units. The Party and the unemployed block committees, I was responsible for both.

In the section, I got two or three people. I got just two or three people I sit down with and we talk, we plan. Each one go back to they group and on down. That's the way we did. I didn't go running around to every little bunch to have to see everybody. Maybe we going to have a leaflet put out—say we meet Friday night and we have a report to get word we going have a city-wide distribution of leaflets Wednesday night.

I already maybe done been told where the leaflets going to be. Leaflets going to be brought to Collegeville area, that certain places they going to be left at. So now I got to see to each one of these people getting they share and going back to they group. They go, get every member there involved, get ready to put the leaflets out Wednesday night. It was just like a network.

I didn't have to worry about what was going on outside Collegeville. They going see to they task. I'm going see to my tasks. All I got to do is see my two-three people and they get they people. They put the leaflets out, come on back to the house. That's just how easy it was. In thirty minutes, we'd cover the whole city of Birmingham with leaflets. It was easy because we was well organized, very well organized.

We would always put them out by night, about first dark, when a person could not be identified so easy by another neighbor if they were seen putting a leaflet on their doorstep or on their porch or in their yard gate from the sidewalk. There were many ways that we would work out with members to get their leaflets. Some of us would have a close friend or friends that would take a few leaflets and put them out in their community or in their shop or mine.

We didn't take anything for granted. We had a system there to check up on each other in putting out our Party leaflets, and no one would know who was checking up on who. I remember one occasion in 1933 where we had a leaflet distribution, and a Negro member of the Party, member of the section committee, the name of John Gordon, on the southside of Birmingham, was given a bunch of ten or fifteen leaflets to put out. In the check-up meeting, everybody was telling how they put out their leaflets. John didn't know there's checking behind him. When we check up on John Gordon and his leaflets by talking to the people in that community, it was found that nobody had seen the leaflets in his area. We went to his territory, and we didn't find nobody know anything about the leaflets. They hadn't seen none.

At our meetings we not only had the members to make their reports about how and where they put out their leaflets, we would have a free discussion that everybody was free to take part in. John's telling all about the leaflets, how he had been back in his area where he put out his leaflets and how the people was talking about how they liked the leaflet that they had read, and how the person that he talk with gave they leaflet to another neighbor or close friend. We all just sat there that had been out in his area where he was to put out his leaflets and had talk to several people.

We just let him report all he want to, talk. First we praise such people's report, then we ask questions. Then all we got to do is just to wind him up in these questions: "Where did you put your leaflets? You say certain people's been talking about them, but we went through there." I went through there, I was one of the people who checked up on John. I said, "I went through there, and I found ain't nobody know anything about those leaflets. I asked three or four people, nobody ain't seen the leaflets." So when I get down to that, then he goes to giving in. You see guys go to sweating then, cause the questions getting too sharp.

At that point, John began to scratch and wiggle in his chair and also getting balled up on what he had first reported about his leaflets. And finally someone put the question to him, "John, just what *did* you do with your leaflets? You didn't put them out in that area that you told us you put them out in." Finally he came out and told what he did with his leaflets. He put them in a sewer manhole in the street. And then we all showed him just how he was helping the bosses against the interest of the oppressed Negro and poor white workers who could not get sufficient food to eat and clothing to keep themselves and their children warm from the cold winter weather.

After that exposure of John's lying report about his carrying out of that assignment of putting out his leaflets, we began to find out more and more about him, until it became very clear that he was a police pimp. He was seen more than once talking with the Birmingham police, at a time when none of us had any trust in the police and neither in anyone who spent time with the police. John was dropped out of the Party and the ILD branch, and the word was passed among all the Party and all other friends and contacts about our distrust in John on the basis of what he had been found lying about and also talking with the police.*

* The last time that I can remember seeing him after that exposure was in 1952. I was passing through Opelika Alabama, and spotted him standing on a street corner. He did not see or recognize me at that time. That was the last I seen of John Gordon.

10

National Training School

I couldn't do much reading, but I had a good mother wit. And I had a lot of room in my head to learn. My head wasn't full of this bourgeois education, bourgeois ideas, that if I be a good guy, I can get rich, and that if I don't get rich, it's my fault. I've lived and learned, and anything I was able to learn was through studying the program of the Party, through Marxism-Leninism. I found out where the trouble was, who was responsible for people being poor. First I learned from discussing and listening. I was a great listener and didn't do much talking, cause I couldn't explain myself. I'd get in meetings, but I didn't know what the words meant.

The Scottsboro case had got me interested in trying to read, but I had to spell every word before I said it. If it was "is," I had to say "I-S, is." Then after I became connected to the Party, I still was trying to read a little more but I had a very hard time, especially pronouncing big words, until 1934, when I went to the National Training School for ten weeks.

In early 1934—fact of it, it was January 1st—three of us left Birmingham on New Year's morning to hobo to New York, to go to the National Training School. We were told by the D.O. we would have to hobo, because he didn't have enough money to pay our way to New York. He said, "You can go to school, but you have to hobo." And here in the dead heart of the winter, January 1st, and he said, "You can't go through Virginia, you have to go around through Ohio, cause if you go through Virginia you liable to get picked off by the railroad detectives. They don't allow hobo-ing in the state of Virginia." He didn't make no arrangements for us to ride a bus. Sent us on the freight train. We had $13 among all three of us. It was myself, Eddie, a young fellow from Louisiana (one of those creole fellows—I don't know whether he's white or creole or Negro or what), and Ward Turner.

That last day of December '33 it rained all day. We went out on the railroad that Sunday night, which New Year's morning going to be Monday morning. We were out in the woods there in Woodlawn and went to wait for a freight train. We didn't know when the train was going to run, so we went out there along about 9 o'clock that night. We stayed out there beside a tree till the morning at 6 o'clock, before the train run.

These other two boys, they had been used to hoboing, but I had never been on a train to ride 10 feet to hobo before. They told me to catch the train first so I wouldn't get left. When the train run up, going by, they showed me how to catch the car on the front end, in order not to get swung around between the cars. I caught the car, but when I grabbed the car and went to raise my feet up to climb on that car, my overcoat had me shackled. I had my overcoat buttoned all the way up on me. The train was going slow enough, going up a grade there in Woodlawn. It running slow enough for you to run along and catch it. But when it began to pick up speed, I still hadn't got my feet where I could get them up in that step. So all I could do then was just to ball myself up and fall loose from the train. I helt my legs together where they wouldn't flop under the wheels, and I just strung off and rolled down off the track. The railroad track was up on a grade, on gravel, and I skint all my knuckles of my hand up on that gravel. The other boys hadn't got on then, and we had to wait until another train came.

The next train came by about 6:30, freight train, and that time I undid my coat and got on. It was raining all day that day, so we got under one of these high coal cars, one of these gondola coal cars. We got back under the end of it, back over the wheels. You see, these gondola cars, they slope in like that, and under here there's room. That's the way we rode all the way from Birmingham to Chattanooga.

We got in Chattanooga that afternoon, along about 2 or 3 o'clock. It was getting cold up there. We caught a train out from Chattanooga and went into Knoxville Tennessee. We got in Knoxville Tennessee sometime along about dark. We got a train out from Knoxville to Cincinnati—we got in a boxcar. But now it's getting cold up in that part, snowing.

We got in Cincinnati the next morning at sun-up. When the train stopped, we had to get off the car we was on before it got in the yard. The car we was on was right over a high fill, over a underpass. It was a very small space to get out of that car, out of the door, down, without falling on down in that underpass. I was very nervous, very scared, but I had to get off there. If I didn't, I going to be carried in the yard where the detectives would get me. So we all jumped off out the door, and I was able to hold on and not fall down the underpass, and walk outside the car.

In those days, every city around a railroad, you had hobo jungles. So we inquired of the hobo jungle. We asked anybody. Anybody could tell you where the hobo jungle was around the railroad, just a ordinary person would know. Everybody was hoboing then. You had plenty friends hoboing. Wont no strangers. We went down the hobo jungle, under a big overhead bridge going over the railroad. We were back up under the abutment here. There was a great, large oil barrel, had been knocked the head out of it with holes in the side, like you take a pick and knock holes in the side. It was full of coal, just hot, red, cherry red. We went there and hung around there all day. Every hobo would leave, he leave the fire. Nobody but just us three there.

We found a restaurant up the street. We go up there, get us a sandwich, then try to wait for the freight train to leave. Finally about sundown, a freight train started out. We didn't catch it. It was running too fast for us to catch it. And after, it was a detective looking at us. The detective waved his pistol and told us to get out the yard. So what we did, we went on back up to this restaurant. That was about sundown now. Later a freight train started out, so we got that train. It was a cattle train. We wont supposed to ride that train, but we caught it.

It wont nowhere to ride but up on top of the cars. First I was standing between the cars with a foot on each stub of each car. The car was shaking so, running so fast, till I don't know how long I'm going stay there. I afraid even to move, to try to turn around to try to get them stirrups to climb up on the car. The other boys was up on the train, up on the top of the car. Finally some of them say, "Hosie," say, "come up on top." And I got up enough nerve to hold on with my one hand and move one foot off of this car to come over to the next stub, put both feet on that stub, then I climb up on top of the car. It looked like you was a feather going fly off.

I laid down and my head towards the engine, so the air was

blowing over me. My cap had a rabbit lining over my ears. I had on some gloves with rabbit lining, and I had my arm across my forehead like that, and my face down here. I felt something hit my head, but I couldn't tell what it was. I thought it was cinders from the train—it was just flying down that track. When the train run into this yard in Columbus Ohio, I went to get up and I found out that was sleet hitting on me. I had a cake of ice had done caked on me all back of my neck and all down my back. All on the car was slick. Even the things you hold was slick, cold.

We got off that train, and it was so cold, until we just got off, went on out across the yard, went on out. The first thing we see was a big light. We went through to that. It was where they was sorting the mail at. We just walked out through there, people looking at us, we went out on the street, cause it was cold and we didn't care now. We went out to the highway.

After we got up there in Ohio, I got to the point where I just didn't care. I learnt then about what a soldier's like when he get in a jungle. He just get where he don't care whether he live or die. He don't have no feelings. It was just a matter of you sleepy and you drowsy, and you ain't been to bed, you needs a good bath, you needs a shave. And all that's on you, see. Then you cold. You have on a plenty clothes, but it's cold. I got to the point I didn't want no fire. We got downcast and everything else, but we didn't give up.

Up on the highway we found another place where they stayed open all night, where they sold sandwiches, hot dogs, on the outskirts of the town. There we sent a telegram back to Birmingham for some money. It was snowing. We stayed there till the next morning, and they sent us a little money. We left there, and we got another train. We went to the hobo jungle, got a long government train, fruit cars. It was so long till you couldn't see the engine on either end. All the hoboes was standing off on the side. Nobody would attempt to get that train. Someone said, "You better not get that. It's hot." It mean hot cars, you wont supposed to ride them, was government cars. Everybody stood out and looked at that train till it passed. We wouldn't catch that train. Let that one pass.

We was all standing on the side, on the track, standing on the bank. A whole lot of guys. Finally then came another train, nothing but empty cars. When it came along, everybody got on that train. It was a engine on that end and a engine on this end. And we rode and rode and rode, till finally when it did come to a stop, they took a whole lot of them empty cars and set them on a side track. A man come up the track, said, "If you all want to go on, you better get on up yonder, cause they ain't going take these cars anywhere. They going start up yonder." And everybody went to walking up the railroad track. It was a good ways to walk, maybe a quarter of a mile. That was a long train of empty cars. We walked up there till them cars was took off, and then the engine way up yonder had took them other cars and come up here and hooked up with these others. We got on these up here and that was the one what carried us into Pittsburgh. It was Wednesday night when we got into Pittsburgh.

We went into a place where they selling sandwiches and hot dogs. There was a Negro sitting up against the counter, eating a sandwich. The other boys told me to ask him did he know where we could find a place to sleep. I asked him, and he said, "Go down the street about three blocks down there to the temple." We didn't know what the temple was. He just said, "temple." So we got out and walked on down to the temple.

We got down to the temple. The temple was the police headquarters. We walked in. In those days, people was sleeping in police headquarters.*

We went in there, and a big sergeant was sitting at the desk with his badge on, uniform, everything. He said, "What can I do for you boys?" We wanted to know could we get a bed for the night. He said, "Yes, I got beds 15¢, 25¢, 35¢. Which bed you want?"

I thought a 35¢ bed might have been a little better. I told him, "give me a 35¢ bed." I don't remember what bed the other fellows got, but they broke us up there. We didn't sleep together. They had a key-boy, and the key-boy carried me on around there, and we got in there where all the bunks, three-deck bunks. So mine was on the low bunk next to the floor.

I hadn't been to bed since Saturday night, and this was Wednesday night, near up about Thursday morning 12:30–1 o'clock. I got in there and slept and slept. I got out the next morning and went to shower. They give you a towel, soap, all this was in the jailhouse. So I took a good bath. And you know, it was fellows working and staying in that place, working in the steel plant and living in the jail.

I went on outside, stood out there till the other two guys came

* All over, even down Birmingham, whites was sleeping in. I don't know about putting up the Negroes, but I heard that whites go to the police station to be put up at night.

out. I didn't know whereabouts they's located. We went back up to this place and got us some meatballs and spaghetti. That was the first time I ever ate any meatballs and spaghetti in my life, was at that place that day. We went then back to the hobo jungle. We got down there, and they had a lot of fellows, guys going different directions. They ask you, "Which-a-way you going, buddy?"

"I'm trying to go such-and-such a way."

"Your train leave at such-and-such a time." They know what time to tell you the train leave. So that morning we caught a train out there and went into Newcastle Pennsylvania. It was around midnight or 1 or 2 o'clock when we got off the train. It's snowing, sleet, rain, doing each one a while. It would snow and sleet a while. It would snow a while, then rain a while. Slushy!

When we got off the train, we walked on through the town, and we inquired how to get to the railroad on the other side the town. We went on over through the town—we didn't know anything about it—down to the railroad.

Down by the railroad, twas a beer factory, and the man was firing a boiler. About half of the door was open, the upper part; down here, the part was closed. Just half the door open to get some air. Beautiful light in there, and it was warm. We walked up there and asked him could we come in.

"No. We lose our job. We lose our job. We can't let you in here, can't let you in." It was bad.

But out on the spur railroad track, twas a railroad car, very clean, had a lot of paper, lined with heavy paper. We got in that car and pulled the door up and had a railroad spike—Turner had the spike, I don't know where he find it—where the door wouldn't close up on us. If it close up, we couldn't get out.

We went back in the end of that car. We had some matches, and we just pulled down little strips of paper and light the paper, and kept alighting a little piece, light a little piece, until we had that heat all in that car. And then we laid down in the floor and we slept till we get cold. Then we get up and jump, flip-flip, flip-flip, flip-flip. Just jump till we get hot. And that's the way we spent the night there.

The next morning we got up, went out to a place, we got us a sandwich and went back and sit around there. We sit there in the place where we got the sandwich till afternoon, just talking. Went back out on the railroad—was near the Allegheny River, cause I seen a boat go down the river with these pedals behind it, big wheels turning over and over, big thing. It was the first boat like that I seen. We set on the railroad track and it got real cold. We had to push snow off the railroad track to have where to sit down, trying to wait for a freight train, out there on the railroad. Finally a freight train came along, going to New York, and we got that and we got in Baltimore just about sundown. That was on Saturday evening. The train kept on up to Philadelphia. The trains was running fast, so fast that the wind was just cutting you like a icicle. We was on a flatcar, several hoboes was on the flatcar. It was down between two high cars, big boxcars, and that wind coming around. Oh! Cold! That wind was cutting so till we three got off at Philadelphia. Decided we didn't want to hold it down no further. We got to Philadelphia Saturday around 11 p.m. The other hoboes was trying to make it on to New York.

We three jumped off. It was raining when we got there, but we done got so tired of fighting that wind till we got off the train, walked off, come off the fill, come on down on the street. The trolley came along, and we asked the guy on the trolley how could we get to the seamen's hall.

When we got to the seamen's hall, they taken us out for some supper. We didn't have no money, they given us some food. We didn't eat at the hall, they was having a party there that night, having a dance. After they fed us, they put us up for the night. They give us some food Sunday, put us back up Sunday night. We set round there till Monday.

Monday morning we went to the Party headquarters in Philadelphia. We stayed there all day, try to get a phone call to New York. We done got out of money again. So along when they got ready to close the Party office that evening about dark, we still ain't got no hearing from New York, ain't got no money. So there in the Party office they give us $2 among us three to try to make New York.

We went down on the railroad, we got a freight train, and we rode that train on and on, all in the night, and we got somewhere in Jersey. The train, sometimes it run so slow going up a grade, we'd get off, walk along side the car. We's riding on a car of scrap iron, out in the cold. When it got on a grade, we'd get off, walk side the train, it was just moping along. It was cold. It was uncomfortable to sit up there in the cold on nothing but scrap iron. After the train get over the grade, go to picking up, we get on the car and ride. We just got tired of it.

Finally we got off, walked out, got on the highway, went to walking. About five sets of highway patrols would meet us and ask us where we going. We had our line. My line was I had a uncle in New York and he told me if I could get up there, he could help me get a job. That was my line. The other boys had a nice line. We told them the same line. We said we knowed each other, but everybody was going to New York for a different purpose. I was coming from Atlanta, I wont coming from Birmingham.

Eventually we got a bus somewhere, I don't know where that was, got to a bus. That bus carried us down to the Courtland Street ferry, and the fare over was a nickel. All the money we had between us was one nickel. We had done ate up that $2, and riding that trolley, where we was on that bus to ride down to the river, you paid fare on that too.

I was the onliest one that knew the way over, so I left the others down there, and I caught the boat and came across. Then I walked from the Courtland Street ferry, from the river, up to Union Square, to 35 East 13th Street, to the Party headquarters. I had been there the summer before, and I knowed James Ford and Harry Haywood. I told them what our problem was. Oh, they raised the devil!

Them two Negroes, they pitched a wolf, because the D.O. in Birmingham had put us out in the cold weather, put us on that cold trip to hobo all the way up there. The way they talked, they had the money. They could of payed our way. (I never did know the depths of it, but the D.O., Don, was called to New York and put on the carpet about sending us, having us to hobo up there through that cold weather. Harry Haywood and James Ford, I think they raised the whole question in the national committee, cause they was members of the national committee. Don was up there, but what was said to him I never did know. I know when we got back, he said, "You all cause me to catch hell up there." I know he said that. He was crazy about his prestige, that fellow Don was.)

They put us before the doctor that evening, to examine us to see had we caught a cold. Along about 6 o'clock, they taken us in a big limousine, a Cadillac or something, and lit out to carry us to Camp Nitgedaiget,[1] to the National Training School.

We had supper and they put us to bed, and they wanted us to

stay in the bed a day or two until we got a rest. They brought my breakfast to the bed, up to my room, wanted to be sure I wouldn't get sick, wouldn't take pneumonia. Eddie had wrenched his ankle. He had a tub, and it was quite a while before he was able to walk on his ankle good. I had done skint all my knuckles on my fist, where I fell off the train, and that had got cold. It was all swole up, my hands was popped up.

I stayed in the bed the next day until about 11 o'clock, then I got up, went down in the cafeteria and had dinner. That afternoon I just went on down and set in the classsoom, listen at the others. I was ready to go.

We didn't get up there till the 8th of January, and all the rest of the students was there. Twas about thirty-seven in all, from all different parts, white and black. We had one black woman in the group.

They had one guy there, I don't know where he's from, but he had a very high education from a college, but from a bourgeois point of view. That working-class understanding on that blackboard, it was hard for him to get it. I thought once there they was going to have to put him out the class, cause he would try to fight for his position. All the students was working-class, but some of them's college people. Some of them from steel plants, but here's this guy, he looked more like a white-collar student. And he was younger. One young woman from Florida, she just didn't have no business being in the class at all, cause she wont ready for it. She wont developed, but she was there. We had another young woman from Chicago, and they was completely different in the two outlooks. This one from Florida, her political understanding was very low. And this one from Chicago was a very well politically developed young woman.

The instructor we had there, we call him "Pop" Mindel.[2] He's a elderly fellow, a Jewish fellow, and his English was very bad, his speaking English. I couldn't understand half of what he was saying. But eventually I was able to learn what he said.

We'd have lectures. Pop Mindel would have a blackboard, and he would lecture and write on the blackboard. What you had to do, you had to learn from the blackboard, instead of learning from the book. If he's discussing political economy, how capitalism developed and how it decayed and how it deteriorated, the rise and fall, the crisis of capitalism, he'd put that on the board. You'd be able to learn from his discussion. For an instance, he'd take the words, "constant capital plus variable capital." He'd put "constant + variable capital = surplus value." Then "relative surplus value and absolute surplus value."

Now you'd have to learn that by heart, to explain the difference. Then they'd show the rise and fall of capitalism, you'd see it zigzags, just like the stock market, it zigzags, up today, down tomorrow. He had all that on the blackboard. And then how the economic crisis takes place, how it come about, overproduction, underconsumption. That was his first lecture. He give that maybe for a week or more. Then after that, he call on the students. You'd have to explain, see how much you know about it. I had already discussed some of that back in Birmingham, the imperialist war, in unit meetings. It wasn't all new there, but I was able to understand it more clearly, and the meaning of it. After the lectures, you'd have a reading. You'd read in your room or your group. You wouldn't come out here and read it in the open.

We studied the history of the trade union movement, the history of the Party, the whole question of China,[3] and we discussed Roosevelt in that period. They considered his position was reactionary, at that time, that he was taking a semi-fascist position. Back in those years it was already out at that school that Britain and France and the United States was building Hitler up to attack the Soviet Union. Hitler had already come to power in '33. I remember one night we had a man there who was in Germany, a writer. He lectured there on how they was torturing people in Germany at that time, taking people down in boiler rooms and stripping them, and they push them and push them, till they push them up against them hot boilers, naked, with no clothes on, trying to make them talk.

Everybody was organized into what you call social competition. There was a young white minister, Jim Gray, twenty-six years old, and I was thirty-six. He was a poetry writer, he liked poetry. He was a mountaineer from up there in north Georgia. His people fought on the side of the Union Army, never no slavery in his family. This was the first time I met him, when our instructor assigned him and me together. His task was to get me straightened out on my reading.

Every day for thirty minutes or maybe three-quarters of a hour, a certain time at night, we'd go into a room and he would have me to read, stop me from saying "T-H-E, the" before I say it. That's what got me kind of straightened out. When I left I could read much better. (It's a whole lot of words now I can't pronounce today, because a lot of our Party people writes big words that they don't hardly know. They have to look in the dictionary to spell it themselves. I give them the devil about it.)

After we got there, got started, Pop Mindel organized a leading bureau. I was on the bureau, it was a bureau of about six people, the leadership of that group of thirty-seven. They made me chairman of the house committee of our bureau. My task was seeing to everybody going to bed on time, going to the rooms, not being up all night, keeping order in the building among the students, and then also seeing to who wash the dishes. I had a committee, and me and my committee would set down—this group will wash dishes today, another group wash dishes tomorrow, all the way around. We were getting 50¢ a week for cigarettes, tobacco, what they call the subsidy. They give me all the money, and I pass around to everybody 50¢. I'm the paymaster, so I'm getting along pretty good.

We had to take so much exercise every morning, volleyball. We got friendly, but everybody had fictitious names. You didn't use your regular name, and you didn't tell where you's from either. Sometime, after you come to know a guy, you'd say, "You know, I'm from Chicago," but you just didn't get up, open, and say, "I'm from Alabama." I was from the South, but I didn't say from Birmingham. It was like that. My name was Henry Thornton.

We had one incident happen there that I settled myself. It was a guy going in one of the women's rooms at night. And they was carrying on all in the open, practically, had got to the point where they was acting like man and wife. They didn't care who see it. Now this Jim Gray, the minister that learnt me how to read, he was as sharp as death in the middle of that stuff. He didn't believe in that stuff. The South, you know, they was religious people. So me and him was rooming together, and he says to me, he says, "Comrade Thornton, I just don't approve of this stuff. I think it's a disgrace, and you, as chairman of the house committee, you ought to do something about it." I didn't know just what to do. I didn't want to go to Pop Mindel about it, so I called the house committee together, and I raised this question about these people slipping into each others' rooms.

I knowed that if I just came out and raised it, the guy slipping would ask, "Who's saying these things?" I didn't want to tell him it was Jim Gray was saying it, because I felt if Jim raised it, being white, these white guys would tear him apart, the North and the

South. You had that. So before the meeting of the house committee, I go and get Comrade Hill, a boy from Camp Hill, a eighteen-year-old Negro, and I get him to say that *he's* raising it, because he wasn't used to all this stuff, being a young fellow, *he* thought it was a disgrace.

So when we got in the meeting that night, this guy who was slipping,* he says, "Nobody tell me how to live my life, as long as it don't affect nobody else, I don't see why . . ." and blah, blah, blah. And he wanted to know who was saying it. He was talking all out loud, "Who is saying it?"

I says, "All right, Comrade Hill." I says, "All right Hill, explain to them what you discuss with me." And Hill just come out and tore them apart.

He said, "I think we here to learn Marxism-Leninism, and the comrades at home have sent us here, sacrificing. I think we ought to lay all this personal stuff aside," he said. "I know it's affecting me to see all this going on at night, and I'm the one raising the question." Then that give Gray a chance to come out and say what he wanted to say.

I played some smart politics that meeting. And I broke it up. At least, I might not have broke it up, but it made them more careful. So that's the way I worked it. You regular have to use your head. It ain't what you do. It's how you do it, what effect it's going to have. That was one ordeal then, but it wont hardly the biggest.

We had a case of white chauvinism there in that class. You'd be surprised how this racism and white chauvinism can develop. We had a young black fellow, Miller, in his early twenties. He liked to put lotion on his face. He liked to do his hair up, primp up. So these two girls was rooming together on the women's hall, one from Florida, named Gloria, one from Chicago, both these white. The one from Florida, he had borrowed a little pair of scissors from her, to cut something up there in his room. Whatever he was fixing, he needed a pair of scissors. So she loaned him the scissors. He didn't carry them back. She asked him about them, and he said, "I got them, I'll bring them back to you."

Then he borrowed from the other girl a little jar of face cream. He taken that up to his room. He used some of it, and she asked him about bringing it back. "Yeah, I'll bring it back. I'm a bring it

* I think he was killed in the Spanish War over there fighting Franco.

back." But he still didn't bring it. So she got vehement, "When you going to bring my cream back? I need my cream!"

"I'm a bring it, I'm a bring it." So finally, when he did bring the cream down to her room, the two girls and two white guys was sitting there in the room—in the girls' room. So when the fellow brought the cream in, he handed this girl from Chicago—it was hers—and she said, "Why, Miller, you done used up half my cream out this jar!"

"No, I didn't! I didn't use none but one time."

She say, "Yes you did. This jar of cream was just about full. You done about used it all up."

"No I didn't. I didn't use it all up. I didn't use all that cream up!"

So she turned to the other girl from Florida and say, "Wont this jar of cream about near full?"

She said, "Yes, that jar of cream was just about full of cream." She from Florida, she made the remark, "Now Miller, listen. You know you borrowed my scissors and hasn't brought them back. If you don't tell the truth about this cream, I'm going to call you a thief and a liar."

Whew! That's a typical racist remark, to call a Negro a thief and a liar. So that set off one of the worst battles you ever had. He flew hot, "Calling me a thief and a liar!" He flew hot. Quite naturally he would. The other two guys sitting there, they didn't say nothing.

They was raising sand down on the lower end. I knowed it was going on, but I'd stay out of these places. When I see something developing, I didn't never see nothing. I'd get away.

It was about noontime, and Pop Mindel come up and say, "What you all doing in here? Get out, take a hike, take a hike! Get some fresh air!" So when I hear them down there raising sand—he's all up at the top of his voice—I get my coat and hat. Snow out here about half-knee deep. But I hurried and got out cause I knowed twas something going on down here. I went out in the snow, went walking. I don't want to be no witness for nothing.

So Pop Mindel went down that end of the hall, "What's wrong? What's wrong in here?"

Miller say, "She called me a thief and a liar," and then he start to tell how it happen. Pop Mindel calm everybody down, send them outside. After we got back from walking, we take lunch. Then we got to deal with this thing.

After lunch, Pop Mindel called the class into session. He assigned the young woman that was more or less his helper, he assigned her the task to take over the class. Then he called a meeting with the bureau members. He called us all up in another room for a big bureau meeting.

Pop says, "Comrades," he says, "we got a situation here where I was hoping that we wouldn't have, wouldn't develop in this little school." He told us all what had happened, then he says, "We going have to postpone our class tonight. We going to have to have a discussion on this thing."

At the night session, after supper, we have to have out with Miller and these two girls—we ain't going have no class. So I'm up here now with the rest of the bureau members at the table at the front. All the bureau members was sitting behind the table.

Pop Mindel got up, and he lectured and he explained and he proved that this was a act of white chauvinism, something that the Party did not tolerate. He had Miller and the two girls sitting over here, and after he outlined and all, he had Miller to speak. Miller, he got up and told the story, what about the cream and everything, and what he had done and what he hadn't done. Then he begin to tear these girls apart, "They called me a thief and a liar," and how that was a blot on his integrity as a leader, cause it wasn't just him, but it was his section what sent him there, as a leader from that section.*

When he got through making these charges, then these girls, especially this one from Chicago, she got up to show her side of the picture, on the basis of defending herself, because he took her cream. She still hadn't seen this as a act of white chauvinism, not there, not yet. She said it wasn't her intention and she was sorry. But you had to go beyond the words of sorry, you had to prove a little more than that.

When she got through, they called Gloria, the girl from Florida, to make her statement. She just didn't know what to say. She was just a amateur on a point like that. She tried to make her statement the best she could, she's sorry, she cried, and all like that.

Then these two guys was in there, one of them named Bogart and the other was Evans. Now this girl from Florida, Evans had been slipping in the room with her at night, see, and I knew it. I had spoke to Pop Mindel about it, cause I didn't want it to get out, they

---

* We found out later he was from Harlem, but that didn't come out there.

say I know it, but I won't say nothing, I don't know how to handle the situation. So I goes to Pop Mindel, tell him, I said, "Listen here, you got something up there and I don't know what to do with it." I said, "I'm chairman of the house committee, and my job is to see that these people all in their rooms after 9:30 at night. "Now after 9:30," I said, "Evans had been seen going into this girl's room." And I said, "The other comrades see it, and they brought it to me." I said, "I don't know what to do with it."

It wont no rule against the getting together, they could get together after 9:30 if they was a class or a discussion or something. But you couldn't walk around. You going to class the next morning early, you getting up early. You couldn't stay up late at night. (Except Saturday night. Saturday night we'd be up late, have banquets and all.) But you couldn't be walking in the hallway, because you had other people on the second floor. You had guests there from the trade unions and everywhere, was on the second floor. This was a place where everybody came, so these students, they's not there by theyself. The other people there, trade union guys' wives and different people, they come out there for a couple of days, some be there for a week, for a vacation, to get a rest. You can't have these students disturbing them.

It wont a rule against sex, unlessen it come to be a problem. Long as you can do it and it's not known, one person know it, or two, it's all right. But don't let everybody—everybody not supposed to know it. And Evans was doing it and this one knowing and different people began to raise the question: "Evans is slipping in that girl's room at night." And I don't know what to do with it. I can't handle this one like I did the other one with Gray and the boy from Camp Hill. So I talked to Pop Mindel. And Pop Mindel said, "You can't be too rigid, unlessen it come to be a political question. If it come to be a political question damaging to the Party, then we have to deal with it."

So now Evans was on the bureau. And this girl done got in trouble. After she explain herself, Pop Mindel call on Evans as a member of the bureau. He's sitting up there at the table, as a leader, but he been going to bed with her, with this girl, slipping in there.

Evans spoke out against her. Oh, he was vicious against her. I mean he was a political orator. The idea of she accusing Miller of being a thief and a liar, and Miller a Negro, and all like that. When he got through, Pop Mindel says, "Comrade Evans, what have you done to try to develop Comrade Gloria?" (Oh, he was a *mess,* that Pop Mindel, he was something!)

So Evans explain he done this, he done that, and "I've discussed with her," and everybody know about he been slipping in the room. Everybody looking at each other. But Evans didn't know that everybody know, and Pop Mindel know he been slipping.

Pop Mindel come to his final point. He's asking Evans, "Do you think you was helping Comrade Gloria when you was slipping in her room at night when the other comrades supposed to been in their rooms asleep?"

Evans couldn't say nothing. I'm telling you, he looked like a minnow. He had been a big shot, been a big fish, but now he looking like a minnow. Right there, in front of all the students, everybody, Pop Mindel asked Comrade Evans to resign his post as a member of the bureau—took him down, sit him out there in the audience with the other people.

Well, now, there's Bogart. Bogart was sitting in there too that afternoon. He wasn't going to bed, he was just there. Pop Mindel asked Bogart, "Comrade Bogart, did you hear this discussion?"

"Yeah, I heard it."

"What did you say?" He was the prosecutor, Pop Mindel.

"I didn't say anything."

"You didn't take no part in it, either way?"

"No. I felt it wasn't none of my business."

"Do you think you being a leader of the Party, and you hear such a discussion as this, acts of white chauvinism, and you have no part in it?" There he begins to choke him. What Bogart done, he was indulging white chauvinism. He didn't fight against it. He didn't take no part, but that's indulging. After a while, Pop Mindel got through, and he got nearly all the bureau members to speak. I was so scared, I'm telling you.

Then Pop Mindel call on me. I wasn't used to talking out in public, afraid that I don't know how to explain myself. I was automatically afraid, don't ask me why. I just was afraid. And I was the onliest Negro on the bureau. So here I am. We done heard practically everybody speak, and I ain't said nothing.

"Comrade Thornton!"

I said yeah.

"In the South, when a white landlord accuse a Negro of stealing chickens, of stealing some corn, of stealing some cotton, and yet the

Negro might be innocent, and that landlord begin to whip that Negro, what do the other landlords do, if they there in the presence, Thornton?"

I said, "In most cases, they don't say anything. They might sometime turn they back, don't look at it, but they won't say nothing."

"They don't tell him to stop, do they?"

I said no.

"Don't care how much he whip, they won't walk up there, stop him from whipping."

I said, "No, they won't stop him from whipping. I ain't never knowed that to happen."

"Wasn't that what Comrade Bogart was doing?"

I said yeah.

"Wasn't he acting like this landlord in the South, who don't take no part and don't say nothing, don't stop them?"

I said, "That's right." You see where he done place him? Well, we finished for now, but we going to talk tomorrow night, come back again.

After that discussion got so hot, Miller seen that he hadn't got to the depths of it, when he's making his charges at first. So that next day, he comes to Pop Mindel told him, "I wants to make a statement before we open the meeting tonight." So that night, Pop Mindel says that Comrade Miller wants the floor before further discussion.

Comrade Miller, he got up, and he said he felt that he had exaggerated the charges of white chauvinism, and he wanted to say that he should be severely criticized for making such drastic charges of white chauvinism. He felt that the charges wasn't as serious as he had put them.

When Miller made his speech, Pop Mindel asked me, said, "Comrade Thornton, don't you want to have a word to say?" He called me after Miller. That's where I like to bust.

Now here I am. I started off by saying, "I think that Comrade Miller last night presented a very clear picture of a act of white chauvinism," I said. I pointed out that the Negro in the South was accused of being a thief and a liar, and that was exactly what this girl here was doing. On the cream, she was accusing him of being a thief—he done took her cream, and he said he didn't. I said, "In the South, if a Negro is accused of stealing cotton, and he say, 'I didn't steal it,' but the white landlord say he did it, he's automatically guilty." I says, "Then the Negro's lying. He's a thief and a liar. Coming from Florida, Comrade Gloria, she says he's a liar and a thief. To my belief that's been proved beyond a doubt, and this was a gross, rank act of white chauvinism." And I said, "Now tonight, Comrade Miller come back and ridicule hisself by saying he feel that he should be tore apart because he exaggerate the charges." And I said, "I consider that this is *capitulating* to white chauvinism." Oh yeah, I done learnt to say that much, "This is a capitulation to white chauvinism, right in the heated line of the battle against white chauvinism." I said, "I think that Comrade Miller should be severely, severely criticized for his position."

And that was my statement. I know I was doing pretty good, cause here we had about three or four young women, they would sit in on the discussions. They not students, they out there for rest. They would come down in our regular sessions and sit in the back and listen, but they didn't take no part. When I was talking, I see one of them looking at the other, and bow they head like that and smile. That give me more encouragement, and I know I must have been doing pretty good.

Oh, that thing wound up everyone in there! White and black had to make a statement about white chauvinism. Some was capitulating and some was indulging, some had the right line. But it brought out everybody. Twas nearabouts a whole week, every night, before we got over.

The final analysis of it was that Miller had to write a statement criticizing himself and present it to the class. This girl from Florida couldn't sit in the classes no longer. She could be in on the lecture, but her studies, she had to be with the four women who were setting in. They taken her over. Pop Mindel said to the bureau members, "We can't have this big a battle and come out without making a decision. We can't just exonerate her and let her stay in class. We got to expel her out the class." Now the girl from Chicago, we didn't expel her, but we did severely reprimand her. And we sent reports back to both districts, Florida and Chicago, about acts of white chauvinism.

But that one battle of how the Party handled discrimination, white chauvinism against Negroes, that give me double determination that I had somewhere that I could fight for against the oppression. That one thing in itself established great confidence in me. I surprised myself, when I was able to stand up there, when I spoke out. Comrade Mindel congratulated my remarks. And here I was from the South, I hadn't been talking. That was the first major speech I made out in public. I had talked around among our people in the units, but not with no big top leaders like that before.

11

Back South

Our school closed about the third week in March, and we all went back to our various homes with our literature. We came back in a little car, a roadster. It was some minister from Atlanta, was in New York, had this little roadster, and they wanted somebody to take it back to Atlanta. So here's a good way now to get all five of us guys back South cheap, in the car: me, and Jim Gray, from Georgia, and Hill, the guy from Camp Hill Alabama, and the two guys I came up with, the creole guy Eddie, and Turner, from Birmingham.

It was something like a Ford, had a rumble seat. In them days, white and black riding together was pretty tough. We couldn't drive, me and Hill couldn't, so we put the creole guy and Reverend Gray and Turner in the front, they's white. And me and Hill was in the back, in the rumble seat. It was cold as the devil back there. That winter of 1934, that was a *cold* winter up north. But it was just a situation where we had to be arranged like that. It couldn't of been one white behind with one black. We might of been stopped on the highway. We had so much literature that we had it all packed and tied on the fender of the car, and some in the car. We left New York on Wednesday, about 11 o'clock at night on our way back south. It took to about 11 o'clock before we could get things straightened out.

So we left out of New York and come on out and come on down through, till we got to about Philadelphia, somewhere along about 2 or 3 o'clock in the morning, riding in our car. Then two motorcycle cops got alongside us, ordered us over to the side.* We stopped. Gray was driving the car at that time. Gray was from

* It was one motorcycle with a sidecar. One police was driving, the other, he sitting in the sidecar. I don't see them no more in Philadelphia now.

214

Georgia and didn't have no driver's license. In them days in the
South you didn't have to have no driver's license, but up here, you
did. He didn't have no driver's license and didn't have no ownership
of the car. So they carrying us back to the police precinct. West told
them that he was a minister and some lie about all us going back
with this material.

They carried us in there and sit us all down on a wooden bench,
long board, side the wall, the police did. One stayed in there with us
and the other one, he went back out, got a batch of our material.
Ha, ha! The guy come in there had opened up our material, throwed
it up on the long counter across there, says to Gray, says, "You's a
minister from Georgia, eh?"

Gray says yeah.

"These are your God damn Bibles! And these are your God damn
disciples you got here!"

They kept us there in Philadelphia and kept us and kept us, and
finally came up here with a paddy wagon. That paddy wagon had a
police driving it, and had the back door open and a window behind
the driver up in the front, and had these old wooden seats on the
inside. Two police was setting at the back, on each side the door in
the back, and the door was open. Two more police was riding up
there in the front. They carried us to about six different police sta-
tions that night. It was cold, and the wind blowing through the
doors and windows.

One of these police was a Negro. He was from Atlanta, a brown-
skin Negro, and in Philadelphia he was a police. He said to me on
the side, "Yeah, I'm from Atlanta Georgia myself." (We were going
back to Atlanta, that was our line. We didn't say we were going
back to Birmingham.) That Negro police said to me and Hill, "You
all shouldn't let these poor white trash be misleading you all up here
and getting you all in trouble like this." This was the Negro police.
He was our "good friend." In Philadelphia I learned about Negro
police, and that give me enough of Negro police right there, cause
along about day, they came and taken us out the last place and carried us over to another station. We set there all day, from morning
to afternoon. While we was setting there, I seen a Negro police going
at a boy about fifteen or sixteen years old. He done whipped that
boy's head like a artichoke. That Negro police, a old, gray, kind of
low, chubby, real black guy, had a old police cap. He didn't have on

a new cap, and he brought this Negro boy in there. I don't know
what the boy had done, but the Negro bleeding all in the face and
head, and that dirty police standing around with his blackjack.

At that place they's waiting, trying to get the records from Atlanta, about whether the car was stolen or not. They had accused
us of stolen car. We still ain't had no sleep now, still ain't had no
breakfast. They had carried us all around during the night before
day, mugging us and taking our pictures with a number on our
chest. The old white guy was mugging us, police, he was a old man,
he said to me, he says, "You all shouldn't let this white trash get you
up here in trouble like this." Said, "You see, we Yankees look out
for you all. We fought, we came down and helped to free you all out
of slavery." And said, "You shouldn't let them get you in trouble
like this." He was my great friend, but he was mugging my fingers
while he was talking.

Then about noon they carried us to another jail that had a great
open space with a lot of cells around the wall, like lion cages. It was
a big old space, just like lion cages, iron pickets, just like you got a
lion in something. The toilets was automatic. They start down there
on the end and automatically, they just flush, one after the other,
"Arrrrwwwww," all day and all night.

This was still Thursday. They put me and Hill in a cell together.
This place was another place like the first jail where it was just a

Hudson's mug shot, Philadelphia, 1934

board. Wont no space, was just a piece of wood and wont big as the other place. The board was something like about two feet wide and about two inches thick, just a board, and too short to stretch out on. Hill'd lay up on that board a while. When you lay down, you had to prop your knees up. You couldn't lay down. You turn on your side, you had to double your legs up. While one on the board, the other either be standing up or squatting down on the floor or setting on the concrete floor. And the toilet, it had a top on it, but not a top you could set on. It just had that lever on it, and it set up all the time. It had a spring, and when you get up, it fly up. You'd have to mash it down when you want to set on it. They automatically flush theyselves, but in order to set on it you had to pull the seat down. The start flushing up here and go one down, this one flush then the next one flush, then the next one flush, like that.

That evening they call theyselves bringing us dinner. They bring us some white beans, some pieces of boiled white meat, and some old hard French bread, I reckon you call it. It was real hard, old. That's what we had to eat for dinner. We hadn't et no breakfast. The next morning, they brought us some oatmeal with some banana cut up in it and a piece of this here shreaded white bread, and some old coffee, no sugar. It was bitter. Look like it was made out of coconut hulls or something, black and bitter, no sugar, no milk. That's what we had for breakfast. Wednesday we had started on the trip and they took us off. We done went all day Thursday. Thursday evening we got this little junk, and Friday morning we got this other little junk. That's all we've had to eat.

Friday morning they put us out on a big lineup. They put us on a big stage, like a show place, and they had a big blue curtain come across. You go in front of that curtain. They had some lights down here on the edge of the stage shining right against you, up in your face, inside that curtain. They setting out in front, behind the lights. When they get to you they say, "Boy, what your name?" I said, "My name Henry Thornton."

"Where you live?"

"Atlanta Georgia."

"You ever been arrested before?"

I said, "No, I never been arrested before." I had been arrested before, one time, but they didn't have that record. So they tell me to stand aside. Everyone, they tell you to stand aside.

In that lineup they had a white man and his wife. They asked her,

"You ever been arrested before?" She said no. "Wasn't you arrested such-and-such a time, such-and-such a place for selling whiskey?"

"Ah, yes sir." They put them in another line.

Them they found charges against, they put in one line, the ones they free, they put them in another line. I don't know what they done with them. When they got through, they took us all out from there and put us in the paddy wagon and we lit out from there into this big rock jail, in North Philadelphia on the railroad.*

At the time the tool and die makers was on strike in Philadelphia, big strike in '34. They had loaded us with a whole lot of strikers that had been arrested on the picket line. The strikers told us about getting in the jail. They said, "If you all got any tobacco or chewing gum, or anything like that, you better hide it, cause they going take it away from you when you get over there." Up in New York, before we left, they had give me a whole lot of chewing tobacco, and four or five packages of chewing gum. So I commenced trying to hide that chewing gum and tobacco. I took the chewing gum packages apart, put separate sticks all over. And the way I done the tobacco, I taken it, torn it all to pieces, put some in all my pockets.

When I went in the prison, they stripped me down, they stripped me off everything, down to my naked flesh. Then they examined my pockets. Well, the guy just get tired of going through *every* pocket. They took everything away from me but my money. You keep your money. And you walk out of that room after you put your clothes back on, and you come out in a great open space, inside, and there you have a little commissary over on the side. Anything you want to buy, you can go over there, and you can buy chewing tobacco, whatever you want to buy. All that they done took away from you, you can go there and buy, cigarettes or whatever, crackers, chewing gum, anything like that.

Me and Hill got split up in that prison. They put Hill somewhere else, put me in a cell with a guy who had done knocked a guy in the head with a automobile crankshaft, about a woman. The guy he hit with the crankshaft was expected to die, and they had him in there, waiting to see about the outcome.

That was also the first time I hear talk about a grown old man raping a seven-year-old girl. They had a guy in there, he was reddish. He wont white. I don't know whether he was a Negro or

* [Holmesburg prison.]

whether he's what, but he wasn't white. I know that because he went out in the yard with the Negroes, he didn't go out with the whites.*

The next morning, a man come around, whupping on the door, waking us up at 6 o'clock. Then we have to scrub our cell. They had a brush about as wide as your three fingers and about four inches long. You'd have to get down on the floor with a bucket and soap and scrub the floor with that brush. You get down on your knees and you start yonder and go back, you scrub all over. He do part and I do part. You start over yonder, washing, and you wash backwards, come backwards. Then you had you a rag, you dried your floor as you moved backwards, so you wouldn't spot the floor whilst it was wet. That was the first thing you do every morning after you get up. And you had to keep your bed clean. You couldn't sit on your bed, cause the inspector going come in and inspect it. Then they bring your food around, stick everything through the pigeonhole. They brought some hard bread, some syrup, some coffee, little bit better than the first. That was Saturday morning, Sunday morning, Monday morning.

While we in prison, didn't nobody know where we were, we got no way to send out no word, we just there. I'd be in there and hear the trains running, coming by there, but I couldn't see them. I seen that prison since I got free. Everytime I pass there, I look for it, cause on each corner they got a guard post, a little steeple up on the end, on the corner where the guard sit and look out. You can see it from the railroad.

On Saturday, Gray and Turner and Eddie, somehow they got out and they know where my window at. I was up on about the second floor and I got a window, it's a little small window, iron bars. They came out back of my window, kept acalling, "Thornton, hey, Thornton! Hey, Henry!" I heard them, went to the window. They told me, "Don't worry, we have made contact." Just like that.

What had happen, the ILD lawyer in Philadelphia, he read in the paper where they said it was five educated agitators with 500 pictures of Stalin and Lenin was headed south to break up the peace

---

* That prison is where I found out they had jim crow in the North. They had a big yard out there, and they put all the whites out there in the morning. Then they take the whites in in the afternoon, around noon, and they let the Negroes out in the afternoon. And I mean it wont no two or three men, it was hundreds of them was in jail.

and happiness in the South.* When he seen that, he didn't know who they was, but he came down, went down to see who was it, asked for his name. Gray's name was there, he was head of the car. And that's the way they found us there, told them to tell us, "Don't worry, Tuesday morning at the trial we'll be there to take care of you."

That Monday night after we'd all gone to bed, they came around and woke me up. They won't call you by name, they go, "Hey, boy! Hey, boy! Hey, you over there!" You jump up. "What's your name?"

This guy want me to tell him what my name was. My name— now I ain't Hudson, I got to be careful. When he call me, I won't answer till I get good and woke up, where I could study on it: "Now what is my name?" I said to myself, "What is my name?" It come to me, "Thornton." I done had so many names. If I had said "Hudson," I got a wrong name. That's why I had to be so careful. So I said to him, "My name Henry Thornton."

"Get up, get ready, let's go."

After I got dressed and everything, I had to go to the desk to get my belongings they had, my pipe, my watch, such things like that. After they load us up then, they carried us back to that first jail, where they put us when they first arrested us. That's where we stayed all night, the balance of the night on Monday. All of us was in there in that one little cell.

It was one little room, all us packed up. That little place had a great big board upside the wall you could set on, had a toilet over there in the hole, and all five of us in that little place, in that pigeon coop all night Monday night. Some sit up and some had to stand up. The thing wont over something like about five or six feet long and three or four feet wide. It was just a closet.

We had a little money, so we got the key-man to order us some food. We bought a whole lot of sandwiches and bread and cheese and crackers and coca colas. We had a big feast, in that little hole. That wont considered a jail, that was the place they put the prisoners until they bring them up for trial.

Tuesday morning they brought us out for trial. We all came before the judge, and the police dropped the charges, because they had found the car wasn't stolen. We had proper credentials. So they didn't have no charge, and the old judge—I never will forget—he sit up and say, looked at us, say, "Yes, but these is agitators going

* We didn't have nary a picture. That was they lie.

down to break up the peace and happiness in the South." He said to the police, "You should have put a charge against them of insurrection. But since you didn't put it against them, I'm going to dismiss the charges. The Ku Klux will meet them at the river and take care of them when they get down there."* He was setting in the judge seat, and he said, "I want you to escort them out of the city."

Our ILD lawyer spoke up, said, "Judge, your Honor, my clients can't leave the city right now, cause they have some business to take care of here."

"I'll turn them over to your custody, until they take care of their business." Then he said to the police, "If they are found in this city after sundown, I want you to bring them back and charge them for insurrection."

We went out and we all got shaves and haircuts, then we went to the lawyer's office. He had got in touch with somebody and they had got us some money. When the sun went down, we was in Harrisburg Pennsylvania. We didn't go south, we changed our route and went west, around through Harrisburg, Pennsylvania and down through West Virginia, all down through Virginia, and we came through Knoxville, Tennessee, went on in to Birmingham. We missed going through Atlanta. We didn't go to Atlanta, cause we thought they might have got the Klan waiting for us there.

We got back to Birmingham, the coal mines on strike, ore mines on strike. And we just right fresh out of the National Training School. And then also Mack Coad was back from Russia. We was all then high hoping and full of fight among the miners, issuing leaflets and talking to miners, and trying to get the members of the Party units in the mines more active in the strike. That was the year when they had some big, major battles between the coal miners on strike and the National Guard, when the miners was in the bushes with shotguns, from there on, '34, '35, '36. All them years was battle years. Them Negroes had they shotguns, and they was shooting them too. It was quite a struggle there in them years.

I stayed in Birmingham and I went to work on the CWA.[1] In the CWA they was paying $6 and 30¢ for six hours a day for three days a week. You work three days at six hours a day on a big pipeline, digging a big ditch to put a pipe in. (I don't know what that pipe

---

* We had to cross the Chattahoochee River down there before we went into Atlanta.

was for.) And they'd pay you $6.30. The whites was over here in another area of the site from the Negroes, but they's working the same money. What the whites did, they organized a flying squad to go from one project to the other and call the CWA workers off the job on strike. Their demand was for 30¢ an hour, eight hours a day, five days a week. That would have give us more than $6.

Just hundred and hundreds, if not thousands—I never did know the exact number—was on these CWA jobs. They was all around Jefferson County. So when these workers begin to walk off and organize these wildcat strikes, the hod carriers' union organizers came out. (The hod carriers was carrying brick and mortar to the brickmen building buildings, they call that the hod carriers. That was a AF of L union.) The hod carriers' union organizers came out, made a talk to all these welfare workers, charged them 25¢. They signed a card, and they'd bring them into the hod carriers' union. And that's when these workers really got to striking then, when 'they thought they done got into the union.

So when these hod carrier union officials call a mass meeting, instead of they talking in favor of the workers, for more money, they come out telling them to be quiet, you couldn't strike against the government. This was a government job, you can't strike against the government. That was all the big talk, all among everywhere: "Here these welfare workers strike against the government." The preachers was preaching from the pulpit, some of them. Newspapers every day, headlines: "Workers Striking Against the Government." Some of the strikers was Party people, I wouldn't say they were not Party people at all, but the Party wasn't head in the leadership. We was accused of being at the head of it. We was accused of everything that come along in the interest of the workers. *Whatever* come along, we's accused of it.

That $6 and 30¢ a week on the CWA was the first money that was received there for welfare work, after we beat all the way from '32, '33, up to '34. Before, when you work, they give you a grocery order, and you go to the supply house. That was the city relief. That CWA was the first federal job.

I stayed there, then, till July '34. July was when Solicitor Boykin* of Atlanta launched his drive against the ILD and Party leadership. They going clean out the Reds. Angelo Herndon was in jail at that

* [Solicitor General John A. Boykin of Fulton County, Georgia, was the equivalent of a district attorney in Atlanta.]

time also. The Party leaders there, the whites, they left the city. Jim Gray and Tom Johnson was in charge of the Party and ILD there, and they and they wives, they left the city and left nobody there. Some of the most active Negro local members also were going to hide out. Otto Hall had already gone back to New York. He went back after that whipping they gave him in Birmingham.

The Party sent me from Birmingham over there to try to pull things back together in Atlanta. I guess it was the district there in Birmingham that decided, but I'm sure that the national had something to do with it, maybe suggested it. I was to go over there and stay about four weeks. I went over there and stayed the four weeks out, and then when I went back to Birmingham, the D.O. asked me how would I like to go and live in Atlanta? Well, I had been long wanting to go back to Atlanta, and so it just suited me to be going back.

When I left Birmingham in July, I was working on the CWA, and twas a young boy there, and he couldn't get no job. He was living with his grandmother and grandfather, couldn't get no job, and he didn't have nothing to bring home. When I had to leave to go to Atlanta, I gave him my work card and told him, I said, "Now you work my job. You take my job and work it," I said, "and you don't make no to-do. When they call Will Holton, you answer to that name." And I said, "You draw the check. But if anything comes up against you about it," I said, "don't come hunting for me. Don't try to get that check. You just leave the check there. Let them have it."

This was in July '34. It went on '34, it went on '35. Sometime in '35, all of a sudden, I had a letter telling me come over there, that they done caught up with what happen, that he was working my name, but he wasn't me. I had done told him, "If they ever catch you," I says, "you just hit the woods, hit the bushes, don't look for me." So when they did cotton on, the first thing he done, he wrote me. I didn't never answer that letter.*

* I never did see him any more since I put him on the job there in 1934. They tell me he's somewhere living in Chicago, selling peanuts in Chicago.

12
Atlanta

WHEN I went to Atlanta, I went first to Ben Davis and John Geer.[1] They had a orderly boy named D'Antignac was studying law, and he finally passed the bar, after Ben left there. So Ben was my main contact. My name there was Larry Brown.

Ben and me, our relationship was not exactly the same as it had been in that trip in '33. Now I had been to the National Training School ten weeks and I felt like I'm somebody. I'm telling *him* something now. I'm talking about political economy, about the society itself, how it automatically would breed war and fascism. I'm discussing about the danger of imperialist war. I felt like that I know his education was above mine, but I had something he didn't have. I had an understanding of Marxism and a Marxist approach to conditions that he didn't have then.

He called together about fifteen schoolteachers, there in Atlanta for me to talk to. He introduced me to the school teachers, two-three men and several women. I was very shy. I practically didn't want to do it, cause I told him, "I can't talk to them schoolteachers."

He said, "Aw, Brown," said, "you know more about the world situation than they does. You got something to tell them. They can't tell you nothing about what you can tell them."

My language, words, was poor, couldn't half pronounce my words right. I was saying "de" and "dis" all back in them days, see, but at the same time, I'm talking about the conditions of the world and the danger of fascist war, and I showed how the economy itself would automatically breed war. When I got into it, why I dropped all my scared ideas about these people and went to talking about what's on my mind. I forgot they was schoolteachers and I just went to talking about things that I know. When they left that night, all of them talking among themselves, you know how they do, talk-ing, using big words.

Ben told me they said, "You know one thing," they said, "his English is very bad, but he knows a lot, don't he?" They said, "He knows things I never thought of, the things he brought out there."

Ben told them, "He's a basic industrial worker, he's a proletarian. That's why he's able to know these things and say them." When he told me about what they had said, that give me confidence.

When I go in the office, Ben and Geer, and they had some time off and somebody there, they would start conversations. I would never talk, but they would start talking about something, about the conditions of the world or what they thought. I didn't know they were doing it in order to get me started, but after a while, they get to talking, and maybe I wouldn't say nothing until they ask me, "What do you think about that?" And I'd go to expressing my views. I'd get into it then, and I'd just keep on talking on and on and on. But I didn't know that's what they was doing. You see, they didn't want their friends to see them as communist, not at that time. So here I'm a known communist. Ben was a communist, but he didn't let everybody know he was a communist because he had certain legal work to do, and it wasn't advisable for him to come out. When he give up that position as a lawyer in Atlanta and went to New York and come to be the editor of the *Daily Worker,* then more and more he come out. He laid down his attorney's law practice and picked up the whole question, come to be a known communist.

His father—I knew his father in Atlanta, old man Ben Davis. He was there when Ben was there. He used to come in the office. He had a newspaper he wrote, and he would come in there with his paper, all his material under his arm, and look around, and talk, and he go on out. That's where I come to know old man Ben.* After Ben left there and went to New York—I think the first and last case Ben had was the Herndon case, I don't remember he having any other case of hearing about it—so he come in the office, old man Ben. He stand around and say, "Out of all the money I spent on that boy, finished him for a full law practice, and here he thrown it all away, go to New York to edit that God damn paper!" And he said that more than one time.

---

* The Odd Fellows building was where his office was at. Old Man Davis was head of the Odd Fellows. They claim way down the years that old man Ben Davis broke the Odd Fellows. But that's a whole lot of gossip.

Old man Ben wasn't progressive at all. He was a Republican. But he was militant, he was very militant. He had quite a struggle hisself. He didn't come up no easy street. He get sorely tried publishing his paper. He had to get his shotgun and guard his house at night, getting threatening letters and all that. Just because he was advocating such like the right to vote, the right to put out his paper, they was threatening his life. He didn't have no easy going.*

Old man Ben would come in Ben's office and talk, and so would this pastor, a big pastor named Reverend Martin. He was a great big man, large, robust, and he was the man that took some of his deacons, when Ben was defending Herndon in the courts. They was afraid that someone was going to try to lynch Ben. Reverend Martin, he and two-three of his deacons, they put on they overalls and they pistols in they pockets, and they went in and sit in the courthouse. Ben didn't know it. Nobody didn't know it, but him and his deacons was armed, sitting in the courthouse like workers, while the case was going on. When Ben would leave the courthouse, they'd leave, follow him, stay some distance, see that nothing happen to him.

At first I went to Ben's office, two or three days I went down, talked with him, and eventually then, I began to move out, try to find people in the community. My first place was called Peoples Town.† Then also there was people on the westside, out among Mr. Weaver, the Matthews, and the Moores. These were all new people to me, I didn't know none of them. Fact of it is, it wasn't too many people when I left there in '24 I could find when I went back there in '34. I found some of them, not all of them, because I was a different person now. I wont doing what them people wanted to do. They wanted to be out in the big time. I'm here trying to organize. So I was organizing the Party people. I regrouped some of them. Some of them I never did get straightened out.

In Peoples Town, I sort of got them folks lined up. The westside, I got them lined up. The people in Summerhill, I never was able to get them straight. I had contact with them, go by they house, give them literature to read or sell them a piece of literature and talked with them. They wished me well, but I couldn't get them active to

---

* [Benjamin J. Davis, Sr., was a Republican national committeeman and edited the Atlanta *Independent*.]

† Peoples Town is on the southeast side of Atlanta, beyond Summerhill section. Summerhill, it's out there also on the southeast side.

do anything. They had been active before. But I don't know whether they's frightened now or what. See, a lot of people, my thinking was, when they first meet the Party and get to playing with the Party, they's all ready to do something, you think. But they find out really it's work, it's responsible work, and at the same time you liable to get arrested. Then they friends begin telling them, "You better leave that thing off." That way a whole lot of them would drop off. It take some courage when you start off, to keep on, because you'll go so far, and you get to the point now, you begin to make your decision, whether you going to keep going or whether you're going to stop. I don't know what went on in Atlanta, but over there in Birmingham, when we was first contacted by Murphy, we were told that we would have to be prepared to make a sacrifice. He said sometimes it might be sacrifice near to your life. Maybe it be that.

To show you what I mean, in that period, in '34, we had contact in Memphis Tennessee. And they had some arrests up there. Mack Coad went up there from Birmingham to look into that situation up there in Memphis. That was in the time of Mayor Crump, when he was the Daddy of Memphis. Mack Coad went up there, and he though he was going to the right people, went to some Negro business people, undertakers. He was there talking with them, telling what he's there for. He thought he was talking with some friends, but he was talking to Crump's people. They turned him over to the police. The police got on to Mack and they whipped him unmerciful at the railroad, he said. He told me that hisself. That night some of them wanted to lynch him, and some of the rest declared, "No, we shouldn't lynch him." What they decide to do, they whup him, give him a good whupping and put him on a freight train to Birmingham. They near whupped him to death. That's what kind of terror we had. He got back to Birmingham, and he got over that whupping, but he never stopped. He kept on.

These people in Atlanta wasn't willing to take that chance, most of them. Now there in Birmingham, you got these steelworkers and coal miners, what been used to hard going all the time. If they got any nerve or courage, they make good fighters. I ain't saying that you didn't have no basic industrial workers in Atlanta, cause you had that there then. You had basic industry in Atlanta, you had a steel plant. You had molding foundries in Atlanta, small ones, you had railroad shops, railroads, all kinds of railroads. The industry was there. The workers was there, but they had a petty bourgeois outlook. They going to get rich tomorrow. They going have them a nice home tomorrow. That's the way they was looking. They was working class, but they wasn't like the working class of Birmingham.

Here in Atlanta you had some different people altogether—insurance writers, college graduates, little homeowners. You just had a different element to deal with. So the industrial workers, you wouldn't find them in a community, just workers living in together, like you would in Birmingham. In Birmingham, you got all the steelworkers, all coal miners living side to side. They ain't got nothing to do but here to that job and back to the house. In Atlanta they wasn't congregated together.

It was the neighborhood, the working class, industrial neighborhood that make all the difference. You miss one worker here, you get the other next door. But over there in Atlanta, you got to go from here over cross town to see the next steelworker. He'll talk well, but getting him to go from over yonder to over here and this one over here to meet together, that was the problem I had. And it kept me running around, just running around.

I moved to Atlanta to stay along in August, and then I was there, trying to do what I could from then until the balance of the year. They had two of the Scottsboro boys' mothers there, Mrs. Montgomery and Mrs. Powell. And you had another one of the Scottsboro boys' aunts was there. So these was contacts of mine. I could go to them and give them a few leaflets to put out or something, but still, I didn't have that organized group what I would like to have. The Scottsboro mothers were working-class women, just poor, working-class black women. They were enthusiastic about the Party and the ILD, they knew what was going on. Mrs. Montgomery, she was very active around there, around Atlanta. She'd attend meetings, her and her common-law husband. I forgot what his name was now. He was a Party member. Now Mrs. Powell, she was sympathetic, but she was a different woman. She wasn't like Mrs. Montgomery. She was more or less a woman that's around home. She wasn't active, and her family, I considered, her daughter and what I could see around there, was what we used to call on the side of the rough type of people, the rough-rowdy type. So that was the difference in her and Mrs. Montgomery.

I had regular contact with Mrs. Montgomery. I visited her more often than I did Mrs. Powell or Miss Lula Jackson, the aunt of one of these boys, cause Mrs. Montgomery was more active in the organization. These others just wished us well but twont nothing they was doing. I used to carry they money.

The International Labor Defense, they had what was known as a prison fund. And Mrs. Powell and Mrs. Montgomery, I carried them $100 each and every month. Miss Jackson, I don't know whether they give her the money. She wasn't a mother. But the other two, I carried them $100 each several times. The ILD didn't write checks, they give me the money to carry. The money would come down through Geer and Ben Davis' office. It would be sent in from the ILD national. I'd get the money there and carry it out. And one of the other mothers, Mrs. Noyes, I carried her money also. I contacted her at Mrs. Powell's, but she didn't live in Atlanta. It might have been dangerous, taking that $100 at once, if anybody know. But didn't anybody know I had it. I had the money and nobody know where I had it until I came and give it to them. I had them give me a receipt as soon as I gave them the money. So it was just me handing them $100 and get a receipt.

I was at Mrs. Montgomery's house the first night Angelo Herndon got out of jail. He spent the night at Mrs. Montgomery's house, him and the white lawyer who got him out of jail. They came there first of the night, and I happened to be there when they came, and I stayed there till about 8–9 o'clock. We just talked, drank coffee, ate cookies. That's all we done, we talked. Herndon, he sit there and told us some of his experiences in jail, some of the things that happened to him. He didn't do too much talking. We talked about other things, first one thing then another. Talk about unemployed conditions, talk about no jobs, and our opinion of what it's going take to change things, what's going happen. Was a general discussion. It wont pinning him down, asking questions. So I left and went home, and they left for New York.

WE had several Jewish sympathizers and members of the Party there in Atlanta. And it was a mass organization among the Jewish people known as the IWO, it was burial insurance.* That was a

* In the McCarthy days, that organization was destroyed. The insurance companies lined up with the government or the government lined up with them, and I don't hear no more about the IWO now. [The International Workers Order was a largely Yiddish-speaking fraternal order independent of the CP but informally allied with it. The Pattersons and Ben Davis were members.]

national organization all over. Well, William L. Patterson's wife, Louise Patterson, came to Atlanta and contacted the Jewish people there. Louise Patterson's main task in Atlanta was to organize a IWO branch among the Negroes. They had very good policies. In other words, it wasn't something you sent all your money off. You kept your money here in your group. And also it was a organization that supported such cases like the Scottsboro case.

So Louise came there in Atlanta, and a lot of these insurance people, Party people that used to work in insurance, Weaver, Moore, Matthews, and all them, these insurance writers, they thought now they got them something good, where they won't get arrested.

They got together about 28–30 people, they friends, where Louise could speak to them about the IWO. She organized a IWO branch, and they elected secretary and treasurer and chairman, etc. And Weaver, the Party member, he was elected as chairman of that branch. He took all the members' names of that branch, sat down, put them in a notebook. Then he went to Chicago to the peace conference that Dr. DuBois[2] and others called in the spring, this was in '35.

When he got back from the peace conference, twas a white schoolteacher and her daughter lived over in DeKalb County.* So she trying to do something. She invited some of her neighbors to meet at her home on Sunday night, where Weaver could make a report on the peace conference. At that same time, twas a young white lawyer in there from New York, was working out of Geer's office with me on the case of some white Party members had got arrested, getting out some leaflets. He's just down there, he wont there for good. He just coming through. He tried to carry me that night. He was going to the meeting, he had contact with this white woman and her daughter. He said, "Brown, don't you think you'd like to go over there tonight?"

I says, "No," I says, "it don't do to get everybody piled up in one place. You going. You's enough." That night, Weaver was there and the white woman was there and her daughter and this lawyer from New York, and I think one or two other people. All the neighbors invited to the party, ain't none of them come, they knowed about the police.

* Atlanta has two counties in the city, Fulton County and DeKalb County. She was living in the DeKalb side.

The police came in and arrested the house. If I had of been there, I'd of been picked up. So when they got Weaver, he had this notebook of all these other people's names. When they arrested him, got this notebook, all these people's names in Atlanta, they just went around from house to house and got all them that same night before day, got them out they beds. All these IWO people, they was all communists too, so far as the police was concerned. Everything was communists in they eyes. And they put them in jail. Oh God! You talk about a mess, you had a *mess*.

If I had of been there, I'd of been in jail that night. I wont involved in the IWO because it wont no use of me getting involved. I had enough to worry about. There were other comrades there working, supporting they getting together. Maybe I would have got in it later, but it was just something just started. Louise hadn't hardly got away from there before everybody's in jail.*

ABOUT a year later, the D.O.—from Birmingham—and another fellow from New York, they came through Atlanta to see me. And while they's in Atlanta, the New York guy says, "Brown, you get some of your people together, I would like to make a talk to them."

I first went to Miss Jackson, to the Scottsboro boys' aunt's, and got her to agree to I could hold a meeting there. Then I went around one by one. I invited thirteen people all told, Negro and white, men and women. I told them where the place was at, the address and everything. So that night, in time the meeting set for, they were there. Now I don't know, I never did know the full meaning of what happened, but just about time we got in the meeting, we got in and started, somebody knocked at the front door. They knocked at the front door just when I was making my introductory speech. Miss Jackson said, "Who is it?"

"The law." When he said "the law," the D.O. from Birmingham, he didn't know where he's going, but he went out the window. The house was high up off the ground, was on a hill, and where that window, was on the high part. It was about 10 or 12 feet from the ground. He didn't want to get caught, you know, and he just jumped out of that window. And was some palings outside. It's a wonder he hadn't fell on his face and killed hisself. But he jumped out. He was O.K. The other fellow from New York, he was left in there with us.

* They all got out, it wasn't nothing to it finally.

So at the same time they knocks on the front door and says, "It's the law," the other detectives come to the back door. Now I didn't know that the woman of the house, Miss Lula Jackson, was running something like a transient.* She was running her house like that, but I didn't know it. So there was these people, a woman and two men, they had come there for a room, one of these fellows had brought his friend and the girlfriend there, he knew them. They was setting in the back of the house in the kitchen. I didn't know they was there. Because Miss Jackson, instead of she telling them that she having a meeting tonight, she puts them back in the kitchen somewhere, till the meeting is over.

When the detectives knocked on the back door, this guy with the friends, he didn't know nothing. He got up and opened the door, and here these detectives come in there in the back and brought them on out of the kitchen on up here with all of us. When I seen them Negro men and woman come walking out, I thought they was police pimps. I thought they brought the detectives there. They had their clothes on and all, but the question of it was, where did these people come from? Who was they? And Miss Jackson hadn't told me nothing.

One of the boys in our meeting, a white boy, his name was George.† He was from New York, but he had come down Atlanta and he had married Gloria Clark. She was also a Party member, about nineteen years old, a beautiful white girl. So George was standing over there, and I'm over here, and he's trying to give signs for something, cutting his eyes at me, and I don't know what he's talking about. And these detectives are watching me and him. Whatever he was doing, he was just about to get both of us killed. We didn't have nothing to fight with, but he would look at me and cut his eyes, and I'd look at him. I was out in the middle of the floor, and the detective watch me, and he said, "All right, big boy, back over side the wall." That's when he talking to me. This detective had me get back side the wall, where he know he could see me move. Then he say, "You, there, you better stay where you at over there," talking to the white boy, George.

Now they done called the paddy wagon, and they got everybody in the house waiting for the paddy wagon to come. It's so many

* A place where a man could take his girlfriend to be alone for a hour or so in a room.
† He got killed in World War II. I seen the picture in the *Daily Worker*.

people in the house, till the detectives' cars had some of them and the paddy wagon had some. One of the fellows there, Singer, the scrap iron dealer, a Jewish fellow, he was in the meeting that night, him and his Negro helper. Me and his helper was put in the cell together.

But all that finally came out, and all the charges was dropped somehow or another. It panned out to be nothing. Only thing about it, in the lineup that day, this here white girl, Gloria, she wouldn't allow them to fingerprint her. We were the last two, and she tried to get me not to let them fingerprint me, neither. She kept telling me, "Let's don't let them fingerprint us."

I said, "No, I can't do that." They called her before me. All the rest of them, they done carried them on, put them in the cells somewhere. They come to her she said, "I ain't going let you fingerprint me."

They said, "All right, then, young lady." Then they said to me, "Come on here, nigger!"

So I gets up and go ahead on, cause I knowed I didn't have nothing to buck up there with but get a bloody head, so I went on and get my fingerprints, and I left her there.

I heard that they turned her over to these old women, matrons in the jail, and they turned a cold water hose on her and she was menstruating. She came to the first trial that day all dressed in red. She's at the trial, but she looked very pale to me. She looked sick. I was sitting over there, and she walked right by me and she say, "How you coming, Brown?" I sort of nodded my head. I was afraid the white folks looking at it. And she went on out.

Gloria was sick with a bad cold that day she was at the trial. The next trial, the next Friday, she wasn't at the trial. She went into the hospital with pneumonia and it turned to tuberculosis. And she died. Her daddy buried her over there at the foot of Stone Mountain.

13

The Neighborhood Union
and Lint Shaw

I never did have a job in Atlanta, never did have enough to buy food. I don't know how I lived, I just made it somehow. While Ben Davis and Geer was there, the ILD national office, in New York, they was making a finance donation of $5 a week, help carry on the work there. I don't know what twas for, I don't know how it go. All I know, they was supposed to give it to Atlanta for organization work, and sometimes I get a little something.

When the whites ran out of there and left, some Jewish people decided, it was about six of them, promised to give me 50¢ apiece, that was $3 a week. Three or four of them was merchandisers running stores. And another one, he was working some kind of little industrial, making hats. They had a little IWO get-together every Sunday. I don't know how many's in the group, but out of that gathering, they supposed to lay aside $3. One person in that group, a young white woman, her and her husband was in a business. I go to her job Monday morning, see did they dish out any money for me. Sometimes she have it, sometimes she didn't. I'd go down, and she say, "I'm sorry, Brown, nobody give me nothing for you yesterday." So I'm missing this $3 here. I just couldn't never plan nothing.

My wife was working some in a private home, and she would bring pans of food home from the white folks' house. I wouldn't be at home when she come. Her and the kid would eat all they want and leave the other food sitting open on the table, just all open. I come home at night, it sitting there, it had got stale, and no doubt flies had been around it. That's just how she treated me. That's what I went through, in 1935 to the last of '36.

I found out long years later that she wasn't no angel all the way up through our married life. But she had a big front to me. She done a whole lot of devilment that I didn't know about and found out way later years.

Now when she was working in Atlanta, it come a ice storm, sleet, snow, and rain, and all that stuff turned to ice, the first of '36. Sophie couldn't go to work because of the ice. Me and her was sitting there at the house, at the fire, and a great big old husky, half-ugly Negro came and knocked on the door. I ain't seen him before nor since. She know him, she told him to come in.

I say, "Have a seat."

"No, I just happen to come up here. I see Mrs. Brown didn't go to work, I didn't know whether she was sick or not." That's the way he put it. I didn't dig into it in my mind. He stood on this end of the mantelboard with his elbow on this end of the mantelboard, standing up here. Sophie sitting over here, and I'm sitting here. He just stood there. He looked at me, he looked at Sophie. Then him and her talking. I'm trying to act intelligent. I didn't get mad or nothing, but I took note of it. Finally he left.

About ten or fifteen minutes after he's gone, she took a notion, all of a sudden, "I want to go up to Mama's." Her mother lived back over here about two or three blocks, and she just had to go over to mama's. She went off and stayed about a hour and come back. Down here, twas a little street, just one block off the hill, and twas some houses all in there and some people, some women in there she knew. She had to go down, go up that way to go to her mother's. I always will believe that her and that Negro had a place around there, and she went out and went down and went around to meet that Negro. I hadn't seen him before that day, but they knew each other, very well. Cause he act strange to me. But I'm got so much confidence in her, till I just didn't see that then. I had so much confidence till she carried me all these years. I'm telling you, she had a good front.

I was from Birmingham and I was a stranger in Atlanta. I couldn't get on welfare. If I went to get on the welfare, I had a reputation back in Birmingham, so I had to stay away from the welfare. I had to make it the best I could.

My house rent was $7½ a month. When the time come to pay the $7 in advance, I didn't have it. I went down and told him I didn't have it, didn't have no job, soon as I could get some money, I'd bring it. They told me, "If you don't have money, you just come down here every Monday and let us see you." That's what they told me. I'd go down every Monday, reported I didn't have money. Every Monday, I ain't got no money. That's all they charged me, come down and let us see you. I had to walk too.

The onliest thing that helped me keep my head above water was that I played the numbers. Every once in a while, I'd hit for a penny or two pennies. One Sunday, I looked in the Atlanta newspaper, looking at the cotton market of New Orleans. Sitting there, trying to look, I see 052 in that cotton market. That Monday morning, I had three pennies, all the money I had. I went round to Mrs. Williams, she wrote numbers, Mrs. Williams did. She sold coal and ice, had several grown kids, that's where I get my coal at. Wont but just two blocks away. I was living around here on this block, walk down the corner, walked up on the corner here, and she's on this block. So that morning, I went around there, I said, "Mrs. Williams, I want you to put down a number for me today."

She said, "What is it? What number you like?"

I said, "Give me 052." So she wrote 052, and I gave her three red pennies. She put them on it.

That evening—the number came out at 3 o'clock—I walked back around there, said, "Mrs. Williams, what you heard?"

She said, "052 come out." I had $15. $5 for a penny. I told Mrs. Williams, I said, "I can't give you out of this money, cause I got to go down, try to take care of my rent." She'd let me have coal, a quarter's worth, 50¢ worth at the time, till I get some money. But I went with that $15, went on downtown to that white real estate office, and I paid him that $15. I was already a month behind. I paid him two months, out of them three cents. If it hadn't a been, I didn't see no other place but I'd go on the street. They going set me out.

I wont doing a whole lot of Party organization there in Atlanta, I just more or less was making contact from one individual person to the other. Get two or three people together, we sit down and have a discussion, but it wont no real Party activity like we had in Birmingham. So I became active meeting with this women's union, neighborhood union.

The membership was about 125 members, and they's all around there, around Spelman College,* in that area there. One of the women that I knew there, member of that union, her husband cut

* [A prestigious college for black women, founded in 1881, now part of the Atlanta University complex.]

the hedges around that girls' college. But was a woman lived right on that hedge on the outside of that college, her name was Mrs. Latimore. She had quite a few daughters, three or four daughters, and had a little boy. At that time he was five or six years old. That was the time Joe Lewis was in his high days boxing, and he's always said he'd be a Joe Lewis. He named himself Joe Lewis. I can see his little brown-skin color now, kind of chubby and fat.

Mrs. Latimore was the president of this neighborhood union of women. She knew I was a Party member. She wasn't a member, but we consider her a friend. I don't know how sympathetic she was, but she was sympathetic enough to allow me to come to the meetings and have me talk. All the other women, I didn't think, would know that I was a Party member. I don't think she'd tell anybody, cause they was regular hunting communists there in Atlanta then. The Scottsboro case was still hot and had that big arrest there about Boykin, the prosecuting attorney, they's going around, beating up and whipping Party people.

The neighborhood union had some men, two-three men and a houseful of women. It met every Monday night. I'd meet with them. They didn't make no special fuss over me cause I was a man, but then I was always a little more advanced in ideas than the average person. They'd always want me to talk. "We have Brother Brown with us tonight. Maybe he have something to say." And I'd get up and tie what they were doing with something I read in the *Daily Worker,* or tell them something happen about the unemployed or the importance of getting together, what it meant by being organized. I sold a few of them papers. I didn't want to broadside selling papers, but I had Mrs. Latimore and three or four other people I'd sell the paper to, individuals. Depend on the kind of material I have. Sometimes I give them a leaflet to read. They had a idea of who I was. I wont just ordinary Brown, but I didn't go out there being a representative of the Party publicly.

One Monday morning, Mrs. Latimore went down to Grady Hospital, went down to carry one of her daughters. While she was there, two white men came and brought a Negro. They didn't seem to be guarding him, they just brought him in there. They sit down over there to be waited on. The Negro had one of his arms bandaged up and had a bandage on his forehead.

When she got chance, Mrs. Latimore tipped over and asked him what was his name. He told her his name was Lint Shaw. He's from up to Colbert Georgia.* She didn't ask him what had he done, cause she's afraid the white folks would see her talking with him. But she got his name. Lint Shaw, and he's from Colbert Georgia.

That night at the meeting, she made a report about him, this man was brought in there, where he's from. She asked who would be able to go down to the hospital on visiting hours, which was at night at about 7 o'clock, and ask for this name and see what happened, what kind of trouble he's in. Nobody wouldn't volunteer. I wasn't doing anything. I'm a big man, I volunteer.

I went down there Tuesday evening about visiting hours at the hospital. I went to the woman at the desk, Negro woman, and asked did they have a man there by the name of Lint Shaw. She said yes. She told me he was up on the second floor, and his bed number. It was just great, big open space, men's beds was just down the line, down the line, down the line. So I went up there and I found him.

He was in his bed, and he had a little gallus and a whirl up there at the head of his bed, and he had a weight on a cord down here. That cord come through that whirl, and had a stick about the size of a broom handle in his hand. He had his finger taped around where it keep his hand on there. His arm was lying out flat that way and his hand like that, because he had been shot in his muscle of his arm there, and that big bone was broken in his right arm.

I went there and told him who I was and what I was there for, who sent me. He called me "Bubba." He was fifty years old, he was black, dark-complexioned, had beautiful hair, black, wont no nappy hair. He was a medium-sized man, had a dark mustache, dark eyebrows. He was the father of eleven children, was a sharecropper up there in Colbert Georgia, working for a old white man by the name of Huff. He was living outside the outskirts of the little old town. Down below his house, he told me, was a branch. Was a little meadow down there before you get to it. His house was kind of up on a hill off the side of the highway.

About dark, that Friday evening, some women was hollering down there towards that branch. One of his boys, about nineteen years old, he was at the woodpile, cutting wood. The boy come in and told him about the people down there hollering. Lint Shaw had a sick headache, was laying on the floor there, on a pallet. He told the boys, said, "Don't you all go out the yard, go down there, cause

* [Colbert is about 10 miles northeast of Athens, on the then Seaboard railroad from Atlanta to New York, between Elberton and Athens.]

you don't know what's happening. Stay here in the yard." So they didn't go. He let the women holler long as they want, till they got through.*

So along about 1 or 2 o'clock that night, the law come to his door and knocked on his door. He got up, open the door, and they came in, wanted to know who was that went from his house down towards there where the people was hollering. He told them nobody hadn't left his house, cause he was laying on the floor with a bad headache and he wouldn't let his boys go down there.

They said, "It was three women with a car down there, and they had a puncture, and they said that some man come from towards out his house, come down there, claimed he going to help them get the tire fixed, tried to rape them." They were white women.

Lint Shaw said, "Well, it wont me. Ain't nobody left my house."

"We going take you up, come on, we going put you in the callaboose." They didn't have a jail, called it a callaboose, which was this thing like a jail. They said, "Come on, go up there. There won't be nothing to it, till day in the morning."

So he left well satisfied that it wouldn't be anything. Went on up there, and they put him in jail. He knowed now he innocent, he can get out the next morning. He said around 9–9:30, they came in there and brought these white women, come in to look him over to see was he the one. They walked in, say yeah, he was the one. He went to say, "No, no . . . ."

"Shut up your damn mouth. Don't you dispute these women's word. Shut up!"

He couldn't even defend hisself. They didn't allow him to dispute they word. After they took him out, then they took him from Colbert, was carrying him, they claim, to Royston. That's the big jail, Royston Georgia. That was on Saturday morning.

He say he had a barlow knife. He don't know what become of the knife, he said, but on the way up to Royston, he went blank, thinking about what a mess he's in now. And when he come to hisself, these two dogs—or whatever you call them, deputy sheriffs—had got out they car, and one's on one side the radiator, and one on the other, was shooting at him in the back seat. He said he didn't have no handcuffs, and he hollering, "Oh Lordy, what has I done?"

One of them says, "God damn it, you done cut me!"

* [10 April 1936.]

And he was apologizing, he didn't know, he didn't know. But he didn't see no blood, he said. And he didn't know what become of his knife.

Well, they shot at him. One of the balls hit the edge of his hair and went over the skull, and the other one hit him in the right arm and broke that big bone. That Monday morning they took him, brought him to Atlanta, put him in the hospital, and that's when Mrs. Latimore had chance to see him.

The neighborhood union members had told me to tell him that if he didn't have a lawyer, that they would get him a lawyer and raise the money to defend his case, if it was something that they would be able to defend, a case they could get involved in. So I told him what they said. And he said to me, said, "Write my wife." He give me her name and address, told me to write her, and "Whatever my wife say about it will be all right with me."

I said to him, said, "Don't you think, by writing your wife, the white folks might get hold to the letter up there before she do, or maybe she show them the letter and it might make it bad for you?"

He said, no, he didn't think so.

So I said, "I advise you, I wouldn't write my wife," I said. "You have to write her before you get a lawyer? You the one in trouble, not her." I done all kind of talk to him. I couldn't convince him. He got to have that letter wrote to his wife.

Now he told me at the same time while I talking to him, that the two white men had been back there that day to see him—the two that brought him down there. (I don't know whether the two that brought him to Grady hospital was the two that shot him up.) One of them give him a 50¢ piece and told him, "It wouldn't of been nothing to it if you just hadn't of cut that officer."

And Lint Shaw told him, "Well, I'm sorry if I did," he said, "I don't know nothing about it."

"That's all going make it hard to get you off, cause you cut the officer." He thought he could get him out of the arrest if it hadn't been for that.

So Lint Shaw told me he wanted some peanut candy. This was when they was selling this peanut candy in blocks, 10¢ a block. He wanted some peanut candy and a apple. He give me that 50¢. I went out there, and I bought him two apples, and the apples was 5¢ a piece. I brought the two apples and the peanut candy back to him, but I paid for it myself and give him his 50¢ back. And oh, he thanked me so much, said, "Bubba," said, "thank you so much, thank you, Bubba." He called me "Bubba" and told me to come back to see him.

I left and came back and brought the address back to Mrs. Latimore that next day, went to her house and told her what he said. Mrs. Latimore wrote the letter to his wife, told her I had been to see her husband and how he was getting on and asking her about the lawyer and what they wanted to do, as he said. She put a stamp on it and asked me to put it in the post office box. I put it in the mail.

A few days after that, along about Saturday, same week, she got a letter back from the wife, stating that she had showed the letter to Mr. Huff, and Mr. Huff said wont no use bothering about a lawyer. It wasn't nothing a lawyer could do about it. She said, "I'm going just leave it in the hands of the Lord." That's what she said in that letter.

That Monday morning, the white folks, they come up there and got Lint Shaw and carried him back to Royston and put him in jail. It hadn't been but a week, you know his arm wasn't cured. That evening, about first dark, they taken him out of that jail and carried him down right below his house and swung him up to a pine tree and shot him up all to pieces.* And they say they had his kids, the boys, to go down, look at the body.

Now a fellow by the name of Ratcliffe was reporting for the Atlanta *World* at that time, a young fellow, light-complexioned. He went over there from the Atlanta *World*. He was real bright,† had pretty good hair, and they allowed him to snap the pictures of Lint Shaw hanging from that limb, feet was touching, toes was just touching the ground, the rope round his neck, swinging there side that pine tree.

They allowed Ratcliffe to make the picture, put that picture in the paper. I guess they thought that would keep the niggers in they place, a lesson to the others. Ratcliffe then came out to Mrs. Latimore and talked to her about it, get what information that she know about it, what they were planning. Mrs. Latimore give me Ratcliffe's name. I went down to the Atlanta *World* and I talked with Ratcliffe personally about how it happened and what all about it. So what the people did do then, they went and got a whole lot of clothes,

* [The lynching occurred Monday night, 27 April 1936.]
† [Light-skinned.]

women's clothes and children's clothes and boxed them up, big boxes of clothes. That union sent them to that widow, and that was the last I heard of it.[1]

But that's what I call a hen-pecked man. He couldn't do nothing unlessen he consult his wife. And his wife, she was leaving it to the Lord and the white folks. He took that and got shot all to pieces.

I continued to go to the neighborhood union meetings for a while after that. The biggest thing they'd do, they'd have prayer meeting and they'd collect dues, and they'd have dinners from one's house to the other's house, you know, on a Sunday. One Sunday, we all was at a lady's house, having dinner. They had a undertaker there named Murdock at this dinner that day. He and I was the onliest men—all the rest of them women. And he was just talking about

MOB VICTIM

LINT SHAW
—handsome 225-pound, 45-year-old father of eleven children and pioneer resident of Danielsville, Ga., who was tied to a tree and his body riddled with bullets by an infuriated mob at Colbert, Ga., around midnight Monday.

NAACP Alert;

45-YEAR-OLD LINT SHAW IS TIED TO TREE AND BODY RIDDLED WITH BULLETS

Saddened Mother, Eleven Children Left With But Scant Means Of Livelihood By Stark Event

FRIENDS CONSOLE FAMILY

By ROBERT M. RATCLIFFE

COLBERT, Ga.—(SNS)—The wife of Lint Shaw and their eleven children huddled together in a little room of the Shaw home Monday at midnight and listened in sorrow as a mob of approximately 50 white persons riddled with bullets the body of the husband and father for the alleged attack on a white girl near here April 10.

Lint Shaw, the 45-year-old farmer, was shot to death within hearing distance of his own home and in the vicinity of the alleged attack.

Mrs. Georgia Shaw, a brown skinned woman with coal black hair and Indian features, who speaks only when spoken to, said the automobiles carrying the mob began passing their home as early as 11:30 o'clock Monday night.

how much he loved women, "I just can't do without the women," and all that women, women, women.

I told him, I said, "My position," I said, "is that there's much more things important that we should be interested in besides just being interested in women."

Oh, he tried to take me apart, "What's any more sweeter than the women?" And these women, they was more or less agreeing with him. I don't think I went there no more. I don't think I went to another one of they affairs.

The first of December 1936, the D.O. called me back to Birmingham. Maybe it was for security reasons, but they didn't tell me that. They thought it was best for me to come out of Atlanta, cause I had done been arrested there twice within the same year. I left my wife and kid there in Atlanta with my brother, cause in '36 I had moved in with my brother. He told me to come on, move in the house. He had a big brick apartment, and he decided there was enough room for me too. I should come into the other room of his apartment, he didn't need it. So I moved in there, me and my wife and son, with him and his wife. We use the same kitchen, and we had one bedroom. The boy had a cot out in the hallway. My brother give me the works again about the Party. He had done give it to me before, when I first lost my job, back in '32, but he done cooled that off. He was speaking to me again.

So I left my wife and kid with him, come on back to Birmingham. I done starved out there for two years in Atlanta. Jobs here and yonder began to open up, and the D.O. thought I might be able to get a job. When I first went back to Birmingham, I was staying with Mayfield. Mayfield was batching. Him and his wife done separated. He was batching, and I stayed with Mayfield from along in December till along about July in '37. He was working in the mine. He worked at night, so I slept in the bed at night. He used the bed in the day.

But the Party wasn't what it was when I left. It wasn't well organized like it was in '34. It was a new D.O., Hall, and this was beginning to get coming up in the New Deal period.*

* [What Hudson calls the New Deal period extends from about 1935 to about 1946.]

14

CIO Organizing
in Birmingham

The D.O., Hall, called me back to Birmingham, but I existed on practically nothing from the first of December 1936 until February 19th, 1937, before I got a job. Now here I had left my wife and kid in Atlanta with my brother in the dead heart of the winter. She had a little job working, day working, but I didn't have nothing to send back there to give to them to live on. She had a hard time, and this is part of the trouble we had, she and me. All of this over the years helped to build it up. It ain't just a one-way street, when you go to get to looking at all of this. I didn't have nothing to do and nothing to do anything with. No money. I'm walking around and trying to find a job in these plants with no kind of subsidy, no kind of support.

I stayed there and stayed with Mayfield. He was paying the rent and buying the food. I took a dollar now and then from the Party people at the office. I just figured something had to be done till I could get a job. I'd say, "I ain't got no carfare."

And they'd "Here, here's 50¢, here's a dollar."

But that's all I got from the Party in them days, a dollar here and 75¢ there. No money, and I didn't know how to fight for no money. Didn't know how to stand up and demand it, because I thought Party people was all going to be good enough to know what your condition is and try to work out some solution. I'm so loyal, see, to carry out the decision, until I didn't question. It wasn't that I didn't have a right to question, but I was just a loyal Party person. It was racism and white chauvinism and everything else with it, cause it was the D.O.'s job as the Party head and the white was to see what my problem was, that I didn't have no money. I knowed somehow, somewhere, the Party, the national Party organization, was paying this guy, giving this guy so much money. I don't know how much it was, don't know whether it was enough or not, but he was getting so much money to operate with, cause he was subsidized. And I was a part of the Party. But he never one time asked me what was my status of my home, of my kid, how they was living.

But I want to keep this clear. It's not the Party itself was practicing white chauvinism. I don't hold the Party responsible, but I hold that there is individuals in the Party which have to be reckoned with. You see, some Negroes be so narrow-minded, until they fought the whole Party for that. But that was that one individual D.O.* I have never raised it yet. Finally, I got a job, went to work, then I got on the level again, back to the family, got them over to Birmingham, moved them over.

In this New Deal period the Party was different from before. Now we got this open Party office, and you go up there, walk in, have classes on a Sunday. And they broke the Party units down from Party units to Party clubs. The decision came down from Browder to Hall that we organize Party clubs with bigger memberships. Instead of having two or three little units, we have a club where everybody come, a community club or a industrial club, where all the coal miners and steelworkers meet, a regular goulash for the stoolpigeons. This was in '37, '38, all down through those years. We had to organize a club, would be for a given area, like North Birmingham would have a club, Woodlawn would have a club. We'd have a southside club. But these clubs begin to deteriorate, the Party begin to deteriorate by not having this close contact, like in the units. There was a lot of members who was members of these Party clubs, who's maybe a coal miner, been unemployed, got his job back in the mine. He become involved in the mine local and he wouldn't come to his Party club meeting. So the Party we had wasn't organized as strong. The Party deteriorated on through '37. But at the same time, several of us was active in helping to build the CIO unions.

When the steel union begin, there's nothing in steel. Everywhere you look around, you had people wasn't in the union. So we Party people, one of our main points to the program in the Party was industrial concentration. Industrial concentration meant to help to build the union, and also to recruit members in the Party among the steelworkers. There was a twofold approach. You didn't recruit just

* He eventually got out of the Party. He was one who turned coat too, in the Stalin period, in 1956.

anybody for the Party, you recruited the best people you think would come up to the qualification of being a member of the Party. If you see a guy, excess drinker, you wouldn't bother him about the Party. You get him to read the paper, read a pamphlet, sell him a pamphlet, and see can you get him to give a finance donation to the Party, cause in those days we accepted any donation anybody offered. We had people that pledged to say they'd give a dollar a month to the Party. We get enough of them dollars, we'd have some money. That's the way we operated, but we didn't recruit everybody to be a Party member.

Contacting people to join the Party wasn't so hard as in the early period. It was less Red fear. Things had opened up and became much more better for the Party to operate itself, cause we had been able to open up the Party headquarters.*

When the unions came in and the steel drive began to hold all these big meetings in the halls and what not, it give our people a kind of breathing spell. Where they been cramped up, dodging and hiding to get to a meeting, they could go to the union meeting and they wouldn't be bothered, wont afraid at the steel union. It was a devil of a turnaround. The CIO was hiring known communists as organizers among the steelworkers. This was under the leadership of Lewis and Murray.[1] One or two of the communists there in Birmingham was put on the union payroll, under Noel R. Beddow,[2] head of the steel drive.

Beddow was responsible for the steel drive from the CIO point of view in the steel mills of Birmingham. He was a lawyer. Beddow was a Red baiter. He was a communist hater. But he had orders from Philip Murray and John L. Lewis and them, "You got to work these guys, cause they's good organizers. They's the ones that know how to organize, know how to contact people." Joe Howard, Eb Cox, and a white guy named Dave Smith was some of the Party people that organized in the steel plants for the CIO. Joe Howard and me had been in the Party together since way back. Dave Smith was a local white communist, so I was told, but I never was ever meeting with him, because he was in another club out in another section of the city.

* We always had a Party post office box, box #1700 was the post office box. We had a certain person to go to the box. The person never was arrested—to my knowing—going to the post office box. So at least we could go to the post office box and get mail.

One of the shops that Joe Howard and Smith was responsible for organizing was the Jackson foundry. They had a strike on Christmas eve day, sitdown strike. Sitdown strikes was popular in the union back in those days. Stay in the shop, don't go out. So they had a sitdown strike at this place. And they stayed in there Christmas day, the Negroes did, and one or two whites. Most of the whites jumped the fence, they say. (I wouldn't doubt it.) They left, but the Negroes stayed there.

So they won the strike. But after they won the strike, the boss, old man Jackson, he canceled his orders and shut the shop down. Put everybody out.

Right in that period, after that strike, Joe Howard lost his job with Beddow. Beddow never did like communists, and as soon as he got the chance, he dumped them. The strike was under Howard's and Smith's leadership, and both of them became inactive among the steelworkers organizing drive after that strike. Whether they charged them as communists who called this wildcat strike, the strike the fault of the communists, I never was able to know. But the strike was finally lost, and Howard didn't work with the steel organizing committee with Beddow no more. And where was he supposed to get his money from? Through Hall, the D.O. The Party was subsidizing Joe Howard.

Joe had six children, and his wife died with the dropsy, and the baby wont over three or four years old, and the girl about fourteen. He had a boy about fifteen, he and the girl were the two oldest. Him and my boy's along together.

Along in January or February, I was in with the D.O. and Joe Howard, we had to meet. That was in '37. We had the meeting out there in Hickman Jordan's funeral parlor. Jordan would give us a place to meet when he didn't have a funeral to meet there. They won't bother us so bad, the police wouldn't. So me and Joe Howard and Hall meet that Sunday, Joe asked him, "Do you got any money for me?"

"No, they ain't sent you nothing."

"I ain't got nothing for the kids."

"I'm sorry. There's nothing I can do because I don't have any money." Now they done dropped Joe Howard, they had done stopped his subsidy, whatever he's getting from the Party. I don't know whether it's from the district or from the national, but it had been stopped. Hall told Joe Howard he ain't got no money for him and he ain't heard nothing. I don't know where he's going hear it from. Hall was the head of the Party there in Birmingham.

Then me and Joe Howard walked home down the railroad. He said to me, said, "I think I'm going quit the Party," he said, "I can't stand this."

I told him, I said, "I don't know what the score is," I says, "but I don't think anything could make me quit the Party on account of what some individuals do." I says, "I think you have a right, you ought to fight through it." We walked on down the railroad. We walked about a mile together, and I turned off to the right to go to Norwood, and he kept on the railroad. That was the last time me and Joe Howard walked together.* He quit the Party. Now who's responsible, I don't know, but I do know one thing I think was responsible. That's white chauvinism.

White racism. Now who's responsible for it, I don't know. I don't know whether it's from Hall, I don't know whether the national knowed anything about it. I don't know whether it's from Beddow. I never did know the set-up. All I know, I know Howard quit the Party.†

You understand that I'm not saying that the Party responsible, it was individuals responsible. And it's a lot of that went on in the Party in the South from time to time. The Negroes turned heels to it, instead of standing up and fight. Just like Howard did. He walked. He left. And I say he should of fought it out. He didn't tell me what it's all about. He didn't even tell me what his trouble was, and we had been in the Party together all the time, from those hard, rough days, up until 1937.

I went to work on February the 19th, down there molding in a job called the Wallwork foundry. The Wallwork foundry made material for the TCI†† wire mill, draw wire. That's where I started to work,

---

* I don't remember getting in contact with him anymore until along in '38. Twas at a ball diamond, Acipco ball diamond, and he was there. I seed him and asked him how come he didn't come down to the Workers Alliance meetings. He was setting in the stands, and he says, "I'm coming. I'm coming." That's the last time I seed him.

† In 1939 he had the locked bowels [intestinal obstruction] and died. That was the end of him. He left all these kids, these kids just wandered. I really don't know what become of them, cause he had one sister, I think she took them. She wasn't married. It was a bad situation. They just drifted and scattered about.

†† [Tennessee Coal and Iron.]

and it paid me 40¢ an hour. That was big money, cause I hadn't made no money in a long time. I had been unemployed from 1932 until I got on the CWA in 1934. A little while out there, then I left there and went to Atlanta. I made no more money on a job until 1937.

My wife was relieved then, because I was making money again. She was working, but her money wont help to me, whatever she made. (When I think about how she treated me, I ought of left her long ago. I should of walked off and left her long ago. Just thinking about how she treated me when I didn't have a job and didn't have no money. How she talked to me. I was a fool for staying with her long as I did.)

At the Wallwork foundry, they didn't have no union, and they didn't allow no union person that they knowing to work there. I worked there from February till November '37, and all that period I was recording secretary of Steelworkers Local 1489, at a big steel plant in Ensley.* The union had a policy then, if you was working in a steel plant and wont no union here, and there was another plant that had a union local, you could be a member of that local over there. That's what give me a chance to be a member over here in Local 1489. I would slip to these meetings, cause if the old boss—they called him "Poor"—where I was working find out where I was going, he'd fire me. So I wouldn't tell none of them I was going. I didn't trust any of them.

At first in the local, you didn't pay no dues. You sign a card, you tear off the stub, and you don't pay no joining fee. Long as you held that stub of your card, you's a member of the union. Then when Phil Murray got the first steel contract signed in the big steel plants in Birmingham, all members was to pay dues out of their pocket. It was $1 month.

When the union began to tighten down and the members had to pay dues, it was in early '38, when they began to collect the dues in the big Ensley steel plant where I was in the local. They got the contract signed after I was out of work. So I'd go up there to the gate and stand for the guys when they come out. The guys would see me and know I was recording secretary, and they come and give me they dollar dues.

The CIO came in and began to show to these white and black

* [A suburb of Birmingham to the southwest of the city.]

workers the differential in the wages of the steelworkers in Birmingham and the steelworkers in Pittsburgh. And yet they working for the same company, both is owned by the same industrialists.* They brought the wage-scale books into the union halls to show the workers, white workers particularly, what they were working for and what the worker in the same job was getting in Pittsburgh.

The president of that local took that book of the union wage scales and showed the white electricians. The job that was making $12 for eight hours in Birmingham, in Pittsburgh, they was making $16 in eight hours. That's CIO wage scales. One of the electricians, the union taken his grievance up with the company and got him that $16, that other $4 a day. Then a lot of people joined the union, especially the whites, in order to get their grievance took up. The union would only take up the grievance of the members of the union. The union could represent the members of the union, but not the workers who wasn't in the union.

At the local meeting one night, a young Negro man, a coal miner, came to our local meeting and spoke, urging our local to elect a delegate from our local to the Southern Negro Youth Congress convention that was to convene in Chattanooga Tennessee.[3] Since I was unemployed at the time, the local elected me as a delegate to represent that local at the SNYC convention up in Tennessee. There was only four delegates there from Birmingham: myself, Henry O. Mayfield, Emory O. Jackson[4] of the Birmingham *World,* and Hartford Knight, a Negro leader from Birmingham in the coal miners' union.

I was on the resolutions committee at that SNYC convention, and I work in that committee and got a resolution brought out of that committee to the floor of the convention, presented by Mayfield, Jackson, and Knight, calling for the next convention of the SNYC to be held in Birmingham Alabama, in 1939. The resolution was adopted. When we got back to Birmingham, it was a group of twenty-five or thirty or more, met in the YWCA and organized a provisional committee to lay plans for that 1939 SNYC convention. Later the headquarters was removed from Richmond Virginia to Birmingham.

Most of all of them attending meetings of the union local I went to was Negroes, three or four whites and a whole lot of Negroes, and some of them had been to college. I came to be recording sec-

---

* U.S. Steel up in Pittsburgh was the company that owned TCI there in Birmingham.

retary because none of them would take the book. They tried to nominate them for secretary and they declined. Bill Crowder, he was the president (he has white), he tried to appoint them, and they said, "No, no, cause I'm afraid I couldn't handle it, Mr. President." So he looked over at me, and I didn't have no idea he going try to give it to me.

He looks at me, say, "Here's a brother, he be here every night, and he don't never miss a night. I'm going to appoint you recording secretary, and I hope you won't decline." That's what he said, the white president. And all these guys, some of them had been to Tuskegee. I took them books and read the minutes, too, for a whole year.

Most of the minutes was to pass a resolution to do a certain thing, send a group of men to a certain place to another local meeting, like that. I put it down. I'd jot it down the best my way of jotting it down, and then I'd go home. I'd remember who made this motion and who second it, and I'd write down in longhand in my minutes, "motion made by Brother So and So, the second by Brother So and So," and what the motion was about. I'd fill it in, then I'd take it and rehearse it all the week. When I got back to the Tuesday meeting, I'd know it all by heart. That's the way I done it, all by memory.

I held that office and read my minutes well, until April 1938. They elected officers every April, and the next April, when it come time for elections, I had done got unemployed again. I got laid off at the Wallwork foundry, and since I wont working in the foundry, I were unqualified to be elected again to office in the local. But I still could attend meetings.

The unions held big, open mass meetings on Sunday. They's be having a meeting somewhere every Sunday. Eb Cox, he was more or less looked upon as the most active Negro organizer among the steel organizing committee, and me and him got chummy-chummy. I had his telephone number. I'd call him and ask him where the meeting going be. He got to know me and he'd call me. Then I'd know about the next meeting. I'd take the trolley car so I'd always be in the meetings Sunday.

We wont doing nothing but talking. And what was actually happening was, the white coal miners was coming from the coal mine locals over to the steel plant locals and talking, in order to encourage the Negroes to stick to the union. Because it was the Negro steelworkers who built the steel union, not the white steelworkers.

But the white coal miners—I didn't know a white coal miner from a white steelworker—the white coal miners would come out to encourage the Negroes to where the Negroes wouldn't quit coming to the meetings. The Negroes thought these guys was coming from the steel locals who get up all that talk, "You all boys stick with us. We going build this union." You didn't have no trouble, though, cause it was all under John L. Lewis' wings.

The union drive got started in '36, but it really got going in '37. On the Fairfield hill, all the big churches, big preachers, they was preaching these sermons on Sunday morning against the union. (I don't know what the whites done, but I know what a whole lot of Negro preachers was doing.) They had seven Negro churches out there. Reverend Williams was the pastor of the First Baptist Church in Fairfield. I know Reverend Williams was against the union. His name stuck out all the time. All this was TCI property. These communities, like Fairfield and Westfield, they was on the company land, company houses. And these preachers was preaching against the CIO. Calling John L. Lewis and Philip Murray "sending them agitators to the South to break up the peace and happiness between the workers and the managements, with their Moscow gold."

Some of these biggest deacons of these churches was members of what we called the "popsicle union,"[5] company union. Company unions was very popular back in those days. So these deacons was a member of the popsicle unions, and they having they little groups meeting off here somewhere and carrying the Negroes off. "Why don't you come and join us, where you won't get fired. You can get fired, fooling with that thing over there," and all such as that.

So in the spring of 1937, one Sunday, all these CIO coal miners and steelworkers got together. The whites had come to a local meeting there in Fairfield and we had organized a march. They put out that "we going have a march through Fairfield Hill." We started down in the business section where the hall was at. We marched up the hill, went round, circled up across the streets, down the hill, up and down, up and down. It was a mountainous hill right in the main area where these churches was, where the big shots lived. The churches wasn't all right together. They's a church on the hill then a church over younder, church over yonder. We had the route laid out in such a way that it went right by Reverend Williams' church.

We was four deep. I never did know how many people was in that march, because I wasn't able to ever see the tail end. It was so long, it coming twisting around. You look up, far as you could see, you see men, all the way down. (Wont no women in the line.) It did go a long way, up the hill, down through the most important sections.

They tell me them deacons, them popsicle deacons, when they heard that march was coming across the hill, they left Fairfield. Reverend Williams, he took his wife and went to Tuscaloosa. They done seen that strength of the union, white and black together. That was something unusual, to see white and black together. We used everything to show them our strength. That's the only way we had. We had to bluff our way through. We had to pressure folks in, you know. We didn't threaten them, but we done everything.

At the head of the line was a man, wont a boy, a man, William Norman. He was a very healthy-looking, tall, handsome-looking, real smooth black Negro. I think he was about thirty years old. He was tall, over six foot. He wont bulky, just solid made.

Willie Norman's heart was the CIO, building that union. He wouldn't want to talk with you about nothing, if it wont talking about the union. He say, "I ain't got time to throw away. Let's talk about how we going build the union." He was at the head of that march. I would say I was about half a block back in the line, but he was at the head. He just wanted to be at the head.

Down in December of that same year, he went to work on a Thursday. I was out to his house, and I was to go back that Saturday. He was a Party member. He hadn't been long joining the Party, hadn't been long in. I was out to his house that Thursday. Me and him talked, and we walked from his house to the trolley line going to Fairfield, where he worked. He was a steelworker, went to work at 3 o'clock. He went on up, he caught the trolley going to Fairfield, the number 7 trolley that went to Ensley and on out to Wylam mine. And I caught the car, the trolley coming to Birmingham. He had a pain in his side, talking that Thursday about it. He said he'd been using olive oil, olive oil supposed to been good for appendix. I kept atelling him, I told him, said, "You better have them see about that."

He got off at 11 o'clock, and when he come in, his appendix was bothering him. Before day, at about 4 o'clock, he woke up deathly sick with that pain in his side. His wife rushed him to the hospital. So they got him in the hospital, but his appendix had busted. His wife told me she was talking with him at the hospital about buying

Christmas. He had three kids, three little boys, and he was crazy about his kids. But she said she noticed he just didn't seem like he was interested. She asked him, "What you think we ought to get the kids for Christmas?"

He told her, "You get whatever you want to," you know, just like he didn't care. And he died off.

15

The Right
To Vote Club

WE had a Depression. We got out of the Depression. Then we had a recession, last of '37. When that recession came in '37, everybody what had done got a job, practically, was throwed back out in the street. And the first of '38, along about January 1st, they sent out public statements that they would start paying unemployed compensation to the unemployed workers. Now the first day—if it wasn't New Year's day it was the next day—they opened up a old vacant building there in Birmingham, and they had lines of people, coal miners, steelworkers, white and black. But they had a jim crow line. This here was for the federal government, now, but the jim crow line. The whites go in one way, the Negroes go in the other.

I was in that first line. I was among the first ones that signed up for my unemployed compensation, the first of '38. I had worked long enough to draw ten weeks, ten checks at $9½ a week. Not much, but I'm not talking about much. I had to live on it. Now you see what our living was. And you had to wait so long, you didn't get it right then. You had to wait it was something like a month or six weeks or so before you got it. Finally I got that unemployed compensation, $9½ a week, until July in '38. In between I lived the best I could, just did the best I could. I couldn't tell you how I lived myself, because I'd get, say, a quarter, and I would go buy 15¢ worth of pork chop and buy a loaf of bread. That was the way I had to buy dinner sometimes for my wife and kid and myself. Pork chop, say for an instance, wasn't but about 15¢ a pound. Or maybe I get something like this here what you call "ends," 10¢ a pound, and neck bones was 5¢ a pound, 7¢ a pound. Pork liver was 10¢ a pound.

While I was on unemployed compensation, I got started trying to get people registered to vote. Joe Gelders[1] was a member of the Party, and he met with the bureau every once in a while. He spoke to me about organizing a voters club.

When he first spoke to me, it was just like somebody talking about something over yonder blue. I never did hardly turn down anything, though, so I told him I could try. He told me, "See can you get somebody, start off with two or three people, start a committee where we can maybe be able to organize a club." He told me it would be good if I can get somebody outside of just our people involved in it, but at the same time, have some of our people. I had to think about it a while, but I know who was the first person I went to.

It was a young minister there name of Murphy. I never did know all of his name, just Murphy—great big husky fellow. He was a hod carrier, he worked carrying mortar. But he was a jackleg preacher. He was a Baptist then. He eventually turned and went Methodist. Just him and his wife lived together, not too far from me. I was giving him the *Daily Worker* to read. He was one of these outside contacts I was talking about. I hadn't been knowing him too long. I didn't have to work on him long at all. I just went to him and talked to him about it. He was ready to do something. I spoke to him about it and he said, "Yeah, Bro'." (They all called me "Bro'." All of them called me "Brother Hudson."*) He said, "Yeah, Bro' Hudson, I think that would be a good idea." He said, "I'll be one."

We talked about it and who else we could get. Not too far from him, right down the corner, was another little jackleg preacher who's working in the operating room in the Norwood hospital, Reverend Joseph. He was another little preacher, wont no pastor, but he was a member of the church right there near by. So I contacted Reverend Joseph, and Reverend Joseph was interested. I got these two down, I got them all right. I got to get somebody else. Then I went and I got Cornella Hibbard and Mack Coad, and one or two other people that I knew. I had five or six or seven people, including Hazel Stanley and Jimmie Hooper.

Jimmie Hooper was active at the begin with in the Young Communist League. He was along with Mayfield, and he was keeping company with Hazel. I never did know Hazel to be a member of the

* [Hudson used his own name after he returned to Birmingham from Atlanta at the end of 1937.]

YCL, but she became active around in the voters club with Jimmie. That's the way I come to know her. She was a Party person. She came in the Party while I was away.*

Hazel Stanley, she was a onliest child of her mother, and her father died of pneumonia. I didn't know her father. It was Hazel, her mother, and her Aunt, Aunt Lucy, and her grandmother and her grandfather. They was all living in the house together. Hazel was the sole provider. She was what you might call a white-collar worker on the WPA. She went in that category. She was a very nice young woman, I would say.

I took the responsibility for the voters club, and told them, "I'm going see can I get a hall up in the Masonic Temple." I come back, I get the hall, that same hall number four. I always asked for that hall. It wasn't a big hall, but it helt about a hundred people. Then I went back and contacted all my people, and I told them I got the meeting for next Tuesday night, hall number 4, for 7:30. And we all met.

At the same time, there was a little white lawyer there, worked with Joe Gelders, wasn't married, and I don't think he had passed the bar, named Laurent Frantz. He was from Birmingham. Joe Gelders and I had contacted him, and had him to be down there that night. So when we got all these people there, I got up and made the introductory remarks about what we wanted to do, get people to register to vote. Then Laurent Frantz—he was the onliest white— he got up and he talked, and he told them what they rights was, so far as he know about the law, what it took to become a qualified electoral voter.

We decided we'd set up this committee. We elected Reverend Joseph as the president. We elected Reverend Murphy as the vice-president. And we elected Hazel Stanley as the recording secretary. The people there elected them, but quite naturally, I told Hazel and them who was the best for what we trying to do, and some of them was nominated. It wont a hand-picked-put-them-up-there. The people elected the president, the vice-president, and the secretary, out of the people what was there. That was a committee to build a voters club. Everybody was to come back, they bring somebody next Tuesday night.

---

* Hazel became ultra-left in later years, in the Stalin period [late 1950s].

We went to the Birmingham *World*. Emory O. Jackson was the editor then, and we got him to run a statement in the paper announcing about the meeting.

We assigned Laurent Frantz—he pledged, more or less, wont no assigned, hardly, he pledged—that he would get the United States Constitution. The Party at one time put out a small pamphlet, was about a half inch thick, of the United States Constitution and the Bill of Rights, and all these things, where all the Party members had them. That was what Laurent Frantz had. We had several of them. Then he got the constitution of Alabama, it was very small. It wont no size. And one of those blanks from the courthouse you had to fill out to register to vote. We had took this one blank and we had made a whole lot of blanks, just like the one—the same questions— mimeographed. We had to get two or three stencils to make it, cause it had so much on this side and so much on the other side. We had to make up about two or three different ways, to get it all on one sheet. You got long paper. So we made about two or three hundred of them.

At the next meeting, we had more people. Everybody brought somebody, all of them was ordinary people. Reverend Joseph explained the purpose of the meeting. The joining fee was 25¢ to join. Wont no dues. After he announced about it and everybody was there had their question asked, then we go into our study. We more or less elected Laurent Frantz to be our instructor.

We passed these blanks around to everybody. "Now you keep that blank. Don't turn it back in, and every time you come back, you bring that blank, cause there's instructions on it." We'd go over every night what was on the instructions, and what the rights to become a qualified electoral voter in Birmingham was at that time.

The constitution of Alabama—that was the law from 1901—the constitution explained what to do to become a qualified electoral voter. It was one clause in the constitution pertained to soldiers who had deserted the army, like that, they was unqualified, they rights had been taken away from them. And they spoke about foreigners and all such like that. But for ordinary people, in order to become a qualified electoral voter as a citizen of Alabama, you had to live in the state for one year, live in the county six months, and you live in your precinct three months. I think that's right. I don't think it went any lower than the precinct, like district or ward.[2]

Anyone who had $300 worth of taxable property, but couldn't read and write, was eligible to become a qualified electoral voter. Anyone who couldn't read and write and they wife or husband of that person had that much property—the wife who couldn't read and write could become a voter on the strength of her husband's $300 worth of taxable property.

Also required then was the paying of the poll tax. The poll tax was $1½ a year, from twenty-one to forty-five years old. That was also in the constitution.

Now if anyone went up to become a qualified electoral voter and was denied the rights to become a qualified electoral voter, they had the right to petition to a circuit judge, I believe it was a circuit judge, for a hearing. And if it was found that that person had been denied the rights to vote by the Board of Registrars, and they come up to qualifications, the judge would call that Board of Registrars into question, and a hearing would be helt with a jury trial. And if it was found that the person had been discriminated against and denied the right to vote, that judge would instruct that jury, would instruct that Board of Registrars, to register that person, there and then, and give them their voter's certificate. That was the law at that time in Alabama, in 1938.

Now these questions that you had to fill out was just like the same questions that the Board of Registrars was supposed to ask you: how old was you, where were you born, had you ever been arrested for a felony, crime, and how long you lived in the state, and how long you lived in the county, in the precinct. And it may have asked you about your mother and father. Was you employed, how much taxable property you had, like that. And they asked had you paid your poll tax when you twenty-one. They didn't ask nothing pertaining about the constitution.

But what the Board of Registrars, what they was doing and the law there was allowing the board members to do that, when the whites go up, they would ask these questions. If they answered them, they wrote them a certificate, right there. But when a Negro go up, they give you this blank, and you'd have to go over there and try to fill it out the best you could. Wont nobody supposed to help you. When you fill it out and bring it back and hand in the blank, they would say, "You'll hear from us, we got to investigate your case." You never hear from them. That was the regular way they was carrying on. So it was a very few ordinary Negroes went up. Cause first of all, they was afraid of white people, shy, and they didn't know how to talk and afraid they couldn't fill out the questions. So they wouldn't go.

Then we started this club, the Right To Vote Club, and we begin to advertise about the meeting nights in the paper. We had school-teachers, we had steelworkers, coal miners, everybody coming down. Laurent Frantz would give everybody a blank, ask, "Do you got your blank?" say no, then everybody pass the blanks around. Now he done already went over it last Tuesday night, but he'd go all over, he explain about the constitution, the rights under the United States Constitution and under the rights of the state of Alabama, and then he proceed to go around, to carry the people over these questions again, how to answer these questions.

Then the Board of Registrars cotton on to people learning all the regular questions, so when you fill out what's on that blank and you go up, they go ask you other questions, questions that's not on the blank. Negroes that did go up, call theyself passing, the board'd ask them who was the president in such-and-such a year of the United States, which wont no part of the blank. They'd ask you how many senators you have, how many congressmen was in the Congress of the United States, all these big questions people had never studied up on. It wont nothing in that blank pertaining to that. And I did hear (I can't prove that), but I did hear that some of them was asking such questions as "How many drops of water was in the ocean?" All that kind of stuff, anything. They turn these people down, say they unqualified.

We organize this club in the spring of '38, and the primary election came off in May. When the primary opened up in May, we had got—wont no thousand, I won't tell that, it wasn't a thousand—but we had got numbers of people, around the hundred, coming through that class.* Everybody what did get registered, they's voting as

* At that time also, all the CIO unions was under the leadership of John L. Lewis. In that period, the CIO was progressive. So in the union locals themselves, they had announcements telling the whites to go register, telling the members to go down, go register. So when they all got down to the courthouse to register, you'd have a long line of Negroes and a line of whites. They would ask the whites the questions and they was passing the whites, and the Negroes was just standing. They bring up just one every now and then. Sometime Reverend Murphy went down to the courthouse in time for registration, he went down to try to assist the Negroes, show them how to go about registering, and the officials drug him away from the courthouse.

Democrats. Didn't have nobody Republican. Republicans was on the ballot, but it wasn't no Republicans.

The club got very active. But it was a hard job, a hard job even in our own Party, to get black folks to go to register to vote. Twas a hard nut, and it ain't overcome yet. Some was afraid, some was bashful, some was shy to go down. You'd be surprised how people felt. I know how I felt, and that's the way I know how them people felt. You just get nervous, you just nervous. It's a very uncomfortable feeling. Going down to a new place, you don't know whether you going to make mistakes, going down among these white folks, to face these white folks, you ain't been used to facing white people. You just was nervous that's all. I was nervous too. Telling people to come out to meetings and to register to vote is one thing. But going down to the horse's mouth to register to vote is another. But at least I had the courage to push through.

Going down to the white people, to walk in there, just walking in now, and say, "I came down to register to vote." It took courage. You all don't have no idea! I can't explain how deep the oppression of the Negro people was, and how backward the poor whites was. That's what the thing's all about. Cause the whites could go down, but they was so backward they wouldn't go. The poor whites had that same backward feeling. Some of the whites was very bashful. Some of them wouldn't go. You had to preach to the whites just like you had to preach to the Negroes. They didn't feel comfortable at all. You'd be surprised the problem we had among the poor white.

After we all got our Right To Vote Club in 1938, and then after I got active in the Workers Alliance among the poor white, all that kept building me up, giving me courage, till I was bold enough to get four white guys of the Workers Alliance, just ordinary—no Party people now—they just raw, poor white. We went down to the Board of Registrars together. They walked up here to the members of the board and line up. They wanted to register to vote. So they asked them the questions, said, "Where you live? How old are you? How long you been in the country, in the state?" And when they got all that information down, they wrote them out a card and handed them they card.

But they give me a blank, and I'm over there by myself, to fill out this blank the best I can. They didn't read off the questions to me, that's the difference. I done the best I could. So when I got through all these questions, I walks over and hand them my blank.

The white guys standing there looking. I hand in my blank, and the woman says to me, "You'll hear from us."

I says, "I don't get my certificate now?"

She says, "No, we have to investigate."

So we went right out from there, these four white guys and me. We know what we going to do, we know before we left the union hall. We march right on out from that office to Attorney Shores's office, and I filed a complaint against the board for discrimination.[3] And they signed the affidavit that there was discrimination.

It took nerve to do that. You couldn't get everybody to do that. That's the point. I can bring it down so you can understand what the feeling was like. I had done been the secretary of this Local 1489 for a whole year. I had done been to the Southern Negro Youth Congress convention in Chattanooga, and I done moved a long way along here, to give me a little more courage. But think about the guy ain't had this experience. That's the picture I can make of it.

In this Right To Vote Club we had schoolteachers coming out there at night, every Tuesday night and going over those questionnaires with somebody to tell them, just like everybody else. Some of them went down and attempted to register and were turned down. And they went down to Shores, and they made out affidavits. We had several people going down to Shores. Shores had a pile of petitions. But he didn't file all of them. He picked out some he thought was the best, to see could he make a breakthrough. He picked out five schoolteachers and me, as a worker. I was the onliest worker he had.

Six people. He presented the case, with these six names as a petition for a court hearing. He thought we would be the people he could depend on to stand up. So he presented our names to the judge.* In his court, this judge issued a statement to the press all about it, naming all of us who had filed this petition. He said he would not call this Board of Registrars into question concerning this case.

When the names come out in the newspaper that Friday, all those Negroes, schoolteachers that had petitioned to the courts against the discriminatory practices by the Board of Registrars, my name

* I think the judge was Judge McEleroy, if I make no mistake.
[According to Ralph J. Bunche's "Political Status of the Negro," (1940), Hudson remembers correctly.]

and they name were there: Hosie Hudson, so and so, and all. Them Negroes went running down to Shores to tell him to "take my name off! Take my name off!" They afraid they lose they job teaching school there, cause some of them was teaching in the high school out there in Westfield. Westfield was dominated by the TCI coal and railroad company.

Shores told them, according to what he told me, they went down to him and said, "We want to withdraw our names," and he told them, "No, wait a while, wait a while." That was on a Friday when the names come out. On Monday, everybody, me and them too, got they voter's certificate in in the mail. Nobody lost their job.

So then the NAACP came in with us, and we was able to establish a united front. We'd have the NAACP coming in our meetings on meeting nights, speaking. We had one night—you had a guy from the NAACP, you had a guy, Hartford Knight, from the United Mine Workers, and you had Emory O. Jackson from the press. We was making a big splash. Place was filling up then with people. We was moving.

What we did, we went on till the primary and the election. There was a general election in November, a governatorial election. We issued our own leaflet. Joe Gelders got the records of all these candidates running in the state, like the governor and the senator and what not. He give us these names. We took all these names, took them name by name, and we made a leaflet. The leaflet told the record of what they had did and what they hadn't did. Them that had did something, we would give them credit for it. Them that hadn't did nothing, we told it just the way it was. And we put them leaflets all over Birmingham, to everybody, and telling people who to vote for.

When we did that, that's when the president of the Negro Democratic Voters Club, he got in contact with Joe Gelders. He didn't come to the meeting, he got in contact with Joe Gelders—figured Joe Gelders knowed something about it. So here the president of that Negro Democratic Club wanted to meet with some of the representatives from the Right To Vote Club. Joe Gelders got in contact with me and set up a appointment—the guy be at the National Cafe at 6 o'clock one afternoon, and told me what he looked like, so I would know him.

When I walked in, I seed this slender, brown-skin man setting over at the table there. He looked like a kind of little white-collar guy, businesslike guy. He was a World War I veteran, but I never did know what his job was. He didn't look like no ordinary worker. So I walks over to him. I says, "Pardon me, is this Mr. White⁴ from the Democratic Voters Club?"

He said, "Yes."

I said, "This is Hosie Hudson from the Right To Vote Club."

"Have a seat." So he immediately begin to outline about our club and their club. He told me straight out. He said, "Mr. Hudson," he said, "I wanted to talk with you, because you all's Right To Vote Club have put me and my club on the spot."

I said, "How's that?"

Then he went into all the details. He said, "When the communists first came into Alabama and begin to raise the slogan for the rights to vote to the Negro people and the right to hold office," he said, "we didn't have no voters. We wasn't voting." And he said that the communists was agitating, continually agitating for the rights of Negroes to vote, and some of the white politicians thought some of these undereducated, ignorant people might get out of hand and go over to the communists.

He said, "Some of the white politicians contacted us and told us they wanted to give us the right to set up a Democratic Voters Club." He told me that when they told them to set up the club, give them the charter, said, " 'We only going qualify those that you all will recommend, send down or bring down. Your friends, we'll qualify them. But don't send everybody down. Don't bring no common nigras, and don't bring over fifty a year. We ain't going qualify everybody.' " They had it well sewed up, White and them, thought they did.*

Then we sent down all these people, said they want to register to vote. A lot of them in the crowd was our Party people, and they a little more advanced then the rest of them. So we give them some real headaches up there at the Board of Registrars with so many people. That's why they got on White and them.

White said to me, "You all has organized you all's club, putting out your material and naming your candidates for you all's people to vote for." And says, "The white politicians is calling us into question, say, 'Why is it we give you all a charter and this Right To Vote

---

* They felt themselves superior to the ordinary Negroes like us was in overalls. Sure, they felt superior. If they didn't figure that, we felt that they felt that they were superior to us, looked down on the ordinary person.

Club doing all this here? We chartered you all and you ain't called they hand. You ain't saying nothing.' " White said, "I'm with you all for what you all are doing. But what I want you all to agree to do, if you'll do it, is to come and affiliate with us. Come under our wings, and we'll get you all a charter. That don't mean you stop doing what you doing, but just come under our wings so we can all be working together."

When he got through telling me all that—I just stayed till he got through talking—I told him, I said, "I'm just only one. I can't speak for the club. All I can do is take your question back to the membership, and whatever they decide to do, that's what I have to abide by." And I told him, "I will go back and make your position known and will let you know."

I went to the next meeting, and went up and made the report of what White had told me. When I got through reporting and got in the discussion period, everybody wanted to stay independent, not to get with them. We stayed independent like we was.

WE had a long struggle to get people to register to vote. We always would try to urge them and encourage them to not go by theyselves, to go down with a group of people, so that one could be witness to what happened. We wouldn't just try to get them to go down one by one. But it was a long struggle. Many of them wouldn't push through. They'd turn around and go back. They wouldn't admit they was scared or they nervous. They would find some kind of excuse, something they have to do, and all like that.

I would say, "You going down today?"

They say, "No, I won't go down today, cause I got to go see about my rent. I got to go pay a bill, I got to do this, I got to do that." But the final analysis, they never would get down there.

That's the way a lot of them was. But some of them, especially like coal miners, they would. But these people got these little pie-back jobs—you know, domestic workers, bootblacks, and all like that, I call them piebacks—they wouldn't go down. It was different with the basic industrial workers. Now schoolteachers, a whole lot of them, they would go. Preachers would go.

When I first actually voted it was in 1938, and you had to vote by a ballot. You went there, you sign your name in the book, and they passed you a ballot. All you had to do, you know what you going to vote for, they had a block there to mark with. You mark your ballot

—it had a circle and you mark x in it, circle at the end of the party. You mark that and fold it up. They had a ballot box with a hole in it. You fold it up and drop it in the box. So that wont so bad. It was the question of going down to that Board of Registrars, that was the biggest hump to get over.*

Getting people to register, that was hard. But we got them to go down to register. But after they register, they wouldn't pay the poll tax. They wouldn't sacrifice. That part, we didn't get over that hump. We got a whole lot of Negroes qualified, but we couldn't get them to pay they poll tax.

Cause say if you was forty years old, and got qualified to vote. You'd have to go pay the poll tax a $1½ a year from the time you twenty-one up to when you forty. (That's $25–$30.) So a whole lot of them wouldn't pay the poll tax. That was a big problem we had. You had to be very conscious of the importance to pay that kind of money.

I paid mine up by lying. I didn't say I was younger than I was. But in view of the fact that I had been in and out of Birmingham and hadn't been in Birmingham regular, and a lot of the years I was there I wasn't under the name of Hosie Hudson, they didn't have no record of how long I been in Birmingham. So I cut my years down. I said I came to Birmingham and Alabama in 1936. So I paid up from 1936, up then, to along in 1938. I didn't have much to pay. And I paid every year from then until I came to be forty-five years old. I was there when I came forty-five.

Quite naturally the Right To Vote Club come to be Red-baited. "Here's the communists. This here's a communist outfit." We were moving. We were doing things ain't anybody else been doing. It got so hot, till finally Reverend Joseph, he says he got so busy he couldn't serve as president no more. So he resigned as president of the club. This was still in '38. So then we put up Reverend Murphy.

* In the unions we even had a problem getting the whites to go register. We had a hard job there getting the white union leaders, such as the president and grievance committee members to register to vote. They was against the union getting involved in politics. They talked that from the floor. They wont registered theyselves, say, "I'm not interested in politics. That's politics. That's somebody else." So you had to hammer away, hammer away, hammer away to the white and the Negro, particularly the white, in order that you be able to safeguard the legislation that's already on the books pertaining to the rights of labor. You got to become qualified voters, and you got to become active in politics. Especially in voting. This was preached from the union locals and everywhere, to the whites, all the way down into the '40s.

He took over as president. Hazel was still recording secretary. Eventually Reverend Murphy, he got called off somewhere else, and he had to resign. So he resigned. We had another guy there who was a member of the club—I forgot what his name was, I can see him though. He was a very brown-skin Negro, and we elected him as president of the club.

Along in the spring of '39, we was running trucks, open trucks with bodies where people could ride, we would hire at night. Twas a place, they had a dancing hall a way out, in a little park out there 12 or 18 miles from Birmingham, in a Negro community. We'd get one or two trucks and sell tickets for people to ride out there. The tickets was a dollar or something. Everybody would pile on the truck and go out there. That way we try to raise some money, put in the treasury of the club.

The last trip we made out there, that's when the club fell apart. We had about two-three trucks we had full of people. We went out there to this park that night, had a dance. And we carried a whole lot of these roughnecks from the southside. The dancing hall, I think they was charging 25¢ to go in. And around the club, they had just ordinary screen wire. So these Negroes on the outside, they put they friend on the inside the club, and they go there, cut the screen, these guys climb up on the outside and climb over and come in the dance without paying. (These were people we had carried out, we carried anybody.)

We had a fellow there from the southside, Glover. He was a member for a long time in the Party. He wasn't a old guy, he was about in his thirties or early forties. He was one of the watchmen, on the side to keep these guys from climbing in. We had two-three watchmen, after we find they was cutting the wire, getting inside. This guy Glover seed these guys coming in, and so he challenged them that was getting in, and called the rest of us there to try to make them get back out. They wanted to stand us a fight.

On the way back to Birmingham, they was on this truck that Glover was on. It was a devil of a time. They wanted to gang this Negro for trying to keep them out the dance. And twas a big, black woman, her name was Flossie.* And Flossie, she was very militant, big, stout, she was a young woman, she wont old. So Flossie and one or two others, they was able to keep these Negroes off of Glover

---

* The last time I seen Flossie was in 1950. She went to Chicago.

on the truck till they got back to the southside. That southside was rough.

And this guy was called the president, the money that we raised out of the trucks—it was $30 or $40—and being the president, somehow or other, we turned the money over to him. That Negro never did come back to meeting no more.

He never did come back to meeting, and after we had this big skirmish on the truck that night, a lot of the people on the southside, the members, they fell out, didn't come back to the club. So me and Hazel and Jimmie Hooper and Cornella Hibbard and a few others, we helt that club as long as we could. Finally it dissolved itself. We had to give it up. We didn't have money to pay the rent with. That was the downfall of that Right To Vote Club.

We done a lot of things. In fact of the business, when we started that club, Emory Jackson, he had studied the number of Negro voters on the voter roll in Birmingham. Jackson made the report that they had less than five hundred Negroes on the rolls when we started this club. It was less than five hundred live Negro voters on the rolls. The names was on the rolls run way up in the hundreds, but a whole lot of the people had died. They didn't take the name out the roll, just let it stay on the list. You'd have to know that this person was dead, by the names.

When we begin to send down so many people, they had to let some go by. Just like I got by. Because every time we'd attempt to have a court case, that's when we got a whole lot of people qualified. They couldn't get away with keeping everybody out and being challenged in court all the time. They couldn't get away with that.

16

The NAACP
and Community Work

BETWEEN '32 and '38 I devoted all my time to the Party. I didn't see anything to be gained running around to the churches singing and giving money. So I quit singing. Cause in quartets you didn't have but four members of the quartet. If one fall out, you couldn't sing. And also, the people always have invitations to the church or social club, or something. It kept you always going, but nothing coming back.

Then in that New Deal period, the Party issued instructions for everybody to become active members of mass organizations, cause all through the years, several of the Party members isolated themselves from the mass organizations. They got so involved with the Party work, till it was just Party work, Party work, Party work. Church members quit going to church. So the Party said that people that was out of the churches, go back to the churches. I went back to church, and I started back to singing in 1938.

I had a little spare time, wont working, wont slipping and dodging to go to a meeting. So I organized a singing group known as the Smithfield Vocal Singers, singing notes. It wont a quartet singing. I was singing in a choir. If I had a meeting on a Sunday, I'd tell them, "I got a meeting," so they go ahead on to the singing, and I attended my meeting. They get mad a lot of times, but I didn't put nothing in front of my meetings.

We had a vocal singing convention, about twelve or thirteen choirs around Etowah* and Jefferson County. Anytime a group get together of choirs, they call that a convention, singing conven-

---

* [Etowah County is northeast of Jefferson, separated from it by St. Clair County. The city of Gadsden, a manufacturing center on the Cosa River, is located in Etowah County.]

tion. The Etowah and Jefferson County convention had about thirteen classes, and we'd meet on a Sunday morning, start to sing about 10 o'clock in the morning. Sing until about 12:30 and have lunch, and then sing from there till about 4 or 4:30 in the afternoon and break up.

There was different classes, just like different churches. Each church had a class. They'd come from the church, maybe made up out of the community, but they usually named themselves from the church. Now my class, I didn't name it from the church. I named it Smithfield Vocal Singers, we was come up from different churches.

Say you had a class from 23rd Street Church over to the south-side, the 23rd Street class. Now you'd be the first in the convention and the next, say so-and-so, would follow. Then they'd say, "Smithfield Vocal Singers, get ready!" After you call one, the following is called and this third one get ready, so that they follow the next one. They go around, and when the sing around, they come back, they start here at 23rd Street and go around again. By the time they go around, now it's time to eat dinner. Then they go back in after lunch and they go back around, each sing one song, take up a collection and the thing's all over.

Only on the fifth Sundays was the two-county singing convention, it maybe in Gadsden or Birmingham. You always have a fifth Sunday every three months. But it got to where it was just about at the breaking point between me and this guy Johnny Streeter, the president of the Etowah and Jefferson County convention.

He didn't like me cause I could beat him singing and he was the president. He was evil. You talk about black and evil, he was a black and evil man. So when I'd get up and make these announcements about how it was time for everybody to register to vote there in Birmingham—I'd always catch the floor and make a announcement that the books was open for registration and urge everybody to go down and try to become registered to vote—he tried acting like the preacher. The preacher would get up and tell the Negroes, get the last word, say, "You better leave the white folks' business alone."

Streeter'd tell them, "You all better get out of politics and trust God."* He was always trying to throw cold water. He got to the point when every time I sing a song, he get up and make some kind

* All of them dead, though. God has let me stay to see them all go.

of remark when he get ready to sing. He'd throw some kind of slang remarks at my class. Maybe I'd sing a song of something pertaining about death, and he'd "You have to stay out the cemetery!" All such things. I just got to the point where I told him I was going to quit. We quit the whole convention and went out to Muggins mine where they had a little convention out there, just three or four classes. We'd sing with them.*

EVERYBODY that could go back to church went back. A whole lot of whites had never been in the churches, so they didn't have no church to go to. That didn't fit with the whites much, cause they didn't have no mass organization to go to, only into the unions, become active in the unions. That's where they more or less was in. Beidel went back active in the church. But what he did, the church swallowed him up.

He came to be a deacon. He didn't stop going to Party meetings altogether, but every time you say something to him about doing something, he got to go to church, "I'm one of the deacons, and I got to do this and I got to do that." He got more active in the church than in the Party. He never quit the Party, but he put his church first and the Party second. And the church will *always* find somewhere to have you working.

We members of the Party at every meeting, nearabouts, we'd hammer and hammer on our people, especially Negroes, to become members of the NAACP as a mass organization. Before, we just knew it was there, but we didn't go, that was the better class of folks was in the NAACP. A ordinary Negro didn't feel that was his place. The onliest thing we know, the national leadership of the NAACP was fighting the International Labor Defense in the Scottsboro case. They was regular trying to take that case away from the International Labor Defense. That was Walter White and William Pickens.[1] When they first started, Dr. DuBois's name was along with Pickens and Walter White, but later it was Walter White and Pickens.

When the NAACP put on a drive for membership, I joined and went to going to the meetings. Mack Coad, he joined with me. Beidel didn't join, but Mayfield, he joined, and several other peo-

---

* I was a leader of that Smithfield Vocal Singers from 1938 until 1946. That's when we broke up. My wife trouble broke up the singing.

ple joined there in Birmingham. In the membership drive, they'd have a good turnout. They'd organize in committees, have like a little competition between committees getting members. But all they did was sign up members. Members sign up, they get the money, then they wont doing no more.

The meetings, there'd be forty or fifty people. When we first joined, we didn't go in there talking. We go sit, go to the meetings and sit up there and listen and look, for a long time, afraid to say anything. But finally we broke out of it. We fought out of it, we Party people.

I remember very well at the begin with. People in the NAACP like a old woman by the name of Miss Brooks. She was head of the old folks home they call it, out there in Graymont. She's one of these better class people. And the president of that NAACP was then Dr. Macklin. There was different names I could call, and all these was doctors, schoolteachers, or some kind of little business-man.

When we began to get up and talk, bringing out certain sugges-tions, how to build the organization and all that, these better class Negroes was caught by surprise. These kind of people had never had the chance to hear ordinary Negroes talk like that. They was shocked to find out such people could make such a wonderful presentation. They didn't know that they had people among the low class that could talk like that. But we was just talking and trying to get the NAACP to fighting issues that they ought to have been bringing up, like when the police let whites get away with murdering Negroes.

There in 1938 out there in Norwood, that's out there in North Birmingham, there was a Negro woman. In those days in Birming-ham, some Negroes was living in the rear of white folks' houses. And this Negro woman, a widow woman, she had a boy fifteen years old. She was living in the alley around some white folks. Right by her was a white guy, a steelworker, working at the steel mill. He ain't the poorest kind, but he not no rich guy. He would always come and get this woman to let her boy stay with his two kids when him and his wife go out at night. He had a four-year-old boy and a eight-year-old girl.

One night, the wife got the Negro mother to let the boy stay with the kids. The man was working. And the wife goes out. Wherever she went, she went out and stayed longer than she should have. Her husband got off of work. He didn't get off till 11:00 out there at the steel plant. He gets off to work, comes home, finds this fifteen-year-old boy sitting around seeing after the kids, and his wife still ain't come in. That must of been at least midnight. When she did come in, the boy went home.

I don't know where this wife was at, don't know what lie she had to tell, but what this dirty rat done, he took it out on the Negro boy. His wife was out, so he was mad, and he taken it out on the boy by claiming the boy raped the eight-year-old girl. The next morning, he put out a statement that this Negro boy had raped this eight-year-old girl that night. He had the widow woman's son put in jail.

Some people living out in Smithfield by me was at the courthouse to be in on another case, and they happened to be there when they had this boy's trial. That's how I know about the case. They told me that the boy was sentenced to be executed. Then this judge, he wrote a note and passed it to one of the officials in the courtroom. When he passed that note to this next official, this official looked at the judge and frowned. When he frowned, and looked at that note like that, the judge said, "Give me it back, hand it back here." So he hand him the note back. And then this official which hand the note back to the judge, he went over to the side with his hand behind his back and went to looking out the window. After a while, the judge told the deputy sheriff that he might take the prisoner— this fifteen-year-old boy—on back to the jail. The jail was there in courthouse.

Just as they took the boy through the two double doors of the courtroom, a pistol fired. When the pistol fired, the boy's mother jumped up: "Oh, Lord, is they killing my child?"

Then other people jumped up, but the judge hollered, "Sit down! Sit down!" He made everybody sit down and be quiet. He wouldn't allow nobody to go out the door who was in the court room until finally somebody came in and said something to the judge in a whisper. The judge says, "All cases dismissed for the day. You all go home now. No more cases for the day."

The man what told me the story said when they come up and walked out of the courtroom, this custodian had a bucket and a mop, and had done mopped up the blood, and were going on back up from the door to the court up the hall. Everybody went out. All they see was where he mop, but they ain't seed no boy. What happened, the judge and the official had allowed this girl's daddy to shoot this boy and kill him when they brought him out the door. And they had done moved the body, and wiped up the blood before they allowed the rest of the Negroes to come out the courtroom.

At the NAACP meeting, this question came up. And they're saying, "These people, you can't get them to come to the NAACP meeting." Talking about the boy's mother and all the ordinary Negroes. "They won't come to any meeting. If they come down and let us know what's the trouble, we could do something for them. But we don't know what to do for them because they won't come out and make a report." They didn't even know where the woman lived at. They were still compromising. They didn't want to face the facts, take the responsibility.

I got out myself and went over to that area in Norwood. I walked around through that community, and I found where the woman lived. I went to about four or five houses back there behind these white people. I went to one Negro woman, I told her, I says, "Lady," I says, "pardon me." I says, "I'm over here looking to try to find the woman they killed her son in the courthouse," I said. "I'm a member of the NAACP," I said, "and we, the NAACP, is interested to trying to help the woman, if only we could find where she is and get her to come to the office."

The woman showed me where she live right there. The house was about rock distance across a little open lot behind the white folks. "But she ain't at home now," she said. She let me wait on her porch until the woman got home. When she came back, I went to her house.

The boy's mother was in the house, and I spoke to her and told her who I was and told her what my business was. I told her that the NAACP was interested in that case and would like to help her, if there was any way we could. The woman was glad to see me. She was surprised. I told her she would have to come to the secretary's office—he was a doctor. I give her the office number of the doctor's secretary to take a complaint and eveything. The woman told me she'd be glad to come over there and talk with them. She would like somebody to do something. I made it my business to be over there next morning when the doctor opened his office—Negro doctor, in the Masonic Temple—and told him what I had done, and the woman was coming. So he was ready for her when she got there.

The woman came in and went in to talk with him. (I wasn't in there when they was talking. I don't know what the discussion was.) It was going to be one or two nights till the meeting night. She came to the meeting. They introduced her to the meeting—she's the woman what they killed her son at the courthouse. And oh, everybody raving, you know, all the big shots were talking and shooting the bull.

Twas a Negro setting there in his overalls. He looked just like a ordinary worker like me, but I didn't know him, didn't know nothing about him. When they making they fuss over the woman, he got up, said, "Now you all talking," he said, "but I'm going to show you. I'm going put my money where my mouth at." Said, "I'm ready to do something about this thing." Now he was one of these low class. But he gets up and walks to the table, saying, "I'm laying $10 on the table to start this case off, to raise the money." And everybody there was "Ohhhh!!" just surprised. They had to get up and say something about this wonderful man. Everybody then come up and lay a dollar or something on the table. That was a breakthrough.

They went and had a warrant, had this guy arrested. They went through the motions. Now Shores—that was before a Negro could practice law in Birmingham—he couldn't practice law.[2] He was representing the NAACP, but all Shores could do was work with the prosecutors to get evidence to prosecute the case. He could set in there, but he couldn't say nothing.

When they come up for the preliminary hearing on the case, Arthur D. Shores was setting on the end of the front bench, in front of the judge. The white man what shot the woman's boy come up before this judge, and he had his little boy in his arms. The prosecuting attorney said to the judge, "Judge, Your Honor, I been knowing this man for twenty-five years." Said, "I been knowing him for twenty-five years, and he's a real gentleman."* That's what he told the judge, he standing up there, and Shores sitting there and all the place is packed up with these Negro big shots of the NAACP.

The judge says, "I'll bind him over to the grand jury on the bond of $2500." And he bound him over to the grand jury, but the grand jury hearing came out with no bill and turned him loose. That was it. That was the end of case.

After that the NAACP had a big meeting, but the general saying

---

* The prosecuting attorney said that. Can you figure that?!

was still that "we got to get more of these people, these Negroes, to become members of the organization. We got to get more of them to join, come into the organization, where they pay their money, where we'll have some money to fight these cases. We don't have sufficient money to fight these cases." That was their regular saying all the time. They was always saying they didn't have the money and "These people, they won't support the organization." They was always putting it on the Negro people, particularly what you call the lower class who's always been in front of the gun.

WE had another case there in 1938. I was living out there in Smith-field, in Birmingham, and it was a Tuesday morning. I was pretty near known in the area now. I was always the agitator about coming to meeting, NAACP or building the CIO or something, all the time. I still wasn't working in the shop. So I went up there on the block that Tuesday and there were three or four Negro men standing around. They said to me, "Hudson, what are you going to do about that?"

"Do about what?"

"Did you see where that white man shot that nigger there in that drugstore Sunday evening?"

I said, "No, I didn't know anything about it." It was right there in Smithfield, Birmingham, on 8th Avenue and Charles Street. A Negro walked in a drugstore to buy a package of cigarettes. Cigarettes was 15¢ a pack, and he give the guy a quarter. The guy at the drugstore was a white guy, name of old man Warden. The Negro was a kind of well-dressed young fellow. And the Negro say he didn't give him his change out of his quarter. Warden say he did, and so they got back and forth, words back and forth, "I did," "you didn't," and "you didn't," "I did." So the Negro throwed the cigarettes back on the counter, told him, "Give me my 15¢." He gave him his 15¢, and he was turned around and was walking to the door and this white guy shot this Negro in the back, in the right shoulder. Not a direct shot, but more or less a glancing shot around the shoulder blades. They told me the story and asked me what I'm going to do about it.

I said, "What I'm going to do about it? Don't ask me what I'm going to do about it. Ask me what you all going to do about it!"

"We'll do anything you say to."

"All right, you say you do what I say to do, so all right, come on." About a block away up there is this community center in the housing project, Smithfield housing project community center. I walked up there to the community center, with me and all these men talking, all the way up there with them. The fellow who was on the community center was named Myron Jackson, that was Emory Jackson's brother.

We walked in there and I told him what we had been talking about, and I wanted to know could we get this place for a meeting tomorrow night, that would be a Wednesday night. He told me, yeah, we could get the center and have the meeting. Then I told them, "Now you all go around and tell everybody in the community we're going have a meeting here tomorrow night at 8 o'clock." We didn't put out no leaflets, this just by word of mouth.

That Wednesday night, we had the community center packed with people out of the community. All the big shots, all everybody. We had a guy named Gilliard. Gilliard was a contractor, a plumbing contractor. He was Mr. Gilliard, he was a big shot. He was there.

I got up there that night and I opened the meeting, told them what the purpose of the meeting was for, and "What you all want to do about it?" I made suggestions what ought to be done. I suggested number one, that a committee be elected to go see this fellow's sister. And number two, that another committee would be elected to go and raise some money. And number three, that the other committee be elected to go see a lawyer. Now what the committee was going to the sister for, was to see would the sister be willing for us to have the guy Warden prosecuted. (The Negro was in the hospital now.) Would she be willing for us to work with her to have the man prosecuted, including going to have a warrant swore out for the guy for shooting. That was what that committee was for.

The next committee's on raising finances and the other one to see Attorney Shores. Mind you, I was the chairman, the daddy of the whole thing. I served on all them committees. I was with the committee that went to see the sister. We went to the sheriff's office, and the sheriff told us to go down to see the police department, it's the police department's duty to recommend indictment.

We went to the police department, and we asked them what had they done about it, about indicting this man for shooting this Negro. They had a big old wide table in the room where we went in there to see the police. We was in overalls, and the man's sister was with us. They asked her, "Who is you?"

She said, "I'm his sister."

Then they wanted to know, "Who you all?"

"We came down here with her."

The sister wound up doing all the talking. They told her, "We ain't doing nothing about it. Who is that nigger out there who insulted that white man in that drugstore? We ain't going do nothing about it. He oughta killed the so-and-so."

So we went on out of there and went on back to the courthouse. The sheriff had said if he hadn't been indicted, to come back and he would issue a warrant. We went back down there and the sheriff wrote out a warrant. She's the one got the warrant out.

Same time, I went to Shores's office, me and two more, including a Negro woman. We went and talked to Attorney Shores and told him what we wanted to do, and he agreed that he would represent the community at the case.

Then we got on this finance committee, me and the same woman was on the other committee, her name was Mrs. Smith. At that time she was very active in the Eastern Star. She was just a ordinary working woman. She wont no big shot.* We went round to every little business and different people's house out in the community, including downtown Birmingham among the Negroes. Shores said he would take the case for $150. We raised about $190 in nickels and dimes and all that in practically one day. So we had the money. All right.

We went down and paid Shores. I was the one carried the money to Shores, me and Mrs. Smith, and he give me a receipt. He let us know when the trial going be, the guy was arrested. When the trial come up, we had people down at the courthouse. There again, Shores was sitting on the bench and the prosecutor was there representing him. The Negro was at the court, he out the hospital now.

This old judge was the same as in that other case, the NAACP case with the boy. He asked the question, "Where was this Negro shot at?" The white guy, old man Warden, claimed the Negro

---

* I seen her when I was in Birmingham here Christmas a year ago. She's a very old woman now, and she's dragging one side. She had a stroke. She's a very old woman now. She was a young woman then.

was advancing on him, and he shot him in self-defense. Then the judge asked the Negro, "Where did he shoot you at?"

The Negro said, "He shot me in my back, a glancing shot as I was walking out the door. He took my dime. I told him 'give me my 15¢' and I laid the cigarettes on the counter. When I turn around to walk out, he shot me walking away from him." Shores was sitting on in the prosecution, but the judge asked the prosecutor, said, "Do you have his chart showing he was shot in the back?" And the prosecutor said no.

And this old judge said, "I'm going to hold this case up until I see the chart." Said, "If the chart show that he was shot in the back, I'm going to bind him over to the grand jury. If the chart show that he was shot in the front, I'm going to turn the man free."

Me and Shores walked out the courthouse together. I asked him, said, "What you going do about this chart?"

He said, "I'm sorry. I should have got that chart from the hospital." He hadn't done nothing! Hadn't done no more then went up there to sit down on the end of that bench.

Me and him walked back through that park to his office, hurrying to come back to call to see about the chart at the hospital. I'm involved in this. Everybody in Smithfield looking to me for this, cause they all done said they didn't want to get Shores, because they said the Negro lawyer couldn't do nothing. But me and Mrs. Smith, we just held powder and we got Shores anyway.

We went to Shores's office and Shores got on the phone and called the hospital. I was sitting there. He said he wanted the chart, and they told Shores at the hospital that they couldn't let the chart out of the hospital without the consent of the head doctor, "and he's away now, he's out of town." They said, "We can tell you where he was shot. He was shot in the chest, but in back of the chest." That's right, they said he was shot in the back of the chest.

That was the first time Attorney Shores said he ever heard such talk. He asked, "Do you mean shot from the front or from the back?" They said he was shot from the back, in the chest. And that's all he had, word of mouth. He didn't have nothing to prove to the judge. So that was the last of that case. That white man went free. Shores give me $3. Said I had done more in the case than he did.

I had to take the rap then about Shores didn't do anything, like some of them had done said. But they went along with me, cause me and Mrs. Smith, we tried to give Shores a chance because he was a Negro.

Then some Negroes, I don't know who they was, went there to the drugstore at night and shot, not in the door in the glass, but up there above the door. They shot two-three holes up there. Them holes is in that building yet, in that drugstore. Old man Warden left there then, after they shot in there. He left.*

Even after I went out and got the case for the NAACP and the community got organized around this shooting in the drugstore, the NAACP didn't change much, not much. They didn't do anything. They still didn't want to rock the boat, make they good friends mad. The leadership was still trying to make deals. I kind of stood out in the NAACP individuals' minds—"Mr. Hudson," cause I could go find things they couldn't find. Some of them tell me, "Man, you just like a detective," said, "you'd make a good detective, find these cases like that."

IN 19 and 38 me and Mayfield was delegates to the national Party convention in New York City. They was electing a Southern Regional Committee, from the national. They nominated me and a white guy from North Carolina, somebody Mayfield didn't know nothing about. They put it to a vote of all the Southern delegates. Mayfield voted for that Southern white guy out of North Carolina, and me and him from Birmingham together.

I took him aside, and I said, "Mayfield, what has you got against me?"

"Nothing, er, nothing."

I said, "Why you vote for this white guy you don't know nothing about and here me and you from Birmingham and you voted against me for him?"

I don't remember what lie he told, but I learned from that time don't never put nobody in your bosom. Treat them right, but don't

* And mind you, just about a month ago in the barbershop—it's a Negro detective always come in there with a big pistol sitting up there, get his hair cut. Some of them say, "Mr. Hudson, this man from your town, Birmingham." I forgets his name. So I got to talking with him, and I asked him did he remember that drugstore incident. He said, "Yeah, I was a boy then." I said, "Didn't you used to live right next door to Dr. Bradford?" He said yes. I said, "You was the big old fat boy I used to see there, back in 1938." Now he's a big detective here in Atlantic City.

put them in your bosom, not menfolks. People do things like that to me, but the good Lord let me see them go, I'm still here. Look how long Mayfield been gone* and I'm still here. Me and him supposed to be buddy-buddy, but that's what he done to me.

After the national convention, I had two women, two Negro women at that time was members of the Party from Mississippi, from Oxford Mississippi. They wasn't young women, they was middle-aged people, not overaged people, just in their forties somewhere. And I had a Negro man from Camp Hill Alabama. They was delegates. My task was to carry them back to Birmingham and see to them being put on the right buses back to Mississippi and back to Camp Hill. They hadn't never been North before, and I had to carry these delegates back. I had a time!

They give me some money to feed them, to buy food, cause buses didn't travel like they do now. It took you about two days and a night and some to get back to Birmingham from New York then on a bus. I didn't have but about $20 to feed everybody, myself and them too. So I first give them some money. I didn't give them all the money they supposed to have. I divide it up, give everybody some.

They was out the country, wasn't used to buying none. And they commenced to buying everything they seen. Just everything they see, they buy. So I know that money wasn't going to last to Birmingham. We got along about Roanoke Virginia, and by that time they done spent all the money I had give them. So I got in Roanoke Virginia, and I went out and bought a whole lot of sandwiches, and some apples and fruit, and I fed them from there to Birmingham myself.

I haven't seen them since I put them on the bus, any of them. They got home, but I never did see them no more. Always somebody else would come, and they didn't get back to convention. Finally the terror run them all underground down there in Mississippi.

* Mayfield died December 31, 1963.

17

WPA and the Workers Alliance

You couldn't get on WPA until your unemployed compensation give out. When that give out, you go to WPA and you register for a job. Then you get on the waiting list. And you wait until you get a assignment. I got on the waiting list and they signed me out for a job on July the 8th, 1938. Then I had to wait to get paid. I think it was a month you had to work before you get the first pay, which was $20 and 20¢ every two weeks. You had to put some time in, you work here before you get this check, then you done got another check in. It was only $40 a month, but it was welcome.

We was fixing streets. Streets which had been narrow, little narrow roads, we was opening them up and paving them. The whites worked on one gang. Negroes on another. But everybody getting paid the same. There was a union of the WPA workers, called it the Workers Alliance. John Buckley was the man who got me involved.

When Roosevelt first came in with the NRA, he elected a committee, and John Buckley was on Roosevelt's committee. He was a critic. We read about him a whole lot before he ever come to Birmingham. He wont old, was a young guy, but he was a critic of a lot of the NRA rulings. He was a kind of troublemaker for good, to try to push them ahead.

In that period, that was when Garner was Vice-President, John Garner of Texas. And you had Bankhead from Alabama, and George from Georgia and Hill from Alabama, all very reactionary.*

* [John H. Bankhead, II, Senator from Alabama; Representative William B. Bankhead of Alabama; Walter F. George, Senator from Georgia; and Lister Hill, Representative, then Senator from Alabama, all in the 75th Congress (1937–1939).]

They's fighting Roosevelt. A whole lot of things Roosevelt was trying to do, they was fighting. And some of Roosevelt's things wont
good, either.

So Buckley was on this committee, and this was when every
time things would reach the Supreme Court, the Supreme Court
would rule against Roosevelt's plan, in favor of these reactionaries
of the South. That's when Roosevelt come out and spoke about
these "nine old men," and he tried to change some of them on the
Supreme Court.[1]

John Buckley got so militant and he's such an outstanding critic
by hisself, till they finally wire-worked him off that committee.
Then he came to be a national representative for the WPA workers
union there in Birmingham. David Lasser, the president, and Herb
Benjamin, the secretary-treasurer, was the national officers. They
sent John Buckley down to organize the WPA workers in Alabama.

John Buckley, he was a Party member. I don't know if it was
widely known, but they called him "communist" all the time. You
don't have to be a Party member, they don't have to know you're
a Party member to say so. Anytime you begin to talk too militant,
too progressive about certain things that favors the poor people, you
automatically you's a communist. (Sure enough, whether you believe it or not, it ain't no way for a honest person who wants to see
real progress made to avoid being called a communist. Automatically you fall in that category. Cause communists is the onliest ones
fighting for such things as that. I mean fight. Some of them make a
lot of noise, then they back up. But the Party fights all the way
through. It's like a bulldog. We don't give up—some of us.)

So Buckley came to Birmingham. He was the right man to come
to Birmingham, cause he didn't give in to these white racists. He
didn't give in to the bosses. They didn't want no unified union.
They said, "Let the whites join, but keep the niggers out." All that
stuff. Buckley went foursquares. He had to deal with these raw
white workers, coal miners and steelworkers, who had never been
round Negroes before, cause the Workers Alliance was mostly
white.

He came to our Party meeting one night along in August or the
first of September. It was something like a leading committee,
several of us. He made a report on the WPA workers union. He
said, "Here we trying to build this union," said, "and you all, our

leading Party members ain't out there, none of you active. It's time for electing officers, and none of you all there. We need you all to come out to the meetings where we can elect some of you." He seen somebody was going to get in there wont going to stand up like a leader. Buckley told about the meeting going to be held Saturday in Fairfield to organize this county council. And he asked for some Negroes to be there.* This meeting was to organize locals from Bessemer and different places. They meeting in Fairfield in the steelworkers' hall as a kind of unique meeting place for all the locals that ain't got no meeting hall.

Me and Mayfield went out to Fairfield. I had just started working on the WPA, and Mayfield was still in the coal mine. But he went as a WPA worker. They didn't know one WPA worker from another. Mayfield had been in the unions, in the local, and he done learnt how to talk pretty straight. Me and Mayfield was at this meeting, and we was discussing. We done lost a lot of that fear of whites, of speaking out in public with whites. So Mayfield gets up and made some kind of talk about organizing, about the council, about electing officers, something like that. Then he made a motion, and I said, "I second the motion."

These poor whites had never heard of a Negro making motions. So the old chairman of the meeting hollered, "Look at them! Look at them! They making motions! Look at them! Making motions! Let's go!" He stopped chairing the meeting and got his grip and got his gavel and walked out. It was a lot of people there, white and black, men and women were there, and he carried about ten or fifteen of them crazy crackers with him. I ain't seen him since. Some of them stayed. Then we broke for lunch. When we went back for the afternoon session, we carried on the business. They picked another chairman and elected a president, secretary, and treasurer. This was out in Fairfield.

Along in September, Local 1 in Birmingham was having a mass meeting, open meeting, Negro and white. They was meeting at the courthouse then. They had a great big house full of people, and they's telling about how we need to elect officers there. They still hadn't elected officers of that local. They just meeting and talking

* That's the way I know he was in the Party, cause he was in our Party committee meeting. That was the onliest meeting I ever saw him in, was that committee. He didn't come every time we turned around for a meeting.

and talking, but no electing of officers. I signed my card. Didn't pay but 25¢ to join the Workers Alliance, to join the union. They give you a card, offer you the stub with a number on it.

We was in room 608 in the courthouse, and it had a balcony all around. Down here was the whites. All up here was the Negroes, in the balcony. Negroes all around up here, looking down here at the whites. I'm up here too. It was still segregated cause that was at the beginning of the Workers Alliance. They didn't have nowhere they could hold a meeting with white and black sitting down together. They still abided by the jim crow law, so they could meet at the courthouse.

They got to electing officers that night. They nominated a white president, a white secretary-treasurer, and they wanted a Negro for vice. Well, automatically, up here's two or three of our Party people, they up and nominates me for vice-president. I don't know if we had arranged that before. Maybe so and maybe not. I think it was Cornella Hibbard that nominate me, if I make no mistake about it, her or Hazel Stanley or some of them. They was all up there. We all was Party people up there. So she nominates me. I think we had arranged that beforehand. We always discussed things before we went anywhere.

After they nominates me, they nominate another young Negro woman, Edwina Collins, for recording secretary.* Then we all was elected. When they got ready to swear us in, we had to come out the balcony, me and Edwina Collins, we come down to the main floor, come up the desk where the judge at, be swore in. When they swore us in, we took the oath of allegiance. Then we had a seat back over here where everybody else. I'm at the meeting down here with these white folks. So the next meeting night, we got ready to go back to the courthouse, and the officials of the courthouse wouldn't allow us to hold the meeting there, because they wouldn't allow us to sit down there with the whites.

That fall, in October, I went from Birmingham to Cleveland, to the Workers Alliance convention, me and Buckley and Tom Howard, the president of the local. Tom Howard was a ex coal miner. He eventually was elected president of the Jefferson County council, and they elected me vice-president of the county council. We went to Cleveland, came back through Washington, to see

---

* I hadn't met her before. She was just a woman on some part of the WPA. She wasn't a Party member.

Harry L. Hopkins,[2] because we had some grievances we wanted to discuss with Harry L. Hopkins about. We couldn't get settled there in Birmingham.

The major grievance still hanging was where two brothers, working on WPA, way out from nowhere, one of the brothers was a waterboy.* This brother went off, go bring the water, had to go a long way to get the water to bring it back to the job. He went and he stayed so long, they got suspicious. He didn't never come back. So the other brother stopped work out of the crowd, went to see where he was.

When he found him, he had dropped dead. I don't know whether he was going or coming, on the route, but they found him dead, where he had a heart attack and died. This live brother, he stayed out there with the body till they could get somebody to notify some undertaker to go out there to get the body. In other words, he lost the balance of the day's work. The WPA officials there in Birmingham wouldn't pay him for the day.

So we come around from Cleveland Ohio, me and Buckley and Tom Howard, and we stopped in Washington to see Harry L. Hopkins about that case and some other business, but particularly about that case. Harry L. Hopkins was out in New England, the time it was a big flood up there, so we seed Aubrey Williams.[3] We hadn't been able to get any settlement there in Alabama. Buckley and Howard, they had talked to the officials in Birmingham, and they wouldn't give in on it. They contacted the state officials there at Montgomery, and they wouldn't agree to pay him for the day's work. Then we went to Washington, decided we would raise the question up there in Washington. That was the case that I was most concerned about, and that was the first time that I learnt the position of the government about certain cases.

Now here's what Aubrey Williams said when we asked him about pay. We asked him about paying for this job, paying for this day's work for this fellow—it wont nothing. You know $40 a month, it couldn't a been much a day, maybe $1 or $2 a day or something, that's all.

Aubrey Williams asked the question, "Why should we pay him?" He said, "We can sympathize with him as a brother, it's humane. We can understand that." His brother died, and he was out there to

* The two brothers was Coxes, Eb Cox's brothers. Eb Cox was the first Negro who came to be at the head in the steel union.

see to his brother getting got out from there, back to the under-taker's. "But why should the government have to pay him for that day's work?"

We argued backwards and forwards, but we didn't win our argument. "Do you think the government should have to pay him his day's work when he quit work and went to see about his brother?" It was a pretty stiff question. Whether it's right or wrong, we didn't win the argument. I learnt something from that argument that day. I learnt that just to look at a natural point isn't enough. Automatically I would have paid the man for his day's work. His brother had done died. But Aubrey Williams pointed out that "we sympathize, we sorry he lost his brother, but why should the government have to pay for his day's work?"

Aubrey Williams turned out to be one of the progressives in the South, but since I wasn't developed then, I didn't know whether he's progressive or not. But he was nice. He wasn't rude, nothing like that. I didn't consider he was a racist. He was over the Youth Administration at that time. He was a southerner, and eventually he came back South, I think down in Auburn, somewhere down in Alabama. That's where he finally died, down there. He's always, all the way through, had a liberal approach, more or less. The leaders of the Southern Negro Youth Congress, after he came back from Washington, they used to go have conferences with him.

After that trip to Washington, we came back and organized a meeting out in the park on the back side of the courthouse to report on our trip. We put a leaflet out in the WPA projects that caught a whole lot of people. It was on a Friday night. It was thousands of people out there, white and black, men and women, way out in the park. We had a loudspeaker. I think Buckley might have made the first speech, and Howard last, I wasn't last. We spoke and told them what we found there in Cleveland and Washington.

In my appeal in particular that night, I pointed out what we had to do, the importance of registering to vote, of putting people in office that was going to represent the interest of the people. Cause we had one congressman, Luther Patrick, was up there, he's fighting for the WPA, and another congressman was up there fighting against it. He was from Gadsden, Congressman Starnes.[4] I can't say word for word my remarks, but I also I pointed out the importance of more strongly organized organization among black and white, not only just on the project, but also in the communities, unemployed people, to send postcards and letters. I was pulling no punches. I was saying what ought to be said.

Then the AF of L tried to take over the mike at the meeting, they tried to break it up. I don't know whether it was the hod carriers or who they was, but the AF of L wanted to take over the mike. They was against the Workers Alliance all the way through. One of them wanted to have a right to speak, so John Buckley made an announcement, said, "These gentlemen from the AF of L union wants to take over this platform. It's up to you all brothers and sisters. What is your pleasure?"

"NO!! NO!! NO!!"

Then Buckley said, "I would suggest that a few of you all strong-armed men would come up to this platform . . ." And they had white guys come up there, and them AF of L guys got off there fast. But some of them whites was running among the Negroes, "Where that nigger live, that nigger Hosie Hudson, where do he live at?" Trying to find my address, what part of town I lived in. But none of them wouldn't tell them where I lived at. I was living out there in Smithfield, but wouldn't none of them tell.

This same time in '38 was when the Southern Conference for Human Welfare had a conference in Birmingham. This was the time that President Roosevelt sent out a committee to make a investigation of the conditions of the South.[5] It was last of '37 or the first of '38. When the committee came in, they made a report to President Roosevelt, and when President Roosevelt made a statement, he said that on the basis of this committee's findings, that the South was the number-one economic problem of the nation. On the basis of that, all these leaders, particularly the whites, but many of the blacks—not all of them—but a great many of them in the South, from Washington all the way down, they became very indignant. Professors, big professors, some of the congressmen, and doctors, cause Roosevelt said the South was the number-one problem of the nation. They said, "Look, we got to do something about it."

So they called this Southern Conference for Human Welfare in Birmingham.[6] The woman who helped to organize this conference was Louise Charleton. And also Luther Patrick. He was the congressman from Jefferson County at that time, he and Cooper Green. At that time I believe he was the head of the post office department, Cooper Green. He later come to be mayor of the city of Birmingham. And William Mitch, head of the United Coal Miners,* he also was the district director of the CIO, and president of the state CIO. And they brought in such people as Mrs. Mary McCloud Bethune and Mrs. Roosevelt was there. Hugo Black was there.[7] And about three or four was elected to attend the conference to represent the Workers Alliance. I was a delegate to that conference from the Workers Alliance.

The conference open on Monday, and we had a mass meeting in the city auditorium on Sunday, the Workers Alliance and the unemployed. The place helt about 16,000 people, and it was about full of people. I was up on the platform. I spoke that evening on the question of more relief for the unemployed people, more jobs, and an increased wage scale, because we were then only getting $40 and 40¢ a month on the WPA. These was the things we talked about, was hoping the conference would address itself to, that something would come out of this conference on the wage question of the South.

A lot of these delegates was attending that conference, they tried to put that under the rug. It was a ticklish question, cause it would infringe on their relationship with some of the good white industrialists in the South—these schoolteachers, professors, them kind of people at this conference. When you talk about a wage increase, you're hitting over here on the industrialists, some of them is they friends, and they tried to avoid them kind of issues at that particular conference. And then you had the whole question along with that about the differential of wages in the South, between the South and the North. Common labor making 30–40¢ an hour in the big steel plant. No overtime, just straight time, 40¢ an hour—had been 30¢ an hour. But northern common labor was much higher. So they was touching on a dangerous question here, this question of differential of wages.

Coming out against lynching, the resolution on lynching was another very ticklish question. A lot of times people wouldn't take the floor. It was only the Party people, or somebody very militant would stand up and raise these questions. Everybody didn't speak up against lynching. The rights to vote for the Negro people was another hot issue. Them was automatically Communist Party

* [United Mine Workers. Hudson makes the distinction because the coal miners belonged to the UMW, the ore miners to the Mine, Mill and Smelter Workers union.]

slogans. These people didn't want to have no part of it, cause they didn't want to be accused of being a communist.

So we had that mass meeting Sunday, then had the conference session Monday and Monday night, and all that was at the auditorium. All these leaders, Negro and white, from all over the South, not just Birmingham, all over the South, come there, going work out something to give answers to what President Roosevelt had said. Here in the first meeting, we got a seat where we can find it. We registered in, had seats, had speakers. People sitting everywhere, Negro and white, all over the place, all mixed up, on Monday.

Now Tuesday morning, we get back, here's the jim crow sign, the little city sign, city ordinance. You see, the front of the city auditorium then was a big, beautiful green lawn. The auditorium sits in the middle of the block. You had a walkway going from this corner and one going from this corner, and then one go straight in. And the Birmingham city officials, they come up this walkway come straight in and set up a peg there and put a line on it. They had done got them a white cord, we call it a plow line, like what you drive a mule, and got out there on the avenue, on 8th Avenue. They put that peg there and put that line on it, carried it up the steps, straight to the door (it was a double door), carried it right across, right on through the door, right down the aisle, right on up to the speakers' stand on the platform, on back to the back. It was about 2–3 feet from the ground, and one side say "white," and the other side say "colored."

And all these leaders, law-abiding citizens, Negro and white, they said, "We don't want to be law violators." If they had of challenged that jim crow white cord and that jim crow sign there, that's the time they could have broke the backbone of jim crowism in the South, not only Birmingham, but the whole South. Old lady Bethune, Mrs. Roosevelt, Hugo Black, all of them abided by that doggone jim crow sign.*

In our Party, we had a meeting on it that Tuesday. The Party had a meeting, cause in that period, we got together every day to summarize what took place today, and we discussed it. We had a big discussion in the Party right at that time, and we were saying this is the time that sign, this law, ought to be challenged.[8]

---

* And I say today, all that stuff that Reverend King and them went through, trying to break down segregation, what they had to suffer, and some people's murder, could have been stopped that day.

This meeting was Tuesday afternoon, not a whole lot of people, four–five people, including the D.O. and a guy who was there then from the national office of the Party, Gene Dennis.[9] Gene Dennis was there in Birmingham representing from the national leadership of the Party to give guidance in the discussions. And I was in the meetings. The position that was taken in the discussions was that certain people was trying to see if the Party wouldn't run out and grab the bull by the horns. But what the Party would do was try to maneuver against some other people who had more influence, to get this person to take a stand. That was the role that Joe Gelders was trying to play. He was a professor, and he had a certain group of people, supposed to be liberal, and he had contact with people like Hugo Black and Hugo Black's law partner, Crampton Harris, and Louise Charleton, and three or four more that he could go sit down and talk to. They recognized him. Joe Gelders would try to maneuver behind the scenes, but he wouldn't come out and take a forthright position. But he did approach certain people to try to get some of these people to challenge that law, to correct the law. But all they wanted to say was "I don't want to be a law violator."

Nobody in the Party meeting wanted to act alone. We didn't see that it would of made a good case. It's a question of you going out there by yourself. The Party position was we don't run ahead of the masses. We move with the masses. The Party don't just go out and do things, not real Party people. We moves, we wants to be militant. Our position is militant, but not super-militant. Not to do something here where we going to create a situation we not able to back up and get support, because if you don't get the mass support, you can't get nowhere.

That was our trouble down there all the time with our backs against the wall, because we couldn't get that mass movement. We had to fight practically single-handed. People admire us, but they wouldn't move. So the question of it was, if a Negro had of went over and challenged that law, if a white had of violated that law, would they have been able to build the public support enough to raise the issue? Even five or six or ten, even at that rate, when you got all your leaders of the South here, abiding by it. Do you think we'd of been able to get them involved in fighting to defend those violating the law? It was just a question of getting your head bloody.

Nowadays if you get arrested, put in jail, you may put in jail like Reverend King and them. They put so many they couldn't whup everybody, so some of them didn't mind going to jail. But when we went to jail in that period, it meant to be beat half to death maybe. So this is why we didn't want to get kilt for nothing, unlessen it was necessary. But here, this leadership of the South accepted this jim crow plow line, Judge Louise Charleton, Cooper Green, Luther Patrick, William Mitch, all of them accepted. You think we little fellows there going go out and do something that we know they ain't going to do? We would have been ahead of the times. These things is important to talk about, cause this is the crust of things. I said people can't imagine what we Negroes in the Party was standing up against. We were standing up alone, practically. A whole lot of Negroes and two-three whites. That's the way it was. The mass of whites wouldn't fall in.

18
End of the WPA

ALONG in February of '39, I was at the Workers Alliance conference in Washington. It was a two-day conference. Sixty-five delegates from all over the country was there, and they elected a delegation of five people, including David Lasser, who was the national president, and me to go see President Roosevelt. Secretary Watson* said Roosevelt had the flu, he wasn't seeing any visitors that day, but he took us into the Oval Room and he took our message and promised to deliver it to Roosevelt. In the South, we was asking for a wage increase and also for more projects. We was asking for $70 a month, instead of the $40. We got $50—they did raise it to $50, but everybody was on WPA eighteen months or longer had to take a thirty-day vacation. All that went together.

At the conference of the Workers Alliance, quite naturally, the word got around who's the best people, and somebody around said, "Hosie Hudson, he's a Party member down there in Alabama." So Herb Benjamin, he's the national secretary-treasurer, he was a old Party member—while I was up there at the national office, Herb Benjamin told me to give him my home address. He said, "Whenever anything coming up in the WPA nationally," he said, "whatever I send out, I'll send yourn to you," and he'll send to the Workers Alliance headquarters in Birmingham, to the secretary-treasurer of the county council. But he'd send me my bulletin to my house.

Sometimes I'd get my bulletin before they get theirs at the council. But I wouldn't carry my bulletin out. I would get up and talk about what's going happen. When I talk about it, it would happen. Now I ain't said I got no bulletin. On the job, I'd get up there and

* [General Edwin M. (Pa) Watson was President Roosevelt's appointments secretary.]

293

I'd make a announcement, tell the guys what to be looking out for, according to Washington. So the little foremans and everybody on the job, they waiting for me, wanted to see had I got anything new this morning. When I walk in a meeting meeting nights—we meet on Tuesday night—whites and Negroes, men and women, all the crowd would come around me. "Hi, Bro' Hudson, how's we coming along? What you see new now?" The Negroes was very bashful, they'd stand back there, but the whites come up.

I tell them, "Such-and-such a thing is going to take place, it seems like, what I can line." I wouldn't say where I get my information. The Negro women stood back. They wont used to coming up, walking up among white folks. So I made them welcome.

One night when we was meeting good, a Negro woman was hanging back, she wanted to speak to me. But she stood back. I had to call her up, "Sister, you want to talk to me?"

She said, yes, and she told me her daughter bought a set of furniture from one of these little old furniture dealers. They had a knack there, where Negroes would buy a set of furniture. Whatever you pay for it, you pay down, maybe $20–$25, and you get behind where you can't pay your each week. Then they come take the furniture. In that way, they sell it again, beat the Negroes. So this woman's daughter had bought some furniture and she had paid on it, $3 a week, and she had paid all on the furniture but $9. She missed one or two payments. When she did carry a payment down, they wouldn't accept it at the furniture place, because she's behind and didn't pay on time. This was a scheme to come out and take it. The woman wanted to know from me what did I think she could do, cause they going come take her daughter's furniture.

I thought of it there out of a clear blue sky—didn't nobody tell me. I thought right quick, said, "I tell you what you do. You tell your daughter to go down to the post office and buy her a money order. Buy her a money order, and make the money order out, $9, the whole amount she owe, and send it to them, send it registered mail, so she know they'll get it. They'll have to take it, the government's money."

The next meeting we had, the woman come round to me just all smiling. "Bro' Hudson, me and my daughter we done just what you told me. We done all right. She kept that stub from the money order, and when they got that registered letter, he come out to the house and asked my daughter, 'Who learnt you how to be so God damn smart?' She said to him, 'You got your money?' He said, 'Yeah, I got it.' And they never took the furniture."

I helped several people like that, and doing so, I came to be very outstanding among white and black. So then the president of the Workers Alliance, he got very jealous, Tom Howard did. Not only he jealous, he begin to go around and build up hatred, try to build up hatred among the other whites against me. He commenced talking about me, "I don't see what the hell these damn white women see in that Hosie Hudson. Every time you see him, they all up in his face." He only seen the white women. "What is that they see in this Hudson? I don't see nothing all that grand about him, but they always up in his face talking to him."

We had a white minister from Leeds Alabama, named Reverend Maple. He was one of our Party people, but he was a pastor of a church up there. And Reverend Maple, he was representative from Leeds at the Workers Alliance, so he'd be around among the whites and he'd hear Howard making these expressions. He'd come back in the Party and tell us what Howard be saying about me. That's the way I was able to keep up with what's happening.

It kept on to the point I called a meeting one night, one Wednesday night. I invited about fifteen people, including Howard, and the secretary, Harold Crawford. Crawford also had joined the Party, and Crawford also was telling us in the Party what Howard was saying. He lived out from Birmingham. He was a ex coal miner like Howard, a white guy, but he didn't think what Howard was doing was good for the organization. What Howard's doing was tearing up the organization.

The meeting wont just the officers of the Workers Alliance, it was individual people, white and black, and it wont just Party members either. It was people that I thought was of sound judgment that we could be able to talk this thing over. That night I was going get up and tell what's been coming to me what Howard was saying, and find out why Howard was saying that, and let's see could we iron it out without it getting out to all the organization. But Howard didn't come. All the rest of the people come but him, Negro and white. Since Howard wasn't there, we couldn't do nothing.

I did explain to those that came what the meeting was called for, though, what Howard been saying. Not only was he tearing up the unity, but also he's making personal remarks, dangerous for me, cause some of them racist whites would want to take a lynching attitude towards me, try to do some bodily harm to me about them white women.

At the next regular meeting, on Saturday, Howard was sitting up here at the table, the president, and I was sitting here, next to him, the vice-president. When it got down to the question of new business, he passed the gavel over on to me, said he wanted to make a special point of privilege. He got up, saying that he understood that twas a little wildcat meeting get together Wednesday night, and he was invited to come, but he didn't come, because he felt anything that was inclement before this organization, the membership should know about it. He wont for little rumps going around holding secret meetings unbeknownst to the membership. Therefore he stayed away. "It was something pertaining to Bro' Hudson. He's got some disagreement about something I said about him." He didn't say nothing about communist, didn't Red-bait me, but he just put it as sharp as he could without saying communist. He said, "I'm going make a motion that we appoint a committee, elect a committee here today to thrash this thing out, what Bro' Hudson got on his mind, and get it cleared up. And in this motion I want it understood that no members was at this wildcat meeting Wednesday night be allowed to sit on this committee." Somebody seconded the motion, and I called for discussion of the motion, not for the question.

There was some people it was news to. They didn't know what's all about, "What is this thing?" They was talking backwards and forwards.

I pushed the gavel then back to Howard, pushed it back over here to him, and I get up and take the floor. I told why the meeting was called. "The people was there because I called them, and I called them because certain accusations was being made that was against the interests of this organization which would destroy the unity between the white and Negro in this organization. I thought that we might be able to thrash it out without it getting among everybody. But since Bro' Howard has brought it here, put it on the floor," I said, "I'm going to make a special appeal and further call for this motion that a committee be set up to iron this thing out, but I want to appeal to you all, ladies and gentlemen, do not support the clause in this motion that will prohibit any member that was here at that meeting Wednesday night from sitting on this committee. Anyone you all want to nominate on this committee, I urge you to nominate," I said. "I will agree that I not serve on that committee, and neither Bro' Howard. But any of these members was here Wednesday night, they wasn't here because they came here to frame up something. They was here because I invited them. They didn't know what they was going to come here for until they got here. So I think it would be a disservice to make them victims."

They took my advice. They turned down Howard's position and accepted my position, and some of these people was elected on that committee. The committee was nine members, one or two Negroes, all the rest of them white. When they got in the hearing, they went in there and they read over these charges I made—I had done drawn up my charges and presented them to the committee.

First they called me in, and I went in. They wanted to know about these charges, was this true. I begin to tell them how they's coming to me and who was telling me about this thing and why I called this meeting Wednesday night and why I was wanting this meeting now. It was all in they hands to save the organization and the unity between the white and the black. I felt that these charges of Howard was creating animosity against me and really creating lynch ideas among some of the anti-race-unity elements, because of what he was saying about white women. These racists were saying, "Lynch that Negro, white women going for him like that."

Things got sharp, and they sent me out and brought Howard in. One old fellow in there, white fellow, he was from out of town somewhere, some of these outlying mining towns, he come out to talk to me, said, "Bro' Hudson," he said, "this thing going tear up this organization, and this organization is too important for the unemployed people and to us, to destroy it. I wants one agreement out of you," he said. "If Bro' Howard will agree to apologize to you, will you shake hands and drop this thing?"

I said, "If he apologize and recognize his mistake," I said, "sure, I'll shake hands with him and I'll lay the ax at the root of the tree."

So he went back in there and he told what I had agreed to. They talked, then they call me in there. They made that statement that I would agree to drop the charges against Howard and we wouldn't bother, wouldn't discuss them no more if he would agree to apologize. So I was standing over this way, by the wall, and Howard was standing this way, facing me. He reach his hand to me, and he say, "Bro' Hudson, I beg your pardon," but he not looking at me, he looking out the window. The windows was out that way. He wouldn't look me in the face. Everybody saw him, and it was a strange look. He deliberately wouldn't look me in the face. All the other people in the committee looked at him, took stretching note to it. But I accepted it, I accepted his apology. But the organization then was fast fading away.

It was hard to get appropriations for the WPA in Congress. They wanted to cut the WPA out in Washington. Newspapers came out saying it was a communistic program. The industrialists was against it because "it was making the workers lazy. When they get the job back at the plant they wouldn't work." They had a line about leaning on the shovels and all that. Fact of the business, when the jobs did open up back in the plants, for a good while, if you tell them you working on the WPA, you couldn't get a job. They wouldn't give you a job. You couldn't say you worked on the WPA. They wouldn't hire you, until when the war really got going and they had to open up to hire these workers.

Orders come down from Harry L. Hopkins' office in Washington, and everybody been in WPA eighteen months or longer had to take a thirty-day vacation. That destroyed the Workers Alliance, because more or less all these staunch union members, white and Negro, had been on there more than eighteen months.

At that time you had a host of people sitting out, waiting to get on the WPA. The officials' claim was they couldn't put them on because they didn't have the jobs. We said if we get more jobs, then we'd have somewhere to put these people to work. That's the kind of battle we had going on all the time. So while this was going on, all through the whole thing, you had the agents behind the scenes, buttonholing individuals, saying that everything done was communist. They still branding the Workers Alliance as being a communistic organization, since we went up there and got a hall with one toilet for men, one for women. White women and black women use the same; white men and black men use the same. Those guys pick out individuals and work on them: "You all shouldn't be up there, white and nigger sitting together, nigger women going in the same toilet white women going in." The members would get all confused and come to us—essentially myself, and Hazel Stanley and Jimmie Hooper, and people who more or less acted as spokesmen in the union—come buttonhole us and tell us "what the public is saying."

I always answer back to them, "What is the public doing to help us get more WPA jobs or to give these people more relief? What are they saying about that?" They couldn't answer. "We don't listen at them. We don't let nobody tell us how to be seated if they ain't helping us do nothing for the unemployed, for the people." And that's where we set these people down at.

We would have them come in there, might of been FBI agents. I remember one very well. He wore a blue serge suit, clean-dressed guy, wont so tall, chubby, had a blue serge suit. He come in to me with all that crap, you know. "Ahhhhh, Hudson, I think . . ." I was well known now. He trying to tell me "what the public is saying," trying to hurt our organization.

I say, "How they going hurt us? They can't hurt us no worse than they is hurting us. People ain't got no jobs, ain't getting no relief. How they going hurt us?"

"It's going endanger your public relations." He took me out one evening and me and him had it out. Right on the street, he trying to convince me what the public is going to do. But I think since I learnt them pretty good, I think that he was a agent himself. Cause he always come, sit in the meeting, never say anything, sit quiet and never say nothing.

The first day of May 1939, all these people on WPA for eighteen months or more was laid off. At the union meeting, everybody poured into the hall, white and black. Our Party took the position that this thirty-day leave was going to be longer than thirty days. A lot of these people would never get a job back on WPA. The important thing was us trying to organize the people in such a way that we could hold the Workers Alliance membership and continue to fight for at least unemployed relief for the unemployed. So we tried that.

But things went so fast we couldn't keep up with it. First of all, when this first layoff first came, we had a meeting up there in the hall one day. This particular meeting was packed out. Down where they was interviewing people to re-register for a job, they didn't have enough staff people to interview people. Big lines of people would be standing out in the street, couldn't get in, in the weather. People go down, stay all day trying to get registered up. They couldn't get re-registered for after the thirty-day period was up, because they didn't have enough help to register. So we had this meeting at the Workers Alliance headquarters and we elected a committee to go down and see the officials of the WPA about it. On that committee was two white young men, one of them was a minister, and me. The people all waiting for us to come back at the hall where they elected us. We didn't have far to go.

Now here these guys, I ain't never met them before. I don't know what they are. You see, more or less, when we go on a committee, we'd be on there with someone we know. If it's a white person, you'd know him, about how he thinking or what. But here these two guys, I don't know what they going do. We hadn't elected no chairman or nothing of the group. We just walking down the street together. I was very much out of my place, tell the truth, cause I didn't feel altogether at home with these new folks. I looked at them, I said to myself, "I don't know about these folks. I don't know what they going go down there and say." So I raised the question, first of all, "What about who going to be chairman of this committee when we get down?" I thought this little white preacher would say, "I'll chair."

First thing he say was, "I can't handle it, cause I don't know what to say. I'm not too well acquainted with the situation." So that put him off.

I asked the other one, "What you say about it?"

He said, "I don't think I can handle it cause I can't talk well enough. I ain't no public speaker."

That don't leave nobody now but me. So I told them, I said, "Now if neither one of you all won't take it, nobody left to take it but me." I said, "I'll take it, with one agreement. When we go in, if we get us a conference in with the officials, whenever one start to talk on the subject, the others don't butt in till he finish. When he finish his point and the others trying to talk, don't he butt in till the others finish. And don't talk too long." And I said, "Try to stick to the point that we set out to clear up." I said, "Now what we going there for is to try to get the WPA to rent this vacant hall down here, and put some desks in there where they can wait on more than one or two people at a time." (Twas a vacant building down there, and that vacant building could put a whole lot of desks in there, and hire some of these people to let them write these people up.) I said, "If you all don't act chairman, I'll act chairman, but when I speak, don't cut me off. When you speak, try to stick to the point, and I won't cut you off. Just work together." That was our agreement.

We went in there, and we told who we was and where we from.

I'm the spokesman, told them we was there to see Mr. Reed. After a while he was available and they come out and got us, invited us in. We three went in and had a seat. I opened up the conversation. Mr. Reed, he wasn't hostile, he became very agreeable. He thought it was a good suggestion, give him a few days and he'd let us know what he could do about opening this place up, putting more desks in there, where the people wouldn't have to be standing in line outside the door like in the other place they was at.

We went back, and sure enough in the next few days that place was opened up, and desks and chairs was put in there and everything. These people was interviewed and they re-registered and they put them on the waiting lists. Some of them is waiting on the waiting lists till today. They never did get off the waiting lists. They hired a few of these other people, but then the WPA went to dwindling away. The appropriations commenced to giving out. The PWA came in.[1] That was private contractors, in order to give the private contractors some working business cause they making no money. That was the way it was organized. In that way, these people never did get back on WPA. They commenced to wonder, then to try to look for a job. I stayed, I helped that organization, the Workers Alliance, but then we had to give up that office up there where we was at cause the members wouldn't come to meeting.

I moved the office to the Negro Masonic Temple, in that same number 4 hall, for $1. I'd meet some of the white members on the street and ask them, "Why won't you come to meeting?" They'd promise to come, but they didn't come. One thing about the whites, I had moved the meeting down into the Negro community, and they wasn't accustomed to meeting in a Negro hall at that time. Tom Howard, the president, he moved out of the city. He moved out. The secretary quit coming. The council quit meeting. People scattering everywhere.

The last Workers Alliance meeting I attempted to hold was right there in that hall. It was two old Negro men and the Negro woman her daughter bought the furniture. This is way up in '39 now, something like up in the summer. The meeting was on a Saturday. That Saturday I paid $1 for the hall, and one of these old men, he got to looking at the brick, at the building. He was a old man, and he said, "You know, I made all the mortar you see in this brick wall here. I was the mortar maker for to build this building." And the other old fellow, he nodded. He was very old, and he couldn't hardly see good.[2]

AFTER I got off the WPA I first went to work at the Sloss coke oven company, out there in North Birmingham. They was expecting a strike among the coke oven and coal miners of District 50. That was part of John L. Lewis' United Mine Workers, chemical section, and this was in chemical. I went out there to the coke oven and worked ten days, eight hours a day. I was only learning, but if somebody lay off, then I work they shift, and I made what they would make. I went to work at 8 o'clock, and sometime I get a shift where somebody lay off from 3 to 11, and I'd work till 11 o'clock. Now I wouldn't get no pay for the 8 o'clock shift, for that eight hours of the day. Of the ten shifts I worked there, I made two shifts that I got paid. I worked eight shifts for nothing, just to learn. They paying somewhere pretty close to $4 a shift.

I kept on going out there to work, and it was hot as the devil. That was a hot job, that was working on the oven itself, where that coke come out. I worked out there, paying my transportation to get out there, and when I get out there, I go to work, do the work, but wont getting nothing.

I was on the furnace, on the block, they call it. The block was where they put the coal in and burn that coal. And where they burn out that coal, different pipes would bring out different ingredients from the coal. Some parts there you'd get sulfur and some you'd get salt. And some you'd get tar and oil, and some you'd get coke. Coke is just like a great big lump of coal where all the ingredients been burnt out. It'll burn just like coal, but it gets much hotter than coal. That's what I was on.

I worked that devilish thing ten shifts, got paid for two. I went to the man, told him I wanted to get a regular job. I wont getting no pay. He told me to wait a while. Finally he told me, said, "I'm going to let you go back home today. I ain't got no way I can place you. If I need you I'll send for you." He never did send for me.

I rocked on from there, walked up there to the Alabama Stove Foundry. (That's where I was working the day when Lindbergh crossed the pond, going to France. I was working in this place in 1927. Everybody's talking about "he's going fall in the ocean." That's where I was working, this Alabama Stove Foundry. This was the foundry where I spoke about when they first opened up, we went there, and we found it wont paying nothing, and we left. That was in '27. Then I got in bad times and I went back to work there again.) This was coming down through the winter then, 1939.

I just happened to walk up by there, and the foreman was there. My wife used to work for his wife back when I was working at Stockham. He give me a job there, working one day a week and two days a week. I stood out there in the cold weather, working. One day it was snowing, and that sand is wet, cold. It ain't warm, ain't got no way of getting it warm. I worked in that cold sand, and I wouldn't go over to the fire till I felt pain hitting me in the wrist. You got a big old oil barrel sitting over yonder, full of hot coke, and everybody get over there soon as they feel their hand get cold. They'd go there and stand around, warm their hands around that big oil barrel full of hot coke. But I'm out here, no fire.

I felt this pain in my wrist, and it went up my arm and all over my side. That pain stayed in my side round there a *long* time. While I'm working in that cold sand, I feel the pain when it start in my right arm. Look like it was in the blood vein or something. It just went on up, went on up, it just kept on up, and went on up and come on up. And that pain was in my arm for months, at least six months to a year.

I didn't make enough money to hardly pay my rent, when they got through taking out expenses for cutting the sand and all like that. There you didn't have to rap out your casting. You didn't have to do anything but pour off and go home. They had men what they called "shake-out men," and these shake-out men, you had to pay them so much out of what little you made. Time I got through paying them, and they got through taking out the scrap, I would clear about $2 or $3 a week.

Ain't got no money, no income, and Sophie, she was working a little day job. I stayed at the house till I got to move, the house was $9 a month. I stayed there and stayed there, and I couldn't pay no rent. Finally, when I got a notice to move, a ten-day notice, I found me $10, hustle up $10, and I went over to see about another house. Plenty houses for rent.

I went to the real estate place and went up there and told the man I'd been living with some friend, Beidel or Mayfield. I stop by them and tell them to say I been living with them, renting from them, in case they question where I been living at before. I say, "I live down there with Beidel, address so-and-so, and I thought I'd see the house you got, thought I'd get out and get me a house on my own, me and my wife." So they rent it to me. I paid my $10 and stayed on there that month, and the next month. Then I got a ten-day notice because of no rent. That was the second time.

I'm working at this Alabama Stove Foundry, but when I get paid I gets about $2 on Friday. Just enough to buy a little something to eat, nothing to pay no rent with. So I went to this guy, went to Otis Real Estate Company. He had a house there for $11. And somehow or another I got the $11 and told him another lie where I been living somewhere else, moved in that house. It was a nice three-room house, nice place. I paid the $11, stayed there that month, and wont able to get up no more money. Next time come down for rent, rent come due, no rent. Two weeks pass, no rent. So I was in a position that I wont able to move no more now. They done give me ten-day notice from the courthouse three times. I can't go back up there now no more. That was the law. They had to give you ten days' notice, and if you didn't move then, they send out the sheriff and put you out, set you outdoors. I just missed that setting outdoors.

I can't go back to the courthouse. So every time I get a notice from Otis, I go up and tell him, "I ain't got no job." I said, "If I can find a job," I said, "I'll pay the rent." Wont but $11, but I'm still getting behind. I went one week, didn't have it. Went the next week, didn't have it. But the next week was the third week I went up. I didn't wait till they come out there, I went up.

He said, "You look like a good fellow." He said, "I can't let you stay there in that house and not pay any rent because the owners wants their rent." He said, "But right down Short John* I got some two-room houses down there." It wont but just about rock distance from where I was living. He said, "It's got a front room, bedroom and a kitchen, back porch. Toilet on the back porch." He said, "They's $6 a month." He said, "I'll let you stay there until you be able to do better, but I can't let you stay up here in this house you got."

I went down there, and there was two or three of them, wont nobody in them. Worse mess you ever seen in your life. I went there and cleaned that house, and oh my God, I washed and rubbed and done everything and cleaned that house out. They

---

* It was one little block. You had John Street and they called that Short John.

called theyself had it sealed, weatherboard on the outside and had this stuff they throw out the railroad car boxes, they was laying up on top of each other just like that, with big spaces between, big spaces. Called it putting the groove together, but it was only near about come together. We plastered that house, took newspaper, me and Sophie, and plastered that house all around, and moved in. That was at the first of 1940. Sophie seen I couldn't do no better. So whatever move I made, she'd go along with me, "It's all right with me." But her mind would be elsewhere.

That's when that wife of mine, Sophie, she was cutting up like a pony. She wouldn't wash me a shirt, and she accused me of everybody come along, accused me of other women. She was the one doing the dirt and accuse me. She accused me of going with some of the women in the singing class. Money was part of it, I reckon. I didn't have no money and she couldn't understand why, that I didn't have money like other men.[3]

I never did accuse her, I really didn't have no idea she was messing around. I thought she was just mad at me. I was just that big a fool. Since I joined the Party she never did get used to me going to meetings, and I'd just go to meetings anyway. It just kept on and she got so fine at it till she got too common, too careless with herself.

One day, we was just talking, and she say, "Hosie . . ."
I say, "What?"
She say, "You know them things what I think about?"
I says, "What is that, Sophie?"
"I believe if I would go with another man, I don't believe you'd get mad about it."
I said, "You try it and see."
That's what she said to me. Another time she came up to me and she said that she had a spiritual reading, and the spiritual reader told her she was going marry the second time, and it was going to be to a bright man.

19

The Alabama CP
in the 1940s

ALONG about in '43, the D.O., Rob Hall, he went to Party meetings in New York, and when he come back, he made a long report about what the decisions are. The decision was that we liquidate the Party. That was Browder's line.[1] We voted on it. In Birmingham I was just as much responsible for helping to liquidate the Party as anybody else. I didn't speak out against it. I went along with it. We all did. We was just following, we thought, correct leadership then. All of us, just members in Birmingham, we said we didn't understand. We considered that the national leadership knows more about what they were doing than we did. So we voted to dissolve the Party. It was me and Andy Brown—I think Mayfield was already in the army—but there was three or four who was still on the district bureau there. We discussed it, but when we got through discussing it, we voted for it, and we went to carry it out. It wont just one person, it was the whole leadership there was responsible. We was all responsible.

When we came to our final agreement, come down to that final decision, everybody went along. We agreed to liquidate the Party and set up the Alabama People's Educational Association.[2] This organization would be open to everybody. We set our date, try to decide where we going get a hall, what Sunday would be our meeting Sunday, how would we popularize the meeting—should we do it by contacting individual people and inviting them out, or should we do it by putting ads in the paper. After we got it going, we thought we wouldn't be arrested. Everybody come in the Alabama People's Educational Association. We thought things was getting real good.

Our line of discussion in those days was that people talk about shortage of houses, shortage of coal, rations of food, couldn't get no meat, we said, "After the war, we're going to have everything." Browder had us through this thing. We said, "We'll have plenty of houses, going to build houses, going to have plenty of jobs." That's how far he had gone. He had left the line of Marxism and Leninism. That was our talk.

I had more battles in Birmingham with workers tell me, "Man, how in hell you going to have jobs?"

I say, "All right, we got to win the war, and after the war, jobs going to multiply, we'll have plenty of jobs."

I believed it, sure, I believed it! I thought the bosses going to lay down with the workers, the wolves and the lambs going to lay together. I was teaching that, I was preaching that everywhere I went, in the union and everywhere. Not only me, but the union leaders was preaching that stuff. We'd work together, you had what you call in the unions "labor relations committees," where the company and the men and the union would get together, discuss the problems, would iron out their differences without having strikes and strifes.

Some people couldn't understand that the Alabama People's Educational Association wasn't the same as the Party. We had one old Negro communist, couldn't explain hisself clear, said "Comrade" all the time in the meeting. Everybody look at him. The Party people would look at each other, try to treat him nice, wouldn't call him down, let him finish talking. Then they try to smooth it over. The other people sitting there looking at it. They think they in the wrong place. We say it's not the Communist Party, and they said, "Ain't you all communists?"

"No, we ain't no communists. We done liquidate the Party. This here's the Alabama People's Educational Association." But the same people had been seen as being Party members, now they something else. The people couldn't understand it.

They put me out in front. I was the onliest one left, all the rest of them, Negroes, was in the army. I being too old for the army, they makes me vice-president of that group, more or less in Birmingham. They elects a guy, white, that I had never seen before but two other whites knew him, they elected him as president, Charlie Wilson. Then after Wilson wouldn't serve, they elected Ordway

Southard. He never sat in the chair nary a time. I had to preside at all the meetings. Once or twice he come to the meeting and set over there. I'd say, "Come on, you preside."

He say, "It's all right. It's all right. You handling it."

What made it so hard after the Party was dissolved in 1944, when these racists in the union was attacking me, these racists in the Steelworkers, because I was fighting for the rights of Negroes to vote and for the men in the local, then these so-called members of the Alabama People's Educational Association, had been Party members, they would tell me not to criticize. When Cary Haigler and Ben Gage and W. J. Shewmake* and them making racist remarks, then Southard and some of the rest of them, like Andy Brown, they would say, "You got to work with these people." Ordway Southard, he would be the sharpest. He was a racist hisself. He was from New York.

Everytime when I'd come to a meeting and get up and report about what's going on in the Birmingham Industrial Council, they'd tell me not to criticize. One time, I was talking about this John Henry Jones case,[3] this steelworker from London England, and I was criticizing how these guys in the union was fighting me because I took a position and presented a resolution against discrimination. These so-called Party members said, "You must go easy, you must not criticize. You must work with these people."

But as I understood it, it was something that come down from Browder. We must cease our rigid criticism, in order to have more unity, more harmony with such people like Haigler and Shewmake in the union. These people in the union were doing their dirty work, and I wont supposed to fight back. And this is coming up to the period when they getting ready to start the real chop-blocks against the left-progressive forces in the CIO.

We tried to go through with the Alabama People's Educational Association, with open doors for everybody to come in and have a seat. We wont taking no kind of precautions. We had stoolpigeons, pimps, everything. We had about fifteen or twenty guys from the mines all in this industrial club of the Alabama People's Educational Association. And to show you what danger was in it, we had a little young cat there, Negro, his name was Israel. He was just flippy-flippy. You couldn't hardly keep him from talking. He talk

* [Representatives of the United Steelworkers of America, Birmingham District, native white Alabamians.]

without addressing the chairman. He wanted to say something, he wanted to ask questions. Oh, he was a mighty energetic young fellow. I was always suspicious of him, and I'd raise the question with other comrades. I didn't have a bit of use for him.

He wanted to go to the National Training School, he just wanted to work hisself right on up. That's why I was suspicious of him. But Rob Hall and all the whites, they all praise Israel. They liked him, oh yeah, they liked him. But finally he turned out to be what I thought he was. He was a stoolpigeon for Bull Connor and the city detectives. It was said that he sold whiskey or had blind-cat whiskey or something. They caught him and give him two years in prison.

AFTER the Duclos disclosure[4] we had a big discussion to see where we made our mistake at. We came out criticizing Browder's position. The national office set up a temporary committee to reconstitute the Party, and we had a guy from New York who came down, was working through Texas, Louisiana, Alabama, and the Carolinas, trying to pull the Party back together after it had been liquidated. When he got in Birmingham, he tried to use the people in the Alabama Educational Association thing.

When they got to talking about "who going lead," they elected me and Ordway Southard to attend the national convention. We couldn't be delegates there, cause that was a Party convention, and we wasn't a Party in Alabama. They accepted us as observers. I was the spokesman, for the people in Alabama and Birmingham.

When this convention coming up, it was some young white women, they didn't want Ordway to go. They didn't want Southard to go at all, but they had nobody else to send, just to have white and black together. Then all the filth come out. We Negroes didn't know it, but it was some young white women, wives of white comrades who went into the army. The D.O., Rob Hall, and this Ordway Southard, they had tried to makes passes at these young women. We Negroes didn't know this was going on, this was all among the whites. Now come time for the convention, these young white women, they had some charges they wanted brought up at the national convention against Rob Hall and Ordway Southard, moral conduct with them. Rob Hall, he wont no more D.O. after he come out the army. He left Birmingham, he didn't come back to the organization. But Southard, he was just there. He was married to a Birmingham girl.

Howbeitsoever, me and Ordway Southard went up to the national convention. We got up there, and they had a lot of discussing, you had a lot of one criticizing the other. One night Ben Davis was calling Jack Stachel,* said, "Jack get up here with his old slimy, slick, slimy stuff." I never did understand what they was talking about. But we stayed up till 4 o'clock the next morning, and they was pulling and criticizing and talking and talking. I was so sleepy! I wasn't developed then. I didn't understand all the discussion.

Ordway wasn't reprimanded at the convention, because I didn't raise the issue up there. I didn't want to get all in a hassle. I always shun fights if I don't have to get into them. It was just Ordway and me, and we got up there, and I didn't push it. I knowed it was going to be a whole lot of stink, and it was only me there to try to tell what everybody else was saying. I didn't fully know about it, so I let it go by. I always shun battles if I didn't have to fight them.

I don't know how it worked out, but when they got to nominating the national committee, after they put Browder out, then they nominated Ed Strong (he had been in Birmingham with the Southern Negro Youth Congress, but in '45 he lived in New York.) And they nominated Foster[5] and Ben Davis and James Ford, and anyhow, the national committee consisted of forty-five members. And they nominated me for the national committee.[6] It was my job then, as national representative down in the South, to try to pull the Party back together, especially in Alabama and Louisiana.

The first thing we did after we had the conference in New York, we had a meeting in Birmingham. It was called down in the little Masonic on 7th Avenue and about 15th Street, Saturday and Sunday. Ben Davis came down. He was down there with us that Christmas '45. That was when we reconstituted the Party in Birmingham, in Alabama. We stop that meeting of the Alabama People's Educational Association every Sunday, that everybody meeting together. We decided to build the clubs back. We tried to organize clubs in Smithfield, one in Woodlawn, one in East Birmingham, not units, but clubs. And we had an industrial club, coal miners and steelworkers.

Ordway Southard was pushed aside in the leadership. Rob Hall was gone. Don Rose brought in Sam Hall and introduced Sam to us.

---

* Jack Stachel, he's dead. All of them dead. [Both Benjamin Davis and Jacob Stachel were among the Foley Square Eleven, communists convicted in the Smith Act trials in 1949.]

Sam was a Alabama boy, he was from Anniston. Sam I think was in the Carolinas before he went in the army. The Party recommended Sam to come into Alabama, so we accepted Sam as D.O. He taken over as D.O.

We re-established the Party in the Black Belt, down in Camp Hill and Reeltown, in that area, also in Montgomery. Andy Brown did. And we had one or two Party people up in Huntsville Alabama. I was working on the job in the shop, so I didn't move around a lot like some of the whites, like Sam Hall. They'd meet a lot of people. The only way I'd meet people was in the state committee meetings. It was a big brown-skinned fellow from the union up in Huntsville, I met him on two occasions. Then they had that same Reverend Maple, he was still very active around Leeds. He had a big church, Reverend Maple.*

We went down to Louisiana to try to reorganize the Party down there. In the last of '46, we went down to New Orleans, me and Mayfield and Andy Brown. We had a two-day conference to re-constitute the Party. We got down there Friday night, stayed down there Saturday and Sunday, broke up Sunday night. People there from all around Louisiana. I spoke because I was a representative from the national. Henry Winston,[7] he was down from the national office. Henry took me and Mayfield and Andy and somebody else out. We all went out to a place called Hayes Chicken Shop, a cafe or something on Louisiana Avenue. It was a night spot. Everybody ordered a bottle of beer. That was the first time I drink a bottle of beer in my life. I never drinked no beer before.

In Birmingham my assignment was that club out there in Smithfield, try to work in Smithfield, and also the industrial club, what met every Sunday. Then I tried to set up a club out there in the shop. I had five or six guys I wrote up in the shop, and we was doing pretty good meeting until they started to raid against me in '47. I was carrying the *Daily Worker* in the shop there. Wont slipping, just going in, passing around, different guys would take it. I had all kinds of literature, pamphlets, *Political Affairs,*† I had guys out there taking it in the shop.

Then one morning, Adam Wilson, the vice-president of the

---

* I don't know what happened to that fellow from Huntsville. Reverend Maple, he died there in the McCarthy period, he died of cancer.

† [*Political Affairs* is the official Party monthly magazine. Before 1945 its title had been *The Communist.*]

local, he made a announcement there in the bathroom, gave them all the devil. "Mr. Jackson say he don't want no more of these communist newspapers in this shop." I'm in one aisle, and he over yonder in his aisle, and everybody changing clothes. He didn't come up to me to tell me what Mr. Jackson said, and wont nobody bringing newspapers in there but me. He just got up, "Mr. Jackson said he don't want no more of these communist newspapers in this shop! Whoever fooling with them going lose they job!" Everybody looking at me. I already had several of them in my locker then. I had more than I could distribute.

Now I got to figure how to get them papers out of here, take them out, cause I don't know what's going start next. I didn't know when they'd go around and go in the lockers. I had a few leftover papers down at the bottom of my locker, cause I was getting a bundle of papers every week, about ten papers. I had five or six guys I'd give them to in the shop. Well, I had some extra I hadn't put out. I'd just take them, put them in my locker. I had done got very tame. I don't know whether I had two weeks' papers or one week's, but I know when the announcement was made, I had some papers. When he made that big public announcement, then I began to figure out how to take them out of there. I don't remember whether I carried them out the shop or whether I took them and put them in the garbage or what. But I got them out the locker.

After that announcement, all the guys fell away from me. I tried to get them to meeting. I couldn't get them to meeting. They wouldn't say they ain't going meet, they'd promise but they wouldn't show up. We had got to the point there after we got out the shop, we'd hold our meetings after work hours around a fellow named Wash's house. But after that announcement, I'd tell them, "I'm going down to Wash, you all," they'd say yeah, but they'd go on home. Left me setting there.

That was before November, cause it was along in November when they started the real raid against me.

20

Local 2815, USWA

I went into the American Casting Company, went to work, trying to keep myself hid, didn't want it to become known who I am there among the little foremens and bosses. I went there the 5th of June 1942, and along about July or August, some of the men, the guys among the Negroes, they knew me from the Workers Alliance, had known me from way back. They asked me, said, "Hudson," said, "can't you do nothing about this thing?"

They wasn't paying common labor but 30¢ an hour, and they paying 40¢ an hour for iron pourers, grinders, and shake-out men, and they paying the Negro molders 48¢ an hour,* making hand grenades and torpedoes and incendiary bombs. They paying the cupolo† man 50¢ an hour, running that cupolo, where you melt your iron. He have to fix it up, got a certain way it got to be fixed, put that ring on there, everything, so when that iron melts in there like water, it's able to hold it without coming out. It's a very dangerous job, an important job. When that iron get hot and come through that mud and brick, you got a hard job to stop it. It run like water, you get burnt, you got a hard job to stop it. So the guys said "Hudson, you know how to get folks together. Can't you do nothing about this thing?"

I said no. I told them, I said, "No, I ain't have to do nothing. Now if you all want to do something, I'll show you all how to do it. I'll help you, but I ain't going to stick my head out."

"We'll do anything you say. Anything you say do, we'll do it."

I said okay, and I went down to the district steel office, district

---

* Paying the whites about $1.25 an hour, wont but two-three of them.

† [A cupolo—which Hudson pronounces "cubelo"—is a melting furnace in which gray (cast) iron is melted.]

313

office of the United Steelworkers union, and I got twenty-five membership cards. You didn't have to pay nothing to join the union then. You just sign a card and you's a full-fledged member.

I went back to the shop, and I told the guys, said, "You all say you want to do something . . ." I went around and I picked four guys, excluding myself, told them, "Now you all say you want to do something. Let's get together tonight and sit down and decide what to do."

Sure enough, we all met. We didn't meet in my home, cause I was living out in Smithfield. We met somewhere around the foundry, around in East Birmingham. I give all four of them five cards a piece, and I kept five. I told them, said, "Now your task is to talk to the guys you think is the best guys, see can you get them to sign a card. Don't try to write up just anybody." Then we going to meet next Wednesday night, check up, see how many we got signed. We met. We had signed up them twenty-five cards.

I went back down to the district office in the Steiner Bank Building, that's where the hall was, and I went down and seed old man Stevenson, who I got the card from, one of the field representatives. I asked him when could we have a meeting.

I got the meeting set for Saturday, down there at the district office. Saturday was the Saturday before Labor Day, '42. We went down there, every man bring his own men, met down there in old man Stevenson's office. He was there with us with his one arm—he had his right hand cut off a long time ago. He give us a good pep talk, all twenty-five of us. Old man Stevenson told us what we had to do now was elect officers and everybody pay $1 joining fee and send off after the charter. They elect me president and elected another boy as vice-president, another boy as financial secretary, and one recording secretary, elected a inner door guard and a outer door guard.* We all paid out the money, and we sent off for the charter.

That was Saturday evening. Monday we was off for Labor Day.

---

* There was the inner door guard and the outer door guard. See, back there when we first started building the union, we had to have watchmens. The inner door guard stands at the door or sit at the door, on the inside. And the outer door guard would sit on the outside of the hall, watching to see who coming in, see who on the outside trying to sneak up, see what being said. The inner door guard would let you in if the outer door guard done passed you. It meant your neck back in them days to be in the union.

Tuesday morning we went back, all of us went back to work, nobody said nothing. That evening we got through work, we poured off. The foreman come by. He fired everybody of the twenty-five that they done knowed who was in the union, fired seven or eight people all told, told them, "You pour off. When you get through, go to the clock, punch your card, you go to the office and get your time."

When the guy ask, "What you firing me for?" the foreman say, "I understand you one of these smart alecks around here, trying to get a union started." They fired the vice-president, the financial secretary, the treasurer, and the inner door guard, just about all the elected officers and some of the members. They didn't fire me, and they didn't fire the recording secretary. He was on the cupolo. I learnt that he was the man that turned everybody's name in. Turned mine in too, but they wouldn't fire me, because they needed molders too bad, but soon as they got a chance, they was going let me go.

When they fired the guys that Tuesday, everybody come running to me out there in front of the gate. They had a little place right across the street, little shade bushes, nice shade, right across the street from the office. That's where he held our meeting at, right out there in that shade right across the street from the office after we got off work. All the guys getting around me, asking me, "Big Red," said, "they fired us. What we going to do now? They fired us on account of we was members of this union."

I'm talking, telling them the best I can. I said, "I tell you," I said, "you all meet me back here in the morning." I lit out, went down to the United Steelworkers district office to see old man Stevenson, told him what happen.

He said, "Get all the boys down here tomorrow night."

The next morning, I come, all of them's standing around. I said, "Down at the union hall, they wants everybody there, whether you been fired or not, down there tonight at 7:30, without fail."

They all wanted to know, "What about getting my job back, what about my job?"

I said, "Come down, they'll tell you tonight."

All of them poured down there. Old man Stevenson give them all a talk, told them, "By God, we going make them pay you for every day you off and don't work in that plant. Every day the plant

run and you don't work on your job, you be sure to write it down."
He give them a big talk, but that's all it was. I knowed that wouldn't
be enough for very long if they was firing people. And I was looking
for them to fire me.

I said, "Mr. Stevenson, do you have any membership buttons?"

He said yeah. Them buttons shine like new money, they was red,
small, about like a dime. "CIO," that was on it, "CIO." He give me
a handful, and I give everyone wasn't fired two or three. I said,
"Now you go in the shop in the morning, put this on where it can
be seen. Put you one up on your hat, on your shirt, suspenders, when
you go in the shop where you going to work. And give everybody
one and tell them to wear it."

There in the shop in the morning, buttons shining all over the
place. Everyone put on the buttons, but they didn't know what it
was, what it was all about. They didn't know what danger was in it.
I knowed what danger it was if I didn't get some mass around me
there. So everyone put on the buttons. They just thought it was a
pretty button. They didn't know the meaning behind it. But the
little foremens standing, looking—look here, you got a button,
look there at you, you got a button. They didn't know who was a
member and who wasn't a member. That made them afraid to fire
anybody. That was what saved me. They think they can't fire me
now, cause if they do, these guys liable to shut the whole place down.

But they didn't take the men back they done fired. Old man
Stevenson told them all to keep count of the days the place run and
they didn't work, they make them pay for everything they lost. Well,
in March, about the middle of March, the company put up a sign
over the clock saying no more discrimination against the members
of the union. And these guys they had done fired, they name them
by name. They was subject to get their job back if they call in, make
a report for their job within the next forty-eight hours. But some of
the guys was way up North. I never did see them no more. The
treasurer, he had done left, went to Detroit. Only two came back,
one was the finance secretary.

When we got the job back, we call ourselves "won a victory." It
was all right for them all to get their job back, but $25 was all the
back pay they paid. The guys had gone from September till March.
All they go was just that $25. But when the "victory" was won, the
other guys, sitting around there, scared, you couldn't get them to

come to a meeting, They kind of perked up. Every time they perked up, I take advantage of it, call a meeting.

IT come up for Christmas, this was 19 and 43. We had petitioned for an election, cause we figured we had the majority of the workers signed union cards. So the labor board[1] election going to be the 12th of November, in '43. So what old man Jackson did, old man Jackson closed down the American Casting Company. We going to have the election on the 12th, which was on a Monday. He closed that shop down on a Friday, and he told some of us to go to his other shop—which was Jackson foundry—on Monday morning to be placed up there for a job. Some of them he put them on a waiting list. That automatically destroyed that election for Monday.

We petitioned against it. We said it was discrimination, union discrimination. But we couldn't prove it, so he won that point. But all the time he trying to get a chance to fire me. All the time. Charles Rivers, he was a custodian in the office, he been there since the company started. He'd tell me everything going on up at the office, he kept me posted.* He told me they had as many as five superintendents that old man Jackson told, said, "If you get that Hosie Hudson out of my shop, you got a job." And I seed five of them go, and they still haven't got me out.

So the shop officials put me on the machine between two guys, Bob and Robert. Bob and Robert been there eighteen years, and they told them, "We want you to tell us everything he have to say."

I got to working there. I didn't make no noise, didn't never say nothing, never grumbled, just done my work. Finally one went to the bathroom, and the other one said to me, "Look-a-here, man, do you got any chewing tobacco?"

I said yeah.

He said, "Give me a chew."

I said, "Here you keep it."

He said, "You keep this under your hat, but you be careful, cause they say that you that union man, they aim to fire you."

I said, "Okay, thank you."

Now turn right around, and when he went to the bathroom, then

---

* I checked up on him when I was in Birmingham in April '77, and he's done about lost all his sight, Charlie Rivers. He's still living. His son come and got him, taken and carried him to New York.

that other one come, and he told me the same thing. Each one told me not to tell the other one, cause the other one would talk.

I never was late. Be on time all the time for the job. Go to the bathroom, didn't go there, hang around talking. Go in there and come out. I had some of the foremens to follow me in the bathroom. The bathroom had a white side and a Negro side, but they walk in the Negro side, claim they looking for somebody, looking behind me. They come in, look around. They wanted to see what I'm doing. When I come out, they come on out. So I went on, and they couldn't get nothing on me.

I was setting the cores of the hand grenades. I could just set them cores! Just like a chicken picking up corn. When I set them, I could place them just right. See, when you put them down, your print was over here, and your core set here. If you press it here, it would be thick on one side, thin on the other. Be thick and thin. But if you put them down, put them down, put them down, right where they hit, they fit. And oh! I could set them cores!

After we lost that election in November, when old man Jackson moved the shop, we had to have the election again. In February '44 we had the election. Now the machinists and mechanics, the whites, they was in the American Federation of Labor. The CIO was only Negroes. The whites was in the AF of L, they didn't try to get no Negroes to join they local. But when we petitioned the labor relations board for the election, for Steelworkers, CIO, they came out and put up a petition that they also would be in the ballot. In order to have a certain amount of members, they forged the name of some of the members of our local, saying they was members of the AF of L, paying-dues members. They had Beidel's name in the crowd. You know Beidel wasn't a member. They did get on the ballot, and after getting on the ballot, I don't think they hardly got 90 votes. Quite a few people voted for no union. Everybody was eligible to vote, office workers and everybody. But our vote was about 280-something. Not too many people, but we had the overwhelming majority.

We done that in February, but down in August we still didn't have no contract. Finally I went up to the office there one day and told Mr. Jackson we wanted to have a meeting with him. We had a committee, me, Beidel, and and a little guy named Alexander. He told me he would see us when we come off work.

(The way I got that committee was the way I had to run that

local for them six years. What I do, I maneuver around among the guys in the union and tell them I think Beidel or Alexander would be good to put on that committee, and get them to nominate them. I had to do a lot of buttonholing, a lot of working behind the scenes. At noon, I got to the point at noon in the shop, I never sit down and eat my dinner. I walk along and go from the foundry department up to the core room up to see some guy. I eat as I walking along.)

When we, the committee, knocked off work, we went out there and saw old man Jackson. We come out, he come out, we was waiting for him. He walked out in the yard with Mr. Lloyd and Len,* said to them, "I invited you all to come out here with me, cause Hosie told me he wanted to have a meeting between me and the committee. I thought he might want to lynch me." That's what Jackson said. He call hisself teasing.

I told him, "No, Mr. Jackson, we don't want to lynch you. We just wants a contract signed."

He said, "You all boys want a contract signed?"

I said, "Yeah, that's what all the fellows there in the shop say. They said we done got the bargaining rights in the union, and they asking why we can't sign a contract."

"Why you all want to have a contract?"

I said, "Number one, we won the election. We wants a check-off system. We wants a better grievance procedure, settle grievances, and we also want a wage increase."

"I can give you a wage increase without signing a contract. You don't have to have a contract to get a wage increase."

I said, "All these things go together."

He said, "Tell them to give me a little more time and I'll set a time for a meeting. We'll get together on a contract."

When they did meet us, it was him and Lloyd and Len and Lawyer Young, four of them. It was five of us, Shewmake and Ben Gage from the Steelworkers Union district office, they was white, and me and Beidel and Alexander from the local. We got to discussing about wages. At that time, the molders' wages, to begin with, was 55¢ an hour. After he's there a while, it automatically be raised to 60¢. Common labor wages was 50¢ an hour. Had one nickel between molders and common labor an hour. When we got

---

* That was Len Argyle, the man that fired me at Stockham in 19 and 32.

to negotiating the contract, they agreed to give a raise. Molders begin at 60¢ an hour and after the thirty days, they raise automatically to 65¢ an hour. Iron pourers and molders was making the same. Everybody got a 10¢ raise. The molders automatically going get a 10¢ raise, but I was asking for a raise on the premium too.

Three hundred and fifty molds was your day's work for the eight hours a day. After you make 350 molds to 400 molds, then you get something like a penny a mold. And all over 400 molds, we got 2¢ a piece for each man. I was after trying to get 3¢ or 4¢ a mold, because the molds had got heavier.* Jackson said he couldn't raise the percentage on the mold. They begin to talk about what they paying, they couldn't give no raise. Then I happen to grunt. I make a noise.

Lawyer Young, he setting across the table, he said, "What is it, Hosie? What is it, Hosie?"

I said, "Nothing. I was just thinking."

"Well, what is it? Whatever you want to say, say it. Don't hesitate. We all here to talk."

I said to him, "If you all keep insisting, I will say it." I said, "What I was thinking about, I can't understand Mr. Jackson when he say he can't give a increase on the percentage rates on the mold. At one time," I said, "we had three cores in a mold, six castings in a mold, and we had four men to the machine. Now we got up to eight cores in a mold, sixteen castings, we done changed from six castings to sixteen castings, and done cut one man off—three men doing what four men doing. And yet Mr. Jackson say he can't make no money. I can't understand it."

When I said that, Shewmake, supposed to been representing the union out there, representing my interests, jumped up, said, "Mr. Jackson, you don't have to answer that question!" He was one of the district representatives of the union. He said, "Mr. Jackson, you don't have to answer that question. I think we understand."

Finally the lawyer said, "Gentlemen," said, "let's have a smoke." He got up and walked out the door, him and Mr. Jackson and Lloyd and Len Argyle, and they stayed a few minutes and come back in. Lawyer Young said, "Gentlemen, we going have to postpone our meeting this afternoon, because Mr. Jackson has an ap-

---

* Wont no use to try to get the day's task reduced. You couldn't get them to do that.

pointment with the eye doctor. He got to be there very soon. We have to postpone this meeting and set another date and let you all know in the near future."

Mr. Jackson left that meeting and never did come back to the meeting no more. He never faced me no more after that date, but he did go telling the shop officials that he didn't know that he had a nigger in his plant smart as that Hosie Hudson. Said, "That damn nigger ain't nobody's fool." Later, after that, Lawyer Young said, "Don't play that damn nigger cheap, because he ain't nobody to be played with. Just cause he talk like he ain't educated, like he ignorant, don't play that damn nigger cheap." That was the kind of recognition I got out of them. They recognized me.*

After we got the contract signed in '44, I was the chairman of the grievance committee and president of the local. I settled several cases, guys that were fired out the shop, I was able to get them back to work. One was Jimmie Ziegler. He was working on the shake-out. The shake-out men had to take the castings off the belt before they went through that rattling, cause the materials they was making was very thin, easy to break. The fan stopped, and he called to the foreman, asked him to turn the fan on, it was getting too hot up there in that heat.

The foreman didn't rush to turn it on. So Jimmie walked down and left all the casts, let them go through the rattling, which meant they would get broke up when they fall over into the rattling by themselves.

The foreman told Jimmie Ziegler to go back up there and go to work. He refused to go up. So the foreman told him to go punch out, he was fired. Jimmie come by me, asked could they fire a man for getting hot. I didn't know what he was talking about. I said no.

He said, "But that's what they did to me up on that shake-out." I told him to go tell Johnson about it. That was the procedure we had set up. Johnson was the assistant to the superintendent, and before we carry any grievance to the company, we said let's try to settle it in the shop without carrying it to the next highest committee, to the company.

Johnson told Jimmie, "If the foreman say you punch out, go ahead on and punch out." They said Jimmie Ziegler was insub-

* Charlie Rivers told me that.

ordinate and that he never would work at the plant no more. I carried that grievance to the third step,* and they was forced to put Ziegler back to work. But they didn't put him back on the shake-out, they put him on the molding machine, molding. I won that case, and that was the last I know of it. When I left, I left Jimmie Ziegler in the shop.

Then there was another case with a guy shoveling coke under the crane. The crane was dipping up the coke out of a railroad car. And that bucket, it shut up, but it ain't going shut up all the way. Sometimes it got a piece of coke hanging out, liable to drop out anytime. Them lumps was big as your two fists or larger, weigh maybe 4–5 pounds. If one fell on you it would knock your brains out. When the bucket was flying over his head, dropping coke on the ground, the Negro wanted to stop, move out the way. The foreman wanted the Negro to continue to rake the coke up when the crane coming over his head. The foreman told the Negro to go punch out, he call hisself firing him. The boy came to me and told me that the foreman had told him to punch out because he wouldn't go under that crane while that crane over head, dropping coke. I told him, I said, "You go and tell Mr. Johnson what you told me." He went out and seed Johnson, told Johnson I told him to come out and tell him about it. Johnson told him to go get the foreman and bring him there. So he went and got the foreman, and Johnson told the foreman, "You and this boy go out there and see Hudson, settle this thing."

The foreman come out and he walked by me before he'd speak to me. Went by me like he's going somewhere elese. Then he turned back, walked back to my machine, told me, "Hudson, come out here. I want to speak to you." I had to quit my machine then, go out there and meet with them.

The foreman, he explained his end, "The boy lazy, he don't want to work, he watch me all the time, loafing all the time." The boy started to cut in, and I said, "Wait, wait, let him finish."

Then the Negro told what was happening, he said that every time the crane get this coke out the car and unload it, that bucket, some coke would drop between the car and the pile. The foreman wanted him to keep raking it when that thing come across his head. The

* [Hudson met with representatives of the company and from the United Steelworkers district office. Hudson fought this grievance in March 1946.]

foreman tried to cut him off, but I would just let one talk at a time. The foreman tried to smooth it over, but the Negro was telling the truth.

So I told the foreman that what he was doing, "If you doing that, you know you violating safety rules." I told them that our contract reads that everybody work a honest day's work for a honest day's pay. If you loafing on the job, that's a violation of the contract. It don't say rip and run, but everybody work a honest day's work for a honest day's pay. And I said, "Both of you here for the duration of the war, trying to help to win the war and in the meantime trying to make a living for your wives and kids to live on." That was what the foreman was there for, and that's what this Negro was there for. "Now for that cause," I said, "my suggestion is, lay the ax at the root of the tree, turn over a new leaf, and don't say no more about this." The foreman and the Negro agreed to it, and that grievance was settled.

THE whites didn't join the CIO at first. We would ask them about joining, and they shrug, throw up they shoulders, "Well, I don't know, I'll think about it . . ." But they didn't want to come sit down with a bunch of niggers, that's what they were saying. They wont saying it to me, but the news come to me that they were making remarks. The Negroes had built the local and had all the officers in the local. Then we got a 18½ ¢ raise.

This guy Miller, a white guy, come crying to me, how much wages we got? I said we had got a 18½ ¢ an hour raise.

"By God, we didn't get but a 7½ ¢ raise."

I told him, "You know why, don't you? Cause you all ain't in the union." He wanted to know if I thought they could get it if they join the union. I said, "If you sign your cards up, I'll put you on the check-off. When you name come out on check-off, I'll see can I get it straightened out." The company would furnish us with a list of everybody members of the union, and that was how we could tell who paid their dues. Miller signed up in the union, and I met him out there one evening when I got off from work, and I wrote the grievance up.

Me and Miller went in to see Vice-President Milton, and Johnson, the superintendent, and Lloyd. Vice-President Milton told

Miller, said, "Miller," said, "you didn't tell Hosie that on such-and-such a time and such-and-such a day, we give all a 1½ ¢ raise, did you?" Miller sat there and look like a fool. Vice-President Milton said, "You didn't say that at such-and-such a month and such-and-such a time, we give you a 2½ ¢ raise. You didn't tell Hosie and his committee that, did you?" All along the management had been giving the whites little raises and didn't give none to us, never consulted the union at all.

I thought, and I said, "Mr. Milton, with all due respect, I can understand your point," I said. "I can see clear what you talking about," said, "but you know, you all violated the contract."

"What do you mean, Hudson?"

I said, "Read this clause, right here, what it say." It was a little book, wont no size, little small booklet we had. He read it. I said, "Don't you see, 'all wage adjustment will be mutually agreed upon by a vote of union and management.' " I said, "You all ain't consulted the union at all. You give these guys a raise, but you didn't say nothing to us. And that's where you violated the contract." I said, "Now we come out with a 18½ ¢ raise. You all want to take out the 11 ¢ that you done give them already under the table and just give them the balance of the 7½ ¢ of the 18½ ¢. I said, "They's entitled to this 11 ¢."

"Damn if we'll pay it."

I said, "So I make a motion that we close our meeting." I said, "I don't think we could get no further, and we will call for the next step in the grievance procedure." That was the second step here, and we going carry it to the third step. Wont no use setting there arguing with him. He done told us what his opinion. I said, "We request for another meeting at the earliest possible future date." That's where we rolled it up at. The next time I had the union officials out from the district office and the company had Lawyer Young.

Me and Shewmake and Ben Gage and the other two Negroes on the grievance committee, we went in. We didn't have Miller no more. I opened up the case again. I read the clause in the contract, and I said, "I must say that being that this is in violation of the contract, these men are subject to this 11 ¢." I opened it up and turned it loose; I didn't say no more. Then it was Shewmake and Ben Gage and the company. Twas warfare on. I just sat there and listened at them. When they got through, though. I had got them the 11¢.

We were meeting in the local after all these whites had done signed up, after they done checked off. I told them all to come down and take the union obligation. It was a whole host of them white guys, about fifteen or twenty came down at one time. And if it wasn't for them racists down there at the Steelworkers district office, I wouldn't of had no trouble with them men about race.

I was presiding at the local meeting when those whites came down to take the obligation. I had them all to stand in line—it was more than one line, it was face to face, up here, here's a line, and another line and another line. I tell them all to raise they hand and I give them the obligation, electricians, cranemen, millwrights, and inspectors. All of them helt up they hand, and I swore them in as union brothers. And Brother Gary, he's a old ex coal miner, a very religious man, he always was the chaplain, he open the meeting with prayer, I had him give them the right hand of fellowship of membership. He was a black man, and he went around shaking hands with all of them, and they all shook hands.

I knowed that Shewmake or Proach or some of them from the district office was coming down there. That's why I hurried and give them the obligation before any of them come. I knowed they going walk in, want to give them the obligation, because they's white.

Sure enough, after a while, Proach, he come to the local. I was up, I'm going through my meeting. When we got through with our reports and everything, all the business procedures, it always custom, you say, "We have Brother Proach from the district office, we'll give way and have a word from him." And I give way for him to have a word.

The first thing he said when he got up, he pulled out the constitution and begin, "Hosie, we have our white members come down and join. I will give them the obligation . . ."

I said, "Pardon me, Mr. Proach, I've already give them the obligation." And he turned redder and redder. I knowed that's what he was going to do, and I wanted to be sure I give the obligation. I was the president, I was the one supposed to do it.

The other Negroes, presidents or members of locals, what they would do, the Negroes would step back and let the white man give them the obligation, but I didn't do it. Most of the other Negroes, not all of them but most of them, if anything come up, they had to go down to the district office and ask the advice of the whites, They'd go see Shewmake or Proach or Ben Gage, "I thought I'd come down and get your opinion." I wouldn't go down there and ask them *nothing*. I just settled grievances at the shop. I just come, when you know anything, I'm coming across the floor with what I got. Because of that—I didn't ask they opinion or they permission every time you turn around—the white Steelworkers officials didn't like me much.

The white members of the local never came out to meetings like the Negroes. Miller had done signed up fifty of them. Some never did come while I was there, and the rest quit coming before I left there. We had one little old white guy, he'd come to every meeting. Eventually, though, he quit coming. I asked him, "Why don't you all come to meetings?"

He said, "I can't get the others to come, so I just decided I wouldn't come either." They was tearing at him, getting on his neck about coming, made him stop coming to local meeting. He said, "I have to go along with the crowd." They was threatening to whup him, I reckon, if he keep coming down. That was the kind of stuff they was carrying on.

Sometimes I took very adventurous positions. It just took nerve. It wont all that much education, it was strictly nerve. To show you what I'm speaking about, coming up to Christmas '43, all the little shops, Stockham, McWane, Birmingham Machine Shop, Jules Goslin, Virginia Bridge Company, all of them's paying what was called the Christmas bonus. Sometimes it would be a week's pay and a turkey. I waited about two or three days to Christmas, and never seen nothing about no Christmas bonus. I asked the guys, "When we going get a bucket?"

They told me, said, "No, man, they don't pay no Christmas. They don't give you nothing. They ain't never give nothing here for Christmas."

I went home and dictated a letter to old man Jackson: "Mr. J.O. Jackson. Dear Sir, We the undersigned have been expecting some good news, news that would help us make our wives and kids happy for Christmas. News that we going receive a Christmas bonus, like all the other plants around here saying that they going give a bonus. But as the time is drawing nigh, and we still haven't had any good news, in case that we don't get a Christmas bonus, we all want our time in full Christmas Eve, in order to make our kids happy for Christmas.* Signed, Hosie Hudson, Chairman."

Then I took the paper and had all the guys sign it, said, "All you who want your time in full for Christmas, put your badge number here and put your name." And all them Negroes signed. I don't know how many signed, cause we started up in the core room. The core room's in the far end of the foundry. From the core room on down through the cleaning department, shake-out department, and at 12 o'clock it was in the molding department. It went on up to the cupolo guys, and that was the last. All them shops there signed it. I had some long pieces of paper, about three of them, had got all them names on them.

The machine shop, it wasn't in the foundry. It was over in the next building over there, the machine shop, where they thread the hand grenades. All them was white. At 12 o'clock, here they all come pulling across the yard over there, "Where that paper where we sign up for full time?" All them white guys wanted to sign.

I told them, I said, "We ain't got no more paper now," I said. I should have told them to get a piece of paper, write they name on it, but I didn't. I said, "I got enough names. If we get it, you all will get it too." So none of them signed.

Then I went to Charlie Rivers. I told him, "Put this on Mr. Jackson's desk for me." Great big envelope, sealed up. Charlie Rivers put it on his desk. Old man Jackson had a special office. When he come in, he opened it and he read it.

Old man Jackson's top stoolpigeon, Sturdemeyer, was the first one up in the coal room signed. Old man Jackson walked by me and stopped and stood and looked at me at the machine working that morning after he read the letter. He went off to the coal room, went up to Sturdemeyer, said, "Sturdemeyer, who wrote me that letter?"

Sturdemeyer said, "Letter? I don't know."

"You don't know! I see I got a letter got your name at the top of the list."

"Oh. The boys was signing up here for they money, they said

* That didn't mean we were quitting. That mean everything we had in, they pay all our time in full for Christmas. We wont making but $24 a week. That's what I was making, $24 a week, got paid every week, every Friday.

they wanted all they money for Christmas. I put my name on that."

"That's just what I want you all to do," old man Jackson said that. Said, "If you all get together, let me know what you want to do, I'll know what to do."

That made Sturdemeyer feel now he done something great, cause Mr. Jackson said that's what he wants us to do. News went all over the shop what Mr. Jackson told Sturdemeyer.

But the thing old man Jackson saw, he saw Hosie Hudson, and he saw all these niggers here in this union. They been educated. That's what he's afraid of. So he got his little foremen. They run around with a little piece of paper, "How much time you have in? You been here for how many weeks? You work all week?"

They didn't pay you your time in full. They give you part of your time. If you had $20 in, you could get $15. If you had $15, you could get $10. They didn't pay you all your time, and they didn't pay no bonus. They just let you have that money, cut it out your payroll next pay day. Everybody got some money for Christmas, white and everybody.*

The next Christmas, Christmas of '44, they went out and got a truckload of frozen turkeys. They got the biggest turkeys they could find. They give everybody a turkey, them old great big gobblers. I had one, weighed 35 pounds. His legs was just stiff as a board. And the feathers just picked off the body part, they hadn't cleaned them either. I had to carry that thing home on the trolley car. Great big thing. And he's all frozen stiff, just all hard, great long legs, just as stiff as a piece of two-by-four. Any way you carried it in your arms was wrong—them great long turkey legs in them trolley cars.

I had done went and bought me a 15-pound turkey. So when I got that 35-pound turkey, I took him, thawed him up, and got him limbered up and cleaned him good. I had a big old tin tub, and I took that turkey, when I got ready to do it, cut his legs off and everything, took that salt, and I just salted him, just like I did a hog. I put him in that tub, and I kept it three or four weeks. I just let him stay in that salt. I taken him out, washed him off and boiled him and cooked that turkey, after Christmas. You talk about something good, that was a *good* turkey. Taste just like ham, just like a cured country-ham. Didn't taste like turkey.

---

* Membership increased in the local after that letter. That helped rebuild the local to be ready for that election in February.

21
The Alabama CIO

THE Steelworkers leadership wasn't lukewarm on fighting for the rights of the Negro people. It was worse than lukewarm. When it come to the constitution of the union, the constitution say one thing, but down there, they wanted to do another thing. Constitution didn't mean nothing in Alabama at that time. That's why I was always raising the devil. I'd take the national constitution and just always hit the deck about what the constitution say, reading certain sections. But I was pouring water on a duck's back. They wont listening.

I had all kind of battles with the district office of the Steelworkers and with the Birmingham Industrial Council. Down in '47, I was on the Political Action Committee, me and another Negro, Saunders, he was from Mine Mills in Bessemer. We was on a committee of seven members, the council interrogation committee. We was to interview the political candidates running for office, see who was the pro-labor candidates, report to a joint labor conference that was being held one Sunday. The joint labor conference was chaired by a man representing Philip Murray's office in Washington. He was there the Sunday we going to give a report on the various candidates running for state office.

Now Saturday night at the council meeting, coming up to the conference on Sunday, they already had the meeting with the candidates, and they didn't even notify me and Saunders. They had done went down to the Thomas Jefferson Hotel, that was a hotel where at that time they wouldn't allow Negroes in, not so far as attending a meeting was concerned. That's where they set the hearing to interrogate the various candidates—at the Thomas Jefferson Hotel. They set there and helt the meeting and didn't say a word to us.

We didn't know a word about it. After it was over, then the chairman of the committee come telling me that they done had the meeting and what they decided.

The next day at the conference, they know they done bypass me and Saunders, and I guess they done told the guy who's chairing the meeting, "Now don't let him speak," cause they knew I was going to speak about it. This guy from Philip Murray's office—he was a young guy, he wont so old—everytime I raise my hand up, he look over yonder where he could get somebody else's hand. He look back here at me, I raise my hand up, he look over yonder, call somebody else. That was all the way through the discussion on the report, till the time for to close out the discussion on the interrogation committee's report that they brought back.

I helt up my hand again, he look over yonder, so when they got through, I took the floor, said, "Mr. Chairman . . ."

All these whites come up, "Question! Question! Call for the question, question on the motion!" That's to stop the discussion. When I got up to say something, they just song, "Question, question, question!" That's all whites.

After they put the motion, carried it, then I asked for a special point of privilege. I brought up what I wanted to say at the begin with. I said, "I tried to get the floor on discussing these reports. I was denied the right to get the floor." I said, "It was me and Saunders, we was elected on this committee to interrogate these candidates." I said, "Now if you all didn't trust us to represent you, you wouldn't of elected us," said, "but this hearing been helt in the Thomas Jefferson Hotel where Negroes can't go in, these candidates been invited, and they been interrogated, and me and Saunders hadn't knowed anything about it until last night. This is what I want to make clear here. You asking me, you asking the Negro to go to these locals, and go around, people raising money to support these candidates' campaigns," I said, "and I want to let you know here and now, that since I haven't had a chance to meet the candidates or to speak on this report, and I was denied the floor, I'm not going to ask in my locals for nary dime." And I said, "I'm not going to ask anybody among the Negroes to support nary candidate. If they vote, that's up to them. If they give you money, that's up to them. But I'm not going to encourage them or urge them to give nary penny or vote for nary one of these candidates," I said that. I got my hat and walked on out. And these other Negroes that they wouldn't allow either, they walked out with me. That was my walkout.

I had to battle on both fronts, see, cause many a time I'd hit the floor and other Negroes wouldn't even open their mouths. They would set down, they wouldn't fight back, they wouldn't pick up where I leave off. And the whites would get up there and water down what I said.

The Negroes wouldn't back me up, cause at that time, the Negro in the South, you had to pick certain Negroes to stand up and speak out. Everybody didn't speak out. When Negroes set down, they mind set down, they thoughts set down. They went to sleep, like, and they just couldn't think, cause they wouldn't think. These things they ought to talk about, they wouldn't talk about it.

Now if it come to a vote, they would vote right. But they wouldn't get up and talk. That was the trouble in that Birmingham Industrial Council where I was a delegate from my local. I was always like a sore thumb, standing out ahead, cause I was always raising the issues, questions that the other guys would just sit there and wouldn't say nothing. Some of them would get up and take they hat and walk out and leave me on the floor fighting. To tell you the truth about it, I tells a lot of people every once in a while, I been let down so many times by Negroes, I ought not to *never, never* do nothing but set down in the chair and read the paper and watch the TV.

We heard so much when we was there in the Party in the early years, in the '30s, that Negro leadership wouldn't fight for the Negro masses. That was the regular cry. The regular saying was that what the Negroes was lacking was some good leaders. So when I got to developing and found I could be somebody, from not being able to read and write and still coming forward, I set out to be a leader among the Negro people in Birmingham. I thought, really thought, that the Negro, all he needs is somebody to stand up and speak, and he would fall in line.

But that's where I was let down. That's where I found that they wouldn't do it, they wouldn't. It wasn't a crisis of leadership, it was a question of a crisis of people needing to be educated to the importance of leadership.

Another Sunday in 1947, we had a CIO meeting for political action. Delegates from all over everywhere in Alabama. The hall was packed. That meeting was to report on results of getting members of the union qualified to vote, getting them by the Registration Board. They had a delegation there from Gadsden Alabama, about six or seven. On that delegation was only one Negro.

The chairman, white guy, got up there and he made a wonderful report. Oh, they done so much, what they got in Gadsden, how many members they got qualified to vote, they had so many people went down to register to vote till they give out of blanks. They had to make some more blanks.

Cary Haigler, he was chairing that meeting. He was the state president of the CIO. He said, "We heard the report from our delegates from Gadsden, thank you, you made a wonderful report. You been doing wonderful work. Anybody have any questions?"

Several people got up. "Mr. Chairman, I think the delegation from Gadsden learned us what we should do."

"Mr. Chairman, that was a wonderful report. The brothers from Gadsden set us a fine example."

I was setting there. After a while, I said, "Mr. Chairman, I have a question," and I gets up. I said, "I think all of us have to tip our hats to our union brothers in Gadsden, cause I think the report has showed they've done some good work up there, and I think they can show us all how we can improve our work, getting our members qualified to vote. But I have a question. My question to the delegate is, out of the people that was passed by the Board of Registrars— and I noticed they said so many members of the union went to the board to register till they give out of blanks—could you tell us just what the percentage of *Negroes* that got qualified?"

"No, I, uh, I don't know. I don't know of any . . ." And they had half of the membership, if not over half the membership was Negro members of the unions, members in the unions up there in the steel plants, in the rubber plants. And yet he couldn't tell whether nary a one passed.

I pointed out what the problems was that Negroes had in trying to pass the Board of Registrars. I said that the union local leadership have to take a greater responsibility in helping Negroes get registered to vote. "If you mean what we talk about getting members qualified to vote to support the labor candidates, we got to get the white members to take a more active part in trying to help the Negro members pass the Board of Registrars. Because," I said, "it's like you trying to fight with one hand tied down side of you. Here you fight with one hand, the other hand tied is the Negro."

I said, "Automatically the Negro gets the vote, he automatically will support labor candidates, because whatever benefits labor benefits the Negro as a whole."

When I set down, old big George Mills,* he got up. He said, "Mr. President, I rise to say I think that the delegates from Gadsden done a wonderful job, and I wants to say also, don't let nobody tell you that the Negro is going to turn his back on the CIO." This is a black Negro speaking.

I ain't said nothing about turning the back. But this is what I had every time I got up, practically, from some old stupid Negro. And he had the nerve, after the meeting's over, to come out, when we on the street there, said, "Bro' Hudson, you made a wonderful talk. I'm with you one hundred percent." This was the same man. The same Negro! That's the way they would do. "Yeah, I'm with you one hundred percent." I just walk on off. They'd wonder what they had done. I wouldn't even try to discuss with them.

ME and Eb Cox, we went back a long ways together, back to '36, '37, when the CIO drive was on organizing the steelworkers.[1] Philip Murray sent representatives to William Z. Foster and asked the Party to recommend organizers wherever they had people. In Birmingham, Eb Cox was a member of the Party, and he was a unemployed, militant guy who was there. He was just a member, he wont no important guy way up there, just a member of the club. They recommended Eb Cox and also Joe Howard and Dave Smith. Joe Howard and Dave Smith was the ones who organized that sit down strike at Jackson. That was when the CIO dropped Joe Howard and Dave Smith.

In '38 Cox was still coming into the Party office, having discussions about what our line going to be in the CIO convention, what resolutions we going support. At the same time, Cox is going all out now, he going try to make a career in the Steel staff. And Beddow† and them was calling him into account about being a communist. He wanted to be able to fight back if they Red-bait him. He didn't want them to be able to trace him down to the Party office. Cox asked the Party D.O., asked Rob Hall for a leave of absence from the Party, where his conscience could be clear and he

* I guess he's dead now. He was from the wholesale-retail workers' union Local 251.

† [Noel Beddow was then president of the Alabama State CIO.]

could say, "I'm not a member." It wont no great big meeting, private meeting with Rob Hall. It was agreed that Cox leave the Party. So that's when he got loose. I never did see him come in a Party office after that. He'd always give a little finance donation. I'd go around, he'd take a paper, but he kept adrifting the other way.

In '43, he was still good with us, so I supported his position. He was the onliest thing we had among the Negroes worthwhile to support as a representative. It still wont no Negroes on the CIO state executive board. Everything was elected, so everybody going be white. Automatically you elected a president, he going be white. Elect a secretary-treasurer, he's white. Then all the rest of the representatives, the vice-presidents, come from the different unions. Mine Mills would elect a vice-president, textile workers would elect a vice-president, the longshoremen would elect a vice-president, Steel would elect a vice-president. They take these vice-presidents from the various unions, and that would make the state executive board. All these would be white, because it wont enough Negroes attending local meetings regular enough to see the importance of they sending Negroes here where they get a Negro elected.

The onliest way you can get a Negro in, you got to figure out how you can do it. So I figured it out, and I presented a resolution from my little local,* and I presented a resolution in the convention that the office of vice-president at large would be opened up. There would be two vice-presidents at large, and I said that the two would be Negroes.

I ran into a conflict in the constitutional committee on that question of the two "be Negroes." While the convention's going on, they called me into the committee Tom Howell from the wire mill local, Local 1700, out there in Fairfield, he was chairman of that constitutional committee. (They were saying that he was one of the top leaders of the Ku Klux Klan.) Me and him and the committee, we discussed backwards and forwards. Finally they convinced me to drop the word "Negro" and just say "two vice-presidents at large." They said you would tie your hands, maybe a lot of whites wouldn't vote for it because they was prejudiced, a lot of the whites was. And they said, next thing, you'd have a Chinese

* It won't but twenty-five of us meeting. I wouldn't have all twenty-five at one time. When I got nine–ten I had a big meeting in that period.

or somebody else come up, an Italian, and they want two vice-presidents at large to be Chinamen or Italians. So I dropped the word "Negroes," and said "vice-presidents at large." They said, "We'll support you in trying to get a Negro elected." I had also asked for the vice-presidents at large to have "voice and vote," and I had to sacrifice "vote." At the next convention, I went in that convention with a resolution supporting that same resolution, but the vice-presidents at large would have voice and vote. That was in '45. We didn't have no convention in '44. That was right in the heat of the war. That was when Roosevelt asked everybody not to have no big meeting, on the question of transportation. So we didn't have no convention in '44.

That first time, Eb Cox was elected over Beddow's head, that was in '43, after I had got the resolution passed. Beddow went down from the table at the front of the meeting to these Negroes over down yonder and talked to one of these Negroes in the Acipco new organized local. (Beddow had been the district representative of the Steelworkers under William Mitch, and he helped organize this new local at Acipo.) He said, "If you all pick your man, I'll help you get him elected." Then Beddow went back to the table.

I'm over here in the aisle over side the wall, and the guy Beddow talk to come over where I was and told me what Mr. Beddow had said. I told him, "We'll support Eb Cox." I said, "I'm going nominate Eb Cox."

The Negro brother goes back down there. All right, Beddow got up, come on down again, walks over and asks him who had they decided to run. The Negro said, "Bro' Hudson said he going run Eb Cox." Then Beddow got all mad.

The brother come back to me looking all sick, told me, "Mr. Beddow say, 'Hell, no!' say his men ain't going never allow Eb Cox to held elective office." "His men," that means all Beddow's staff men in the Steelworkers district office.

I said, "Beddow don't tell us who we vote for a leader." I said, "I'm going nominate Cox. If nobody don't vote for him, then leave it." So then the Negro went away from me looking even sicker. He didn't know what to tell Beddow now, so he went on back and sit down. Nobody didn't say no more.

When it come to nominating vice-presidents at large, I went up to the mike. The mike was setting about 4–5 feet from the table, and I'm over here talking. Beddow was setting right behind the table, in the middle. I talked about what this person had done, what a great leader he would make, put him in good position. I ain't called his name yet. When I got through talking, I said, "This person's no other than Brother Eb Cox of the United Steelworkers of America." When I said that, I walked over around here and back around to my seat.

Beddow got up to the mike right behind me. He said, "I got a man I want to put up here . . ." and all what he was, and finally, "It's no other than Ben Gage." Ben Gage was setting there side of him. He was one of the staff guys too. So that made him have four of his own staff men from Steel running for that particular office. Three of them was elected, Ben Gage and Dan Houston and Cox. A Mine Mill* guy was elected, a white guy. At that time they was elected voice but no vote. They could talk all they wanted, but no vote.

The next time, McGruder was put in and Asbury Howard was put in. Asbury Howard was from Mine Mill, we supported him. And we was still supporting Eb Cox. McGruder was from around there in Alabama. He called hisself a preacher, but he wasn't nothing but a stoolpigeon. The white union officials, what they was doing, they had him around, trying to go around among the Negroes, try to win the Negroes over to the union, talking with them, but he wont from no particular union. They paid him. He was some kind of little salaried guy. At the '45 convention, he was a delegate, and he's running for vice-president at large. The white union officials wanted to put McGruder up over Eb Cox.

We had a Steel caucus, and I tried to edge them off, stall them on endorsing McGruder. They wanted a unanimous vote. I asked them, "What union do McGruder come from, is it Steel or what?" They couldn't say. Nobody know. I said, "Since my question hasn't been answered satisfactorily of what union do McGruder represent," I said, "I'm going to withhold my vote from the unanimous." That was the only way I could stall.

They dropped the unanimous question in the caucus itself, said, "Let's just forget about it, let's forget about it. We won't make a unanimous vote." That was the whites, see. I did that in order to get

---

* Mine Mill was the next biggest union in the Alabama CIO.

back in the convention to nominate Eb Cox. I did nominate Eb Cox from the floor. But these white Steel guys, these racist guys among the whites, they was able to muster enough votes to put McGruder in over Eb Cox.

I had done nominated Cox twice for vice-president at large. And I supported him from way back in the '30s. We always called up each other to stay in touch about what's going on. I kind of backed him up. Back in '37, Eb Cox had to fight these popsicle unions, company unions. He had to fight the leading Negroes who was working among these Negroes in Fairfield hill. All the big church deacons and things, all the big homeowners up there, not all of them, but a lot of them, had a hand in the popsicle unions. One Sunday they was having a meeting of the posicles down there in a place called French Town. Eb Cox found out where they was going meet, he come and notified us and wanted us to come with him, me and Willie Norman and another guy. We got with Eb Cox and went to it. It was a private home where they having the meeting.

We walked in there and all these Negroes' eyes buckled. They stopped the discussion, got quiet, and looked around at each other. We just sit there. After a while, the chairman, he said, "Gentlemen, we have some visitors here, some guests, and right here we going hear from them to see what they have to say."

Eb, he was the spokesman. He told them, "We come over to your meeting this evening to discuss with you the question of labor. We would like to unite with you to work together with you all. What will benefit one will benefit all, benefit the Negro as a whole."

When Eb got through talking, the chairman thanked Brother Cox for the suggestions he had offered, said, "We'll take your suggestions under consideration." Then he asked us to be excused, they wanted us to leave, they had some important business to take up. We left. We didn't argue with him. But I never did hear no more about that popsicle after that Sunday. It begin to fall apart. If I make no mistake, old man Jerry Darby was chairman of that group that Sunday. The man who spoke kind of favored him. I come to know him later. He come to be the vice-president of Local 1700 of the Steelworkers at the wire mills.

That was one thing me and Eb done. And it was lots of little things. Labor Day in '44 me and Eb and somebody else, we all lined up and went to a meeting down in Jonesboro, down the other side of Bessemer. A. Q. Johnson was slated to speak at that Labor Day meeting.

A. Q. Johnson was supposed to been a ex coal miner. But he was one who was fully recognized as being a stoolpigeon. A. Q., he was a orator. He could speak. And Eb Cox was as mad as he could be cause here they recognizing this stoolpigeon up here, and there he was in the leadership, vice-president at large, and nobody invited him to speak. That was another little time I was with him.

Me and Eb started to break, in around '47 and '48, when the CIO started Red baiting. When Philip Murray started his raids against the left in the CIO, Eb Cox was all the way on the other side.

At the last CIO convention I was in, in 1947, I run for vice-president at large. I had supported Cox against Beddow and Cox went in, the first time, and I supported Cox against McGruder, McGruder beat him. Now here the third time. Some of them asking me about running. The Negroes was all saying, "We want Bro' Hudson to run. We want to support him for vice-president this time."

We had a caucus of Negro delegates to the convention down at the little Masonic Temple, about sixty or seventy delegates from all the various unions. They got to talking about nominating of candidates for the vice-president at large, who they going support. Somebody nominated me. Then they nominated Gus Dixon. Gus Dixon was from Steel and I was from Steel. Then they nominated Asbury Howard. Asbury Howard was from Mine Mill, no trouble with Asbury Howard. But now here's Hudson and Dixon.

Eb Cox was chairing the meeting of this caucus in '47. All I fought back yonder for him, and here's my payoff now.

He spoke up and said, "I tell you all, you better know what you doing when you nominating these candidates. You better know what you doing nominating Bro' Hudson."

I said, "What you talking about?" said, "Tell these people what you talking about."

"Naw, Bro' Hudson, let's don't get into it. I think you understand."

I said, "I don't understand nothing. Tell these people what you talking about." He was Red baiting, trying to raise a bogey, telling them, if you nominate Hudson here, he's a bugabear, get you some trouble.

All the people started asking, "What, what about Hudson?" So they didn't nominate me there. They didn't agree on me. Everybody was talking, but nobody else said anything but me. I was the only one that challenged Eb Cox.

We went back to the convention. They got up and nominate Gus Dixon, and Asbury Howard was nominated. And Mack Coad, he nominated me. He had just enough nerve to go to the mike and say, "I want to place a name in nomination for vice-president at large, Bro' Hosie Hudson, president of Local 2815," and went on back and set down. Didn't say who I was or what I had done, nothing. In the voting, Asbury Howard got elected, and Gus Dixon won. They counted me out. The guy counting the people standing up to be counted for me, he didn't count a whole slice of people, went on out the door instead of carrying the votes down. I still got 139 votes. Gus Dixon didn't get but 160-some. But I didn't challenge it, cause I done fought till I just said, let them do what they want to. The rest of the Negroes just sit there and wouldn't say nothing.

After the voting, Louie Yates—he's dead and gone to the devil now—he walked by me and said, "Hudson, you got 139 votes. Man, you got a whole lot of support here in this convention. Did you think you's going get elected?"

"Why not? What you think I was running for if I didn't want to be elected?" But I tell you who was voting for me. It wont them devils from around Birmingham. The Negroes, yes, but not them whites—a few whites—but not the bulk of the whites. My support was from them out-of-town textile white women, white members from Huntsville, Talladega, and all them places. Them's the ones. On the basis of what I'm saying on the floor, I gained they confidence. They voted for my position and for me.

Eb Cox and me really broke when Steel raided the Mine, Mill, and Smelter Workers, around '48.* Along in the fall, me and

* When Philip Murray began to raid, they split Mine Mill right down the middle, black on one side, white on the other, with some whites staying with the blacks and some of the blacks part of the whites. The black members built Mine Mill with a help from a few whites. But among the whites, you had all these Klan elements, all these Red baiters. Automatically they was against Mine Mill, "that damn communist union, them communists! Every time you get around Mine Mill

Eb chanced to meet on the corner in front of the Masonic Temple. I asked him, "What is your position about Steel going raiding in Mine Mill now?"

"Well, I tell you, Hudson, I'm a old man now. I can't get back into the plant now, cause they ain't going hire me back. I got a job to do. I got to look out for my job. I got to look out for my wife and family."

I said, "Therefore you forsaking the Negro people now, huh?" I said, "Mine Mill been the union that been fighting against all forms of discrimination in the mines, you know that." I said, "you forsaking the Negro, trying to tear down the Mine Mill union and what they done for the Negro, just to support your boss in the Steelworkers union to try to raid Mine Mill?"

He said, "I got to look out for my family. My job is with the United Steelworkers of America."

I said, "Well, I wish you God speed." We walked away from each other, and that was the last time me and Eb Cox had anything to say.

I saw him one more time around about in '50, just before Bull Connor started to raid against us there in Birmingham. I was coming from Atlanta on my way back to Birmingham. I happened to catch the train he was on, coming from the Steelworkers convention in Atlantic City, one Sunday. He tried to make a great point with the Negro delegates sitting around me on the train.

He was talking to them. I'm just setting there. "Philip Murray's the greatest trade union statesman that ever lived!" Oh, he put Philip Murray high! That was when Philip Murray was raiding and putting the left out of the CIO. I didn't even turn to answer. I just sit there, let it stay. I rode on in to Birmingham. That was the last time I remember seeing him.*

---

you got communists!" But among the Negroes it was a different picture. When it come to a vote, come to election in the mines, whether to vote for Mine Mill or vote for the Steel union, the Negroes voted for Mine Mill and the whites voted for Steel.

* I went to Birmingham in 1961 and Eb Cox had just died.

22

The Marriage
Breaks Up

ONE Sunday in the spring of 1946 my wife Sophie come home talking about Mr. and Mrs. Lester. Wade Lester sang in my Smithfield Vocal Singers. We singing together every Sunday, a capella singing. Me and him was good friends for nine years. So I didn't think nothing of it when Sophie said his wife wouldn't wash his shirt where he have a clean shirt for that Sunday, Sophie said, "I told him to bring it here, I'd wash it for him and iron it." It was a white shirt. I didn't pay no attention to it.[1]

Then a little bit later, not long after, I lay down, me and Sophie in the bed, and I was over in the bed next to the wall. In my sleep, me and her was walking down through a old grove of trees. And in this dream, twas a old barn, and the barn was here, about one foot high off the ground, it was on pillars. The sill of it was on pillars, and me and her was walking this way beside the barn. I was on the outside, and she was on this side. I looked under the edge of this barn, and there lay a red snake, striped like a baseball, red and white, and he was about three-four inches long. He wont laying long ways, he was zigzagged, this way, that way, this way. He ain't stretched out. He wont curled up, he was laying backwards and forwards. Red just like a flag. I looked down there and I said, "Sophie, look there! There's a snake."

She said, "Yeah, sure is, Hosie."

I said, "Bring me a stick." She brought me a hickory, it wasn't a stick, it was kind of like a half stick and a half switch, but twas long. It was four or five feet long. I took it and I hit the snake, and the green stick kind of bent and snatched him out from under that barn.

When I snatched him out, that stick turned to a baseball bat I

341

had, and that snake turned to a little bulldog about a foot long, real white, and he's trying to get me, and I was hitting him down in the head, beating him in the head, till his eyeballs come out of his head, swung way down, and blood's running down his mouth. I beat that dog, trying to keep him off me till I woke up. When I woke up, that dog turned to that Negro, Lester, in my mind. Just like right now when I think back, I see Lester, I see the dog, but I see Lester, so much so until I first turned to my side. I said, "Sophie! Sophie!"

"Huh? Huh?"

I'm all frightened, and I said to her, I said, "What's between you and Lester?"

She said, "Nothing. Why?"

I said, "I had a dream here. I had a dream about you and Lester, and we was walking down. I whupped on a snake and the snake turned to a bulldog and the dog turned to Lester."

"I ain't nothing to that man. I don't know if that man a man or woman. He ain't never said nothing to me in his life." That's what she told me. But that dream stayed with me. I woke up the next day, and I didn't forget it. I haven't forgotten it even today. That was in the spring of the year 1946.

I didn't want to accuse her of Lester—we singing together every Sunday. In the Smithfield Vocal Singers, he was the basson and she was the alto. They sit side by side. The others on the front, seated over the side of them, and I'm here on the front. They sitting right behind me on the back seat. It wont but a few of us, six of us.

One Sunday, we was at a singing convention. The custom, when I sound my song, everybody stand, and we'd sing. That day at the convention, when I got up and sound my song, all the rest of the members of the class stood up, but Sophie and Lester still sitting down. All the rest of the people's up, three or four people stood up, and her and Lester sitting side by side. They sound but they didn't stand up, and it was a custom that when I sound the second time, everybody *got* to stand, but they didn't stand, they sit.

So after they didn't stand up, I waved to the mistress of cere-monies to call on the next choir to go sing behind me. And I sit down. So she called on the next choir was going to sing after my singing, and I said to Sophie and Lester, "How come you all didn't stand up? What's wrong with you all? How come you can't stand up around here? We ain't singing like this, some standing up, some sitting down."

She said, "Mr. Lester said his legs hurt."

Now Lester sitting there and he ain't said a word. All right. We come around—they sung around about five things—they sung around and got back to me. I sound again, and they did the same thing again. It was me and three others standing up and these two sitting down. The tenor standing up and the two soprano people standing up the same way, and myself. So when I told the mistress of ceremonies the second time, she announced to the church, she said, "I don't know what's the matter with Smithfield." She said, "I done passed them once, now they want to be passed again."

Everybody hollering, "Smithfield! Smithfield! Smithfield!" in the church.

I said, "Some of my singers don't want to stand up around here."

So Sophie gets up, says, "Mr. Lester said his legs was hurting him and that's the reason he and I was sitting down, wont standing up singing."

Then the president of the singing convention said, "Well, we don't have anything to do with Smithfield's problems," he said. "We were looking for the Smithfield singers to sing."

So before I would be outdone, I sit down with everybody else, I sit down and sung the song sitting down. I let everybody sit down.

When the thing was over we started home. I said, "Sophie, what's wrong here, you and Lester want to sit down. You ain't said nothing to me that you wants to sit down. And then you got to get up and speak for Lester."

"Hosie, listen, don't start none of your mess here now. The man just said his legs was hurting, and I just got up and told them what he said."

I didn't understand how come she had to sit down with him. Before that we hadn't had no troubles at all. That was the first outcome from my dream. I went on now, I'm trying to figure out, I begin to start to think different.

We had to sing that second Sunday in May before I came to Atlantic City that next Saturday, that next weekend. I was watching, I was trying to see do I see any kind of move between them. I ain't said nothing to nobody. So I couldn't see anything. So I went on to the CIO convention in Atlantic City.

On Wednesday night in this hotel down here, the Liberty Hotel, I was in that hotel trying to figure out what is going on in that dream. Then a voice spoke to me, not outside of my head, but it sound like a voice so plain that it look like your head open up, wake up inside your head, and that spirit or whatever it was deals into my head, and saying, "When you go back home, you go down to Mrs. Lester's and ask her is there anything between her and Sophie." Just like that.

When that voice said that, I jumped up. "That's right!" In there by myself, in my room, down in the middle of this hotel, room 208. I said, "That's right! That woman don't come around to our house there like she used to." She used to come to the house in there to see my wife to do sewing for her. She hadn't been there in I don't know when. I ain't never woke up to she ain't coming. But it come to me she didn't come no more.

I left Atlantic City that Friday night, I wouldn't wait until the convention's over. I left Friday night on the 3:45 train, got into Birmingham the next day. That next day in the afternoon I went home. Sophie wasn't there, but my boy's wife was there.* I said, "Where Sophie, Hazel?"

"I don't know, she went to town about 11 o'clock. She ain't never come back yet." Now it's around about 4 or 4:30.

I went right on down to Mrs. Lester's, about five or six blocks from my house. She was sitting on the porch, and she asked how was my trip and how did I enjoy it—fine—and when did I get back.

"I just got back just a while ago," and I said to her, I said, "Mrs. Lester, I came around to ask you a question I just want to stay confidential between me and you."

"Ask me anything you want to ask." She laid it wide open.

I said, "Is there anything between you and Sophie? Don't tell nobody I asked you."

"I wouldn't ask you that question. Sophie Hudson just about done broke up my home, and ain't just now started. She been giving me trouble the last two-three years. People have come here trying to get me to carry them to the rooming house where that old dog of mine in with her. I just don't want to kill him, cause if I run up

* My son met Hazel when he was in the army in 1944 in Camp Lee, Virginia. He and she got married there before he was shipped overseas. They moved in with me and Sophie when he was discharged out of the army in 1945.

on them, I'm going to kill them. I just want to meet them in the street together."

You could have bought me for 10¢.

She said, "You know when you were in New York on your vacation last year?" That was back last November in '45.

I said yeah.

She said, "I got a letter she wrote Wade Lester, and he loved it so well he toted it around in this pocket till he lost it here on the floor, and I found it. I got it up here folded, unless a thief ain't went up here and stole it."

She went and got a great big old patent-leather women's pocketbook upside the wall, went in there among her papers and got it out and handed it to me. It started off about "Dear Darling, don't think hard of me for not writing before now . . ." and all that stuff. She didn't call my name the first time, didn't say "Hosie" nary a time, in that whole of that one-page letter. It was all about what she's been doing up there and how she's enjoying herself, how "people carried me over to the George Washington Bridge today and it's so high I couldn't walk." She said, "If you had been with me, Darling, I could have walked. I got a lot to tell you when I come home." Now me and her aunt's husband was the ones that trying to get her to walk across there.

I had told Sophie, course I don't guess she thought I meant it, I told her if ever she found anybody she thought she wanted to mistreat me for, to just go away. I said, "Don't try to live with me and ride two horses. You just quit me and go on with him." I told her that several times, cause I said, "If I catch you," I said, "if I don't kill you, I'm going to quit you." I quit her, but it was a hard pill to swallow.

I tried everything but taking violent actions. I talked all I could talk, up to begging. I didn't beg. I talked to her and tried to show her how long we had been together, why we ought to still stick together now after all these years. It was just like you pouring water on a duck's back. It wont even sinking in, not hearing. So there was nothing else I seed I could do. Cause by '47 I had done developed and done got to be the leader in Birmingham. I was known.[2] On the one hand, I'm a local leader, on the other hand, though, here I am in this trouble.

Some friends offered me a pistol. But the Party people was telling me, said, "Don't take that pistol, that gun. It ain't worth it.

Don't get in trouble." It was outside people was offering the guns. One guy was a coal miner. He had a pistol and a two-barreled derringer. I could get either one of them. Another guy named Mills, he was working in the shop with me, he offered me to give me his pistol. I wouldn't take no pistol, cause I felt if I took the pistol I might do something. If I didn't have it, I wouldn't do it. That's the way I stayed out of trouble. If I'd of taken the pistol and shot them, I'd of been in plenty trouble. I was in the Party, and it would of been a blot on the Party. If I hadn't of been in the Party, though, I would have got in trouble. The Party was more or less a kind of balance, was a guide.

Mayfield would tell me, "You'll find another woman. Man, don't get in trouble about one woman. The world full of women." He had separated from his first wife, and he'd married the second wife. And Beidel, he had separated from his first wife. Beidel's first wife, she . . . well, you know sometimes they say, that's my experience, sometimes a woman, some women, they get a certain age, they mind gets bad. Her mind got bad. She done went off and took all his money, left. I don't know if she was crazy, but she had enough sense to take the money. She didn't leave the money. He was working and wasn't making but about 40¢ an hour, and the little money he saved, he give it to her to put up there in the house. I don't know how much he had, maybe $100, it wont much money, but whatever he had, she got it and left. That was back in about '42.

After she left there, he quit keeping house. He got him a room. After she went off and spent the money and stayed, then she wanted to come back home. He wouldn't let her come back home, and she come there where he living, she wanted to raise sand. So he had to call the law for her, get a decree that she not go around where he lived at. Finally she left and went back to Columbus Georgia.

After so long a time, then he went and got to going with another woman, Flora,* and him and her married. They was together when me and Sophie separated in '47, cause he got me the room up there at Mrs. Vesey's where I was living. Wont but a block from they house, after I moved out and left Sophie. I come over to Mrs. Vesey's and went to living. I went down there many

---

* Flora died with cancer. And Beidel died with the same thing I got, mine asthma [chronic obstructive pulmonary disease, probably pneumoconiosis or black-lung disease]. I got it from steel. But he had it worser than I got, I reckon.

times to Beidel's house in the morning, and they give me breakfast.

I don't know what the trouble, but I had a whole lot of little bumps come out, and they's all in the back of my head. None of them would come in the front, they's all back there. All back there, these little bumps, they just as hard! They wouldn't get no size, but they hurt, great God! And Flora, she used to love to pick and bust them bumps. They hurt, and I couldn't see them. That was in the fall of '47 and the first of '48. She'd come and look at my head and she'd mash on them. She say wouldn't anything come out, but it was just several little hard bumps.

And I had a rising on my backbone, between my shoulder blades. I couldn't reach it with my hand. I couldn't reach it from this-a-way, and I couldn't reach it from that-a-way. It was all back there. All of that come in the back, and nothing in front.

I moved in with Mrs. Vesey, clean on out on the east side. I made it my business not to go back over in the west side, cause as long as I was over in there I'd look down towards where I lived. I just couldn't help but looking down there or going by, standing on the corner up there where the street come out down the way. So I moved out completely on the east side. That took me away from out of that community, then I was able sort of to handle myself.

After we broke up, I didn't do nothing for enjoyment. All I attended was Party meetings. I attended union meetings until they put me out the union, in good fashion in '48. The onliest thing then I had to enjoy was when I went to working with the people down there in Bessemer.[3] And I would go around a little bit to the singing, but I didn't do much singing. Singing choked me. Got to be to the point, everytime I tried to sing, I just choked. I got mad with all the women. All of '47, I didn't do much of nothing with myself for enjoyment or social life. In '48 I went back to try to sing a little bit, about the last of '48.

ONE day in the fall of '48, I was standing on a street corner. And a old man, Mr. Johnson was his name, he knew me and Sophie and he was asking had we went back together. I told him no. He was a old fellow, he's from Georgia too, and he come to know us from singing. He was about eighty-five years old. He said, "Boy, don't you worry about that gal." He said, "One of these days, she'll come back and ask you to take her back. My wife done me the same way." But that wont fast enough for me. That was too slow. I wanted something done now.

The light changed, and his light carried him over this way, he went across the avenue, and I'm waiting till the light change where I can go across the street. And it was another old man standing off listening at me and Mr. Johnson talk. When we broke off our conversation, this man walks up, says, "Say friend, I hear you talking to the other fellow. Seem like you had a little trouble. You have some domestic trouble?"

I said, "Yeah. Me and my wife separated, and he was talking to me about it."

"How long you all been separated?"

"Oh, we been separated now since about '46."

And he said, "Do you believe that anyone could do anything for you underhanded?" He meant did I want to try some hoodoo.

I said, "No, I don't believe in that junk. I don't believe in nothing like that." Now why I don't believe it, I already been to two or three people, and they ain't done nothing, ain't done no good. That's why I done give that up.

He said, "I got a friend I'd like you to go see." He said, "It ain't far," he said, "so you could walk down there. If he don't tell you what you want to know—he won't charge but a dollar—I'll pay for it myself."

I said, "I don't fool with them folks." I said, "Ain't nobody can do nothing. I just don't want to fool with it."

I was just all mad, disgusted and tore up and everything. I been tore up now ever since '46, this here's '48. I cussing every woman I see. Sometime a woman would come up, "Mr. Hudson, how you feeling?"

"All right, how you feeling?"

"Why don't you come to see me sometime?"

"All right, I be over to see you." But that was it. I never did go. I didn't want to talk with any women. I was bitter.

But this old man on the street corner kept talking to me till he got me to agree to walk down there. We had to walk from about 22nd Street and 3rd Avenue down to 11th Street where that other old man lived. We got down there, and he was sitting in the yard in his alley. He lived in a alley. He was a old man, about eighty–ninety years old. They called him "Pop." He had yellowish gray hair, nice good hair, and he just sitting out in front, in a chair, and another chair was sitting there. He just sitting here in his chair, and he had his cards right on him. He always carried his cards. The old man what carried me down there walked up to him and said, "Pop, here's a fellow I just met up there. I ain't never seed him before. I heard him talking, and it look like he got a little trouble. I want you to look him over, see can you see what his trouble is."

Pop said, "Have a seat here."

I sit down. I don't believe nothing. Pop took his little cards, shuffle up, shuffle up, and shuffle up, and I cut them. I hand them back to him, three different times.

And this is God's gospel, I don't care what nobody say. He open up this card. The card he opened up, first time he open up, he said, "Yeah, you got a lot of trouble here. Your home, your home all broke up, ain't it?"

I said, "Yeah, me and my wife separated."

He said, "Your wife is kind of nice looking, a brown-skinned woman." I say yeah. "I see another younger woman here in the house, with a younger man. Who is that?" I say that is my son and his wife. "Well, who is this? I see a real light brown-skinned man. He's a lighter color than you are. He's a little older than you. Who is he? Is that your friend?"

I said, "I guess so." That was the guy broke me and her up, Lester. "Yeah, I took him to be my friend."

"You took him to be your friend?"

I said, "Well, I thought he was my friend."

"Oh, but he wont your friend. Now you done been to about three or four different people before now to get them to break them up, ain't you?"

I said, "Yeah, I have."

"How come they couldn't do it?"

I said, "I don't know. They didn't do it."

"I'll tell you why." He said, "It's something they can't handle, that's why. This is too much for them," he said. "You got three crosses on you." He said, "You got a cross on you, first of all, they is trying to feed you for you to die a slow death. You have a whole lot of trouble with your stomach, don't you? Gets a weak stomach and vomit." I said yeah. He said, "They got that on you. And they got a cross on you for you to get in a argument with somebody and get killed. They got a cross on you for you to walk in an argument with somebody, including the police. And then they got a third cross on you for you to walk in front of a automobile and get killed."

And I had just escaped from that. I was just like a rattlesnake. Every time you say something to me, I was just mean as a snake. And just a day or two before, I nearly done got run over getting off of a trolley car.

The trolley car run in the middle of the street, and when you get off, you got to watch for cars coming up, because you'd walk out and a lot of people got killed between the sidewalk and the trolley. It was dangerous for you to step around in front of that trolley car, cause a automobile liable to be coming up on the other side, come on the wrong side to pass the trolley. When I got off the trolley right at the end, stepped around front of the trolley to go cross, just as I got near clear of the trolley, here's a car coming right by. I just jumped, time enough to jump out, back out the front of it. Once or twice I nearly got hit like that, right in that period.

So Pop told me all these things. He said, "You worrying about him and her. You quit worrying about them and worry about yourself. Get yourself straight, cause you is poisoned through and through. But it ain't going kill you right away. It's going to kill you slow."

And it was true. You could count every rib in my side. My cheekbones standing all out. And I was looking mean. He told me, he said, "If you come down here every week, come down, just let me see you, you don't have to pay me no money, just come and let me see you, let me speak with you and talk with you. In a month's time, your friends won't know you. You work in the shop, and in the shop the boys where you work won't know you. Now you got a $150 job. Well, you know how much I'm going charge you?"

I said, "No, how much you charge me?"

"I'm going to charge you $13 and 13¢. Anything you want to give me above that, if you want to give something, you can give it to me, cause I ain't going to charge you but $13 and 13¢."

Pop went in his house and give me a pint bottle of seltzer, look black like coal, and it was bitter as it could be. That's what he give me to take. And he give me nine little things rolled up about the size of your finger in pieces of paper bag, little balls. Just give me nine of them, and he wanted me to take one every night for nine nights. Put it in my bathtub, put it in a tin tub, and just bathe, just let the water run from my head to my feet. Then get out, don't dry off, just put on my pajamas like that and get into bed.

I gave him the $13 and 13¢, then the guy that carried me, I give him a $1 to buy him a drink of whiskey. I promised him that if Pop told me like I wanted, I'd give him a drink of whiskey.

It was November, it was cold. But I did like he told me. That's what I did for nine nights, and I drank that bitter he give me.

In about a month's time, all the spots I had all around my neck where I was just spotted, all the spots cleared up. I commenced to fattening up. I had weighed 163, 164, like that. When I got on the scales the first time, weighed 170, on up to 178. I stood at 178 for a good while, went on to 180, on up to 190, on up to 210. That's what I weigh now, ever since that day. I went down to see Pop, just to talk with him. Sometime he ask, "Hosie, you got any chewing tobacco?" I say yeah. "Give me a piece."

And I, "Here, take that piece there. Here, take that, here, buy you a piece of tobacco," like that. And I never did have no trouble at all after that.

23

Red-Baited

THE Birmingham Industrial Council was made up of delegates elected from the various CIO locals. Then each local paid so much per capita tax to the council for each member. I was elected from my local in '43 some time. I went to the state convention of the CIO, so I was on the council. That was the time I went against Beddow, nominated Eb Cox for vice-president at large. That was in '43.

In the council I was standing out above everybody else on issues. I was always bringing up something nobody else ain't heard of before—things that had happened, things that had developed—nobody else would say anything about it. I'd get up and talk about it in the council. I was reading the *Daily Worker*. That kept me ahead all the time. Come to this point on getting welfare, on getting welfare to the public, I'd speak about it. In the local I'd do the same thing.

It was in October in '47 when they started raiding against me, when the Birmingham *Post* came out with big headlines saying that "Hosie Hudson, president of local 2815, works at Jackson Foundry Industrial Plant, is suspicious of being a member of the Communist Party of the United States, and also is a member of the national committee, the highest committee of the Party in the land."[1]

It wasn't news in the local. Some of the local members knew I was a communist before, cause I was carrying some of them the *Daily Worker* in the shop. Several guys was reading the paper. They didn't seem to care. When this thing came out, a whole lot of the guys said, "Hell, I don't care what Big Red is. Damn, he's my man, cause he get things done here, better conditions, better wages we wouldn't have had it if hadn't been for him."

The local members was white and Negro, but the Negroes was the only ones that attended the local. The whites wasn't attending the local no way. I had a few rats in among the midst of the Negroes, it was about three or four, open. These rats I had was them *old* devils had been there with the company a long time. They always been finding fault. All the rest of the Negroes was with me. When they started on me in the council, these guys in the shop, they all knew that they done started, they seen it in the paper. The newspapers came about the battle I was having in the council. But I'm still working. The superintendent told me, said, "As far as I'm concerned," said, "that's you and the union. As long as you do the work here, I don't care about it." That's the superintendent, but he didn't have the last say.

Old E. M. Wooten, he was president of the TCI hospital workers, he was white, he brought the charges in the council. He brought in the paper, he jumps up and said, "Hosie Hudson knows he's a communist! I move we set up a committee to get him out of there if he don't deny these charges."

I fought them on the grounds of this is my constitutional rights. I told them in the council that night, I said, "If anyone in this council has heard me discussing anything anywhere that wasn't pertaining to the betterment of organized labor and the workers in the plant, get up and speak." Nobody didn't say nothing. I said, "I'm going tell you right now," I said, "the first ten amendments to the United States Constitution, they tell me, is known as the Bill of Rights." I didn't know which one of the amendments it was, I said ten. "And in that Bill of Rights gives every American citizen the right to think politically, religiously, privately as he chooses, whether he's a Catholic, Methodist, Baptist, Sanctified, or whether he's a communist, Republican, Democrat. And since I'm one of these American citizens," I said, "and have that right as all other citizens," I said, "I ain't answering no questions for nobody. Now whatever you all want to do, do it." I sat down.[2]

Then a Negro, old Tom Green, he got up there, "Mr. President, I make a motion for a committee to investigate this thing. If we find these facts to be true, we get these people out this council if we have to throw them out the window!" He was on the committee that was supposed to investigate me of being a member of the Communist Party. It was five of them, including him and Len Wooten, but only him and Wooten met. That committee ain't went to see nobody. The committee never did nothing. The white man doing all the talking. They ain't never met nothing.

At the third council meeting, this so-called committee come back, and this white guy, he made the recommendation about I was from Tignall Georgia, and I moved to Birmingham in 1937—which was a lie, because I had done been there before then, but I been under the name of Will Holton, they didn't know that—and I worked for Jackson foundry, had a wife and one kid. He said, "We made this investigation, and we think we have enough evidence on Hosie Hudson and his activities in the Communist Party that he be expelled out of the council if he don't prove hisself innocent."

It took them to near 1 o'clock at night to get through that scrapping and scrambling, to put me out the council, throw me out.[3]

Old man Jerry Darby, a Negro, he wont no Party member, and once he was a company union man, he was the one who fought more hard than anybody else in that council when the racists that night was trying to get me out. But Tom Green, I had been knowing all the time, he got up there that night all confused, said, "I don't know, I don't know. So much talk being done." But when he vote, he vote with the white folks.

It was some Negroes voted with the whites, but the majority of the Negroes there was voting for me. But they didn't have but two-three hundred members in they local. It was the whites, in that roll-call vote what got me out. The whites was in the minority at the attending of the council, but the voting was by numbers of members from the plant. They voting for two-three thousand members from the plant. These guys from steel plants had thousands of Negro members of the union, but the Negro members of the union won't go to a union meeting and don't know what's going on, they just paying dues. These white guys on the council used they votes, the votes of these Negro members, to put me out the council.

When them whites that night voting against me, that same Miller from Jackson foundry, the guy I had got him the rest of the 11¢ of the 18½¢ raise, he had been elected to the council as a delegate with me and another Negro guy named Archie Edmundson. It was three of us. Miller had the nerve to divide the membership of the local in three parts. Third of them to me, third of them to Miller, third of them to Edmundson. And the biggest part of them members was Negroes. Old Miller stood there, voting Negroes' votes against me in the council. He turned against me.

I went home. I felt very much let down, cause I been let down by so many Negroes. Tom Green and two guys from the local where I was recording secretary back in '37, and this here was '47, these two Negroes was from the steel plant in Ensley. They voted with the white guy from their local. They voted against me. You know that's hot. That was enough to wreck me. But I stood up under it.

When they trying to get me out the council, I wrote to Philip Murray. And I wrote to the attorney for the CIO. At that time it was Lee Pressman.[4] I wrote Lee Pressman, and I sent him a full statement about my case and what's happening now in the council. He wrote me a letter back that he was turning my report over to somebody, President Murray or somebody. The next thing I see, they kicked Pressman out the union. They done fired *him*. Then Philip Murray wrote a letter. In the main he said he was advising the CIO leadership in Birmingham to give my case full considera-tion. My case "full consideration," that meant, "put him out the union." He was trying to get rid of all the left-progressives then and everybody.[5]

The next meeting of the council after they throwed me out, I was out at the shop. Jake Mellon and some of the boys said, "Hud-son, you want to go to the council meeting tonight?"

I said, "Yeah, I go."

They said, "God damn, let's go. Come on. God damn, we'll *make* them take you back in there!"

About seven of them Negroes at the shop got they pistols, (ain't nobody knowed this, I ain't never told nobody), they got they pistols and we went down there and walked up there in that hall to that Birmingham Industrial Council that Saturday night, it was after Thanksgiving.

I walked up there, all of us was standing around, the guys stand-ing around talking. The meeting hadn't started. We's not on the ground, we was upstairs. You go upstairs, you in a big lobby. You walk around, you go in the door here, to go in the regular meeting hall, but out here, we's in the lobby part. We were all out here with everybody else in the lobby.

When they got ready to announce about the meeting to begin,

all the other people walked up to a guy on the door. That old guy, I think his name was Elliott, a great big old guy from Steel—they say he was a big leader of the Klan, he's the guy that stamped out that Mine Mill guy's eyes out down there in Bessemer in '48 when Steel was raiding Mine Mill—he was on the door. That's something they hadn't never done before. They had some white plain cards with numbers on them, might of been names on them. They made these cards that everybody come up, they hand him they card. All the other people going in the meeting had these white cards. They ain't give me no card because I ain't supposed to go in. So me and these seven guys from the shop, we just stand around. They told me, said, "Hudson," said, "if you want in, by God, we'll see you going in or we'll shoot this damn place up." They was going shoot up the place.

I told them, I said, "Jake, they got the cards made out, passing people in. Ain't no use of all us getting in trouble here." I said, "I know you all with me, and I appreciate what you doing," said, "but I don't want to cause you all to get into a world of trouble for nothing." I said, "Let's give it in and let's go."

He told the other guys, "Come on, let's go." We all walked out and left. All the whites and everybody looking at me, nobody didn't say nothing. So I went out. I ain't been in that union hall since we walked out of there that night. It ain't there now, cause they done tore the building down.

AFTER they vote me out the council, I wouldn't stop at that. I went and drawed me up a statement to give to the paper, stating my side of it, cause the people hadn't heard. I couldn't get my side to the public. I went to the Birmingham *World,* to the Negro paper, went to Emory O. Jackson, who had been in the past my right-hand friend. The year before, he had recommended me for Man of the Year in his paper on the basis of my talk on voting in the CIO convention. He wrote also that I was the onliest black trade unionist at that convention that spoke out for the rights of the Negro people. He put me up on top.

I give my statement to Jackson, around at his paper. I had got it typed up nice. That's where he said, "Brother Hudson," said, "these niggers don't want to be nothing but second-class citizens, and that's what I'm going work for." Said, "I've lost money fooling with these niggers. I'm fifteen years behind. From here on in, I'm going try and make me some money."

I said, "You turn your back on the masses, eh?"

He said, "Yeah, I'm going to make me some money."

I said, "Well, I'm going to stick to the masses."

He said, "I glory in your spunk. I don't want to get into none of this controversy now." So he wouldn't run the statement.

I buttonholed about seven Negroes from different locals, called them, got them to meet me downtown Birmingham one Saturday morning after Thanksgiving. I had one or two from the wire mill local over there in Fairfield and had two or three guys from my local. I made it from more than one local, where we could say we wouldn't have all these guys from just my local. I got them down and they met me at the Masonic Temple. I told them what I wanted to do. I said, "The Birmingham *Post* done run a statement against me and caused me to be put out of the council." I said, "I wants to go down there with a group and demand they print my statement."

They said, "We with you one hundred percent."

We all walked down to the Birmingham *Post,* walked in the office, and I spoke. I pointed out what the *Post* had done for me up there in my union, they had caused me to lose my seat: "Now here's my statement. We demand that you either print my statement or we're going to organize a boycott against your paper throughout this city." Oh, I was tough! You ought to seen them guys scattering!

I gave them the statement. They said I was supposed to see the one who wrote the article about me. I said, "I don't care who I'm supposed to see. You paper carried this article what caused me to lose my seat. Here's my statement, which has been endorsed by the local membership." Then we all walked out.

Then we went to the Birmingham *News.* We didn't want to be as sharp as we was at the *Post,* but we left a copy at the Birmingham *News.* Both the *News* and the *Post,* they didn't print all of it, but they printed a whole lot of what I had to say.[6]

On December the 5th, '47, that's when it was, I went out to get my pay, and they had two checks made out, hand me two checks. I took my checks and walked out in the yard. Then the personnel manager called me in and showed me a big envelope, a big letter. He said, "Your union men, your people, don't want to work in the plant with you." It was a letter, said, "We done signed, we refuse to work in the plant any longer with Hosie Hudson." With that letter was 200 names, about 150 Negroes and 55 whites.

What happen, the whites in the local didn't want to set in a meeting with me as president. Because I wouldn't turn it over to them, they all come to the district office. It was the racists in the Steelworkers district office was the ones working against me. They put the white workers up to doing it. They did it because they didn't have no better sense than to do what their leaders told them, "Get that Hosie Hudson out of there, that God damn communist! He's nothing but a damn communist!" They didn't know no better. In the district office they showed them how to go out there and get them some blank pieces of paper, get all the Negroes they could to sign, claim they sign up for seniority, "Six months or longer, put your name, badge number, and sign here." A hundred and fifty Negroes signed a blank piece of paper, with *nothing*. Ain't asked me nothing, and they know I'm president.

Then when the whites got all the names, they wrote a letter refusing to work in the plant along with me. If I was remaining in the company, they wanted they time in full, Friday. Friday was December the 5th, 1947.

When I went out from the personnel office, out in the yard, here all the Negroes. I said, "Well, boys, this is it."

They said, "What is that, Big Red?"

I said, "You all done signed me out the shop."

"What that be? Would that be what we signed that paper on there?"

All the whites standing around there, listening. They had two lines, line of Negroes, line of whites. They stand there looking. And the Negroes commenced to cussing, "God damn it," said, "we going to shut this damn place down Monday morning. You let us have it now." The whites all standing there, long line.

I said, "You all know I was chairman of the grievance committee, and you know I'm president of the local," and I said, "How come you didn't come ask me something about it?" I said, "I been working here with you six years, and here some whites come along and you listen at them before you listen at me." I said, "You're the ones that signed me out of the shop."

They said, "We're going strike this damn thing!"

I said, "No, don't strike." I told them not to strike. They had a contract with a no-strike clause in the contract against wildcat strikes. That would have been a wildcat strike. That was the biggest mistake I ever made in my life. If I had let them strike, they would have torn the whole doggone thing up, that shop. The company wouldn't have fired everybody, there was too many to fire. They would have been more careful about how they handled my grievance than they was, if them guys had closed the plant down. They would be trying to get the guys back to work and the guys wouldn't of went back to work till "Big Red come home." If they had struck, that would have had more effect than I did by going through this grievance procedure laid down in the contract. As it was, I give them all the chance in the world to get me out of the union.

We had grievance procedures drawn up in the contract. First step, second step, third step, fourth step. One grievance procedure, you take it up with your assistant superintendent and your foreman, or the superintendent and the foreman, in the shop itself. Then if you didn't get recognition there, then I'd call a special conference with management, which meant the other superintendent and maybe a vice-president would meet with me and the committee there, that would be the second step. If we can't get agreement in that meeting, then, the next step would be I'd call the representative from the district office of the union with me. That's the third step. The fourth step is the so-called impartial umpire. That would be a federal judge, a representative of the company, a representative of the union. But it was very easy for the federal judge to side with the company. That's what they did in my case.

It was in January, and they stalled around until the middle of March. Old Judge W. P. McCoy, from down Tuscaloosa Alabama, he was teaching law school in that college where they wouldn't allow Miss Lucy in the door.* He was the guy that was chosen as federal judge to set as a umpire on my case.[7]

He come up, issued a statement that the company was justified in firing me out the shop for what happen, after all these Negroes and whites signed that petition saying they wouldn't work in the shop with me.

I fought on the grounds that it was nothing in the union contract would give them permission to fire me on the basis of that petition,

* [After white students rioted to protest her admittance, Autherine Lucy was expelled from the University of Alabama in 1956. Arthur Shores was her lawyer.]

cause the evidence itself was violating the grievance procedure, as laid down in the contract. That's the way I fought it.

The day I resigned as president of the local, they used Eb Cox to come out there when they give the ruling of the impartial umpire against me having the job. Automatically then, that canceled my rights to be president of the local. That was in '48, along in about March. Eb Cox was there that day, him and old man Houston. Dan Houston was one of the staff guys, white guy. He was there to take over the local. Old man Houston was always kind of a friend. I took him to be a guy would tip me off, would tell me things was coming up that the others didn't tell me. He was always, "Hudson, I'll tell you this, but keep it under your hat," whatever was being said around the district office. He was white, kind of quiet little man.

They took over the local. I was no more president. But I went back to the local meeting one Saturday, and Eb Cox was there. They had a little old Negro, name was Gaddy, he was a Party member out there in Woodlawn. When I resigned, I recommended him as candidate for president. They elected him. When I went back there that day there was something I started to talk about.

He rapped his gavel, this little Gaddy, "Pup, pup, Bro' Hudson, you out of order!" I finished making my point. I didn't pay him no attention, and then I set down.

After I set down, Eb Cox come around to him to be recognized to have something to say. He got up to say, "I want to tell you all, Bro' Hudson don't have a bit more to do with this local now than I do. All he can be is just a member. He don't have no voice in this local as a president."

He didn't have to say that.

LATER in the year, the contract come up for signing. When I was president, every contract, I'd get them a raise. First I got a 10¢ raise. Next I got a 13¢ raise, next a 18½¢ raise, next I got a 13½¢ raise. After I'm out, they want a 15¢ raise. Harry Ramsey had done got to be president of the local. Old man Jackson said he couldn't give them but 7½¢, and the union officials in the district office told Harry Ramsey to speak to the old big man's son Dick. They told Harry to "kind of drop the word with Dick that if he'd kind of play ball, kind of put out a little something, we'll get the guys to accept this 7½¢ raise." They said Harry should say to Dick, "It take about $1800. We got to have enough where we kind of divide it around."* Eighteen hundred dollars, going sell out the guys, make them accept this 7½¢ contract.

Harry told the old man's son in the plant. Dick called his dad, he was way down on the Mobile Bay, down in his summer home, so they say. Old man J. O. Jackson came up there by plane. When he got there, he got up on the stand, and he called him a meeting, old man J. O. Jackson. That's where he showed all the union officials up.

Old man Jackson got up and called everybody in the plant to a meeting at noon, white and black. He got up on the platform. He said, "I come here to call you all together because my son Richard" —his name was Richard, they call him Dick—"Richard called me all the way from down at my home in Mobile, said I should come up here, he had some urgent business for me. Now I get up here to tell you what your union leaders is trying to do for you." Harry was standing in the crowd with the rest of his committee.

Old man Jackson said, "I am not able to give you all but 7½¢ raise, and your union officials told my son Richard if I would give them $1800, they would get you all to accept the 7½¢. I come here today because I'm not going to let your union leaders sell you out." He said, "That's what I say about Hosie Hudson. You all put him out of here," said, "but if it had been left to me, Hosie been in this plant now. But you all, you all signed a petition that you didn't want to work with him, and I had to put him out. But one thing about Hosie Hudson. He would not sell you out." Said, "He was a stomp-down leader. He would not sell you out."

They tell me that them white folks, white devils, got so mad, they went out the shop cussing, some of them. They got a committee, went down to the old man Farr's office† and told him they didn't want none of them to come out to that plant no more, to keep all his staff men away from out there, from coming out to the local. They tell me one man said, "Your men had us to sign Hosie Hudson out of that plant."

That Harry, the last I seen him, he was on Utica Avenue down in Brooklyn New York, dragging one half his side. Had had a stroke. And Jackson foundry, finally they had a wildcat strike, closed the place down. Old man Jackson closed down and locked

* That's what I was told. I didn't hear it.
† [United Steelworkers of America, Birmingham District Office.]

out. I was told he was making something for the Chrysler Motor Company, and Chrysler came down there and got all the machines, brought them back somewhere. The last time I seen that building, it was sitting down there, a old hull. All them guys put out in the street. That's how far it went. When I get to talking about it, it makes me mad.

AFTER the whole thing was over, the Birmingham *News* came out and somebody wrote a letter and said that after all they done to Hosie Hudson, they still hadn't prove nothing on him. He was still on the winning side.[8]

That was something, wont it? Them the kind of fights I put up. It was the Communist Party that learnt me that.

NOTES
BIBLIOGRAPHICAL ESSAY
ACKNOWLEDGMENTS
INDEX

Notes

Introduction

1. Autobiographical manuscript in Hosea Hudson's possession. This manuscript formed part of the basis for Hudson's *Black Worker in the Deep South* (New York, 1972), Henceforth cited as Hudson ms, 1965.

2. Hudson ms, 1965, and Hudson-Painter tapes. The tapes are available to scholars at the Southern Historical Collection of the University of North Carolina at Chapel Hill. Unless otherwise indicated, all further unpublished Hudson quotations are from these tapes.

3. This listing of the family's moves from plantation to plantation, within a circle about 30 miles in diameter, is based on Hudson's memory. He has related the sequence to me more than once, and is consistent. I repeat it for what it shows both about Hudson and about the vicissitudes of black southern life at the time.

Wilkes and Oglethorpe counties are located in northeastern Georgia, close to the Savannah River dividing Georgia and South Carolina, and roughly stretching between Athens and Augusta. Birmingham, Alabama, is almost a straight line to the west from Wilkes County, passing through Atlanta, a distance of some 105 miles.

4. Hudson ms, 1965.

5. James D. Vaughn Music Publishers (Lawrenceburg, Tennessee, 1946). Vaughn published shape-note songbooks between 1923 and 1946, at 35¢ a copy.

6. I have named the notes here according to Hudson's 1946 songbook. Hudson says he begins with fa at middle C.

Today shape-note songbooks are written by both black and white composers for a market that is also black and white. The publishing houses are located in the South, several in Tennessee, and each house brings out at least one new shape-note songbook a year. In the best days of shape-note singing, between the end of the nineteenth century and the First World War, shape-note songbooks poured out of the publishers to a public that held singing contests, or "conventions" four times a year. Information from Joel Brett Sutton, "The Gospel Hymn, Shaped Notes, and the Black Tradition: Continuity and Change in American Traditional Music" (M.A. thesis, University of North Carolina, 1976). I am grateful to Sutton's adviser, Daniel W. Patterson, for bringing this thesis to my attention and for sharing with me his insights into southern Baptist life.

7. In March 1978, shortly before his death, Al Murphy wrote me a long autobiographical letter. This material comes from pp. 7–9.

The meeting Murphy attended was held on 21 July 1930, at 2131 24th Court, North. Joe Carr was the organizer who addressed the meeting. On 25 July, a follow-up meeting was held at the same address for those who had joined on the 21st. Technically these were meetings of the Trade Union Unity League, which was closely related to the CP. *Investigation of Communist Propaganda. Hearings Before a Special Committee to Investigate Communist Activities in the United States of the House of Representatives,* 71st Congress, 2nd session, pt. 6, vol. 1, 96; henceforth cited as *Investigation of Communist Propaganda.* This committee spent one day each in Chattanooga, Birmingham, Atlanta, New Orleans, and Memphis, and in several northern and western cities. The committee sat in Birmingham on 14 November 1930. Only in Atlanta and New Orleans in the South did Negroes give testimony.

8. Murphy letter, March 1978, pp. 10–11.

9. Ibid., p. 8.

10. The only participant's account of the adoption of the self-determination position at the Sixth Comintern Congress in 1928 is Harry Haywood's. According to Haywood, Lenin had written of Afro-Americans as an "oppressed nation" as early as 1917, but the process that actually led to the policy adopted in 1928 began with a visit to the United States by Haywood's friend Nasanov—evidently his whole name—in 1927. On his return to Moscow, where Haywood was a student, Nasanov spoke of Negroes as a nation with a need for self-determination. Haywood found the idea "far-fetched."

Early in 1928 a special subcommittee of the Anglo-American Secretariat of the Comintern was formed to prepare a report on blacks in the United States and South Africa. The six members were Nasanov, four American Negro students in Moscow, and one white American student in Moscow, plus two white American ex-officio members. After several long discussions, Haywood saw the correctness of Nasanov's position. But the rest of the subcommittee was not convinced. Otto Hall, Haywood's brother and also a member of the subcommittee, was implacably opposed to the "oppressed nation" and "self-determination" formula. The subcommittee reached no agreement, and the Negro question was debated in committee and on the floor at the Sixth Comintern Congress in the summer of 1928.

Haywood was the only black supporting the self-determination policy in the sixth congress as a whole and in the Negro Commission (a subcommittee of the Colonial Commission). "The strongest opposition to the self-determination thesis . . . was from the Black comrades James Ford and Otto Hall," Haywood says. Nonetheless, the position was ultimately adopted. Haywood says that it marked "a revolutionary turning point in the treatment of the Afro-American question." Harry Haywood [Haywood Hall], *Black*

Bolshevik, The Autobiography of an Afro-American Communist (Chicago, 1978), pp. 218–280.

11. James S. Allen [Sol Auerbach], *The Negro Question in the United States* (New York, 1936), pp. 178–193. Allen taught briefly at the University of Pennsylvania before going South to edit the Chattanooga weekly *Southern Worker* in 1930. Although two other whites, Robert Minor and Robert Dunne, carried more weight in Party deliberations on the Negro question, Allen published widely on the subject. His two pamphlets, *The American Negro* (New York, 1932) and *Negro Liberation* (New York, 1932), and his book, *The Negro Question in the United States* (New York, 1936), set forth the CP position on the national question and self-determination for the Black Belt.

12. Robert Alperin, "Organization of the CPUSA, 1931–1938," dissertation, Northwestern University, 1959, p. 60, cited in Harvey Klehr, *Communist Cadre: The Social Background of the American Communist Party Elite* (Stanford, California, 1978), pp. 80–81; Horace R. Cayton and George S. Mitchell, *Black Workers and the New Unions* (Chapel Hill, North Carolina, 1939), p. 338; Nathan Glazer, *The Social Basis of American Communism* (New York, 1961), p. 174.

13. The NAACP's branches have been virtually all-black since the 1920s. During the association's early period, in the 1910s, the officers were all white, with the exception of W.E.B. DuBois. The tradition of white presidents continues. That means that in the 1930s, the NAACP was interracial only on the highest levels. Members of local branches knew it as a Negro organization.

14. In his 29 June 1977 interview with me in New York City, Aptheker noted that a black and a white walking together in the streets of New York in the 1940s were assumed to be communists. No one else met across the color line. In *A Fine Old Conflict* (New York, 1977), Mitford wrote that FBI agents, "seeking evidence of Communist affiliation, would routinely ask a suspect's neighbors and co-workers, 'Do Negroes visit their home for meetings or social gatherings?' " (p. 134). Genovese says that FBI agents asked the same of his acquaintances in the 1950s.

15. Even the FBI took cognizance of Hudson's growth in its way, noting the contrast between Hudson as he looked in 1934, when he was photographed in a Philadelphia jail, and his appearance in 1947. The informant found Hudson "a more polished and wideawake negro now." U.S. Department of Justice, FBI, Bureau File #100-24584, Dallas office to Director, 25 March 1947.

16. Letter from Hudson to me, Atlantic City, 26 January 1978.

17. Hudson had broken his leg in a motorcycle accident on his way to work. The Bible citation is actually from Ephesians 6:5–6.

18. Harvey Klehr writes that black leaders in the CP "were far less likely to leave the CPUSA by either resignation or expulsion than whites . . . blacks were relatively unaffected by the major organizational schisms of the CPUSA . . . Several blacks did leave the CPUSA at various times as a result of specifically racial issues. All—two were prominent figures, Angelo

Herndon and Harry Haywood—were accused by the CPUSA of being black nationalists or ultra-leftists . . . there were far fewer opportunities of any kind for blacks in American society and this deterrent may have convinced some that their future outside the CPUSA was even dimmer than inside." Klehr, *Communist Cadre* (1978), pp. 91–92.

The only Negro ex-communist Vivian Gornick interviewed, whom she called "Hugh Armstrong" in her book, says he left the Party after Khrushchev's report on Stalin in 1956, which seemed to negate years of being patronized by white communists: "All those years I always felt I wasn't being listened to as seriously as a white [section organizer] . . . it was never anything I could actually put my finger on, just a feeling that never left me." Vivian Gornick, *The Romance of American Communism* (New York, 1977), pp. 164–165.

19. A long-time Negro communist and leader of the Southern Negro Youth Congress, Edward Strong died of leukemia in 1956. He was a member of the national committee of the CPUSA.

20. An example of this interpretation is James Weinstein's *Ambiguous Legacy: The Left in American Politics* (New York, 1975), which dismisses the "third period" for its policy of lumping liberals with fascists under the rubric "social fascists." Weinstein overlooks entirely the third period's push into the South and its attracting large numbers of black members for the first time. "The results of the Third Period," he says, "were horrendous" (p. 43).

21. Hudson is much opposed to my mention of Haywood in his book, and he asked me to insert this statement of opposition to Haywood and his present politics: "I wants to make it clear to readers and friends that I take responsibility only for what I have to say on the Negro question. In particular, I differ with Harry Haywood and other Negro ex-Communist Party members, and their writings on the Negro question and position as I interpret it. [Nell Painter's] comments and interpretations on the question in reference to Harry Haywood and some of these other Negro ex-Communist Party member writers positions are solely [hers], in [her] rights as [she] and I agreed to. I hope that I have made my position very clear and understood by all concerned." Letter from Hudson to me, Atlantic City, 21 September 1978.

22. This book was originally intended to cover Hudson's life up to 1954. But the narrative as edited does not even get to the 1948 campaign; that material will appear in a forthcoming anthology edited by Charles Martin, *Blacks and the Communist Party*.

23. Letter from Hudson to me, Atlantic City, 26 January 1978.

1. From the Country to the City

1. A sharecropper family working on halves received half of the cotton they produced. The landlord received the other half. If the family worked on thirds, they received one third of what they produced. The formula depended on several variables, including who furnished the animals, seed, tools, and so forth.

Three hundred dollars was a great deal to pay for a mule, but this price reflects wartime inflation. Three years later prices dropped drastically. Hudson says that in 1922 "mules had done fall out where they wont worth $50. That $300 mule wont worth $50 then. Wont no price hardly. You couldn't sell a mule."

2. Cotton this tall was unusual but possible in the days before hybrid strains became popular. The cotton grown now is lower, less woody, and produces fuller bolls.

3. Jefferson County, in which Birmingham is located, has been the basic industrial center of the South since the early twentieth century. Iron ore and coal are both mined in and near the city. As the northern iron and steel producing centers of Ohio and Pennsylvania grew after the First World War, Birmingham lost relative standing in the industry. However, it has continued to produce high-quality iron pipe.

4. Stockham Pipe and Fittings (changed in 1948 to Stockham Valves and Fittings) is located at North 39th Street and 10th Avenue North, near the Birmingham municipal airport. It was founded in 1903 by William H. Stockham (1861–1932), who had attended the University of Illinois and worked as an iron molder (Hudson's trade) before migrating to Birmingham. The foundry is still in Stockham family hands, having had four Stockhams as presidents. (Paul Eldfeldt kindly answered my questions about Stockham and arranged for me to tour the plant in 1978).

5. Negroes whose skin color is reddish-brown, like Hudson or Malcolm X, are often nicknamed "Red," usually with a qualifying adjective. Hudson is six feet tall and then weighed nearly two hundred pounds—hence his nickname "Big Red." In Boston and New York, Malcolm X was known as "Detroit Red."

2. Joining the Communist Party

1. Theophilus Eugene (Bull) Connor (1898–1973) was prominent in Birmingham for five decades. He got his nickname from his deep, sonorous voice. As a youngster he relayed reports of baseball games from the playing fields to the Birmingham poolhalls by megaphone. Later he became well known as a radio sportscaster. Connor served in the Alabama state legislature in the 1920s and as police commissioner in Birmingham from 1936 to 1952. A member of the Democratic national committee, he led the walkout of about half the Alabama delegation from the 1948 convention at which Harry Truman accepted the civil rights plank of the platform. Connor was one of the organizers of the Dixiecrat convention held in Birmingham later in the summer and ran (unsuccessfully) for governor of Alabama on the Dixiecrat ticket. He was convicted but later exonerated of sharing a hotel room with his secretary, then was elected police commissioner again in 1956. He was forced out in 1963, after using police dogs and fire hoses to break up civil rights demonstrations in the early 1960s. His most famous statement is "White and Negro are not to segregate together."

2. The tariff was a lively issue in the 1928 presidential election. After

the Republican victory, Representative Willis Hawley and Senator Reed Smoot pushed for high-tariff legislation. The debate resulted in the Hawley-Smoot tariff, signed into law by President Hoover in June 1930. The Hawley-Smoot tariff raised duties to protective levels and set the tone for this country's economic nationalism during the 1930s.

3. The Bedeaux system is named after Charles Bedeaux (1887–1944), an American industrial engineer. The system measures industrial work and pays wages according to a point system.

4. According to the Birmingham police, communists first became active in the city in October 1929. During the summer of 1930, the CP and its closely allied organizations, the Trade Union Unity League and the unemployed councils, held mass meetings in Capitol Park. At the first meeting on 29 May, 700–800 people turned out. The vast majority of the attendance was black at all CP functions. On 21 June, 450 people attended a protest meeting in the park, and on 28 June, 350 people attended another meeting. The audiences included between 100 and 200 "curiosity seekers," as the police chief called them: Ku Klux Klansmen, city detectives, and members of the American Federation of Labor. *Investigation of Communist Propaganda*, pp. 91–93. The committee spent 14 November 1930 taking testimony in Birmingham. No Negroes testified in that city.

5. In the midst of this communist activity, the city commission passed on 17 June 1930 a strict ordinance to curb communism, which was termed "criminal anarchy." The ordinance made it a misdemeanor, punishable by fines up to $100 and imprisonment up to 180 days, for individuals to advocate criminal anarchy by word of mouth and in print or to distribute such literature; to organize or become members of such groups; to assemble in groups of more than two; to permit premises to be so used. This ordinance made the CP a criminal organization and drove it underground in Birmingham.

City commissioner James Jones attended the 28 June meeting in Capitol Park. He stopped in the middle of his speech a Negro organizer named Gilbert Lewis, because he was going to cause trouble. Several communists were arrested then, and the meeting of 8 July was called off.

6. In March 1931 nine unrelated young black men ranging in age from thirteen to twenty were taken off a freight train near Scottsboro, Alabama, and charged with raping two white women who were also riding the train. In a lynch atmosphere, the men were tried in one day and sentenced to death. The case immediately became a *cause célèbre*. During the 1930s the defendants received support from a broad spectrum of progressives and blacks. Even one of the alleged victims, Ruby Bates, recanted in 1933 and joined the defense movement. Although the men were imprisoned, none was executed, a victory under the circumstances. Only one defendant, Clarence Norris, is still alive. He had violated his parole by leaving Alabama in 1946 to settle permanently in New York City. In 1976 the state of New York refused to extradite Norris, then a sixty-four-year-old warehouseman. The eight other "Scottsboro boys" were Haywood Patterson, Leroy Wright, Ozie Powell, Olen Montgomery, Andrew Wright, Willie Robertson, Charlie Weems, and

Eugene Williams. Angelo Herndon wrote a pamphlet after the 1937 compromise that freed four and gave five of the "boys"—including Norris—long sentences, *Scottsboro Boys, Four Freed, Five to Go* (New York, 1937). Haywood Patterson wrote an autobiography with Earl Conrad, *Scottsboro Boy* (Garden City, 1950). The best scholarly treatment of the case is Dan T. Carter's *Scottsboro: A Tragedy of the American South* (Baton Rouge, 1969).

At Camp Hill, in Tallapoosa County, Alabama, members of the Share Croppers Union met in a church to plan activities in support of the Scottsboro boys and were attacked by county officials. One Negro SCU member, Ralph Gray, was killed, and three others wounded. Two white officials were wounded. As at Reeltown the following year, only SCU members were arrested and convicted.

7. Dr. Henry M. Edmunds was pastor of the Independent Presbyterian Church in Birmingham and chairman of the Alabama Interracial Commission. In 1933 he was one of a group of Birmingham citizens who unsuccessfully urged a change of venue, from Decatur to Birmingham, for one of the series of Scottsboro trials.

8. The Stockham management realized that this little restaurant about a block and a half from the shop was where communists made contact with black workers in 1930. Testimony of Lester N. Shannon, vice-president of Stockham Pipes and Fittings, in *Investigation of Communist Propaganda* (1930), p. 181.

9. Angelo Herndon, a nineteen-year-old miner, met communist organizers in 1930 and quickly joined the Party. He went to Atlanta from Birmingham to organize the unemployed, leading an integrated march of unemployed workers in June 1932 that led to his arrest and conviction in 1933 for inciting insurrection. The International Labor Defense represented Herndon through a long appeal process that made headlines in the mid-1930s. Herndon's case went to the U.S. Supreme Court twice. The final ruling invalidated the Georgia Insurrection Statute and freed Herndon and six communists who had been arrested in 1930 on the same charge. Between appeals, Herndon wrote an autobiography, *Let Me Live* (New York, 1937). Charles H. Martin has written an excellent full-length study, *The Angelo Herndon Case and Southern Justice* (Baton Rouge, 1976). Herndon is still alive but is no longer active publicly.

10. Murphy said that he knew who the stoolpigeons were, such as John Mitchell, whom he termed the "top stooge for Stockham Co." and had a Tuskegee education. Murphy did not try to put Hudson off: "I promised to notify him of our next meeting. I did just that." Murphy letter, March 1978, pp. 10–11.

11. Fred Walker was one of the communists arrested at the protest meeting in Capitol Park on 28 June 1930.

12. Harry Simms died of a wound inflicted by a mine guard in February 1932, during the bloody coal strike in Harlan County, Kentucky. His body lay in state in New York City, first at the Workers' Center, then in the Coliseum. Theodore Dreiser and Waldo Frank showed the terrorism in Harlan County mining fields in their *Harlan Miners Speak* (1932).

3. Sticking to the Party

1. In the midst of the civil rights movement, a bomb exploded on Sunday, 15 September 1963 at 10:25 a.m., while children attended Sunday school. Four girls were killed: Cynthia Wesley, 14; Denise McNair, 11; Carol Robertson, 14; and Addie Mae Collins, 14. Until February 1976, it seemed that this would remain one of some fifty unsolved bombings of Negro property that had occurred in Birmingham between the war and 1963. However, Attorney General William J. Baxley reopened the case and prosecuted Klansman Robert E. Chambliss, who was convicted of first-degree murder in 1977.

2. This is the text of a leaflet distributed by the Trade Union Unity League and the unemployed council, after the city ordinance outlawed the Party in Birmingham:

MASS DEMONSTRATION AGAINST UNEMPLOYMENT AT CAPITOL PARK, TWENTIETH STREET AND SEVENTH AVENUE, MONDAY, SEPTEMBER 1 [1930]

Workers of Birmingham:
The conditions of the workers grow steadily worse. Each day sees more men out, cut off in the shops and mines of Birmingham. White and colored workers are being evicted from their homes and thrown out on the streets to shift for themselves. Gas and water is being cut off because the unemployed workers can not pay their bills. The workers who have jobs are given wage cuts and forced to work faster and faster. Not a working class home in Birmingham is free from the menace of unemployment. Thousands of workers and their families will face starvation in the black winter ahead.

CHAIN GANG FOR THE UNEMPLOYED

The Government and the bosses for whom we made millions of dollars when we were working are doing nothing to help the unemployed. The reports of the Government even state that there is no unemployment worth speaking about. But every worker knows that this is a bare-faced lie designed to cover up the failure of the Government to provide work or wages for the unemployed.

When the unemployed workers of Birmingham organized in unemployed councils in order to fight for their demands for unemployment insurance and immediate relief their meetings were broken up by these lick-spittle tools of the bosses, the police. Their organizers were thrown in jail and sentenced to long terms on the chain gang. But these brutal attacks of the police, the gunmen of the Tennessee Coal and Iron Co. and of the Fascist Ku-Klux Klan will never stop the workers, driven on by misery and oppression, from organizing and fighting for their rights.

FELLOW WORKERS, FIGHT—DON'T STARVE

White and negro workers of Birmingham, organize and fight back against unemployment. Demand work or wages for the unemployed. Demand the immediate enactment of the bill for social insurance proposed by the Communist Party to provide every unemployed worker with a minimum of $25 per week unemployment insurance. Unemployed workers and those still at work, attend the mass demonstration of the unemployed in Capitol Park on Labor Day, Monday, September 1. Force Congress to pass the workers' social insurance bill. Demand "work or wages."

TRADE UNION UNITY LEAGUE,
BIRMINGHAM UNEMPLOYED COUNCIL,
2117½ Second Avenue North.

The TUUL "Program for the Intensification of the Revolutionary Struggle," also from 1930, includes demands that figured in all CP material, but in this statement they are presented in detail:

Program for the Intensification of the Revolutionary Struggle Against Unemployment and the Building of the Revolutionary Unions of the Trade Union Unity League.

Demands:
1. *Work or Wages.*—The Government shall guarantee every worker, regardless of race, sex, age, or creed, a job at the usual rate of pay, or if unemployed, insurance compensation equal to full wages. All workers partially employed shall receive compensation sufficient to bring their income up to the amount of full wages. This unemployed insurance shall be administered by committees elected directly by workers, working in the shops, and the unemployed through their councils.
2. *Emergency unemployment relief.*—Until the unemployment insurance is operative, the Government shall make an emergency appropriation for emergency relief equal to the insurance of full wages, to be administered as in point 1. The funds to come out of Government, city, State treasuries, and raised by a tax on all profits, inheritances, by reduction of salaries of high officials, removal of tax exemption enjoyed by churches, etc.
3. *No work no rent—Housing of unemployed.*—Public buildings shall be thrown open and accommodations made for the emergency housing of the unemployed. The sum of _____ shall be immediately appropriated as an initial sum for building workers dwellings, which shall be rented by the city to the workers, preference being given to the unemployed, without discrimination against or segregation of negroes. All evictions of unemployed for nonpayment of rent shall be prohibited.

4. *7-hour day, 5-day week.*—The 7-hour day, 5-day week shall be established for all workers, without reduction in wages. No overtime work shall be allowed. A general law for the 7-hour day, 5-day week shall be proposed to the State legislature.

5. *Free employment agencies.*—Free employment agencies shall be established under control of workers committees, and unemployed councils.

6. The 6-hour day, 5-day week, and two 15-minute rest periods for young workers.

7. No night work for women and young workers.

8. Free lunches in schools, and Government maintenance of children of unemployed.

9. Abolition of child labor.

10. Against the speed-up.

11. Equal pay for equal work for women and young workers.

12. For the right to organize, strike, and picket.

13. Against police terror against strikers organization activities and unemployed.

14. Down with lynching, Jim Crowism, and discrimination of negroes.

15. Against injunctions used against workers in any way, shape, or form.

16. For the immediate release of the unemployed delegation: Foster, Minor, Amter, Raymond, and all class-war prisoners.

17. For social insurance against sickness, accidents, invalidity, and old age.

These demands shall serve as a basis for concrete demands that must be worked out in accordance with the conditions peculiar to each city or locality.

These demands shall be closely linked up with the campaign to build the Trade Union Unity League and our struggles in various industries.

These documents with several others were inserted as an appendix in the record of the *Investigation of Communist Propaganda* (1930) by the Birmingham chief of police, Fred H. McDuff.

3. Although no law prohibited blacks and whites from meeting together, the city's traditions and segregation ordinances made it unlikely that they would meet as equals. The 1930 General Code of the city of Birmingham prohibited whites and Negroes from traveling together on common carriers, from gambling together, and from eating in restaurants in the same room unless a solid partition at least seven feet high separated the races and each had a separate entrance from the street. These ordinances and the anti-communist ordinances adopted in the summer of 1930 created the racial climate Hudson describes.

4. George Padmore [Malcolm Nurse] (1903–1959) was a Trinidian pan-Africanist who spent several years in this country and in the Soviet

Union. Here he belonged to the African Blood Brotherhood, a black group that gave the CP its first Negro members. He also edited the *Negro Worker* during the 1930s. Over the years, Padmore grew more interested in Africa and pan-Africanism, influencing the first generation of post-colonial African leaders, particularly Kwame Nkrumah, first President of Ghana. *Pan-Africanism or Communism* (London, 1957) is Padmore's best-known book. James R. Hooker wrote his biography, *Black Revolutionary: George Padmore's Path from Communism to Pan-Africanism* (New York, 1967).

William L. Patterson (1891–) joined the CP in 1927, after taking part in vigils for Sacco and Vanzetti in Boston. He served as executive secretary of the International Labor Defense from 1931 until 1946, when it merged with other organizations to form the Civil Rights Congress. Until the CRC was dissolved in 1956, Patterson was its executive director. Patterson now plays an elder statesman role in the CP.

5. John W. Goodgame (1898–?) was a prominent black clergyman in Birmingham well into the 1950s. He had pastored a church in Lexington, Virginia, before moving to Birmingham in 1938.

6. The Interracial Commission was formed in Atlanta in 1919, as an attempt to dissipate the racial tensions of the First World War. Its guiding spirit was Will W. Alexander, a former Methodist minister. In the 1920s the Interracial Commission began its long concern with lynching and peonage. It enjoyed support from a broad spectrum of respectable southerners, black and white, partly because of its avoidance of the issue of racial segregation.

7. The *New York Times* reported this incident on 14 May 1932: "Fifty Negroes addressing each other as 'comrade' marched to the city hall . . . to demand food, but scattered as their self-styled leader was felled with a policeman's billy. No arrests were made."

4. A Party Leader in Birmingham

1. Otto Hall was the brother of Harry Haywood. Hall joined the CP in the 1920s and was in Moscow when the self-determination policy was adopted. He was strongly opposed to the "oppressed nation" formula in 1928. Nonetheless, he was elected to the central committee of the Comintern at the Sixth Convention in 1928.

2. The International Union of Mine, Mill and Smelter Workers was a left-leaning union that grew out of the Western Federation of Miners in 1916. It was one of the original CIO unions and had always had an egalitarian approach to Negro workers. During the Cold War years the union was said to be communist-dominated and was expelled from the CIO in 1950. Even before the expulsion, the United Steel Workers had been raiding Mine Mill locals for members. In 1967, the USWA and Mine Mill merged. Horace Huntley of the University of Alabama, Birmingham, is preparing a full-length treatment of the Mine Mill union.

5. First Demonstrations, 1932–33

1. According to the Federal Bureau of Investigation, the Reverend J. H. Patterson's church was located at 13th Avenue in east Birmingham. File number 100-743, Hosea Hudson, Birmingham, Alabama. Report made for 17 and 27 June 1942, p. 2.

2. A 1930 resolution of District 17 (which then included Chattanooga, Birmingham, Atlanta, and New Orleans) suggests that "workers defense corps" be organized to counter attacks of the "state forces and of armed fascist bands and the gunmen of the American Federation of Labor on the party, the revolutionary unions and the working class of the South in general." The emphasis was to have been put on unarmed defense corps, who were to meet once every two weeks and drill in exercises aimed toward crowd control and use of sticks and stones as weapons. J. T. Watson's committee may well have been such a corps.

3. Al Murphy's grandfather was a minister in the African Methodist Episcopal Church and his mother was a self-made minister. She died when Murphy was five years old, but before her death Murphy said that she wanted him to become a preacher. "She would set up an empty orange crate on its end and teach me the Lord's prayer and recite the 23rd Psalm." He was close to his mother, who taught him to read and told him about her experiences in slavery and Reconstruction. Murphy letter, March 1978, pp. 1–2.

6. Reeltown

1. Hudson retells the story of the Reeltown shoot-out between members of the Share Croppers Union and sheriff's deputies as he heard it in 1932, and there are significant differences between his version and that of Ned Cobb, an actual participant. Cobb describes the events of December 1932 in detail in Theodore Rosengarten's groundbreaking oral autobiography of Cobb, *All God's Dangers* (New York, 1974), pp. 305–316. That book used pseudonyms for people and places. These names occur in both books:

Actual names	*All God's Dangers*
Tallapoosa County	Tukabahchee County
Reeltown	Pottstown
Camp Hill	Crane's Ford
Ned Cobb	Nate Shaw
Clifford James	Virgil Jones
Milo Bentley	Little Waldo Ramsey
Jug Moss	Boss Hatch

2. Mark Solomon writes that Clifford James was taken to the Tuskegee hospital, where Dr. Eugene A. Dibble questioned him. The sheriff located him there and took him to jail. He died in jail on 27 December 1932. Solomon cites "What Happened in Tallapoosa County," *Labor Defender*, IX (February 1933), p. 4, in his "Red and Black: Negroes and Communism"

(dissertation, Harvard University, 1972), pp. 538–539. An excellent work on the work of the Communist Party in rural Alabama is Dale Rosen's "The Alabama Share Croppers Union" (B.A. honors thesis, Radcliffe College, 1969, housed in the Schlesinger Library, Cambridge, Mass.).

8. Reverend Sears and the Reds

1. James Allen wrote several books and pamphlets on the Negro question and southern history. Joe North was a journalist, born in Pennsylvania, and in 1934 he helped found the weekly edition of *New Masses*. He was an editor of *New Masses* for fifteen years and since then has served as foreign editor for the *Daily World,* the successor of the *Daily Worker.* His autobiography is *No Men Are Strangers* (New York, 1958).

2. W. G. Binkley was southern district organizer for the ILD. Irving Schwab had established the Atlanta office of the ILD where Benjamin Davis, who defended Angelo Herndon, was branch attorney.

9. To New York and the Birmingham Jail

1. Benjamin J. Davis, Jr. (1903–1964), was educated at Amherst College and Harvard Law School. He defended Angelo Herndon and then left the South for good. He edited several CP-related periodicals, such as the *Daily Worker* and the *Liberator,* before running successfully for the New York city council, where he served nearly two terms between 1944 and 1949. A member of the national committee of the CPUSA, he was one of the original eleven Smith Act defendants tried in Foley Square in 1949. Davis' autobiography is *Communist Councilman from Harlem* (New York, 1969).

2. Communists led a bloody and unsuccessful strike in the Loray textile mill in Gastonia, North Carolina, in 1929. The combination of communists like Fred Beal, southern workers like Ella Mae Wiggins (who was killed), and the staunchly antiunion southern textile industry inspired songs, articles, and novels about the Gastonia strike. Fred Beal wrote an autobiography, *Proletarian Journey: New York, Gastonia, Moscow* (New York, 1937). The standard account of Gastonia and the strike is Liston Pope, *Millhands and Preachers* (New Haven, 1942).

3. The fourth of July 1933 was a cool, cloudy day that set a record low. According to the *New York Times,* at 5:30 a.m. it was 56.6 degrees.

4. Pokeberry (Pokeweed) has clusters of purplish-white flowers and reddish-purple berries. The roots and berry seeds are poisonous. Mullen is a tall plant of the figwort family with downy leaves and variously colored flowers. Hudson's "seven year itch" may well have been a case of hives (Urticaria) brought on by the stress and discomfort of the long motor trip.

5. William Mitch was vice-president of the Indiana district of the United Mine Workers when he was sent to Alabama in 1933. He served as president of District 20 (Alabama) of the UMA from 1933–1946 and was president of the Alabama State Federation of Labor from 1933 to 1937.

Philip Murray appointed Mitch director of the southern region of the Steel Workers Organizing Committee in 1936. After the AF of L and the CIO split in 1938, Mitch served as president of the Alabama State Industrial Union Council, CIO. He is credited with introducing the UMW formula for selecting officers in steel locals, where the president is white and the vice-president Negro. Alabama AF of L and employers considered him a sort of carpetbagger and denounced him as a communist.

10. National Training School

1. "Nitgedaiget" is Yiddish for "not to worry" or "carefree." The camp was run by the International Ladies Garment Workers Union, whose well-known anticommunist leader, David Dubinsky, had not yet come to power in 1934.

2. Jacob Mindel, then national educational director for the Party, had immigrated to this country from Russia in the first decade of the twentieth century. He was among the thirteen communist leaders convicted in the second round of Smith Act trials in 1953. His statement at that time is published in *Thirteen Communists Speak to the Court* (New York, 1953).

3. In the early 1930s the army of the Republic of China under Chiang Kai-shek attacked Mao Tse-tung's communists, succeeding in October 1934 in forcing the communists to retreat from Kiangsi to Shensi. At the same time, the Japanese occupied Manchuria and organized a puppet state in 1932. For American communists the situation was complicated, for although the Chinese Republic had opposed European colonial powers in the 1920s, it had purged all communists and other socialists from the Kuomintang in 1927. After the Long March, the communists called for a united Chinese front against the Japanese.

11. Back South

1. The Civil Works Administration was the New Deal's first experiment with work relief. Acting through state relief agencies, the CWA provided work and paid wages to the unemployed.

12. Atlanta

1. John H. Geer, the other Negro lawyer defending Angelo Herndon, was a native of South Carolina. Geer left Atlanta in 1935 and died at the age of forty-one in Louisville.

2. W.E.B. DuBois (1868–1963), the outstanding black intellectual of his time, earned his Ph.D from Harvard in 1895 and wrote or edited several important scholarly works, including *Philadelphia Negro* (1899), the *Atlanta University Studies* (1897–1911), *Souls of Black Folk* (1903), and *Black Reconstruction* (1935). DuBois was active politically from early in the twentieth century. In 1905 he founded the Niagara movement, and he edited

the NAACP journal *Crisis* between 1910 and 1932. He served as a professor of economics and history at Atlanta University from 1897 to 1910 and headed its department of sociology from 1932 to 1944. DuBois had shown an interest in Africa very early, taking a leading role in the pan-African conferences from the very first, in 1900. He and Kwame Nkrumah cochaired the fifth pan-African conference in 1945. At the age of ninety-three DuBois joined the Communist Party. In 1962 he settled in Ghana and died there a few months after becoming a Ghanaian citizen.

13. The Neighborhood Union and Lint Shaw

1. Robert M. Ratcliffe wrote a front-page article on the Lint Shaw lynching in the Atlanta *Daily World* (a Negro newspaper) and published three photographs of Shaw's home and family in Colbert, but none of the body. Ratcliffe's account agrees with Hudson's in all aspects, describing Mrs. Georgia Shaw as an extremely shy woman who was afraid to claim her husband's body. Convicts cut Shaw down after several days and buried him in the county graveyard. The Atlanta branch of the NAACP sent Governor Eugene Talmadge a telegram the day of the lynching, calling on him to stop the "growing disregard for law and order and the sanctity of human life in this state" (Atlanta *Daily World*, 29 April 1936).

14. CIO Organizing in Birmingham

1. John L. Lewis (1880–1969) was the international president of the United Mine Workers of America between 1920 and 1960. He was the leading figure in the establishment of the Committee for Industrial Organization within the American Federation of Labor. When the CIO outnumbered the other AF of L unions, it was expelled from the parent body and became the Congress of Industrial Organization in 1938. Lewis and the United Mine Workers sponsored the organizing of iron and steel workers through the Steel Workers Organizing Committee, formally under the AF of L affiliated union, the Amalgamated Association of Iron, Steel, and Tin Workers. The Amalgamated Association dissolved in 1942, and the SWOC became the United Steelworkers of America. Despite the official role of the Amalgamated Association, the mass of workers in the iron and steel industry were organized by officials of the UMW. Lewis split off the UMW from the CIO in 1940, when he backed Wendell Willkie and resigned the presidency of the CIO. The United Steelworkers remained in the CIO. The standard biographies of John L. Lewis are Saul Alinsky, *John L. Lewis, an Unauthorized Biography* (New York, 1949), and Melvin Dubofsky and Warren Van Tine, *John L. Lewis: A Biography* (New York, 1977).

Philip Murray (1886–1952) was born in Scotland and immigrated to this country in 1902. He was a vice-president of the UMW from 1916 and served on an advisory board of the National Recovery Administration in

1933. In 1936 he was appointed chairman of the SWOC, and was elected president of the CIO after Lewis' resignation in 1940.

2. Noel R. Beddow was executive director of UMW District 20 (Alabama), of which William Mitch was president. Beddow had been the general superintendent of a large steel company in Birmingham, then Labor Compliance Director of the NRA, later head of the NRA for the state of Alabama, before joining the SWOC in Birmingham. A longer discussion of Negroes and organized labor in Alabama may be found in Herbert Northrup, "Negro Labor and Union Policies in the South" (dissertation, Harvard University, 1942), and *Negro Employment in Basic Industry* (Philadelphia, 1970).

The UMW alone could not furnish enough organizers to reach the workers in mass production, but it is not clear whether Lewis and Murray approached Foster and asked for the CPUSA's help or Foster offered seasoned organizers to the CIO. It is true that communists made a great contribution to the organizing drives of the CIO unions. The issue of the CP in the CIO is discussed in William Z. Foster, *The History of the Communist Party of the United States of America* (New York, 1952; available now only in the Greenwood Press edition of 1968), Max M. Kampelman, *The Communist Party vs. the C.I.O.* (New York, 1971), and Bert Cochran, *Labor and Communism, the Conflict That Shaped American Unions* (Princeton, 1977).

3. The Southern Negro Youth Congress was allied with the National Negro Congress and had its headquarters in Birmingham between 1939 and 1948, when the organization collapsed. The SNYC was a very liberal organization, and like the Southern Conference for Human Welfare, with which it shared several prominent members, it was considered a tool of the Communist Party by critics. Hudson vehemently rejects this interpretation, because the organization's membership was mostly noncommunist. However, its leaders, Edward Strong, James Jackson, and Louis Burnham, were members of the CP.

4. Emory O. Jackson (1908–1975) was the editor of the Birmingham *World*, founder and first president of the Alabama Newspaper Association and of the Alabama State Conference of the NAACP. Before he gave full time to journalism and civic affairs, he was a teacher.

5. The term "popsicle" was given to the company union because the Tennessee Coal and Iron company furnished free popsicles at each meeting. Horace Huntley of the University of Alabama, Birmingham, kindly shared this information from his interviews with former members of the Mine, Mill and Smelter Workers Union.

15. The Right To Vote Club

1. Joseph Gelders (1898–1950) was a moving force behind the Southern Conference for Human Welfare. He was born in Birmingham and educated at the University of Alabama, where he taught physics between 1930 and 1935. Thanks to contacts with other southern liberals, Gelders met

Franklin Roosevelt in 1938 and had Eleanor Roosevelt's support in the SCHW. As a result of his defending political prisoners, in 1936 he was severely beaten and this hastened his death.

2. According to the long appendix on Alabama electoral law included in Ralph J. Bunche's manuscript, "The Political Status of the Negro" (1940), Hudson is correct. Hudson appears in an interview with Edward Strong. Although he related in 1940 the same story of his attempt to vote as he did to me in 1976, Hudson is said to have tried to register in 1936. This is a mistake on Strong's part, however, because Hudson was in Atlanta in 1936. Hudson's FBI file corroborates the 1938 date. A summary of the Strong interview is in Bunche's *The Political Status of the Negro in the Age of FDR* (Chicago, 1973), p. 260.

3. Arthur D. Shores (1904–   ) was a teacher at Dunbar High School during his early days as a lawyer. He was president of the Alabama Progressive Democratic Political Association for several years in the 1940s and 1950s. At present he is a member of the Birmingham City Council.

4. M.D.L. White was a tailor. He and Henry Harris split off from the Alabama State Federation of Colored Civil Leagues, founded in 1933, to form the Negro Democratic Council. According to Bunche in "The Political Status of the Negro," p. 1007, White and Harris had reached a "working understanding . . . with the white Democratic organization of Jefferson County." In *The Political Status of the Negro in the Age of FDR,* p. 85, Bunche writes at length of the "class feeling" among Negroes in the South: "it is not unusual for 'upper class' Negroes . . . to take the attitude that the great mass of blacks, being uneducated and illiterate, are not yet ready to exercise the franchise."

16. The NAACP and Community Work

1. Walter White was executive secretary, William Pickens a field secretary, of the NAACP. Pickens had been a professor of languages before joining the NAACP in 1920. Both White and Pickens outspokenly blamed the CP for sacrificing the Scottsboro boys to the needs of its political propaganda.

2. Arthur D. Shores was licensed to practice in 1937 and says that another black lawyer had been admitted to the bar in Birmingham forty years before he had. Since nothing in either the Alabama state codes or the state bar association prohibited a black lawyer's appearance in court, it would seem that Hudson is mistaken here.

17. WPA and the Workers Alliance

1. In May 1935 the U.S. Supreme Court declared the National Industrial Recovery Act unconstitutional in *Schechter Poultry Corporation v. U.S.* Following the presidential election of 1936, Roosevelt attempted to "pack" the Supreme Court. Although the attempt failed, he was able to appoint liberal justices to fill places vacated by death. In 1937 he appointed Hugo Black of Alabama to the Court.

2. One of the leading New Dealers, Harry Hopkins (1890–1946) accompanied Roosevelt from New York to Washington in 1933. He was Federal Administrator of Emergency Relief in 1933, Works Progress Administrator in 1935–1938, and Secretary of Commerce in 1938–1940.

3. Aubrey Williams (1890–1965) was a social worker from Alabama before joining the Roosevelt Administration. He served as field representative of the Federal Emergency Relief Administration in 1933 and Assistant Administrator of FERA and the Civil Works Administration in 1933–1935. He was Deputy Works Progress Administrator and National Youth Administrator in 1935–1939, and Published *Southern Farm and Home* from Montgomery between 1945 and 1962.

4. Luther Patrick (1891–1957) sat in the House of Representatives in 1937–1943 and 1945–1947. He was censured in Alabama for his part in convening the Southern Conference for Human Welfare.

Joe Starnes (1895–1962) was in Congress in 1935–1945 and was a member of the Special Committee for Investigating Un-American Activities in the 75th to 78th Congresses.

5. The *Report on Economic Conditions of the South* (1938) was sponsored by the National Emergency Council and prepared by a group of southerners who were active in the Southern Policy Committee. The *Report* summed up existing writing by southern scholars Howard Odum, Walter Prescott Webb, and Rupert Vance.

6. Liberal and influential southerners, black and white, sponsored and attended the first meeting of the Southern Conference for Human Welfare, which had grown from the planning of Joseph Gelders and Noel Beddow of the Steel Workers Organizing Committee and the Alabama Policy Committee. For ten years the organization was a center of liberal activity in the South, campaigning for the development of southern agriculture, the abolition of the poll tax, and full civil rights for all southerners. Its reputation for progressive action and the closeness of Gelders to the CP attracted the attention of the House Un-American Committee immediately. The Southern Conference for Human Welfare disbanded in 1948. Two useful sources are Clark Foreman, "A Decade of Hope," *Phylon*, XII, no. 2 (1951), 137–150, and Thomas A. Krueger, *And Promises To Keep: The Southern Conference for Human Welfare, 1938–1948* (Nashville, 1967).

7. Louise Charleton was a U.S. Commissioner in Birmingham. Mary McLeod Bethune (c. 1875–1955) founded the Daytona Normal and Industrial School for Negro Girls in 1904, which grew into Bethune-Cookman College. She was president of the National Association of Colored Women and came to national prominence as a member of Roosevelt's "Negro Cabinet." She was the director of Negro Affairs in the National Youth Administration between 1936 and 1944.

Hugo Black (1886–1971) was Senator from Alabama for two terms before Roosevelt appointed him an Associate Justice of the Supreme Court in 1937. Black was presented with a Thomas Jefferson Award at the Birmingham meeting.

8. Evidently Hudson did not see Eleanor Roosevelt show her opposition

to the enforcement of jim crow seating by placing her chair in the center aisle. The following resolution was adopted by the November 1938 meeting of the SCHW:

> Resolved: That the action of Birmingham city officials in enforcing existing segregation ordinances, as affecting sessions of this conference, demonstrates a situation that we condemn, and be it further Resolved: That this conference instructs its officer in arranging future meetings to avoid a similar situation, if at all possible, by selecting a locality in which the practices of the past few days would not be applied.

Report of Proceedings of the Southern Conference for Human Welfare (Birmingham, 1938), p. 13, cited in Ralph J. Bunche, "The Programs, Ideologies, Tactics and Achievements of Negro Betterment and Interracial Organizations" (1940), p. 678.

9. Eugene Dennis [Francis Eugene Waldron] (1905–1961) joined the CPUSA in 1926 and became an employee of the Party in California and then overseas. Dennis was elected general secretary of the CPUSA in 1945. He was one of the initial Smith Act defendants tried in 1949 and was in prison from 1951 to 1955. He became chairman of the Party in 1959.

18. End of the WPA

1. Legislation in 1933 created the Public Works Administration to contract for heavy construction projects, as opposed to the 1935 WPA.

2. According to the FBI, Hudson was elected to the national executive board of the Workers Alliance of America at the fifth annual convention in August 1940.

3. Other men made money illegally, Hudson says. They committed thefts, fenced stolen goods, or made wildcat whiskey.

19. The Alabama CP in the 1940s

1. During the Second World War, the United States and the USSR made conciliatory motions toward one another. Roosevelt released from prison Earl Browder (CP chairman, 1934–1945), who had been sentenced for a passport violation, and the USSR dissolved the Comintern in 1943. The following year Browder pursued the United Front spirit of the late 1930s and early 1940s by urging that the CP become the Communist Political Association. With one exception, the national committee and all the district bureaus accepted the new policy.

2. A short-lived organization, the Good Neighbor Club, of which Hudson was president, preceded the Alabama People's Educational Association. In August 1944 the FBI reported that the Good Neighbor Club was "a Communist front organization" consisting "mainly of old COMMUNIST PARTY members." By September the club was reported inactive. (Hudson's FBI file, reports for 12, 16, 19 August 1944 and for 26 September 1944.)

3. In 1944 the USWA invited British steelworker John Henry Jones

to visit Birmingham. The Alabama CIO provided Jones an all-white escort committee and gave him a banquet at a hotel that did not allow Negro guests. In response to this blatant exclusion, several black union men, including Hudson, organized a smoker for Jones that was not segregated. Hudson engineered the reading at the smoker of a resolution pointedly condemning racial discrimination, and he insisted that it be sent to Philip Murray. He wanted to press the issue further, but members of both the CIO and the erstwhile CP reined him in. Hudson discusses the Jones visit and his resolution on pages 80–83 of *Black Worker in the Deep South*.

4. In the April 1945 issue of the French communist monthly, *Cahiers du Communisme,* Jacques Duclos published an article sharply critical of the transformation of the American Party into a political association. Duclos branded Browder's position "revisionism." The American *Daily Worker* published a translation of the Duclos letter on 25 May 1945. American communists subsequently repudiated Browder's coexistence-with-capitalism line, removed him from leadership, and re-established the Communist Party in the United States. Browder was ultimately expelled.

5. William Z. Foster (1881–1916) joined the Socialist Party in 1900, was expelled, and founded the International Trade Union Educational League (predecessor of the Trade Union Unity League) in 1917. Foster led the great steel strike of 1919 and joined the CP in 1921. He was its candidate for president in 1924, 1928, and 1932. He was national chairman of the CPUSA from 1932 to 1957. One of the Foley Square Eleven of the first Smith Act trials, he was not imprisoned because of a week heart. Foster died in Moscow.

6. Hudson was elected to the national committee of the CP in July 1945 under the alias "H. Smith" and received more votes then any other candidate. The FBI knew the real identity of each of the other 44 members of the national committee by 1947, when it suspected that Hudson and H. Smith were the same person. The identification was never sure and ceased being an issue only in September 1948 when the CP elected a new and much smaller national committee that did not include H. Smith.

7. Henry Winston (1914–   ) was born in Hattiesburg, Mississippi, and joined the CP in 1931. The Party sent him to Harlem as an organizer for the Young Communist League in 1932 and to the USSR in 1933 and 1937. He was elected to the national committee in 1946 and held the office of national organizational secretary when he was convicted of violating the Smith Act in 1949. Winston spent five years in a federal prison, where he lost his sight. He is now national chairman of the CPUSA.

20. Local 2815, USWA

1. The National Labor Relations Board was established by section 7a of the National Industrial Recovery Act and continued by the National Labor Relations Act of 1935. The NLRB conducts secret-ballot elections to determine whether employees want a union and, if so, by which union they choose to be represented.

21. The Alabama CIO

1. In 1936 the Committee for Industrial Organization and the Amalgamated Association of Iron, Steel, and Tin Workers reached an agreement that led to the creation of the Steel Workers Organizing Committee and gave the SWOC the right to organize on behalf of the AA. The SWOC, instead of strengthening the AA, became the nucleus of a new organization headed by officials of the United Mine Workers. The SWOC's negotiations with steel manufacturers in Pennsylvania set the pace for the rest of the country. Contracts were signed in 1937 with "big steel" (U.S. Steel), but independent steel makers only negotiated in 1941–42, after a bloody strike in 1937. In 1942 at the first constitutional convention of the SWOC, the AA was dissolved and the SWOC became the United Steelworkers of America, with Philip Murray as its president for the next ten years.

22. The Marriage Breaks Up

1. Like Hudson's other remarks about his wife and his marriage, this chapter is to be read as only one side of a complicated emotional story. It shows the far-reaching effects of his public life on his private life.

2. Listing him as the "#1 Negro Communist in this locality," the Birmingham office of the FBI opened a file on Hudson in 1941. He was described then as "6'; 177#; dark brown in color; has regular negro features and generally wears starched overalls." (Hudson's FBI file, report for 17 and 27 June 1941.) Between 1941 and 1949 the FBI identified Hudson as a "key figure" in the Birmingham division.

3. After the Progressive Party convention of 1950, Hudson organized a United Political Action Committee is Bessemer. He was not able to work with it very long before he was forced to go underground; the committee fell apart. Its main issues were voting and housing.

23. Red-Baited

1. On 23 October 1947 the Birmingham *Post* published the following article by Charles Pou:

> The Birmingham Post learned today that Hosea Hudson, Negro employe of Jackson Industries and president of CIO United Steelworkers Local 2815, is a member of the National Committee of Communist Party of the U.S.A.
>
> He functions under the alias, "H. Smith."
>
> Hudson has participated in several policy-making meetings of the national organization and has been active in soliciting party membership in the Birmingham district.
>
> His numerous absences from employ at the manufacturing company have remarkably coincided with important party meetings and sessions of "front" organizations, according to a reliable source.

Solicits Members

The Negro, a long-time member of the Communist Party, recently tried to solicit the membership of a white CIO union official but was unsuccessful after several "baiting" conversations.

"Hudson approached me at least three times in a period of about two weeks," the official said, "meanwhile loading me down with pamphlets and propaganda from the party.

"He argued that every union official should be a member of the Communist Party.

"I strung him along for a while, gathering information about the Communist Party.

Attends 'School'

The CIO-USW official, as a member of the national committee, is one of about 45 Americans in the executive branch of the Communist Party.

Meanwhile, other local officials of CIO-USW, one of the most right-wing segments of the CIO, are quick to point out that "Hudson doesn't represent the views of most of us."

In May 1945 Hudson was one of six leaders of a Communist-front school held in the Massey Bldg. under the guise of "A School for Democracy."

Active in Alabama

Recommended reading included Communist Earl Browder's "Thheran—Our Path in War and Peace"; "Organized Labor in USSR"; and "China's New Democracy," by Communist Mao Tse Tung.

Also listed as instructors at the school were Ordway Southard, Louis E. Burnham, Mrs. Caroline Ballin, Mrs. Pauline Dobbs and Miss Esther Cooper.

Hudson also has been active in Alabama Communist Party, which is headed by Harold Bolton, a former New Yorker.

This article was sent to me by Bill Edwards, of the Southern Office of the United Steel Workers in Birmingham. In a telephone conversation, I read Hudson the article and he remembered the white official—but he approached him to work on a committee of the Birmingham Industrial Council. He says he never tried to get the man to join the Party, that he did not approach whites to join: "I don't remember trying to recruit no white guy." Nor does he remember giving the man any literature.

On 4 November, the executive board of Hudson's local sent a letter to Philip Murray, CIO president, alerting him to the events in Birmingham:

We are writing you about the dangerous plans of certain steel leaders in the Birmingham Industrial Union Council—using a stool pigeon, red-baiting article which appeared in the known anti-labor paper—the Birmingham Post as an excuse. There are some anti-

Negro steel leaders who are trying to exclude Hosea Hudson, who is one of our elected delegates from our local and also is our president and leader here in our local, and we the great majority of our members respect him as such. These steel leaders are trying to exclude Hudson from the CIO council . . . [We urge] you to immediately inform steel leaders to stop this dangerous and company inspired action.

On 20 November 1947 Murray sent the above letter to Reuben E. Farr, director of the United Steel Workers southern district (Birmingham essentially) and asked Farr to see whether "unfair, discriminatory practices [are] being resorted to by any CIO unions, or our own Union, down there." Farr wrote back that he was probably the "anti-Negro steel leader" referred to and that it was not true. Farr and the USWA fought the Hudson grievance to its last step.

2. Hudson was quoted as making the following remarks at the meeting of the Birmingham Industrial Union Council when he was expelled:

This thing we've seen here tonight is no longer a question of red-baiting. It's just plain Negro-baiting directed at every loyal and progressive Negro member of the CIO in Birmingham . . . Instead of breaking up the unity of white and Negro workers, we should be fighting against the high cost of living to put more bread on the tables of workers in this country. That's CIO policy, and that's what I've always stood for and fought for. (*Daily Worker*, 14 December 1947, by Mary Southard, quoted in Hudson's FBI file, report for 13 and 15 July 1948.)

3. On 24 November 1947 Charles Pou of the *Post* published a front-page article headed "THREE OUSTED HERE AS REDS BY CIO COUNCIL." Conventions of southern journalism barred the appearance of Negroes in the newspapers, and so the article is accompanied only by photographs of Malcolm and Pauline Dobbs.

Three left-wing CIO officials were ousted from the Birmingham Industrial Council at a stormy session Saturday night [22 November] in which all three were branded as Communists.

The council, which represents 45,000 Birmingham area CIO members, by a standing vote removed from council functions Malcolm Dobbs, United Public Workers of America representative of the United Office and Professional Workers of America, and Hosea Hudson, Negro, president of CIO United Steelworkers Local 2815.

A three-man committee, comprised of two white and one Negro council members, which was formed shortly after an article in the Birmingham Post asserted Hudson was a high-ranking official of the American Communist Party, recommended the ouster of all three officials . . .

Reportedly, a great majority of the council members stood when a vote was taken following the recommendations and report of the committee.

The council also expelled a young black woman, Florence Castile, who, like Pauline and Malcolm Dobbs, was a delegate of the United Office and Professional Workers of America. An editorial in the *Post* on 25 November 1947 congratulated the council's president, Ben Gage, for "a good night's work" and called the expulsion "a fine beginning." It was a sign of the "robust health of the unions." "We hope the rank and file members from here out will be just as alert as their representatives on the council to detect and to oust every Communist who attempts to bore his way into their organization," said the *Post* in summation.

4. Lee Pressman (1906–   ) served as general counsel for the Agricultural Adjustment Administration, the WPA, and the Resettlement Administration. He joined the SWOC at its inception and became general counsel of the USWA and the CIO. He was forced to resign from the CIO in 1948, on suspicion of being a communist, a charge he confirmed before the House Un-American Activities Committee in 1950. Pressman supported the Progressive Party in 1948 and ran for Congress on the PP ticket in New York. He is discussed in Murray Kempton, *Part of Our Time* (New York, 1955), and Len Decaux, *Labor Radical* (Boston 1970).

5. As David Caute shows in his enormous book, *The Great Fear* (New York, 1978), anticommunism reached far beyond Philip Murray. The Cold War was, rather, a systematic and complete rooting out of communists from American life. Hudson's case is mentioned on p. 368.

6. On 28 November 1947 the *Post* ran an article headlined "CIO LOCAL APPEALS TO STATE COUNCIL ON OUSTED OFFICIAL." The article mentioned Local 2815's decision to appeal Hudson's expulsion from the Birmingham Industrial Council. It also mentioned a statement that Hudson left at the *Post:*

In an open communication to the state council, copies of which were given The Post by Hudson and five members of the local, the union members termed Saturday's action, in which Hudson and three other CIO officials were expelled from the council, as "pure and simple union wrecking."

"Not only has Brother Hudson not violated either the state or national CIO constitution, but he has been for 10 years a constant fighting example to all the workers in this area on how to uphold and defend the CIO policy and program . . . The bold attack on Brother Hudson was a smear on his supposed political beliefs."

The petitioners also asked Benjamin Gage, president of the Birmingham Industrial Union Council, to rescind the action taken Saturday . . .

Mr. Gage commented that the "council will stand firm in its action, insofar as I'm concerned."

E. M. Wooten, chairman of three-man committee which recommends [expulsion] . . . pointed out that one member of the investigation committee was a Negro, in answer to a charge that the expulsion was "an attack on Negro workers."

7. Whitley P. McCoy was a professor of law at the University of Alabama School of Law, Tuscaloosa. In his 1 March 1947 opinion and award in the matter of arbitration between Jackson Industries and the United Steelworkers of America, McCoy found that "Hudson was not discharged because charges [of being a communist] were made against him, but because the charges, the report of his ouster from the Council, and the continued publicity caused dissension in the plant, tended to disrupt morale and production, and brought about demands from employees, including union members, that he be discharged."

In reviewing the evidence, McCoy presents a version of the meeting that is quite different from Hudson's:

> the meeting of the Local at which it was decided to prosecute the grievance was attended by only about 45 members out of over 200, and that the vote was close, approximately 25 to 20. Hudson is a negro; only 6 or 8 white men attended that meeting. It is thus evident that the dissension caused in the plant by the newspaper article was carried also into the Local Union, and that the opposition to working with Hudson was not confined to white men nor to nonunion men . . . the Company was justified in discharging Hudson. I have in the past gone as far perhaps as most arbitrators and farther than many, in holding that the seniority provisions of a contract give real job protection to the employees. But I cannot hold that the Company is bound to retain in its employ a man whose presence in the plant has caused, and presumably would continue to cause, unrest, dissension and resentment, tending toward quits, lowered morale, loss of production, and consequent loss of business . . . no company is under a duty to protect [the rights of freedom of thought and speech] at the sacrifice of its existence. I conclude that the discharge was for a "legitimate reason," namely, the self preservation of the Company. No issue of "discrimination" was raised . . . this decision in no way involves the issue of communism.

I am very grateful to Bill Edwards of the Birmingham Office of the United Steel Workers of America for making this material available to me.

8. No article such as Hudson describes appeared in either the Birmingham *News* or *Post*. An article in the *News* of 3 March 1947 headed "NEGRO'S DISCHARGE UPHELD BY ARBITRATION BOARD" mention that "a faction of the Birmingham Industrial Union Council subsequently condemned Ben Gage, its president, and other officers for alleged high-handed methods. Still later, the council overwhelmingly adopted a resolution expressing the utmost confidence in Mr. Gage and in the other council officers."

Bibliographical Essay

WITH the exception of periodical literature, writing on the Communist Party and blacks is badly out of date. The standard histories of the CP, Irving Howe's and Lewis Coser's *The American Communist Party: A Critical History 1919–1957* (Boston: Beacon Press, 1957), and Theodore Draper's two volumes, *The Roots of American Communism* (New York: Viking, 1957) and *American Communism and Soviet Russia* (New York: Viking, 1960), all give some notice to the Negroes in the CP. Except for Draper's 1960 book, however, those discussions are brief and only in passing. Draper devotes an entire chapter to "the Negro question" in his 1960 book, and that discussion remains one of the best summaries in print. Mark Naison's article, "Marxism and Black Radicalism in America: Notes on a Long (and Continuing) Journey," *Radical America* V:3 (May–June 1971), is excellent but not easily available.

The Draper books form part of a series edited by Clinton Rossiter for The Fund for the Republic, "Communism in American Life." The best of the group is Daniel Aaron's *Writers on the Left* (New York: Harcourt, Brace & World, 1961), which mentions Negro writers. But since its subject centers on New York intellectuals, it does not include southern material. Draper's 1960 book is the most useful for a wider understanding of Hudson's time because none of the others pays much attention to Negro communists or to the South. From the vantage point of the late 1970s, the books in the series appear to be part of the Cold War, not above it as they were intended to be. The authors chose their side and joined the anti-communist argument, pointing to Marxism's antipathy to the American way of life and the utter failure of the Communist Party in this country.

Apart from these works on the CPUSA, which generally ignore Negro communists, a body of writing has attempted to analyze the relationship between blacks and communism in this country. The first serious scholarly attempt was by Ralph Bunche in his essays prepared in 1940 for the Carnegie Foundation as background material to help Gunnar Myrdal in writing *An American Dilemma: The Negro Problem and American Democracy* (New York: Harper & Brothers, 1944). The original typescripts are housed in the Schomburg Collection of the New York City Public Library and are available on microfilm.

From the reports written by Bunche, Charles S. Johnson, Paul Norgren, and others, Myrdal pulled together the most influential book on Afro-Americans of the century. The study concluded that, despite Negroes' pitiful condition in this country, the Constitution and the American creed are far more desirable ideals and that *"the Communists have not succeeded in getting any appreciable following among Negroes in America."* Myrdal admitted that this generalization grew out of "impressionistic observations" (I, 508, 510; emphasis in the original). Only Herbert Aptheker, the Marxist historian, criticized Myrdal at length. In *The Negro People in America: A Critique of Gunnar Myrdal's "An American Dilemma"* (New York: International Publishers, 1946), Aptheker accuses Myrdal of writing with a patronizing "class bias," which led him to talk of the American race problem as a moral instead of a political issue (pages 24–25, 66). *An American Dilemma* reached a far larger audience than Aptheker's book, and Myrdal's conviction that Negroes were not interested in communism prevailed over the years.

The only book-length academic studies of blacks and the Communist Party were both published in 1951: Wilson Record's *The Negro and the Communist Party* (Chapel Hill: University of North Carolina Press), and William Nolan's *Communism Versus the Negro* (Chicago: Regnery). Both books are unequivocally anti-communist in tone, and Nolan's is hardly more than a tract. Record also published *Race and Radicalism: The NAACP and the Communist Party in Conflict* (Ithaca: Cornell University Press, 1964), but the first book is much better known. In *The Negro and the Communist Party,* Record discusses the CP's stance toward blacks since 1919 and concludes on a note sounded by Ralphe Bunche in 1940: the CP must fail in its bid for black members because it strives only to use them for the Kremlin's ends. This view echoes throughout The Fund for the Republic's series, in which everyone agreed that the CP only worked in the interests of the Soviet Union, that Negroes rejected the CP, and that therefore the CP had failed in regards to blacks, despite all its concentration on them. No matter how white Americans treated Negroes, the latter clung to this country and its ideals "with incredible patience" (John P. Roche in the introduction to Record's *Race and Radicalism,* page vi).

On the other side are the volumes written by communists and usually published by the communist publishing house, International Publishers. Some are histories, such as William Z. Foster's *History of the Communist Party of the United States* (New York: International Publishers, 1952) and *The American Negro People in American History* (New York: International Publishers, 1954), and Philip S. Foner's *Organized Labor and the Black Worker, 1619–1973* (New York: Praeger, 1974). Although these books furnish a wealth of detail about the activities of the CP, to the general reader their perspective seems distorted; they present themselves as comprehensive histories, but they treat at length communist activities that touched relatively few people. Foster's work is stridently critical of Earl Browder and thus confuses readers who cannot follow the disconcerting rise and fall of communist leaders. Of the communist publications, the autobiographies are the most interesting for readers who are not students of political affairs.

Angelo Herndon's *Let Me Live* (1937), unlike most others, was put out by a New York trade publisher, Random House, although Herndon was a communist in good standing at the time. Despite its commercial imprint Herndon's story reads like other authorized autobiographies and shares their literary weaknesses. The International Publishers autobiographies are meant to inspire the faithful as much as to reveal the author's thoughts. *Let Me Live*, like Hosea Hudson's *Black Worker in the Deep South* (1972), was edited with a very heavy hand. Other black autobiographies, by men of more education, are undoubtedly their own. William L. Patterson's *The Man Who Cried Genocide* (1971) is one of the best. But good or merely meritorious, such as Benjamin Davis' prison notes, *Communist Councilman from Harlem* (1969), the International Publishers autobiographies seldom help the non-radical reader to understand the social history of the left. They concentrate on the high points of communist history, whether the author was involved or not. And they take to extremes the weaknesses inherent in most autobiographies—making the author seem like the only person in the world, cut off from a setting among family, neighbors, or friends.

A new group of books by former communists is filling the enormous gaps in our knowledge of communists as people and the CP as a society. So far most of these books are by white authors. Among the best are Len DeCaux's *Labor Radical: From the Wobblies to the C.I.O.* (Boston: Beacon Press, 1970), Al Richmond's *A Long View from the Left* (Boston: Houghton Mifflin, 1973), and Jessica Mitford's *A Fine Old Conflict* (New York: Knopf, 1977). The only ex-communist memoir by a Negro is Harry Haywood's *Black Bolshevik: The Autobiography of an Afro-American Communist* (Chicago: Liberator Press, 1978). By and large, these books avoid shrill anti-communism and furnish believable accounts of individual experiences in the communist movement.

Joseph Starobin's half-memoir, half-monograph, *American Communism in Crisis, 1943–1957* (Cambridge: Harvard University Press, 1972), reveals much of the history and mentality of communists in this country after the Second World War. I found it the most useful rendering of the Party in that period. Harold Cruse's long, testy sermon-memoir, *The Crisis of the Negro Intellectual* (New York: Morrow, 1967), ranges over a host of issues bearing on blacks and the left between the First World War and the 1960s. Insightful, judgmental, and useful, it defies categorization.

Recent works by scholars who were children during the Cold War are more balanced than their predecessors'. Outstanding are Dan T. Carter's *Scottsboro: A Tragedy of the American South* (Baton Rouge: Louisiana State University Press, 1969), Charles H. Martin's *The Angelo Herndon Case and Southern Justice* (Baton Rouge: Louisiana State University Press, 1976), and Harvey Klehr's *Communist Cadre: The Social Background of the American Communist Party Elite* (Stanford: Hoover Institution, 1978). Charles Martin is editing an anthology of original articles on blacks and the CP that will give the subject a modern and comprehensive treatment.

The periodical literature is growing, but again the CPUSA in general, rather than blacks in the Party, is the most usual topic. The great exception is the CP's own theoretical journal, *Political Affairs*, entitled *The Communist* before 1945 and still published. Here communists write for each other and openly debate Party policies at length. For readers interested in the evolution of the politics of the CPUSA, *Political Affairs* is indispensable, the best source for communist writings on "the Negro question" over the years. Other well-established journals that are radical but not associated with the CP are *Radical America, Socialist Revolution,* and *Marxist Perspectives.* Two black periodicals are more helpful in terms of blacks and progressive issues in general: *Freedomways,* an old-left publication from New York, and the now Marxist *Black Scholar* from San Francisco. *Southern Exposure* grows from roots in New Left radicalism of the 1960s and is exceedingly rich in social history.

United States government documents are voluminous, particularly the hearings of the House Un-American Activities Committee, which run to twelve volumes between 1938 and 1940 alone (Document number Y4.Un1/2: Un/vol.number). I found useful the 1930 *Investigation of Communist Propaganda, Hearings Before a Special Committee to Investigate Activities in the United States of the House of Representatives* (71st Congress, 2nd session, document no. 44.C73/3:p94; Greenwood Press microfiche of U.S. government documents, no. 576). However, Hudson's Federal Bureau of Investigation file, as it was sent to me, was practically useless. The entire file, from 1941 to the present, runs to over 3000 pages. I saw only the section covering 1941–1949, of which a great deal was inked out. The file is still being maintained, and much of it is classified material.

Readers interested in oral history as a genre (or worse, as a methodology) will find more works in print than one can easily assimilate. I recommend especially James Hoopes's wonderfully clear guidebook, *Oral History: An Introduction for Students* (Chapel Hill: University of North Carolina Press, 1979), which contains a comprehensive bibliography. I also liked Thomas J. Cottle's thoughtful *Private Lives and Public Accounts* (Amherst: University of Massachusetts Press, 1977), particularly the title essay.

The survey text for the South during Hudson's period is George B. Tindall's encyclopedic *Emergence of the New South, 1913–1946,* volume ten (1967) of the invaluable History of the South series edited by Wendell Holmes Stephenson and E. Merton Coulter (Baton Rouge: Louisiana State University Press).

Acknowledgments

IN preparing this book I incurred many debts. The first, of course, is to Hosea Hudson, who extended to me the most difficult thing for a communist in this country to give, trust. Then he was patient through the long processes of revision and scholarly annotation.

Among my friends and colleagues, the first thanks must go to Nellie McKay, who shared the ups and downs from the very beginning. Like Nellie, Larry Goffney supported the work in countless important ways. He drove me down to Atlantic City from Cambridge one freezing January and also fixed Hudson's kitchen light. Mark Solomon has been selfless in sharing his work and all sorts of information on blacks and the CP. Donald Fleming and the Charles Warren Center at Harvard University cheered me on and provided two typists at a critical moment in the transcribing of the tapes. The American Council of Learned Societies made my moonlighting sabbatical possible in 1976–77. *Radical America* published part of the manuscript at an early stage.

In Birmingham, A. C. Buttram and Reuben Farr told me their recollections of Hudson and the union in the 1940s. I owe special gratitude to Bill Edwards of the USWA in Birmingham for checking newspapers and ferreting out invaluable source material. Hugh Bryan and his associates at Stockham Valves and Fittings showed their plant and made their operations comprehensible to me. At the University of Alabama Law School Library, Hazel Johnson searched out Birmingham codes and judicial usages I could not have found otherwise.

Chris Lindsey and Samantha Steinberger typed the manuscript cheerfully and very well, in part because they both fell in love with Hudson. I have been fortunate that my editors, official and unofficial, see what I see in this book and have helped make it clear. I could not have done without Aida Donald, Joyce Backman, and Malcolm Call.

N.I.P.

Index

* indicates pseudonym

092430